'Powerful and meticulously argued . . . Whatmore approaches the Enlightenment on its own terms . . . There is buried treasure in his account of how figures from different intellectual backgrounds negotiated the Enlightenment crisis . . . Whatmore is to be applauded'
Joseph Hone, *History Today*

'An exhaustive and fascinating read on how the Enlightenment came to a grizzly end' *Reader's Digest*

'A brilliant and revelatory book about the history of ideas'
David Runciman

'In this lucid and beautifully written book, Richard Whatmore evokes the darkening vision of the eighteenth-century thinkers forced to confront the failure of Enlightenment. Instead of achieving perpetual peace and progress, they saw Europe fragment into a collection of warmongering states teetering on the brink of bankruptcy and global turmoil. Whatmore carefully reconstructs the historical context for the failure of Enlightenment and presents it as a powerful echo chamber for our own troubled times. This is a fascinating and important book' Ruth Scurr

'The Enlightenment had seemed to promise a limitless bounty of peace, prosperity, rational inquiry and mutual tolerance to a Europe long ravaged by religious fanaticism and war. Why did it come to end in the extreme violence and continental bloodshed of the French Revolution, and how could another such disaster be avoided? Richard Whatmore charts the response to these concerns of many of the greatest thinkers of the eighteenth century, from Smith and Burke to Wollstonecraft. His book is panoramic in scope, always fresh and deep in its analysis, but with a polemical edge for today's readers fearful again for our global future' Jesse Norman

'A brilliant work of intellectual interpretation by our foremost historian of Enlightenment ideas. Whatmore rescues the Enlightenment from today's circular debates and places it where it belongs: in the pulsing, chaotic era of its genesis and demise' Christopher de Bellaigue

'As the eighteenth century progressed, it was increasingly apparent that the Enlightenment was failing. If religious bigotry was in retreat, new evils advanced: revolution, terror and greed, fuelling war, exploitation and imperial expansion. Richard Whatmore shows how thinkers from David Hume to Mary Wollstonecraft strove to find solutions to such challenges. This intellectually exhilarating book is particularly relevant today, when liberal democracy is facing new dangers, which threaten to drag us back into the darkness once more' Adam Sisman

'An accomplished exercise in intellectual history'
Alexander Faludy, *Catholic Herald*

'Excellent . . . suggests that the Enlightenment ended up devouring those who most believed in it, providing the context for the emergence of Napoleon'
Katherine Bayford, *Engelsberg Ideas*

'One of my favourite books on the British Enlightenment . . . the author captures the tenor of eighteenth century British debates about liberty very well . . . Whatmore writes as if he is actually trying to explain things to you! If you read a lot of history books, you will know that this is oddly rare'
Tyler Cowen

ABOUT THE AUTHOR

Richard Whatmore is Professor of Modern History at the University of St Andrews and Co-Director of the Institute of Intellectual History. He is the author of several acclaimed contributions to intellectual history and eighteenth-century scholarship, including *The History of Political Thought*, *Terrorists, Anarchists, and Republicans* and *Against War and Empire*.

RICHARD WHATMORE

The End of Enlightenment

Empire, Commerce, Crisis

PENGUIN BOOKS

PENGUIN BOOKS

UK | USA | Canada | Ireland | Australia
India | New Zealand | South Africa

Penguin Books is part of the Penguin Random House group of companies
whose addresses can be found at global.penguinrandomhouse.com

Penguin Random House UK,
One Embassy Gardens, 8 Viaduct Gardens, London SW11 7BW

penguin.co.uk

Penguin
Random House
UK

First published by Allen Lane 2023
Published in Penguin Books 2024
001

Printed and bound in Great Britain by Clays Ltd, Elcograf S.p.A.

The authorized representative in the EEA is Penguin Random House Ireland,
Morrison Chambers, 32 Nassau Street, Dublin D02 YH68

A CIP catalogue record for this book is available from the British Library

ISBN: 978-0-141-99770-4

Penguin Random House is committed to a sustainable future
for our business, our readers and our planet. This book is made from
Forest Stewardship Council® certified paper.

MIX
Paper | Supporting
responsible forestry
FSC
www.fsc.org   FSC® C018179

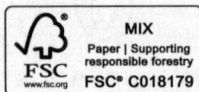

Contents

A dark
Illimitable ocean, without bound,
Without dimension, where length, breadth, and height,
And time, and place, are lost; where eldest Night
And Chaos, ancestors of Nature, hold
Eternal anarchy, amidst the noise
Of endless wars, and by confusion stand.

John Milton, *Paradise Lost*, II, 891–94

Men could not recognise the common good.
They knew no binding customs, used no laws.
Every man, wise in staying strong, surviving,
Kept for himself the spoils that fortune offered.

Lucretius, *De rerum natura*, trans., Anthony M. Esolen
(Baltimore: Johns Hopkins University Press, 1995), 5, 958–61

To John Pocock

LIVONIA

• Moscow

LITHUANIA

RUSSIA

DUCHY
PRUSSIA

KINGDOM
OF POLAND

CRIMEAN
KHANATE

MOLDAVIA

CIRCASSIANS

NGARY

OTTOMAN

Black Sea

A
SERBIA
evo
BULGARIA

Constantinople

ALBANIA

GREECE

After the wars of
religion: Europe in 1648,
when most of the
religious conflicts
between states had
ceased. Although wars
were ongoing between the
major powers, figures
such as Edward Gibbon
and Edmund Burke
praised the diverse
cultures and politics.
Europe became a
patchwork of different
political and religious
communities.

◻ Holy Roman Empire
· Imperial Cities
● The two cities in Westphalia
  where the treaties were signed

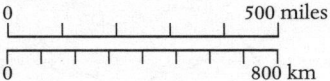

0   500 miles

0   800 km

Map Scale

0 — 500 miles

0 — 800 km

SWEDEN

RUSSIAN EMPIRE

Baltic Sea

• Riga

LIVONIA

Lipawa (Liepāja) •

Mitawa (Jelgava) •

Dyneburg (Daugavpils) •

Tauroggen (Taurage) •

Kowno (Kaunas) •

Polock (Polotsk) •

Witebsk (Vitebsk) •

Königsberg (Kaliningrad) •

EAST PRUSSIA

Gdańsk (Danzig) •

EASTERN POMERANIA

WEST PRUSSIA

Chełmno (Kulm) •

WARMIA

Olsztyn (Allenstein) •

NEW EAST PRUSSIA

WHITE

Wilno (Vilnius) •

• Minsk

Grodno •

Mścisław (Mstislavl) •

Mahilyow (Mogilyov) •

Wołkowysk (Volkovysk) •

Działdowo (Soldau) •

Białystok •

RUTHENIA

Noteć

Toruń (Thorn) •

GREAT

Gniezno (Gnesen) •

Poznań (Posen) •

POLAND

Płock (Plotsk) •

MAZOVIA

POLAND

Drohiczyn •

Bobrujsk •

Warsaw •

Brześć Litewski (Brest) •

Pinsk •

Pripet Marshes

Homel (Gomel) •

SOUTH PRUSSIA

Rawa (Rava) •

Maciejowice •

RUSSIAN EMPIRE

Łódź •

Pilica

Wieluń •

WEST GALICIA

Kowel (Kovel) •

Korosten (Korostyshiv) •

Czestochowa (Tschenstochau) •

Lublin •

LITTLE

Zamość (Zampstyle) •

Łuck (Lutsk) •

• Kiev

SILESIA

Oder

POLAND

NEW SILESIA

Kraków •

Vistula

KINGDOM

Żytomierz (Zhytomyr) •

AUSTRIA

Tarnów •

Przemyśl •

OF GALICIA

Lwów (Lviv) •

Winnica (Vinnytsya) •

Tarnopol (Ternopil) •

RED RUTHENIA

CARPATHIANS

Balta •

Southern Buh

HUNGARY

ROMANIA

Prut

Dniester

OTTOMAN EMPIRE

First Partition, 1772
Lands annexed by:
- Austria
- Prussia
- Russia

Second Partition, 1793
Lands annexed by:
- Prussia
- Russia

Third Partition, 1795
Lands annexed by:
- Austria
- Prussia
- Russia

Black Sea

States ceased to exist across Europe before and after the French Revolution. The best illustration is the Polish-Lithuanian Commonwealth, one of the largest states, which gradually disappeared because of the partitions between Russia, Prussia and Austria, which commenced in 1772 and continued in 1793 and 1795. Smaller and weaker powers across the continent felt increasingly endangered.

Königsberg

Berlin

PRUSSIA

Warsaw

1798
Other German
Principalities

Breslau

HOLY ROMAN
EMPIRE

RUSSIA

Zurich
IC
IC

Leoben • Vienna

AUSTRIAN
POSSESSIONS

lan

VENETIA

NE REPUBLIC • Venice

PARMA

• Bologna

RIAN
LIC

Florence

TUSCANY

• Sarajevo

ROMAN
REPUBLIC

Rome •

PARTHENOPEAN
REPUBLIC

OTTOMAN EMPIRE

Constantinople

Naples

SICILY

GREECE

While the surviving
republics of Europe were
seen to be in decline in
the eighteenth century,
everything changed with
the French Revolution.
The First French Republic
established client
republics across Switzer-
land, Italy and the
Netherlands, but also
turned itself into an
empire, eating up the old
republics in the process.

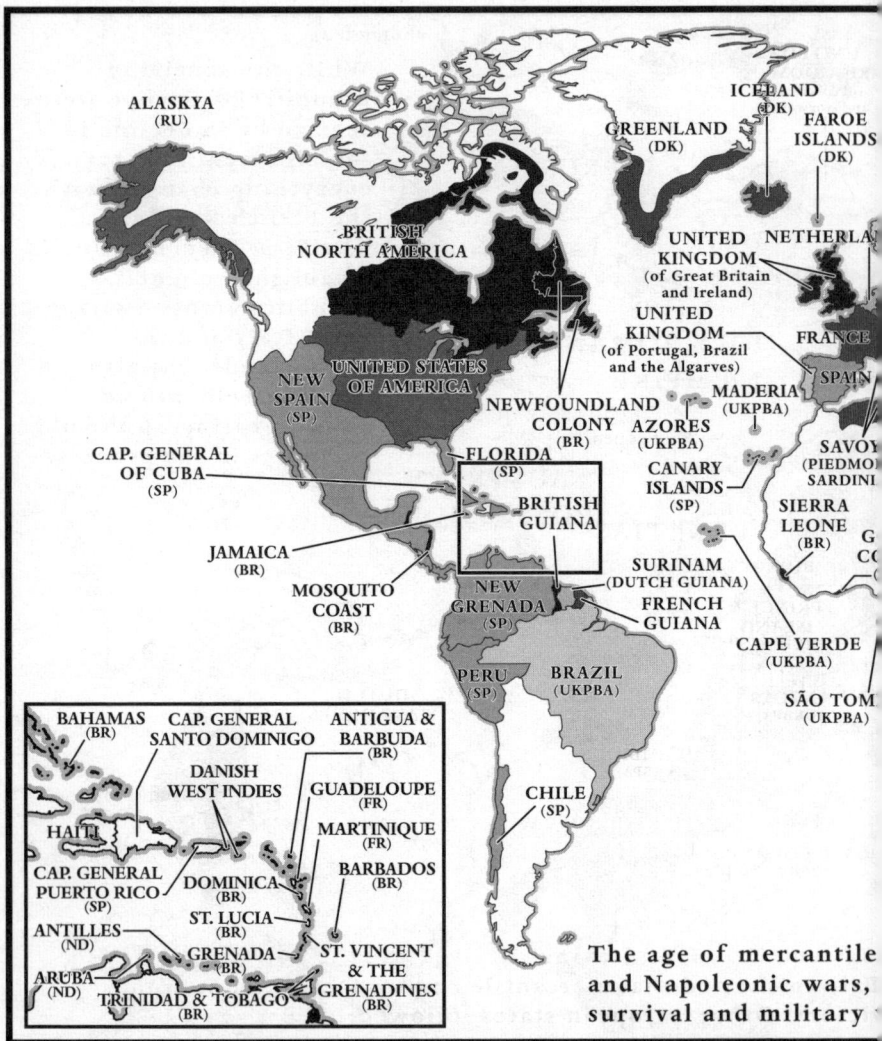

ALASKYA
(RU)

ICELAND
(DK)

FAROE
ISLANDS
(DK)

GREENLAND
(DK)

UNITED
KINGDOM
(of Great Britain
and Ireland)

NETHERLA

BRITISH
NORTH AMERICA

UNITED
KINGDOM
(of Portugal, Brazil
and the Algarves)

FRANCE

NEW
SPAIN
(SP)

UNITED STATES
OF AMERICA

SPAIN

MADERIA
(UKPBA)

NEWFOUNDLAND
COLONY
(BR)

AZORES
(UKPBA)

SAVOY
(PIEDMO
SARDINI

CAP. GENERAL
OF CUBA
(SP)

FLORIDA
(SP)

CANARY
ISLANDS
(SP)

BRITISH
GUIANA

SIERRA
LEONE
(BR)

JAMAICA
(BR)

MOSQUITO
COAST
(BR)

NEW
GRENADA
(SP)

SURINAM
(DUTCH GUIANA)

FRENCH
GUIANA

CAPE VERDE
(UKPBA)

PERU
(SP)

BRAZIL
(UKPBA)

SÃO TOM
(UKPBA)

CHILE
(SP)

BAHAMAS
(BR)

CAP. GENERAL
SANTO DOMINIGO

ANTIGUA &
BARBUDA
(BR)

DANISH
WEST INDIES

GUADELOUPE
(FR)

HAITI

MARTINIQUE
(FR)

CAP. GENERAL
PUERTO RICO
(SP)

DOMINICA
(BR)

BARBADOS
(BR)

ANTILLES
(ND)

ST. LUCIA
(BR)

ARUBA
(ND)

GRENADA
(BR)

ST. VINCENT
& THE
GRENADINES
(BR)

TRINIDAD & TOBAGO
(BR)

The age of mercantile
and Napoleonic wars,
survival and military

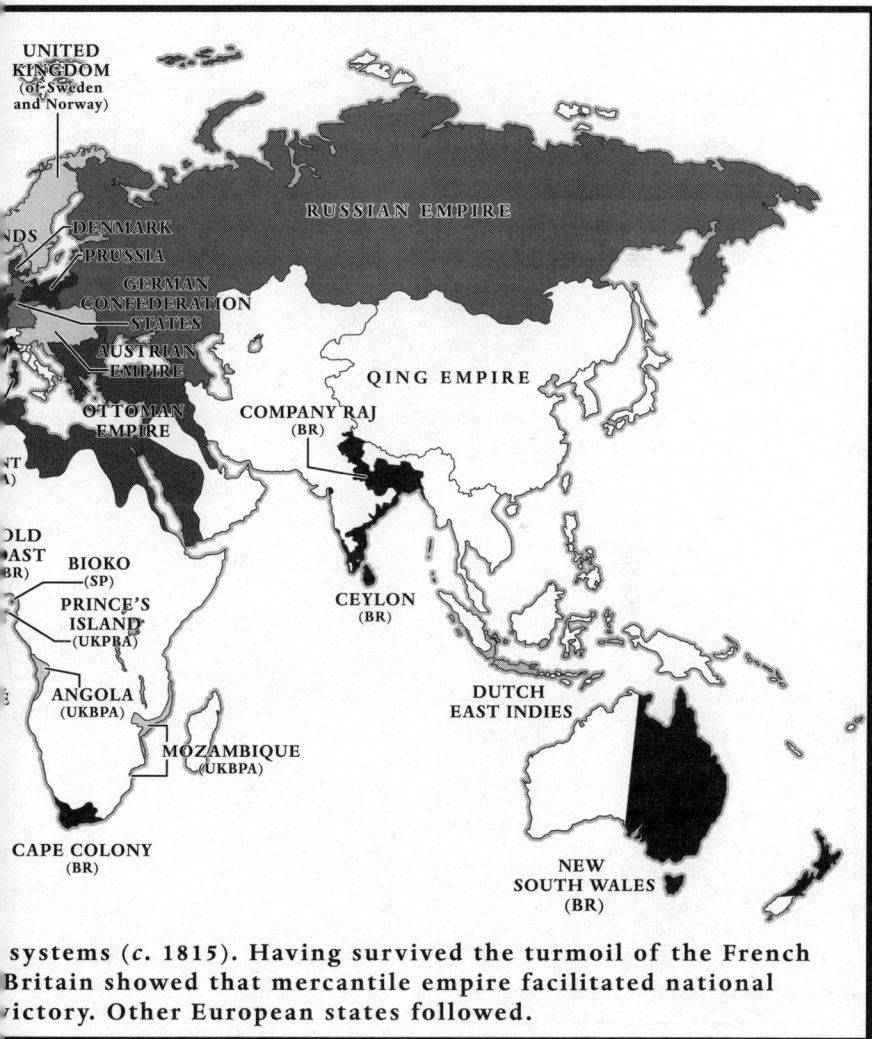

UNITED KINGDOM (of Sweden and Norway)

NDS

DENMARK

PRUSSIA

GERMAN CONFEDERATION STATES

AUSTRIAN EMPIRE

RUSSIAN EMPIRE

QING EMPIRE

OTTOMAN EMPIRE

COMPANY RAJ (BR)

NT A)

OLD AST BR)

BIOKO (SP)

PRINCE'S ISLAND (UKPBA)

CEYLON (BR)

ANGOLA (UKBPA)

MOZAMBIQUE (UKBPA)

DUTCH EAST INDIES

CAPE COLONY (BR)

NEW SOUTH WALES (BR)

systems (*c.* 1815). Having survived the turmoil of the French
Britain showed that mercantile empire facilitated national
victory. Other European states followed.

Introduction

I

On 8 August 1776 the political economist Adam Smith visited his great friend David Hume at his home in Edinburgh. For the past two years Hume had been declining. Although physicians were divided about the nature of the disease, it was evident from the severe pain he felt and the acute loss of weight he had experienced that he was dying. An ill-advised trip to Bath to take the waters in the summer of 1776 further weakened him. On 4 July, just as the American Declaration of Independence was being signed in Philadelphia, Hume returned to Scotland to dine with his closest friends, and to make final alterations to his works and will. There had been some speculation that the famous sceptic might embrace the Christian faith before he died, but this had been firmly put aside weeks before: in a conversation about his soul with the lawyer James Boswell, Hume playfully maintained that 'when he heard a man was religious, he concluded he was a rascal, though he had known some instances of very good men being religious.'[1]

In Smith's company, Hume was much more candid.[2] Together they discussed the prognosis, and Hume assured his friend that a contented end was near. As they conversed, he informed Smith that he had been reading Lucian's *Dialogues of the Dead* and imagining the excuses he might give to Charon for not entering into his boat ferrying the dead across the river Styx to the Underworld. The first excuse was that Hume was very busy 'correcting my works for a new edition', to which the imaginary Charon would patiently reply, 'When you have seen the effect of these, you will be for making other alterations. There will be no end of such excuses; so, honest friend, please step into the boat.' The second excuse was a little grander: 'I have been endeavouring to open the eyes of the public. If I live a few years longer, I may have the satisfaction of seeing the downfall of some of the prevailing systems of superstition.' Charon's reply was significant – through it, Hume admitted that the 'systems of superstition' remained powerful and were unlikely to soon be broken: 'But Charon would then lose all temper and decency. "You loitering rogue, that will not happen these many hundred years. Do you fancy I will grant you a lease for so long a term? Get into the boat this instant, you lazy loitering rogue."'[3]

For much of his life, Hume had held that the great achievement of eighteenth-century Britain was that its religious institutions – those 'systems of superstition' – resembled 'little more but in Name their Predecessors, who flourished during the civil Wars; & who were the Authors of such Disorder'.[4] Zeal and bigotry, he believed, had been replaced by more tolerant and calmer instances of Christian commitment. Hume was attacked for downplaying the link between Protestantism and the civil liberties enjoyed by modern Britons living in their professedly free state.[5] He was violently criticized for playing down the role of the Reformation in contemporary national life, portraying contemporary Protestants as being lesser vessels of the Word of God than their forebears.[6] Hume shrugged off such predictable animosity. What mattered most to Hume during this time was that Europe had finally escaped the bloody sectarian conflicts of the past two hundred years and found itself instead experiencing an enlightenment composed of peace, toleration and moderation.[7] During the sixteenth and seventeenth centuries, the splitting of the church saw the rise of rival attempts to achieve the ecclesiastical and political dominance over populations that in turn heralded religious persecution and wars both within and between states. Attempts to contain this religiously fuelled violence gave rise to various political and constitutional settlements, but ordinary Europeans still faced sustained periods during which fanatics justified actions and laws condoning and encouraging civil and international bloodshed. These movements often justified themselves and generated zealous followers by defining their mission along explicitly war-like terms against those with an alternative faith. The results were often the collapse of pacific modes of behaviour and crisis among communities suddenly overrun by men and women with extreme and uncompromising beliefs. This was one reason why, in the British context, John Foxe's *Actes and Monuments* or 'Book of Martyrs' continued to be so popular from 1563, with its images of the persecuted being burned alive.[8] Europe-wide fears were epitomized by Jacques Callot's prints, published as *Miseries and Misfortunes of War* in 1633, including an unforgettable image of the numerous dead hanging by the neck from tree branches while nearby clerics absolved the murderous soldiers in sacred ceremony.[9]

II

Identifying threats that might transform superstition into fanaticism was, Hume argued, a central duty of the philosopher. As a younger man, he had responded to accusations that he was an atheist who sought the destruction of religion and morality with a refutation founded on the assumption that he was living 'in a Country of Freedom, where Informers and Inquisitors are so deservedly held in universal Detestation, where Liberty, at least of Philosophy, is so highly valued and esteemed'.[10] He portrayed himself then as an advocate of this enlightened attitude, a hard-won spirit of the age that ought to be maintained. He believed he was a defender of the relative harmony he perceived around him, that he was honing tools for society that would help it understand the consequences of its violent past and make clear the measures that could be taken to avoid the return of those dark days.

But, over time, Hume's position changed. And as he approached death, as he rehearsed his excuses for Charon, he had concluded that new forms of superstition had forged new fanaticisms of unparalleled power. Hume believed that this superstition stemmed not from the religious realm, but from that of secular belief. He feared the consequences of ministers and merchants promoting a form of mercantile empire fuelled by spiralling national debts that funded war.[11] He worried especially about one consequence of the pursuit of empire, namely an addiction to the idea of liberty among the populace and politicians.[12] And although he had defended the pursuit of luxury during his life, towards its end he was concerned that the selfishness accompanying the pursuit of material gain had corroded national mores.[13] With these three forces in mind, Hume soon came to the conclusion that the times of the Reformation had been returned to. As they had done then, individuals would pursue extreme ends, but now in the name of liberty, commerce, profit and empire, ensuring that the future looked bleak: once again peace and toleration were being replaced by division, accusation and violence. When such action became social norm, the Enlightenment – defined, in Hume's view, by its aim to prevent superstition-fuelled conflict – had failed. Such threats were real, Hume warned even as he prepared to sail the river Styx.

The fundamental change in the world that Hume became most concerned about as he aged had first been identified in a series of essays that he wrote in the 1730s, and that made him famous by the early 1740s. The young Hume argued that the established rules of international politics had been turned upside down. Hume dated this development to the final decades of the seventeenth century, when states had first started to compete with one another for the control of trade. States had, of course, always sought riches and commerce. In building empires, they had incorporated polities and regions into national domains, always with an eye for spoil.[14] International commerce was traceable to ancient times and numerous seaborne empires had been erected upon such a foundation, as the Dutch had done in the seventeenth century.[15] Merchant empires had risen and fallen since the Renaissance, and since then fiscal-military states had emerged which taxed their populations heavily in order to fight long wars.[16] Britain was such a state.[17] But Hume argued that when the overriding goal of national policy became the expansion of national markets by war or by economic imperialism – through the controlling of the commerce of fellow states and communities by applying political or military pressure, even as they remained notionally independent – then politics was fundamentally altered.

Hume soon too perceived there was no alternative to this new national strategy of commerce increased by whatever means necessary, be it competition, invasion, extortion or threat. The reason, he held, was the link between commerce and a burgeoning military revolution. States had to invest in the latest military technology – canon shooting explosive shells, mortar firing hot-shot, flintlock muskets, polygonal fortifications – to defend themselves against rival powers, as well as often having to deploy vast fleets and huge armies, the latter being frequently ten times larger than they had been in the 1550s.[18] Paying for this relied upon generating revenues through commerce – and the capacity of states to do this was transformed when, from the late seventeenth century, immediate revenue generation through public credit became possible.[19]

This was a moment of historic importance. If they maintained the trust of the financial markets that had loaned them funds at interest, states could now defer capital repayments to a distant point in time. The Dutch Republic had proven to be innovative in generating and servicing debt in this way, with trading in shares of the Dutch East India Company in Amsterdam beginning in the seventeenth century.[20] Britain had followed suit: the Bank of England was founded in 1694, followed by the new East India Company in 1698.[21] By the 1690s equity or risk capital was being issued on the London exchange; the purposes of such exchanges were not solely to finance state or private enterprise, but also entailed trading in stocks, commodities, foreign currencies and insurance. A state like Britain could in very little time generate enormous debts to fund its wars. Yet paying national debts over long periods depended in turn on extended economic success; any long-term downturn would leave a state at the mercy of its creditors – as well as those countries who continued to be able to afford their military expenditure. This was why the British and the French in particular became so worried about national bankruptcy.[22] The need to pay interest upon the national debt in turn focused governments' minds on furthering the reach of their trade, which meant more markets and revenues for the state and a greater level of trust among creditors.[23] Such forces contributed to an ever-greater lust for empire, practically realizable both because of the growing gulf in power between commercial and non-commercial states and the pressure upon states to expand their markets.

As Hume and his friends recognized, one consequence of the turn to commercial empire was that few states in Europe were safe. It was clear by the middle of the eighteenth century that a whole host of traditional powers had declined, from Sweden, Spain and the Dutch Republic to Venice, Genoa and Poland-Lithuania.[24] More were losing their liberty, becoming states ruled by absolute monarchs, the predominant form of government.[25] Smaller states and especially the republics entered a prolonged period of crisis.[26] Traditional survival strategies for such states, from economic specialization to alliances and confederation and, above all else, an emphasis on national patriotism or 'manliness', were no longer sufficient, such was the gulf in strength traceable to commercial dividends. Many states simply ceased to exist. Others found their domestic politics perpetually interfered with by larger commercial powers, who suddenly had an interest in the markets of their neighbours, whether they were traditional allies or enemies. A commonplace assertion in the eighteenth century was that for every state except the global superpowers of Britain, France and a handful of vast longstanding empires such as Russia, China, Japan, the Ottomans and the Habsburg dominions, sovereignty had become a myth.[27] A new form of empire was developing, entailing the economic exploitation of a territory by political control rather than direct acquisition or military invasion. Rome became less relevant – modern Carthages were on the rise.[28]

If the consequence for Europe was a reduction of the number of states that could be considered independent, in other parts of the globe effects were more parlous still. The European capacity to employ military technology to defeat less advanced states, tribes and communities was ruthlessly deployed in the creation of empires intended to generate profits for their national epicentres. The growth of the Atlantic slave trade was one result, with the Portuguese, British, French, Dutch, Danes, Swedes and Spanish battling for control of the supply of enslaved peoples from West Africa to labour in the sugar plantations of the Caribbean and in the mining and farming of South America. In the British case, the plantation economy in the American colonies produced highly profitable cash crops for European consumption, such as sugar, rice, tobacco, indigo and coffee. In addition, raw materials such as gold, ivory and dyewoods were extracted from Africa to support manufactures in the European states. Another instance was the exploitation of India and the Americas, also through chartered companies; significantly, the European power which had yet to establish such a company, Portugal, did so in 1755. Smith accused the Portuguese of making profits only for trading pirates, their actions resulting, as his friend the Abbé Raynal wrote, in the enslavement of all of the northern part of Brazil.[29] For Smith, 'The government of an exclusive company of merchants, is, perhaps, the worst of all governments for any country whatsoever.'[30] Merchant companies made their own interests sovereign, he argued, to the detriment of indigenous peoples who became only a source of profit, and to domestic governments, who became their fools.[31]

The price of such developments was ceaseless war between the larger states for commercial dominion both by arms and by political and economic strategies of control. In addition to the risk of being annexed, smaller states found their own domestic politics to be far more complicated and turbulent, being dependent on the views of the ambassadors from the major powers. New forms of xenophobia developed in which foreigners and rival countries were blamed for the economic health of your own state. In free states, where the people had a voice, it was discovered that elections were much more easily won if voters could be persuaded to blame foreigners rather than national politicians for decline.

War for trade generated enormous profits for particular groups in society. Fears expressed early in the century about 'the monied interest', those whose wealth derived from investment in government stocks or who were able to exploit the commercially dependent elements of empire for vast personal gain, continued to grow. A major worry of contemporaries concerning their own nation's economies centred on this new monied class – and especially the liquidity of their wealth. Rather than relying on the immoveable wealth of land, this group could, it was suggested, move their assets across borders, ruining a state's economy in the process. More dangerous still was the idea that the monied interest could easily establish what Hume's close friend Smith in his *Wealth of Nations* (1776) famously called a 'mercantile system': a corrupt nexus of merchants and bankers, who moved capital for trade, and the politicians they bribed, who made legislation for their own profit rather than the good of society. Smith notoriously put it that 'it is the industry which is carried on for the benefit of the rich and the powerful, that is principally encouraged by our mercantile system. That which is carried on for the benefit of the poor and the indigent, is too often, either neglected, or oppressed.'[32] Traditionally, Smith's mercantile system has been associated with an economic doctrine termed mercantilism, entailing bullionism, the pursuit of gold for your own state, and reason-of-state, the policy of pursuing your own economic interests at the expense of others, beggaring your neighbour wherever possible.[33] Smith is regularly described as the arch-enemy of such a system because he made plain the benefits of free trade in making nations wealthier.[34] This is a mistake. Smith thought all policy prescriptions, including free trade, had positive and negative effects depending on the circumstances in which they operated. This was why he supported Britain's restrictive Navigation Acts, which he called 'the wisest of all the commercial regulations of England' – an example of his preference for discussing specific cases in particular contexts.[35] He found himself writing a book for the ages amid civil war, domestic crisis and likely international war. Accordingly, he defended expansive global trade while depicting various more realistic scenarios, accurately depicting the parlous condition of contemporary states battling for markets.[36]

When he discussed the mercantile system, Smith was mostly concerned about the British Empire: he believed it was likely to collapse because it had turned into a mercantile system addicted to war and empire-building. Smith's *Wealth of Nations* was one of the very last books that Hume read before he died; he was full of praise for it.[37] Hume felt it supported his view, and that of so many of his friends and contemporaries, that Britain *would* collapse, like past mercantile states had tended to, and just as the Dutch and the Spanish empires had declined in living memory. Smith was cautious by character and tended to hedge his bets about the future. But he could not have been more explicit about the ills he perceived around him. The subject on which 'the public prejudices of Europe' needed 'to be set right' was 'the real futility of distant dominions'.[38] Empire was for Smith a policy of madness: 'under the present system of management', he argued, Britain 'derives nothing but loss from the dominion which she assumes over her colonies'.[39]

When states had previously pursued commerce and empire, wealth had come only to the adventurers who travelled and the courts or aristocrats who patronized them. The British were different – politicians from across the political spectrum, in an official capacity or not, owned shares in the East India Company, in related imperial ventures or in national bonds.[40] British politics was increasingly influenced by a coterie of figures who each had a personal interest in the expansion of the existing mercantile empire; waging war brought profit to them at the same time as it damaged indigenous peoples, increased taxes for the British people and reduced wealth for all. Figures such as Robert Clive, who made a fortune in the East as he rose from a simple clerk to major general, were depicted as dangerous 'nabobs', a term derived from the leading officials of the Mughal Empire, who were known as *nawabs*, with influence sufficient to maintain Britain's mercantile path.[41] As Bengal experienced a famine that killed a third of the population from 1769, the more grotesque effects of the system were manifested.[42] Smith's nightmare was that all of Europe was following British policy because of its success in war before the American Revolution. Smith believed that this resulted in an 'unnatural and retrograde' economic development reliant upon the pursuit of war and empire and at odds with the true interests of humanity. Ultimately, he argued, it could not be sustained.[43] For many observers, chattel slavery was the most apparent example of the kind of commerce that resulted from the unnatural order of modern European trade.[44]

However unnatural they considered contemporary economic and political relations to be, Hume and Smith, after the experience of the Seven Years' War, fought across several continents between France and Britain and their respective allies from 1756–63, could not deny that Britain was far better at waging war than any commercial state in history. Britain described itself as a free state whose populace enjoyed far greater liberties and rights than those of other European nations. But this free state amounted to a war machine that used individual liberty as a rationale for the destruction of other states and the subjugation of their peoples. Rather than true liberty, the kind that fostered tolerance and peace, Hume believed that liberty itself was becoming fanatic, that it was morphing into a cynical, xenophobic tool of politicians. Images of John Bull and abstract notions of national glory had begun to be deployed to justify the taxes that sustained the wars that expanded the empire that, finally, generated profits for the monied interest.[45] Traditional strategies for maintaining enlightenment ranged from establishing mutual respect between previously hostile communities to creating separate spheres of influence to laws embodying toleration. Especially in the Protestant German states, an enlightenment/ Aufklärung was emerging entailing a rationalization of religion through the spread of a philosophy that would allow peoples and societies to govern themselves through reason alone. But whatever the nature of the enlightenment strategy, they failed in an era of global wars fought for trade and empire and in which indigenous peoples became embroiled – the Seven Years' War saw conflict across North America, Europe and the Indian subcontinent, with consequences for all of Asia and South America.[46] As we will see, thinkers during this period spent a great deal of time devising schemes to abolish war and empire in perpetuity, using peaceful forms of commerce as a contributing tool, in an attempt to avert what they considered to be the end of enlightenment. Britain, they began to argue, might emerge smaller and weaker and less influential as a result, but more free, tolerant and peaceful.

III

According to its advocates, the Enlightenment ended. Strategies for enlightenment had largely vanquished religious fanaticism from public life. But in the final decades of the eighteenth century, they believed that they ultimately failed in the maintenance of toleration and peace among nations. They braced themselves for an era of civil or international war, the growth of intolerance and the fall of existing constitutions and governments. For many, including Hume, Smith, Gibbon and Burke, the most significant failure was in suppressing ideological zealots whose forebears were deemed to have been responsible for the religious wars that devastated Europe in the sixteenth and seventeenth centuries. They were right: these conflicts broke out again at the end of the eighteenth century, this time in secular guise – but with equally violent results.

Some have argued that fears for the future were a commonplace response to the French Revolution. Enlightenment thinkers had much earlier identified the problems likely to cause the age's end. The French Revolution was, in fact, more of a response to the anticipations of imminent crisis; it was their effect rather than their cause. The view became widespread in the 1760s that new forms of fanaticism were abroad. As societies across Europe became polarized, frightening forms of superstition and enthusiasm were being translated from religion into politics. These terms – superstition, enthusiasm and fanaticism – were employed by contemporaries to signify a person for whom reason was being overwhelmed by passion, delusion or ignorance, and they are of fundamental importance in understanding the eighteenth century. They were employed again and again by a wide variety of thinkers, just as they had been across Reformation Europe, to identify those who had begun to justify civil violence against others, those who argued for war and empire-building and those who promoted forms of selfishness and luxury that were said to corrupt human nature and lead to unnatural forms of living. As a result of such diagnoses of contemporary ills, catastrophic futures were prophesied by numerous philosophers who looked on in anxiety as secular prophets promised their followers incredible social transformation and improvement.

In order to understand the Enlightenment era and its demise it is vital to distinguish between Hume's optimism about what can be termed the enlightenment in his early life and a conversion after the Seven Years' War to the view that enlightenment had failed. Hume's view was that for a variety of reasons existing societies were in crisis, being likely to collapse or be consumed in violence, and the only certainty was that the politics and society that surrounded him could not be expected to survive into the future. This was a view shared by many. As a result, speculation was rife about alternative futures, often highly practical in nature, focusing not just on the desired end but also the means of getting there, the transition mechanism that would successfully move humanity from a state of violence or corruption to harmony – or at least stability.[47] Many of these anticipated futures could be described as enthusiastic, being overly optimistic and impractical, but easily attracting adherents in consequence of promises being made to potential believers and because of the attractiveness of a general message of hope. The rhetorically gifted projector who sold such moonshine was derided but also feared as the 'man of system', Smith's term from *The Theory of Moral Sentiments* (1755).[48] The man of system might be a popular prophet and demagogue who manipulated the people, seeing himself to have special access to truth, or a philosopher advocating rigid laws and policies promising utopia, refusing to adapt to circumstances.[49]

Such men existed in the realms of religion, politics and scholarship. The sort of enthusiasm these schemers might conjure was recognized as being a step on the road to fanaticism, hence Hume's acute concern about the likelihood of civil and international war and all the kinds of intolerance and savagery that would accompany it.[50]

This book tells the story of the strategies to maintain enlightenment that Hume believed in when he was young and his ultimate conversion when older to the view that all of them were failing. It recaptures the views of the many contemporaries who came to share Hume's belief that the Enlightenment had ended and that the world could expect upheavals even greater than those experienced during the Reformation. Hume's world was one where people were expected to adhere to a faith because religion guaranteed promises and oaths, the very foundation of social interaction.[51] Atheism was beyond the pale, and atheists social outcasts.[52] Yet there was ongoing debate about what form of Christian belief was best suited to a tolerant and peaceful society and the least likely to turn fanatic or foment disorder. The legacy of the violence produced during the Reformation ran deep in national memories.[53] The most straightforward employment of terms such as fanaticism, superstition and enthusiasm continued to be in negatively describing forms of Christianity a believer rejected, especially those found in foreign lands.[54]

In Britain the debate was especially acute because it was one of the few remaining free states, albeit a free state with a singularly turbulent history. Free states were associated with civil faction and division, raising the question of whether enlightenment toleration could be sustained only in autocratic states that had entrenched by diktat the rule of law. In the British case, worries about the relationship between liberty and enlightenment affected in turn debates about the dominion of the Church of England or the Church of Scotland, as well as the rights of Dissenting and Catholic minorities. Those who believed that free states could be sustained and remain enlightened are the subjects of this book, those men and women struggling to defend their convictions in circumstances of great upheaval. Some prominent figures – Catharine Macaulay, Jacques-Pierre Brissot, Mary Wollstonecraft and Thomas Paine – were convinced at first that liberty, revolution and republicanism might be sufficient to restore enlightenment. Others, such as William Petty, the 2nd Earl of Shelburne, Edward Gibbon and Edmund Burke thought that a Britain turned away from empire, war and commercial excess might become a beacon of moderation and toleration. These groups accused each other of being destructive fanatics and battled to restore their own version of peace and toleration. As their strategies failed, each accepted Hume's grim prospect: ceaseless global turmoil beckoned as political and economic systems became fundamentally dependent on the practice of war.

The Meaning of Enlightenment

I

The general and accepted meaning of the Enlightenment today is that it was a great leap forward in the capacity of humans to control nature, generate wealth and direct their own destinies. It was, so the story goes, a crowning feat of progress and rationality, associated with some of the greatest philosophers such as Spinoza and Kant. Liberal values expanded, revolutions replaced tyrannical governments and the first shoots of democracy, human rights and constitutionalism began to establish themselves, gradually spreading first across Europe, then North America and then, ultimately, across the rest of the Earth. The assumption is that optimism was the dominant Enlightenment register, not because contemporaries were uncritical, but because they were sure that so much could be solved by the exercise of reason that a future could be forged embodying progress. Such a picture of the eighteenth century has become so rooted in educated minds that almost all scholars embrace this framework when studying the era. It is equally the point of departure for those who reject the Enlightenment for being overly imperialist, colonialist, racist or capitalist.

Sometimes the present prevents us from understanding the past. Precisely this has happened in the case of the Enlightenment. Its story remains the inspiration for many actors in public life, and in politics it is regularly called on to validate stances taken today. The Enlightenment is widely described as the positive origin of our world, a shared Western heritage, emulated in progressive societies and required globally if the human race is to solve some of the enormous problems it presently faces.[1] The mission of defending Enlightenment values against barbarians at the gates continues to inspire politicians and their followers. Countless historians have traced the origins of modernity – our world – back to the Enlightenment.[2] There are continuities, of course, but in doing so they tend to confuse the crucial context of that historical moment. In order to understand contemporary predicaments, it is indeed vital to ask Michel Foucault's question, 'What, then, is this event that is called the Enlightenment, that has determined, at least in part, what we are, what we think, and what we do today?'[3]

If attacks upon the Enlightenment have tended to share the claim that it represents the origin of the modern world, they often then go on to blame eighteenth-century ideas for leading to or for justifying twentieth-century tragedies and crimes. Criticisms of the Enlightenment were initially focused upon a perceived gap between enlightenment values and religious commitment or social order. Religion and order were seen to be the basis of progress or peace, often in accordance with God's providential plan for humanity.[4] Such arguments, that the Enlightenment created a secular world and therefore social and intellectual chaos, persist into modern philosophy.[5] In the 1950s, the Enlightenment was blamed for the rise of tyrannical communist societies – the ineluctable search for perfectibility at any cost was often traced back to the eighteenth century.[6] Liberal philosophers, such as Isaiah Berlin, were convinced that the supposedly monist rationalism of enlightenment philosophy led to the evils of Bolshevism.[7] Conservatives such as Michael Oakeshott worried too about the effects of the enlightenment aspiration to create harmonious societies based on universal laws.[8] The contemporary philosopher John Gray has argued that 'all schools of contemporary political thought are variations on the Enlightenment project.' For Gray this project is 'self-undermining' and 'exhausted', being responsible in part for an 'assault on cultural difference'. The Enlightenment should, in Gray's opinion, be described as the embodiment of 'Western cultural imperialism as the project of a universal civilization' and the source of a 'humanist conception of humankind's relations with the natural world'.⁹ Gray has also blamed the Enlightenment for the evils of global capitalism.¹⁰

Related arguments can be found in Jean-François Lyotard, the prominent French post-structuralist, who called the Enlightenment an 'essentialist' and 'totalising' metanarrative, another failed grand theory incompatible with human diversity.¹¹ Far more influential today is Max Horkheimer's and Theodor Adorno's *Dialectic of Enlightenment*, originally composed during the Second World War, which stated that the 'instrumental reason' that has held sway since the Enlightenment ought to be blamed for totalitarianism and the evils of the twentieth century.¹² It is worth restating again what has been frequently recognized, that Horkheimer and Adorno defined the Enlightenment along rather particular lines: they began with Homer's *Odyssey*, and had very little to say about eighteenth-century philosophy beyond a 'Second Excursus' linking Kant and the Marquis de Sade.¹³

Probably the most revered critique of the Enlightenment has been Michel Foucault's association of the Enlightenment with the modern surveillance state epitomized by Jeremy Bentham's Panopticon.¹⁴ More recently, but in a similar vein, scholars have condemned the Enlightenment for human oppression through justifications of social hierarchy, manifesting itself especially in historic colonialism, sexism and racism.¹⁵ Louis Sala-Molins has argued that Rousseau ought to be admonished for being silent about slavery; abolitionists such as Marie-Jean-Antoine-Nicolas de Caritat, marquis de Condorcet, merit reappraisal too because they did not call for the immediate renunciation of the practice.¹⁶ Some authors go so far as to causally link the Enlightenment with fascism and the Holocaust.¹⁷

II

Even if the last examples are extreme, criticism is increasingly directed towards the historians and students of the past who have played down the levels of injustice that existed within pre-industrial societies, and especially the forms of oppression that arose within the Enlightenment-era European empires as they violated the resources and ravaged the cultures of countless native peoples.[18] Historical actors can be condemned because of their dreadful exercise of power, or their existence within networks of coercion directed for the benefit of the rich and the strong against the poor and the weak. It is often stated that such critiques of the European past are new, a shared and urgent activity by thoroughly modern people motivated by moral conscience. In fact, none of the attacks are original. Indeed, both the positive evaluation of the Enlightenment as the source of civilized modernity and its critique as having justified barbarism can be traced to the nineteenth century. Those who justified the Enlightenment as the embodiment of reason and progress were Whigs or Liberals. Those who rejected the Enlightenment were socialists or Marxists, often inheritors of religious or republican traditions that advocated for social unions or unified cultural communities.[19] And those old schools of thought continue to govern our perspective today.

When the dominant Whig/Liberal ideology in the nineteenth century established itself as a framework for understanding the present, confident histories began to be written of a presumed past, narrating the triumph of representative government, liberty and free markets built on the foundations of progress laid down during the Enlightenment.[20] At the same time, socialists and Marxists indicted industrial society, looking back to the eighteenth century as the time when the rot began, charting the explosion of property-defending laws, the loss of the popular right to the use of common land, and the increasing power of the urban bourgeoisie as they refused to abide by the traditional notions of a moral economy.[21] Liberal and Marxist histories are still being written, whether their exponents realize this or not.

In such histories the Enlightenment becomes a field of battle. For Liberals, toleration, democracy and rights emerge from an ever-growing web of relationships forged through a revolution in human communication. What is deemed most just, global and liberal wins out because it is the most rational – with the caveat that full equality manifested in rights so obvious to us today had yet to be fully realized then.[22] The work of the German philosopher Jürgen Habermas has bolstered such Liberal interpretations of the Enlightenment. He argued that the eighteenth century saw an expanding bourgeois public sphere, facilitating far greater communication through press and print than ever before, as well as the consequent emergence of a new category in politics: public opinion.[23] The Enlightenment that emerged could be defined as secular and cosmopolitan.[24] Against the Liberals, those who see the Enlightenment as an arena for oppression and exploitation reiterate Marxist tropes about the grisly injustices of early commercial modernity and the grotesque abuses of humanity that resulted. Such arguments frequently refer to the imposition in England – purportedly a free state – of the 'Bloody Code' commencing with the Black Act of 1723, which made poaching a capital crime.[25] Between the 1770s and the 1830s the number of offences punishable by death skyrocketed, with many of the new laws focused on the rights of property owners. Smith himself was critical of these sorts of laws.[26] The many thousands who met public execution as a result of some minor theft is evidence, according to the Marxist formulation, of an 'enlightened' middle-class brutally entrenching their assets.[27] Other examples included the eviction of tenants across the Highlands and the Western Isles in a series of clearances from the 1750s, all in the name of agricultural improvement, the Europe-wide enclosure movement and the battle to control the price of grain by populations worried at the prospect of famine. As Marx himself asserted, 'when Christian ideas succumbed in the 18th century to rationalist ideas, feudal society fought its death battle with the then revolutionary bourgeoisie.'[28]

Liberal and Marxist ways of seeing the Enlightenment are mistaken. It is wrong, with the Liberals, to see that world straightforwardly as the origin of our own. They incorrectly assume that the same sorts of questions were being asked about rights, liberty or democracy by significant writers throughout history, a questioning culminating in the age of revolutions at the end of the eighteenth century. In fact, eighteenth-century actors had distinctive responses to their problems. Presumptions of Liberal continuity mask what is alien and significant about ideas at that time – making the intellectual history of the century dull and predictable, simply the passing of a progressive baton from one generation to the next. Liberals forget that assertions of rights can lead to division and fanaticism, the creation of self-proclaimed democracies to further violence and war.[29] It cannot be denied, with the Marxists, that worries about political liberty, poverty and economic globalization are traceable to the eighteenth century. Yet the Marxist attack upon the Enlightenment for ideas which led to later catastrophe has negative consequences. It caricatures what happened in the eighteenth century as a few ink-stained thinkers and rapacious nabobs forming and defending this thing called the Enlightenment. The Enlightenment did exist in the form of genuine strategies for peace and toleration.[30] When these strategies were overwhelmed by new kinds of fanaticism, enlightenment was seen to have ended. But the battle was reconceived and recommenced.

If the Enlightenment is solely perceived as the source of a problematic modernity, the function of historical investigation becomes limited to detecting the errors of the past alone while ignoring the deeper and more complex currents that were in play then and may still be in play today. We cannot learn from the eighteenth century if we associate studying the Enlightenment with just the identification of the presumed mistakes of philosophers working at that time. Finding continuities from the eighteenth century is not wrong. Recognizing that, at the end of the eighteenth century, many observers believed that their own enlightenment dedicated to preventing religious and imperialist wars was collapsing or had disintegrated is the part that has been forgotten; it needs to be restored because it provided singularly clear-eyed evaluations of the prospects for sovereign states in a world which looks much like our own, perspectives now lost.

III

That the Enlightenment exists today mainly in the form of a caricature, a product of a more general turn against history in public life,
has been asserted many times since the turn of the century. James
Schmidt has done more than anyone else to ridicule ahistorical perceptions of eighteenth-century thought.[31] In particular he rejects
those Whiggish accounts in which the Enlightenment becomes synonymous with the progress of reason in the form of human rights
or declarations of the rights of man.[32] Criticism of these standard
approaches raises the inevitable question of whether it makes sense
to generalize about enlightenment ideas at all.[33] If enlightenment
as a whole amounts to a series of strategies intended to put an end
to civil turbulence and religion-inspired international turmoil, it
becomes possible to talk of a plurality of enlightenments that might
be Cartesian, Arminian or Newtonian in origin and Neapolitan,
Scottish, English or Parisian in expression.[34] Within such enlightenments, the contribution of theology to each strategy for peace and
toleration can facilitate a more precise definition. A 'civil enlightenment' derived from eclectic philosophy and seeking a state that
separated religion from politics can be distinguished from a 'metaphysical enlightenment' based on rationalist forms of Christianity
seeking a public theological culture that ensured politics and religion together maintained civil peace. Defenders of the first approach
included Samuel Pufendorf and Christian Thomasius, while the
second included Gottfried Wilhelm Leibniz and Kant.[35] That the
latter won out at the end of the eighteenth century forms a German
version of the end of enlightenment – this is what the Kantian revolution in political philosophy meant – and it was perceived to be
dangerously theological by some of Kant's many critics.[36]

I do not reject the notion of a plurality of enlightenments but
assert that all of the strategies advanced to maintain civil peace
were seen to be failing by major and minor philosophers, politicians
and commentators in the final decades of the eighteenth century. If

we reconstitute this sense of failure and plot the responses to it, eighteenth- and nineteenth-century ideas begin to look very different.[37] The eighteenth century was characterized by uncertainty about the future, so turbulent were the times through which people were living across Europe and the Atlantic world, and in the substantial areas of the globe controlled by the European powers. Problems were especially acute in the self-proclaimed free states, raising the issue of whether it was easier to maintain enlightenment in absolute monarchies or whether liberty and enlightenment were indeed mutually sustaining.

IV

People living in the eighteenth century tended to see themselves as postwar generations. Their parents and grandparents would have had first- or second-hand experience of worldly turbulence traceable to the Reformation. Religious warfare, often bound up with long-burning dynastic conflicts, had devastated Europe from at least the 1520s. Indeed, when, in 1494, Charles VIII of France invaded Italy, initiating a general conflict with the Holy Roman Empire, Spain and numerous local polities, Europeans saw their continent as a constant battleground, a seat of Mars.[38] Those who looked at Europe from other parts of the world came to the same unavoidable conclusion.[39] From the Kingdom of Norway in the north to Portugal and Spain in the west, Muscovy in the east to Sicily in the south, European life became defined by war. Nations were forever invading each other's territories and questioning the right of fellow states to exist as sovereign entities. Shakespeare reveals a great deal about the early modern European experience when he classes the soldier as one of the seven ages of man.[40]

From the end of the fifteenth century a central cause of this ongoing military conflict was the battle between France and Habsburg rulers, with the latter at different times encircling the French in territories ranging from Burgundy, Italy, the Low Countries, Spain, the Holy Roman Empire and even briefly England during the reign of Mary I and her husband Philip II. War occurred across Italy from the 1490s to the 1550s, across the Low Countries from the 1550s to the 1640s, across Germany and Scandinavia from the 1610s to the 1640s and across Europe as a whole during the Nine Years' War (1688–97) and the War of the Spanish Succession (1701–14). Those Europeans in disputed territory faced perpetual danger and hardship. Raids by brigands and pirates were a constant threat. Armies on the march caused carnage by living off the land, often pillaging what wasn't given up. Landowners could insist that men serve them militarily, leaving soil untilled and families dispossessed. Everyone suffered. Joachim von Sandrart, a German painter, wrote of the Thirty Years' War (1618–48) that 'Queen Germania saw her palaces and churches, decorated with magnificent pictures, go up in flames time and again.' In such times, artists experienced only 'poverty and contempt'[41] – it is no surprise that Michelangelo earned his living for a time as a military engineer in Florence. Great cities were sacked and often nearly destroyed, as in the infamous case of Rome by the unpaid troops of Emperor Charles V in 1527, who remained in the city for seven months, raping and killing the populace, pictured like frenzied ants in Pieter Bruegel the Elder's famous panorama.[42]

In addition to intra-European conflict, the continued rise of the Ottoman Empire in the south and east, ranging from Algiers and Budapest to Baku, presented a great external threat to Europe, especially to those states on its frontier.[43] Sultan Mehmed II had captured Constantinople in 1453, and the Empire had threatened to go further, annexing much of Hungary at the battle of Mohács in 1526 during the reign of Süleyman the Magnificent, and launching invasions that reached the gates of Vienna in 1529 and again in 1683. Wars between the Habsburgs and the Ottomans occurred from 1593–1606 and 1683–99. The latter conflict was marked by the creation of a Holy League on the grounds that the Ottomans posed as much a threat to Christianity as a whole as they did to individual territorial states. The Holy League comprised the Republic of Venice, Russia, the Holy Roman

Empire and the Polish-Lithuanian Commonwealth – they ultimately put an end to Ottoman control of Hungary via the Treaty of Karlowitz in 1699. Fear of the Grand Turk, Barbary pirates and the possibility of Muslim jihad was maintained in the eighteenth century despite the eventual decline of Ottoman military power. They became 'useful enemies' to the states of Europe, identified as Oriental despots and used as a warning to Western peoples that they were fortunate to live in polities where the whim of the ruler could not mean life or death for ordinary subjects.[44] Yet during the Reformation, exactly this power was exercised across Europe towards purportedly heretical people and communities.

When traditional dynastic international rivalries were suffused with religious division between Christians, the likelihood of war, especially civil war, intensified. Martin Luther himself stated that war was normal, as necessary as eating or drinking.[45] Luther initiated the Protestant Reformation by posting his 95 Theses attacking the Catholic Church on the door of the All Saints' Church at Wittenberg on the Elbe in Saxony in 1517. Rebellion against Catholicism was sparked and soon raged across northern Europe through the 1520s. By the 1530s martyrdom had become a commonplace. So had the judicial and private execution of individuals for confessing a particular view of Christ. The murder of fellow humans began to be justified as part of a journey of personal salvation, a journey that could encompass the souls of enemies and neighbours alike – necessary victims by virtue of their different perspective upon Christianity. Europe was quickly divided along Catholic, Anabaptist, Lutheran and Calvinist lines. Even if the religious divisions did not always neatly align with dynastic and political rivalries, the resultant instability continually fuelled conflict: from the German Peasants' War and Dalecarlian Rebellion in Sweden in the 1520s to the Schmalkaldic War across the Holy Roman Empire in the 1540s, and from the French Wars of Religion (1562–98), to the Thirty Years' War encompassing Bohemia, Germany, Russia, Denmark, Sweden and France.[46] Between the sixteenth and early eighteenth centuries Europe rarely saw a year of peace.

The Enlightenment began when these religious wars ceased. To its defenders, the Enlightenment meant the project of preventing wars of religion from breaking out once more and destroying communities and states. The message of Thomas Hobbes's *Behemoth, or The Long Parliament* (1681), an analysis of the causes of the civil conflicts that brought about carnage across England, Scotland and Ireland in a war of the three kingdoms between 1639 and 1653, was that theological disputation translated into politics had led to civil and international war.[47] Hobbes explained that when the conviction became generalized among particular communities that they were following the will of God in battling those with alternative beliefs, laws preventing violence ceased to be adhered to. In the worst cases, religious-inspired politics became fanatic, justifying extreme measures such as the assassination and massacre of those perceived to be ungodly. Cultures which defined themselves by war against their unbelieving and heterodox enemies then sprang up. Severe penalties were handed down to those within these communities who failed to adhere to the laws of whatever sect was considered legitimate. This was why Voltaire later wrote that intolerance at this time was ubiquitous across Europe: Protestants, he argued, after freeing themselves from the yoke of Catholicism, turned their societies into monasteries, grim and austere with laws determining every facet of behaviour.[48]

For all parties, fanatical religious wars constituted an anti-Enlightenment. Enlightened strategies for bringing about peace at a local level ranged from challenging community justifications of violence, seeking means of habitualizing pacific behaviour, to the enacting of a series of broadminded, inclusive laws and schemes of education.[49] Equally popular was the embrace of an ethic of toleration known by many at the time as 'right reason', consisting of maxims of behaviour and policy that enshrined moderation.[50] Peace at the international level was even more important. Schemes for peace within and between states included the principle 'cuius regio, eius religio' ('whose realm, his religion') coined by the canon lawyer Joachim Stephani to describe the policy of estates choosing between

Protestantism or Catholicism for their particular lands, enunciated at the Peace of Augsburg (1555).[51] Hobbes's own union of civil and ecclesiastical authority was another enlightenment strategy, giving the sovereign authority to overawe religious communities and prevent them from fighting, a vision pictorially presented in the famous frontispiece to *Leviathan* in 1651.[52] Published blueprints for the establishment of perpetual peace abounded, all of which dealt with religious conflict as much as they did with civil war, from Émeric de Crucé's *The New Cyneas* (*Le nouveau Cynée*, 1623), Maximilien de Béthune, duc de Sully's *The Grand Design of Henry IV* (*Le Grand Dessein d'Henri IV*, 1638), William Penn's *Essay Towards the Present and Future Peace of Europe* (1693) and Charles-Irénée Castel, abbé de Saint-Pierre's *Project for Perpetual Peace* (*Projet pour rendre la paix perpétuelle en Europe*, 1713).[53]

Fortification was another widespread policy enacted to protect populations from war and division, with vast sums spent in early modern Europe to define a community as an impregnable haven through interconnected walls, gates, ditches and ramparts. Star-shaped bastion forts including redoubts, ravelins, hornworks and lunettes, slopes and enfilades made life miserable for those besieging defended walls, following the Italian cities that had replaced ring formations with polygonal structures intended to prevent concentrated canon fire from bringing down walls.[54] But for countless observers it was the act of making peace through legal agreement alone that could restore international accord and relative civil harmony. The Westphalian Treaties (1648), the Treaty of the Pyrenees (1659) and those signed at Utrecht (1713–14) were all envisaged in part as means to enlightenment.[55] Each of these agreements detailed forms of toleration and attempted to definitively establish national borders with the broad goal of preventing the outbreak of wars in general and wars of religion in particular. Advocating enlightenment entailed the development of strategies, treaties, laws, policies and beliefs that could be implemented whenever war and fanaticism arose. For some, the vexed question of religion and dynasticism was ultimately about power; for them, the only enduring solution

would be to forge a new Roman empire, creating a universal monarchy in Europe so militarily powerful as to make civil war or
religious-inspired rebellion futile.[56]

V

Yet plans and projects for civil and religious peace and toleration
were threatened by new commercial forces that were reshaping
national politics, pulling people from the countryside into the ever-
larger towns and rapidly altering physical, social and ideological
landscapes.[57] A longstanding theme of religious apology had it
that the secular lust for commerce could easily develop a fanatical
edge. The kinds of passions that were prevalent in commercial
society – the desire for individual wealth and the jealous consumption of luxury goods – could, it was believed, quickly look like the
sort of fervour that had been unleashed during the Reformation.[58]
When such passions became prevalent in the life of the individual,
it was commonly held that immorality, libertinism and the abandonment of societal duty would soon follow.[59] In this respect,
choosing a life dedicated solely to the pursuit of wealth and self-
interest was akin to the kind of dramatic personal change associated
with religious conversion. Consumer society boomed in the eighteenth century: goods once deemed luxuries, from books and
watches, to lace, porcelain and silks, were now widely enjoyed. For
the richest, varieties of Indian textiles and Chinese vases fuelled
fashion trends that only they could afford.[60] When whole communities and societies became addicted to luxury consumption, sustained
by the new sorts of wealth generated by trade, it was considered by
many critics to be a step into the unknown, potentially leading to
disorder – the bonds of traditional society had been loosened, they
held, and might snap.

Critical contemporaries drew on ancient moral arguments associating luxury with corruption, ultimately holding that the Roman
Empire had fallen because its citizens became addicted to the

consumption of luxuries originating in Asia.[61] A lust for commerce was making people selfish, changing their mores and preventing them from supporting their communities in adhering to social duties in accordance with the good of all. For many, whether it led to war and empire or not, such a development threatened the stability of European states because of the corruption of popular and elite manners. Luxury, it was commonly held, preceded greater vice and effeminacy as men put self-interest before public duty, a process altering social behaviour and risking military defeat as manliness declined. John Brown, the ultimate contemporary doomsayer, held that the lust for gold was the handmaid of effeminacy, guaranteeing the national collapse of Britain, as it had that of ancient Rome.[62]

Writing in his popular journal the *Spectator* of 20 October 1711, Joseph Addison, the poet and playwright, made the parallel clear between change in religious and recent societal developments caused by commerce. Addison warned that 'the two great errors into which a mistaken devotion may betray us are enthusiasm and superstition.'[63] He went on to employ the terms to indict, respectively, Protestant Dissent and Catholicism, in contrast with the moderate nature of contemporary Anglicanism.[64] Another source of fanaticism was identified in the societal division between the landed and the monied interest, the latter considered by Addison to be nouveau-riche products of commercial society, to encompass the desire of individuals to enrich themselves no matter the consequences for others. In this regard, Addison was especially concerned by the conditions created by the vast army and navy employed during the War of the Spanish Succession (1701–14).[65] During this period, he believed that the costs of the war had induced rampant speculation in government bonds, especially among those who had already profited from the war and desired nothing else than to maximize their already substantial fortunes. Addison worried that opposition between the traditional rulers of Britain, the landed interest, and this new social group dedicated to commerce would lead to social and political unrest – and had already, he believed, made civil war suddenly likely in British politics once again:

It gives me a serious Concern to see such a spirit of dissension in the country; not only as it destroys virtue and common sense, and renders us in a manner barbarians towards one another, but as it perpetuates our animosities, widens our breaches, and transmits our present passions and prejudices to our posterity. For my own part, I am sometimes afraid that I discover the seeds of a civil war in these our divisions; and therefore cannot but bewail, as in their first principles, the miseries and calamities of our children.[66]

Addison's observation was taken up by many who were convinced that Britain was on the wrong track in politics and economics in the first decades of the new century. The writers John Trenchard and Thomas Gordon in their popular *Cato's Letters,* in the issue of 6 April 1723, went on to distinguish between two kinds of enthusiast, like Addison drawing a parallel between the wars of religion of the past and the effects of commerce in the present.[67] The first enthusiasts were harmless, being madmen convinced they were directed and inspired by God in all of their actions. The second were deadly, termed in *Cato's Letters* as the 'holy enthusiast' or 'mischievous madman'. Such men became violent and fanatic 'out of a pure zeal for God'. They might, for example, kill, maim, cause plagues and destroy communities in the service of a purported higher good identical with God's true wishes and plan for the world.[68] Trenchard and Gordon's brilliant twist was to redescribe the monied interest explicitly in these religious terms – they could just as easily be potential holy enthusiasts or mischievous madmen. Such a redescription made the threat to contemporaries meaningful, used as they were to the consequences of religious division.

The economic events that were most often described as being akin to these outpourings of religious mania are now known as the South Sea Bubble and the Mississippi Bubble, both of which came to a head in 1720. In the early 1700s, the worry was widespread that politicians, having run up huge state debts through William III's wars, would turn into 'projectors' who promised easy money alongside economic transformation, while in reality maintaining a standing army corrosive of liberty.[69] Daniel Defoe, the indefatigable pamphleteer, wrote in 1697 that theirs was 'The Projecting Age' because improvements in every walk of life had become vital in light of the 'the losses and depredations which this war brought with it'.[70] A singular project in this regard was initiated with the chartering of the South Sea Company in 1711 to supply, for the next thirty years, 4,800 slaves per annum to Spain's South American plantations.[71] When the British acquired monopoly rights over this trade at the Treaty of Utrecht in 1713, the South Sea Company purchased the rights in return for paying off a large portion of the British national debt. Anticipating huge profits on the basis of new South American markets, shares in the Company, issued in order to purchase the national debt, proved wildly popular. This led the Company to cover more of the debt in return for further commercial rights in 1718, resulting in a frenzy of rising share prices: an economic bubble.[72] When profits inevitably proved meagre, the share price and the Company collapsed, leaving large numbers of investors impoverished.

France suffered from a related scheme. In 1716, John Law, a Scottish speculator and professional gambler, promised to pay off the French national debt, commercialize their economy and generate enormous revenues for the state through the development of lands in Louisiana. Law was one of the figures who took advantage of newly developed financial instruments, having as early as 1705 had the idea of stimulating the Scottish economy through the creation of a land bank.[73] Law came to the notice of the French government, mired in debt in the aftermath of the War of the Spanish Succession, and he soon convinced Philippe Charles, the duc d'Orléans, then regent of France, that access to credit would restore French power while reducing the national debt. First, Law established the Banque Générale as a company issuing paper money. Then, in August 1717, he created the Compagnie d'Occident with rights to the enormous Louisiana Territory. Law's idea was to pay off the French national debt by selling it for shares in the land of what was everywhere termed the Mississippi Company.

In 1719, a single company, the Banque Royale, took over all French national finances, from the collection of taxes to the exploitation of imperial lands and international trade. Initially share prices rose ten times over within the first year. Speculation mania spread from Paris to London and Amsterdam with investors believing they were making fortunes at incredible speed. In December 1719, Law abjured his Protestantism and became a Catholic, allowing him to be appointed *Contrôleur général des Finances* in January 1720. Law then attempted to fix the value of company shares by converting them into paper money, but prices began to fall in the spring of 1720. When confidence was shattered in the autumn of 1720 and prices fell precipitously, Law was branded an amoral gambler and a cunning devil who had enriched himself while bringing anguish and wretchedness to the three major commercial states of the continent.[74] He was soon considered to be the ultimate projector, gambling with the lives of the people and the fate of nations, while the Mississippi scheme he oversaw became, to most, tantamount to a dice throw and the antithesis of sensible policy.[75]

In the aftermath of the South Sea Bubble especially it was notable that 'the monied Interest, those pretended Loyalists and Patriots' were redescribed not only as religious enthusiasts but also as fanatic warmongers. War gave the monied interest profit while they refused to pay their share in taxes, in contrast with the landed interest:

> Let the landed and the monied Interest be taxed equally, and then let us see who are the Men for carrying on the War, for humbling of France for enlarging our Trade, and for supporting his Majesty and his Government: Let us both contribute equally and it will soon appear, who are the Friends, and who the Enemies, to our present Settlements. The Government will be soon convinced who are the Jacobites and High Flyers.[76]

Despite such concerns, the pursuit of war and commercial empire by the British especially proceeded apace; rising debt proved intractable, the effects of which became one of Hume's obsessions. The failure to deal with the intensifying forces pulling the world apart prompted the deepest political crises of the late eighteenth century. This was the Enlightenment's end. Recovering the full meaning of this moment is vital – we too live in a time when the political structures we inhabit are fluid and are perhaps on the cusp of great and potentially dangerous change. Our predicament today is very much like that of the eighteenth century in the sense that they too saw themselves to be on the edge of a precipice. If the fall came, civilization would end, liberty would be lost, poverty would abound and new forms of slavery would arise. The eighteenth century was not the origin of our present discontents, but the parallel is clear and important. Due to the way in which we study the past and because of the ahistorical nature of the disciplines we rely upon to solve our problems, we may be less well prepared than our ancestors. It matters then that we recover the ways in which those who first defended the Enlightenment diagnosed the forces that might end it, ever struggling to prevent its demise.

2

David Hume and the End of the World

I

When he was young, Hume believed in enlightenment. He thought peace and toleration could be identified in the world and, more importantly, that there were forces that might be able to sustain them.[1] Victory in the historic battle against religious fanaticism, waged in Europe by previous generations, had been achieved. Hume was not afraid of Christian zeal in his own time, although he subjected to ridicule those who felt its fire.[2] Hume was optimistic about the possibility of Europe's major commercial states, Britain and France, becoming more alike in forming governments of laws rather than of men: he believed that jurists and legislators were finally coming together in each country to enshrine civil liberties, establishing a rule of law for all subjects. Moderate political cultures scornful of war would flourish in consequence, he held, having so much to lose from the loss of law and liberty. Hume went so far as to contemplate a future in which Britain and France would never battle again. He was confident that the Habsburg–Bourbon dynastic conflict would not be replicated in modern Europe with different players. Hume's further reason for optimism derived from the nature of commercial economy. Rich states like Britain could not rely on their trading supremacy being maintained because the prices of their products could, he believed, be undercut by poorer nations paying their workers less for their labour.[3] Commerce was for Hume an inconstant force and would not maintain the supremacy of one particular state over a long period. Competition spread wealth and power, undermining over time the dominating aspirations of national leaders. Equally, commerce flourished best in conditions of peace and necessitated politeness between parties, who might hate one another when it came to religion or politics, but nevertheless were mutually respectful to secure the exchange of goods. All these forces might well ensure that enlightenment was a stable human condition in Europe and even spread beyond the continent.

Regarding religious fanaticism, Hume made his optimism clear in the twelfth essay, entitled 'Of Superstition and Enthusiasm', of the book that made him famous in 1741, the *Essays, Moral and Political*. Here he defined superstition as false or corrupt belief, being the product of blindly following a madman or being foolishly convinced of the truth of opinions that went against reason. Superstition was produced by human weakness, fear, melancholy and ignorance, forces which caused people to accept as true things that were manifestly false. He argued that the forced oppression of individuals, by direct terror or the apprehension of threat, fostered an environment in which superstition thrived.[4] Superstition might lead easily to enthusiasm, when the delusions fed to an individual were embraced to an extent that they wanted to promote them evangelically. Enthusiasm was a situation in which 'the imagination swells with great but confused conceptions.' When the imagination was let loose people began to believe things far beyond the normal because their minds were frequently overcome with 'raptures, transports, and surprising flights of fancy'.

Despite the ludicrous nature of enthusiastic belief, enthusiasts tended to be fearless, certain that they were carrying out the will of God. The individual who experienced the movement from superstition to enthusiasm was likely, Hume argued, to perceive themselves to be both elevated as a person and a particular favourite of the divinity, and it was therefore no surprise that enthusiasm inspired by superstition often resulted in violence. Examples included the Anabaptists of the 1520s in Germany, the Levellers in England in the 1640s, the Covenanters in Scotland in the 1660s and the Camisard rebels in France in 1703.[5] All of these movements were characterized by a 'contempt for the common rules of reason, morality, and prudence'.

In his 1741 analysis of such delusions of the human mind, Hume was most concerned by what he termed the 'most cruel disorders' produced by enthusiasm. At the same time, he identified a positive consequence. It was the case that enthusiastic fury and fanaticism was always short-lived, like its natural parallel of thunder and lightning, and always exhausted itself, leaving all the wildness spent and the air calmer and more serene than before the storm. There was a natural process, Hume said, by which 'dangerous bigots' became 'very free reasoners'. Positive illustrations of the process for Hume included the Quakers, who were devout to the point of rejecting accepted forms of society yet were unquestionably peaceful. This meant that enthusiasm was less to be feared than superstition. Superstition, Hume wrote, 'steals in gradually and insensibly, renders men tame and submissive'. An example of superstition becoming dominant in a society was the rule of priests in Catholic countries; they, Hume asserted, through their social prominence as expositors of God's will, became tyrants and disturbers, creating cultures that promoted division and intolerance and which justified violence towards heretics. Catholicism in the form of the Counter-Reformation and Holy Inquisition in Europe had led to 'dismal convulsions', a parallel to the effects of enthusiastic Protestantism in the times of Reformation.

As was so often the case, Hume ended his essay by expressing his conclusion in the form of a paradox; while there was much to be feared from enthusiasm because of its horrific initial effects, it was ultimately 'a friend' to the enlightened. Superstition, by contrast, was ever 'an enemy to civil liberty'.[6] Hume drew lessons from the English experience of the Reformation and its consequences.[7] He believed that the religious radicalism that had flourished during the civil wars of the seventeenth century had been worth it, because the violence of the radical Puritans, once their force had become exhausted, then led to the foundation of a free state with a moderate and pacific public culture.[8] Hume made the same point in his

History of England, stating that 'the precious spark of liberty had been kindled, and was preserved, by the Puritans alone; and it was to this sect, whose principles appear so frivolous and habits so ridiculous, that the English owe the whole freedom of their constitution.'[9] That British liberty had been erected upon Puritan foundations was a contentious but commonplace theme, becoming more prominent as the century progressed.

The towering achievement of his age was, in Hume's opinion, the neutering of evangelical religion and the drawing from it of a passion for liberty. For Hume, always sensitive to the operation of unintended consequences in history, part of the reason for this success had been the extent of the seventeenth-century bloodletting and the grotesque results of the civil war. However, he nevertheless believed that the barriers erected between religion and politics in the seventeenth century to secure toleration were important in preventing the violence and massacre so prevalent in prior centuries. Hume remained an enemy to superstition, which he continued to associate with established religious authority grown too powerful in society. But the evidence pointed towards modern legislators having discovered means of combating fanaticism. This was the lesson found in France after the death of Louis XIV.

Louis XIV had threatened Europe with the renewal of reformation sectarianism in the form of an imperial Catholicism invading the Protestant parts of Europe, forcibly converting the Huguenot populace in France, and turning his back upon treaties that had put an end to the wars of religion.[10] Louis XIV's policies were readily described as fanatic and enthusiastic, derived logically from a similarly organized church.[11] Propagandists for Louis XIV in turn, above all the Bishop of Meaux, Jacques-Bénigne Bossuet, assaulted Protestants as seditious fanatics and domestic heretics both un-French and dangerous.[12] Louis XIV's war machine had been formidable.[13] Yet Louis XIV's defeat in war and resulting failure to restore confessional religious conflict to the continent for Hume amounted to a message of hope. For many years the profoundly Francophile Hume expected Britain to learn from France, a process that would aid peace by bringing the two states together. Hume noted in 1754 'that my Principles are, all along, tolerably monarchical, and that I abhor that low Practice, so prevalent in England, of speaking with Malignity of France'.[14]

When reflecting on the transformation of political experience during his lifetime, Hume had observed that 'all kinds of government, free and absolute, seem to have undergone, in modern times, a great change for the better, with regard both to foreign and domestic management.'[15] Britain and France were coming together because they were each what he termed 'civilized monarchies', being 'a government of laws, not of men', with all of the resulting benefits:

> But though all kinds of government be improved in modern times, yet monarchical government seems to have made the greatest advances towards perfection. It may now be affirmed of civilized monarchies, what was formerly said in praise of republics alone, that they are a government of Laws, not of Men. They are found susceptible of order, method, and constancy, to a surprizing degree. Property is there secure; industry encouraged; the arts flourish; and the prince lives secure among his subjects, like a father among his children.[16]

France was for Hume 'the most perfect model of pure monarchy' and other monarchies of Europe were following. Here we can perceive the profound influence of Samuel Pufendorf on Hume, who too believed that if the great systems of natural law could be carved into positive law, then future civil and international conflicts could be averted at best and limited at worst.[17] Law could do the work of maintaining enlightenment.[18]

Significantly, France was, Hume held, unlikely to develop as a trading power to the extent of Dutch and British free states, because absolute government rested upon the subordination of ranks and this ensured that 'birth, titles and place must be honoured above industry and riches.'[19] The French law of *dérogeance*, for example, stated that aristocrats involved in commerce risked losing their noble status.[20] This made certain too that successful merchants would sooner or later use their wealth to become landed aristocrats. Despite such tendencies, Hume predicted that absolute monarchies, like France, and mixed or republican polities, like the Dutch Republic and Britain, would become more alike in future times. Monarchies like France could improve by reforming the system of taxation, which could be levied to make agriculture thrive, which in turn would boost trade. France would become richer because its agricultural sector was so strong, if corruptions such as the practice of venality were abolished.[21] Free states like Britain, facing the prospect of degeneration due to rising national debt and reliance upon public credit to fund wars, could learn from French reformers emphasizing agriculture, especially the writings of the Catholic moralist François Fénelon and the physiocratic movement inspired by the physician François Quesnay.[22]

During his early, optimistic years, when his faith in enlightenment held, Hume's grand argument was that the successful battle against superstition in religion created an opportunity for resolving international differences in the economic and political spheres. France and Britain, so often described as eternal enemies with altogether different histories and political traditions, were, Hume believed, very similar in the trajectories of their present politics. When politics was related, peace was anticipated: Hume argued that there was now no good reason for war between these Western empires. In the 1740s and 1750s Hume had a vision of the growth of 'politeness and learning' through 'a number of neighbouring and independent states, connected together by commerce and policy'. Hume stated that 'The emulation, which naturally arises among those neighbouring states, is an obvious source of improvement.'[23] This has been referred to as the *doux commerce* thesis: that commerce could in certain circumstances become a force for peace since trade relied upon toleration, generating soft-power linkages capable of preventing conflict.[24] The possibility of peace between Britain and France was Hume's positive response to what he identified as the most shocking innovation in modern politics: the linkage between war and trade.[25] This linkage was the greatest threat to enlightenment as Hume defined it.

II

War and trade became intimately linked when powerful states believed it necessary to fight for the markets and commerce of their neighbours. In Hume's view this had a profound consequence for thinking about politics. There was no longer much point in turning to the ancient world for lessons about politics, laws and morals, as many of his forebears had done. Ancient societies had never been like modern states in their battle for trade. The parallels traditionally drawn between ancients and moderns became at worst meaningless, or at best only indirectly relevant. As Hume wrote in 'Of the Populousness of Ancient Nations': 'ancient manners were more unfavourable than the modern' and ancient politics contained 'in general, so little humanity and moderation'.[26] In arguing that the ancients were no longer to be considered contemporary models for politics because of economic change, Hume was directly following the London physician, merchant and builder Nicholas Barbon. Significantly, because of their contrastingly active lives in commerce and religion, Barbon was the son of the Puritan Praisegod Barbon after whom the short-lived parliament of 1653 was named (Barebone's Parliament). Barbon had made the claim that the circumstances of the ancients were so distant from those of the moderns as to no longer require scrutiny. Even an author as recent as Machiavelli, writing in republican Florence in the early 1500s, was suddenly alien, he believed, because the economic issues he addressed were a world away from those of modern states. As Barbon put it, 'Machiavel a Modern Writer, and the best, though he lived in a Government, where the Family of Medicis had advanced themselves to the Sovereignty by their Riches, acquired by Merchandizing, doth not mention Trade, as any way interested in the Affairs of State.'[27]

It is worth noting too that in France the great philosopher and jurist Montesquieu had come to similar conclusions. In the decade before Hume was writing, he argued that Rome had existed at a time in history divorced from the present. In his study of the fall of Rome (*Considérations sur les causes de la grandeur des Romains et de leur décadence*), first published in 1734, Montesquieu stated that Romans experienced a world 'not like the world in ours' because of the transformative effect of travel, conquest and trade, and inventions such as the compass, the printing press and the extraordinary distance correspondence could now be delivered. Technological innovation had altered society and ultimately 'given rise, among us, to an art called by the name of politics' the basis of which was that 'every man sees at one glance whatever is transacted in the whole universe.' One consequence was that when a state considered imperial expansion 'all the nations round them are immediately terrified.'[28] Montesquieu argued that 'The Romans were not solicitous to improve commerce, or cultivate the sciences, but ranked them among the attentions proper for slaves.'[29] Drawing a contrast with Carthage, he suggested that Rome was able to survive for so long as a republic and empire because of its anti-commercial nature and manners.[30] Trade did allow states to rise rapidly but they would equally be expected quickly to fall:

> Such powers, as are established by commerce, may subsist for a long series of years in their humble condition, but their grandeur is of short duration; they rise by little and little, and in an imperceptible manner, for they do not perform any particular exploit which may make a noise, and signalize their power: but when they have once raised themselves to so exalted a pitch, that it is impossible but all must see them, every one endeavours to deprive this nation of an advantage which it had snatched, as it were, from the rest of the world.[31]

In his magnificent *Spirit of the Laws* (*De l'esprit des lois*) of 1748 Montesquieu further asserted that 'the Romans were never distinguished by a jealousy of trade. They attacked Carthage as a rival, not as a trading nation.'[32] They did not fear commercial polities or consider them capable of challenging their own power. Modern politics was altogether different.

In his notebooks Hume went further than Montesquieu. He made the point that it was not just the Romans whose politics were distanced from modern concerns but, following Barbon, even Italians of recent centuries such as Machiavelli. For Hume, those who continued to see ancient Rome as a touchstone in politics could only with difficulty speak to a century where politics were determined by wars for trade which in turn funded future conflict: 'There is not a Word of Trade in all Matchiavel [sic], which is strange considering that Florence rose only by Trade.'[33] In 'Of Liberty and Despotism' Machiavelli was identified as being of little use because he had 'confined his study to the furious and tyrannical governments of ancient times, or to the little disorderly principalities of Italy'.[34] The first fact of modern times was the transformation of politics that had occurred when trade became the foremost reason-of-state:

> Trade was never esteemed an affair of state till the last century; and there scarcely is any ancient writer on politics, who has made mention of it. Even the Italians have kept a profound silence with regard to it, though it has now engaged the chief attention, as well of ministers of state, as of speculative reasoners. The great opulence, grandeur, and military achievements of the two maritime powers seem first to have instructed mankind in the importance of an extensive commerce.[35]

Hume's maritime powers were the Dutch Republic and England. Their rise revealed the means of maintaining a state through the aggressive pursuit of commerce, backed up by armed force if necessary, that were, during Hume's lifetime, being adopted by almost all other European powers. Hume recognized that the rise of the Dutch Republic and of England as mercantile empires had been singularly rapid. It signalled to equally small states that they might be able to transform their size and power relative to competitor states by the aggressive pursuit of commerce. The key was that ambitious merchants united in private companies were backed up by military power, itself ultimately underpinned by national politicians, either directly through state enterprise or indirectly, because national leaders were investors in the imperial projects.

For Hume, this meant that the Dutch and English approach was historically different to the practices of other empires. Europe's imperial past was linked to the actions of individual pirates and adventurers or merchants and crusaders, some of whom had state backing and some of whom did not. Rationales for the pursuit of empire were varied. The Christian order of the Hospitallers held Malta and Rhodes to secure passage to the Middle East, always with a view to the conquest of the Holy Land. Individual adventurers from Spain and Portugal took South America partly in search of individual riches and partly, they said, to spread Christianity. The expansion of Portugal, however, was most directly concerned with intercontinental trade. It might have seemed to contemporaries that the Dutch and the English were merely following Portugal – this was not the case. Portuguese explorers unquestionably assailed Brazil to monopolize the pau brasil (red wood) trade, Malacca to secure spices, port cities in north, east and west Africa for slaves and gold, and Goa and Calicut on the Indian Ocean for sugar and cotton. Yet while the Portuguese established a vast trading empire that contributed substantially to their economy, there was no sense of a national mission, or the pursuit of commerce having become the central strategy of Portuguese rulers for security and survival.

Smith made this crystal clear in the brilliant comparative history of colonies in the fourth book of his *Wealth of Nations*. The English and the Dutch Republic were distinctive in pursuing commerce through hybrid entities that were part private company and part state. In the case of the Dutch East India Company (VOC), formed in 1602, imperial strategies were advanced by its warships and armies supporting merchants, creating the wealthiest private company in history by the middle of the century. Significantly, the success of the

VOC was held to be key to national flourishing. The difference was underscored by the ease with which the Dutch seized Malacca from the Portuguese in 1641. In the same year they replaced Portugal as the sole European state able to trade with Japan, via the artificial island off Nagasaki called Tsukishima, which they held until 1854. The Dutch establishment of mercantile empire in the seventeenth century was national policy, sanctioned through the issue of charters from the beginning by the state. The case of the English was identical, from Elizabeth I in 1600 giving legal permission to merchants to create their own East India Company, which was soon active in the ports of Surat from 1612, Madras (Chennai) from 1639, Bombay (Mumbai) from 1668 and Calcutta (Kolkata).[36]

The enterprising histories of the English and the Dutch in the seventeenth century did not overly worry the young Hume. Indeed, they were seen to be compatible with life in civilized monarchies, in states where law held sway. And this was true too, he felt, for the eventual decline of Dutch commercial and military power. Hume followed the views of the diplomat William Temple who had famously said of the Dutch Republic that it had shone like a comet and then fell like a meteor in the year of military disaster that was 1672.[37] This was due mainly to its military inferiority to the English. Anglo-Dutch wars occurred in 1652–54, 1665–67 and 1672–74. These were different to comparable clashes between states because they were 'occasioned by the jealousy of trade', being intended to pave the way for English merchants to humble the maritime power of the Dutch and prevent them from acquiring 'all the commerce of Europe, as they had already done that of the Indies'.[38] Dutch military defeat was traced to their small size and the relative poverty of their natural resources.[39]

England had beaten the Dutch, but as a middle-sized European power they might be expected to go the same way. The process would occur, it was believed, through competition with other states. In short, these two mercantile empires had stimulated the commerce of the globe rather than turning themselves into longstanding despotic or monopolizing empires whose activities, as in the case of historic Spain, focused on bringing luxuries to the metropole. Many believed that there were powerful natural forces in the modern global trading system that spread wealth between commercial states, and that such forces could be relied upon to prevent one state from eating up the commerce of the globe.[40] In the essay 'Of Luxury', which first appeared in the collection entitled *Political Discourses* in 1752, Hume explained that rich countries might cause the loss of their own markets to poorer neighbours. The latter would be jealous of the attractive goods being produced in the richer state. They had an advantage in being able to undercut existing costs of production by paying lower wages to labour, thereby seeing the transfer of an industry into their own realm.[41] Numerous authors had made the same point before Hume, that rich states enjoying the benefits of luxury were likely to see trade fly abroad.[42] In Hume's view this did not mean that rich states overly had to worry, because countervailing forces existed which could be relied upon to maintain their superiority over poorer states. One of these was adaptability in production. Another was the existence of a free government, which Hume believed was directly associated with commercial development. As he put it, 'If we trace commerce in its progress . . . we shall always find it to have fixed its seat in free governments.'[43] Free government was where civil liberty existed and could be expected to last. Britain might follow the Dutch and suffer relative economic decline, but neither state would collapse.

The problem, Hume acknowledged with ever-greater force as he aged, was that free government changed its nature in circumstances of the perpetual pursuit of empire by war. Free governments could become fanatic. When this happened, and Hume was increasingly certain it had in Britain, all reasons for optimism were lost. In addition to competition between states for markets fostering imperialism, Hume emphasized from the beginning of the 1750s another major threat to enlightenment. This was public credit or the extent of the national debt. From the first edition of the essay 'Of Public Credit' in the *Political Discourses* of 1752 Hume had included the sentence 'Either the nation must destroy public credit, or public credit will destroy the nation.'[44] He became more convinced that this destruction was imminent in Britain, in part because of the outcome of the Seven Years' War. It was the national debt that facilitated the pursuit of empire by means of war by Britain, leading politicians away from the public good and causing crisis for future generations forced to pay the debts of their ancestors. And, from 1764, he found it difficult to see a way in which commercial states like Britain could cut free from what had essentially become a dependence upon war-induced debt finance, in part because such a system guaranteed vast profits to the monied interest that had developed a steadfast commitment to Britain's empire and its continued growth, and so was intertwined with the country's traditional patriots and warmongers at court or among the landed aristocracy. Hume was less concerned about France suffering adversely from an excessive use of public credit because absolute monarchs could declare a bankruptcy and ruin the financiers who had lent them money when the debt became too great. The person of the monarch could effectively cancel the debt in return for the transfer of a state asset to a private person or company. Emperor Charles V did exactly this in 1521, amortizing his debt to the financier Jakob Fugger by donating to the latter's company the copper and silver mines of the Tyrol. Free states did not have this option since 'the people, and chiefly those who have the highest offices' are 'commonly the public creditors' themselves. Hume was acknowledging that leading politicians, being likely wealthy, were therefore likely also to be holders of government bonds and investors in public companies. Where there was a multitude of creditors rather than a single financier lending the money, and when public confidence in politics went beyond the person of the monarch, either the debt had to be paid in full, or bankruptcy beckoned. Hume feared the consequences for Britain's mixed government as public credit grew.

One of Hume's scenarios for the natural death of the nation was through a national bankruptcy. Debt would become so high that a choice would have to be made between sacrificing 'thousands' of creditors 'to the safety of millions', meaning that the government which reneged on its debt to prevent the state from going bankrupt would subsequently refuse to pay interest on its bonds, thereby beggaring those who gained income from such investments. Alternatively, 'millions may be sacrificed for ever to the temporary safety of thousands' of prominent and powerful individual creditors, signalling a case where government insisted on paying interest on the debt even if this meant that the general population faced taxes so high that their living standards collapsed.[45] In either case, the capacity of a bankrupt state to defend itself would be drastically reduced because it could no longer generate funds to cover the costs of military action, making it suddenly prey to other imperially minded powers it had battled in the past. In addition, the areas of the empire which the state had used its debt to crush by military action would be tempted to throw off the yoke, resulting in the likely dismemberment of the polity. The consequences of unintended national bankruptcy or monarch-inspired planned bankruptcy were deadly. Hume likened the 'princes and states fighting and quarrelling amid their debts, funds and public mortgages' to cudgel players in a china shop.[46] In Britain's case levels of debt were so high that crisis was imminent:

> . . . all these Inconveniences are slight, in comparison of our public Debts, which bring on inevitable Ruin, and with a Certainty which is even beyond geometrical, because it is arithmetical. I hope you have more Sense than to trust a shilling to that egregious bubble.[47]

Crisis caused by fears of – or the reality of – debt-induced national bankruptcy would lead to civil war and further international war, unleashing forces of intolerance and violence sufficient to restore the continent to a fanatic condition, and so end enlightenment in the process.

III

Hume's sense of the Enlightenment was buffeted later in life by another force that he thought could well be overwhelming, turning him from an optimist about the future into the deepest of pessimists: the nature of the belief in liberty across Britain. As we have seen, Hume considered himself to be dedicated to the study of free states, both those from the past and those in his present. Without civil liberty, the privileges of freeborn Britons to write and speak as they fancied, without fear of being imprisoned or punished by the state, nowhere could be free or be said to enjoy the rule of law. Hume worried, however, that the love of liberty was becoming superstitious – that it had become an ideal detached from reality. He was especially concerned about the growing view in Britain that liberty had somehow been lost and required radical action for it to be restored. Advocates of this position were, according to Hume, dangerously close to the enthusiasts for political violence who had flourished both during the civil wars across England, Scotland and Ireland in the 1630s and 1640s and in the later resistance to James II. He believed that British politics had become increasingly polarized between camps that portrayed those with different views as beyond the pale, as supporters of despotism or anarchy.

Hume blamed two groups for this fanaticism. The first was the Whigs, who he believed used history to argue that true freedom no longer resided in Britain and needed to be recovered by whatever means necessary. The Whigs were defenders of the Revolution Settlement and the Hanoverian succession, holding office from the commencement of George I's reign in 1714 until that of George III in 1760. When they fell from office under the new monarch, and in conditions where the Jacobite threat had ceased to be real, Whigs turned radical, beginning to complain that, with their loss of power, liberty in Britain was suddenly at risk. This was what infuriated Hume. In emphasizing the role of revolutions and revolutionaries in their interpretation of history, and by associating and justifying their political project with it, Hume believed that the Whigs in the 1760s were bringing the lexicon of revolt back into the mainstream of British political discussion, pushing moderation to the periphery. The second group was the Commonwealthmen and the other defenders of England's seventeenth-century republican past, who harkened back to an ancient free and Gothic constitution that ought to be restored against the latest version of the Norman Yoke that free Britons had battled against in times gone by.[48] Although in his *History of England* Hume did not go beyond 1688, he did make clear that he believed that a passion for liberty had turned enthusiastic in the seventeenth century, turning fanatic afresh in his own times.

The authors Hume blamed among the Whigs were Rapin de Thoyras, John Locke, Algernon Sidney and Benjamin Hoadly, whose grand defences of liberty could be drawn upon by contemporary politicians to justify resistance to the monarch.[49] One consequence of such writing, Hume asserted, had been the dominion of the Whig party associated with Robert Walpole and William Pitt the Elder, men who he believed were of the view that the country was not free unless they held power. Whig narratives about English liberty, the false philosophies of Locke and the histories of his friends, shored up the rule of powerful politicians who saw themselves to be guaranteeing the freedom secured in 1688–89. Hume argued that the portrayal of the rise of liberty in Britain had been used by the Whigs for their lone rule of the country, turning dangerously fanatic when their authority was diminished:

> The Whig party, for a course of near seventy years, has, almost without interruption, enjoyed the whole authority of government; and no honours or offices could be obtained but by their countenance and protection: but this event, which, in some particulars has been advantageous to the state, has proved destructive to the truth of history, and has established many gross falsehoods, which it is unaccountable how any civilised nation could have embraced with regard to its domestic occurrences. Compositions the most

despicable, both for style and matter, have been extolled, and propagated, and read, as if they had equalled the most celebrated remains
of antiquity.[50]

Hume later noted that the sales of the second volume of his *History
of England* were improved because he was perceived to have become
more of a Whig. He had, he said, '. . . been taught by Experience,
that the Whig Party were in possession of bestowing all places, both
in the State and in Literature'. Although Hume disliked their 'sense-
less Clamour' and admitted alterations to his *History* were always
'to the Tory side', so corrupt was public culture that to be taken for
a Whig had a positive impact upon trade in his book.[51] An excessive
focus upon liberty, approaching fanaticism, led people to forget that
liberty relied upon law and government, but could quickly erode
both, if it was excessive, becoming the dominant value in a polity.
As Hume put it:

> . . . a regard to liberty, though a laudable passion, ought commonly
> to be subordinate to a reverence for established government, the
> prevailing faction has celebrated only the partisans of the former,
> who pursued as their object the perfection of civil society, and has
> extolled them at the expense of their antagonists, who maintained
> those maxims that are essential to its very existence. But extremes of
> all kinds are to be avoided; and though no one will ever please either
> faction by moderate opinions, it is there we are most likely to meet
> with truth and certainty.[52]

Hume worried that after his death Britain would experience civil
collapse by a revolt of those convinced they were living under a government transformed into a dictatorship since George III had come
to the throne. This in turn would ensure an end to civility, just as it
had during the seventeenth century.[53]

There is often a lot made of Hume's alleged 'conservatism':
that within this vein of thought there can be perceived some
form of reactionary or anti-liberal theme.[54] Such discussion is

anachronistic. Conservatism was not a category that many eighteenth-century writers would have found meaningful; those who saw themselves as friends to the past would have meant something very different to what we today mean by the term. Indeed, maintaining what had gone before necessitated embracing change because the present was deemed to be fluid and likely to alter further. In speculating about the options open to political actors, maintaining what existed was a utopian stance and impractical, such were the forces of change being wrought by commerce and by war. Hume *did* want to maintain the genuine liberties he saw in Britain and the relative toleration he identified across much of Europe. But the forces of change were so great, and the likelihood of violence and intolerance breaking out so certain, that Hume embraced pessimism as a register. He was especially sceptical about those who found solutions in the restoration of the English Republic or an ancient free constitution. Hume considered those who believed that the Enlightenment would last as akin to the Commonwealth fanatics convinced that the civil wars of England could be re-run without Cromwell emerging as a tyrant. Enlightenment had to find new sources of defence against the lust for liberty. Models could not be found among historic or existing republics, when all the existing republics of Europe were themselves becoming failed states. The problem he perceived with the commonwealth argument was that it too misunderstood history: either it made an ideal of republican failure in England or harked back to an ancient constitution that could only be restored in the present by violence, including the widespread impoverishment that would occur by overthrowing commercial society. In Hume's view, reference to an ancient constitution made no sense because of the continual fluctuation of historic politics. There were, in fact, several ancient constitutions in English history. None of them had any relevance to the present.[55] For Hume, the past provided a guide rather than a model. Change had to be managed, as far as this was possible, by new forms of the science of the statesman or legislator.

IV

Hume's optimism did not last about movements of wealth potentially making commercial societies pacific and about the capacity of states to act peaceably as governments of laws and not men. In 1758 he added an essay, 'Of the Jealousy of Trade', to a new edition of the *Essays and Treatises*. In it, he explained that if war and trade were pursued together without reference to law or morality the world would become one where the jealousy of trade dominated politics. Hume was aware that patriotic reasons were being found to justify war for economic gain, entailing behaving ruthlessly towards foreign states and especially towards colonies. Economic practices which entailed the destruction of the trade of neighbouring states became common; the most prominent example being the control and limitation of Ireland's trade by Britain.[56] Another case that became ever-more important was Britain's relationship with India.[57] Since the seventeenth century the cotton trade organized by the East India Company had made commercial centres of Madras, Bombay and Calcutta. From the 1750s, against the background of the disintegration of the Mughal Empire, Company figures, such as Robert Clive and later Warren Hastings, began to take control of Bengal, establishing large armies and replacing traditional governments.[58]

A far less secure world emerged as expanding European commercial monarchies clashed in the pursuit of empire through economic and political dominion. In 'Of the Jealousy of Trade' Hume made the argument that all states could benefit far more by trading freely and openly with one another. Yet such claims fell on deaf ears when national politics became dominated by patriotic ideas of national greatness coupled with the pursuit of global markets. One of the ways of describing this movement was by reference to reason-of-state or neo-Machiavellianism in politics.[59] This was the statecraft of necessity, overriding morality and tradition, associated with the Machiavellian injunction that the end always justifies the means.

The end of national security was identified by British policymakers with the need to expand markets. Such a policy entailed ruining potential competitors, justified in the eyes of the public by a xenophobic patriotism. Imperialist designs towards nations both in and out of Europe were immediately justified on the grounds of economic necessity and national superiority over other nations and cultures. This process resulted in economic and military aggrandizement becoming state policy throughout the eighteenth century.[60] Reason-of-state was thereby coupled with forms of patriotism hitherto associated with expansionist republics reliant upon expressions of a homogeneous and unified national will dedicated to the survival of the state. When states like France and Britain fought for the trade of states within Europe and beyond the continent, war and crisis became norms.

Hume's Francophilia continued to be marked as he aged, bracketing him with those who felt that Britain was naturally the lesser state. Writing from Paris as Under-Secretary of State, Northern Department, at the end of 1763 he asserted 'this place will be long my home', admitting 'little Inclination to [return] to the factious Barbarians of London' and calling the French capital 'the best Place in the World'.[61] Hume blamed the London political parties for the state of Britain and especially, as we have seen, the rule of the Whig Party. He confessed that he himself had been infected by what he called 'the plaguy [sic] Prejudices of Whiggism' and 'Whig rancour', meaning an excessive worry about liberty lost, when he had first completed his *History of England*; Hume asserted that he had removed them from the new edition of 1763.[62] Five years later he combated rumours of a likely return to Paris, but in so doing underlined the extent to which he had come to hate London politics where 'Every event here fills me with Indignation' and where he had to remind himself that 'to a Philosopher & Historian the Madness and Imbecility of Mankind ought to appear ordinary Events.'[63]

Hume always rejected what he termed 'the Prejudices entertained by the vulgar Part of my Country-men' against France, and always advocated peace between Britain and France. Hume blamed the Seven Years' War, which 'spread the Flame from one End of the Globe to the other', on 'frivolous Causes', being 'fomented by some obscure designing Men, contrary to the Intentions of the two Kings, the two Ministries, even the Generality of the two Nations'. Although Britain had emerged victorious, Hume stated that the 'horrible, destructive, ruinous War' had been 'more pernicious to the Victors than to the Vanquished'.[64] The great tragedy for Hume was that the conflict had put an end to the chance of Britain and France becoming civilized monarchies together.

Hume accepted that Britain was a state built upon national difference and division. These were aspects that he himself had experienced keenly, as he suggested in 1764: 'Some hate me because I am a Tory, some because I am not a Whig, some because I am not a Christian, and all because I am a Scotsman.' But the explosion of xenophobia that Hume saw everywhere led him to ask a child-hood friend, 'Can you seriously talk of my continuing an Englishman?' The thoroughly Scottish Gilbert Elliot, a Westminster MP, had no more than the obvious answer to give: 'Notwithstanding all you say we are both Englishmen – that is true British subjects, entitled to every emolument and advantage that our happy constitution can bestow.' Hume was, however, increasingly of the opinion that these advantages were fast disappearing. He saw licentiousness and popular ignorance prevailing around him. Humans were impressionable creatures and easily swayed by foolish rhetoric and false promises. Politicians posing as friends of liberty were selling forms of patriotism that were deadly to the polity but which nevertheless were being heartily embraced. Such politics were commonplace in times of reformation, and hence Hume was certain that a return was being made to the turmoil of the sixteenth and seventeenth centuries, but in the deadlier context of global war, the jealousy of trade and the unstable cultures of commercial society.

Hume blamed and detested William Pitt the Elder, known as Chatham after he was granted an earldom in 1766, the patriotic war minister lauded for Britain's *annus mirabilis* of 1759, when the early reverses of the Seven Years' War were turned into victories at

Québec, Guadeloupe, Lagos and Madras.[65] Chatham had, in Hume's view, expanded the national debt through his warmongering at the same time as he encouraged anti-French sentiments, and corrupted English national character to make it addicted to victory. He discerned what we would now term populism in politics, manipulated by politicians like Chatham increasingly reliant upon an unruly populace and eager to outdo their rivals through evocations of nationalistic patriotism and xenophobia. Hume saw Chatham as a fraud, inculcating a false patriotism in the populace by making the defeat of France the overriding political goal. Chatham in opposition he felt to be fomenting popular enthusiasm, especially among fanatics for liberty, by encouraging the view that the British were not free unless he returned to office. In a rare positive sentence about politics in 1772, 'that the abominable Faction in England is declining', Hume could not resist a further jibe at Chatham: 'I hope that Pitt will have the Gout this whole Session and I pray it may be a hearty and sincere one.'[66] Hume explained in a revealing letter to Strahan the genuine tragedy that Chatham, and the ministers who preceded him, could easily have established a long-lasting peace with France. Instead, war and debt became the norm:

I wish I could have the same Idea with you of the Prosperity of our public Affairs. But when I reflect, that, from 1740 to 1761, during the Course of no more than 21 Years, while a most pacific Monarch sat on the Throne of France, the Nation ran in Debt about a hundred Millions; that the wise and virtuous Minister, Pitt, could contract more Incumbrances, in six months of an unnecessary War, than we have been able to discharge during eight Years of Peace; and that we persevere in the same frantic Maxims; I can forsee nothing but certain and speedy Ruin either to the Nation or to the public Creditors. The last, tho' a great Calamity, would be a small one in comparison; but I cannot see how it can be brought about, while these Creditors fill all the chief Offices and are the Men of greatest Authority in the Nation. In other Respects the Kingdom may be thriving: The Improvement of our Agriculture is a good Circumstance; tho' I believe our Manufactures do not advance; and all depends on our Union with America, which, in the Nature of things, cannot long subsist. But all this is nothing in comparison of the continual Encrease of our Debts, in every idle War, into which, it seems, the Mob of London are to rush every Minister. But these are all other Peoples Concerns; and I know not why I should trouble my head about them.[67]

There was a clear link between the financiers who profited from the expanding debt, the ministers who became popular through war and whose powers increased in time of war, and the mob who fell for the sham patriotism that accompanied war.

One sign of change in Britain for the worse was the nature of the people. Hume had long argued that Britain's mixed government depended upon the republican element of the active populace for the defence of popular liberty: they could, for instance, revolt against a government which threatened to challenge the freedom of the press. This was a freedom sacred for Hume. Yet in the final edition of the essay 'Of the Liberty of the Press' in 1772 and in his last posthumously published corrections in the edition of 1777, Hume inserted a sentence reflecting the bleaker view of his dotage: 'It must however be allowed, that the unbounded liberty of the press, though it be difficult, perhaps impossible, to propose a suitable remedy for it, is one of the evils, attending those mixt forms of government.'[68] Hume likened the excess of liberty among the English to Tacitus's view of the Romans under the emperors, who 'neither could bear total slavery nor total liberty'.[69]

In a letter of July 1767 Hume wrote that, 'For of all our annual confusions, the present seems to be the most violent, and to threaten the most entire revolution, and the most important events.'[70] One of the points Hume regularly made was that a state entirely devoted to the jealousy of trade, such as Britain, was only strong in appearance rather than in reality. When Chatham resigned from office, Hume noted the irony of Britain being presumed the greatest power in Europe while in fact being pitifully weak, because of the instability of parties and ministries, the ignorance of political leaders and the overwhelming costs of servicing the soaring national debt:

> Our Administration is like a Heap of loose stones, where, if you remove one, the rest will all tumble. This is the least of the numberless Evils under which we labour. What do you think of our being such complete Beggars as not to be able to subsist, and yet labouring under the Jealousy and Envy of all Europe, on account of our supposed Power and Opulence.[71]

In the final decade of Hume's life France and Britain diverged. Former hopes of alliance or permanent friendship had been abandoned and both states were on the brink of war yet again. Numerous defences of liberty, in Hume's eyes, had turned both superstitious and enthusiastic, lacking moderation or morality. Yet visions of enthusiastic liberty were attracting ever-more adherents, as the case of John Wilkes underscored. Wilkes was a radical advocate of civil liberties, which Hume might have been expected to favour. But he considered Wilkes to be a fanatic once the forty-fifth issue of his newspaper *North Briton* of 23 April 1763 was published, which attacked the king, and especially his Scots friend and prime minister John Stuart, 3rd Earl of Bute, for too generous a peace with France at the culmination of the Seven Years' War.[72] Opposition to Bute, fostered by Wilkes and his allies, became Scottophobic.[73]

What such developments meant to Hume and so many of his followers and friends was that the Enlightenment, the strategies that had managed to suppress the divisions that had led to almost two centuries of religious war, had failed. New forms of bigotry were dividing society – but these were now found in the arenas of economics and politics rather than religion, and extreme acts on these grounds were being justified. Whereas in the past civil murder had been justified on the grounds of saving souls, it was now being justified to make people free, promising far greater wealth at the same time. Political religions were being formed: new ideologies

that defined exclusive communities worthy of defence – by violence, if necessary.[74] When political religions clashed, it would be
legitimate to kill or persecute those of a different political faith,
returning Europe to violence, long-term war and social collapse.

V

In the final phase of his life Hume anticipated revolutionary
upheaval unless the government took action against the people.
Although Hume was notorious for writing rather tongue-in-cheek
letters, many of his disciples were of the view that Hume believed
revolution alone had a chance of restoring balance to a state facing
the challenge of fanatic ideas about liberty and that was addicted
to the jealousy of trade. Complete collapse might also restore
political sense, overcoming cultures among the Whigs and the
Commonwealthmen in Britain that Hume equated with fantasy
and delusion. Hume wrote to his publisher and friend the MP
William Strahan in 1770, emphasizing the dreadful political state
of the country and the necessity of strong action by George III
against the malcontents:

> Our Government has become a Chimera; and is too perfect in point
> of Liberty, for so vile a Beast as an Englishman, who is a Man, a bad
> Animal too, corrupted by above a Century of Licentiousness. The
> Misfortune is, that this Liberty can scarcely be retrench'd without
> Danger of being entirely lost; at least, the fatal Effects of Licentious-
> ness must first be made palpable, by some extreme Mischief,
> resulting from it. I may wish that the Catastrophe should rather fall
> on our Posterity; but it hastens on with such large Strides, as leaves
> little Room for this hope.[75]

Only months later he informed his friend Strahan that 'The Madness and Wickedness of the English (for do not say, the Scum of
London) appear astonishing, even after all the Experience we have

had. It must end fatally either to the King or Constitution or to both.'[76] Hume was soon writing to Smith to complain about the shocking state of the economy and the likelihood of a general bankruptcy: 'We are here in a very melancholy Situation: Continual Bankruptcies, universal Loss of Credit, and endless Suspicions.' Having listed the impending collapse of numerous enterprises, he asked Smith, 'Do these Events any-wise affect your Theory? Or will it occasion the Reversal of any Chapters?'[77]

As the sensational and anonymous 'Letters of Junius' were appearing in print, containing attacks upon the excessive power of the king, the weakness of parliament and the more general loss of liberty, Hume advised that the ministry wait until 'some Violence or personal Insult be offered to the Parliament, which will not be long'. This would give the government an excuse to take action and as long as the army and militia were faithful order would be restored. Hume wished 'to God we had a Scotch Militia at present'.[78] The danger for Hume was that government and crown had already given up too much. Lord North, a minister Hume admired, had been far too harsh to the French and too placatory towards the Whig friends of liberty so that his powers to constrain the people had become limited:

I own, that I am inclined to have a good Opinion of Lord North, but his Insolence to the House of Bourbon, and his Timidity towards the London Mob appear unaccountable. Only consider how many Powers of Government are lost in this short Reign. The right of displacing the Judges was given up; General Warrants are lost; the right of Expulsion the same; all the co-ercive Powers of the House of Commons abandon'd; all Laws against Libels annihilated; the Authority of Government impair'd by the Impunity granted to the Insolence of Beckford, Crosby, and the common Council: the revenue of the civil List diminished. For God's sake, is there never to be a stop put to this inundation of the Rabble? . . . [Lord North] bullies Spain and France and quakes before the Ward of Farringdon without.[79]

Hume argued further that the collapse of English culture was following on the heels of the chaos of unstable coalition governments in the later 1760s, making worse rather than solving Britain's crisis-ridden relationship with its North American colonies over their contribution by taxation to the national debt created by the Seven Years' War. Writing to Smith in 1770 Hume confessed a feeling 'to give myself up to despair' and called the English 'a deluded People' for whom 'Nothing but a Rebellion and Bloodshed will open the Eyes.'[80] He wrote again to Strahan in 1772 to say that he had observed the decline of literature in England:

> For as to any Englishman, that Nation is so sunk in Stupidity and Barbarism and Faction that you may as well think of Lapland for an Author. The best Book, that has been writ by any Englishman these thirty Years (for Dr Franklyn [sic] is an American) is Tristram Shandy, bad as it is.[81]

Political turmoil had been followed by cultural decrepitude.

Anticipated national bankruptcy was likely to be followed by upheaval, when impoverished creditors would take to the streets. More likely was a social war through the violence of the mob. Hume speculated about the precise process by which this might occur. If there was another war with France, which he thought to be likely because of Britain's continued hostility, he did not expect a clash between the landed interest and the monied interest/financiers who held the debt. Rather, he believed that if the Anglo-French conflict was pursued 'with the usual frenzy', then in the third or fourth year, when public finances were insufficient to pay the interest on the debt, the landed interest who ran the state would retrench rather than face bankruptcy or increase taxes upon the general populace. They would do anything to stave off national bankruptcy. The landed interest would put an end to the war and see Britain defeated by France, rather than see the national debt rise to unsustainable levels.

Hume's view of the monied interest, the men who invested in

and organized the debt, is significant because he presented them as being latter-day religious fanatics selling projects that were ultimately without substance. He considered their power to exist in the realm of fantasy because if the state did go bankrupt they themselves would be the losers in material terms. The identification of the strength of the state with stable public credit was the key fantasy that played such a major role in contemporary politics. As Hume put it, his friend Strahan was wrong in stating that 'if matters came to a fair and open Struggle between the Land-holders and the Stock-holders, the latter would be able to reduce the former to any Composition.' For Hume, 'The Authority of the Land-holders is solidly established over their Tenants and Neighbours: But what Stock-holder has any Influence even over his next Neighbour in his own Street? And if public Credit fall, as it must by the least Touch, he would be reduc'd to instant Poverty, and have authority nowhere.' Assertions of the fragility of public credit might strike modern readers as naive, but Hume's point was that a political system in which the debt dictated politics was necessarily unstable and unnatural in its discussions and priorities. Getting rid of the sword of Damocles that the debt represented in contemporary Britain was vital, although the transition mechanism was likely to be loss in war to France and the acceptance of an impoverished, less influential Britain on the political stage.

Despite the weakness of the financiers, the landed interest would prefer them to the people; this was the core of the problem for Hume that made him anticipate civil war. The landed interest and the monied interest were two orders both intermixed and connected, members of popular clubs and parliament, with heavy investments in the East India Company in addition to Bank of England bonds. When bankruptcy threatened, the landed interest would call upon the people to pay the debt by accepting higher taxes just as Britain could no longer fight war. The people would be sacrificed until they rose against both the landed and the monied, and public violence and a struggle for power would be the outcome.[82]

The revolt of the people if bankruptcy occurred was another likely scenario. If rebellion in America and in India caused national revenues to collapse, the economic collapse of London would follow, with rioting of the mob and disciplining of the people by violence, which Hume anticipated:

O! how I long to see America and the East Indies revolted totally & finally, the Revenue reduc'd to half, public Credit fully discredited by Bankruptcy, the third of London in Ruins, and the rascally Mob subdu'd. I think I am not too old to despair of being Witness to all these Blessings.[83]

In yet another scenario, Hume thought that Chatham might be returned to office and use the Whig cry of liberty lost to organize a rebellion against the crown. If the door was opened 'to Pitt and his Myrmidons' they would 'no doubt, chain the King for ever, and render him a mere Cypher'. If this occurred, the only hope for the future of Britain was for armed force to put down what would amount to the upending of the constitution in the name of liberty. Only when the authority of the monarch, nobility and gentry were restored would the danger have passed. Hume was certain that advocates of liberty among the Whigs would have to be executed for an end to be put to national ills. Although tongue-in-cheek at times about the extreme action he was advocating, Hume was serious in seeing a grim future ahead for Britain and the world. As we shall see, the call for radical and even violent action to prevent the end of enlightenment was something that marked out many of Hume's followers.

3.

Shelburne, His Circle and the End of Britain

I

William Petty, known to all as Shelburne (and from 1786 first Marquess of Lansdowne), had been a follower of Hume from the early
1760s, despite himself being a Whig. Unlike Hume, Shelburne,
who held office under Chatham, was convinced that the Great
Commoner – Chatham's name because he refused ennoblement
until 1766 – was capable of restoring enlightenment through peace
abroad combined with patriotic reform at home and across the
Empire. Reliance upon a prime minister of genius, ably supported
by younger ministers with a zeal for change, could bring national and
then international unity. Yet Shelburne too gradually became disenchanted with Chatham, although he acted as a major patron of his
son William Pitt the Younger.[1] Hume's negative view of Chatham
was in time deemed accurate. After Hume's death in 1776 his dire
predictions about the descent of Britain into chaos appeared to
Shelburne to be coming to pass. America was throwing off British
rule, George III was increasingly seen by many to be a tyrant, and
notions of liberty were causing turbulence as the imperial economy
shuddered, all while the national debt continued to soar.[2] It was in
such circumstances that Shelburne gathered a circle around him
who saw him as their patron and leader. They acted often as one,
united by the view that great change was on the horizon and that
new strategies had to be formulated to prevent enlightenment from
disappearing, signalling the dominion of fanaticism across Europe
and its empires, that philosophy had to be employed as a tool to
defend enlightenment against the forces of violence and bigotry.[3]

While Hume had focused upon evidence of a deepening malaise, emphasizing his own failed battle against superstition, Shelburne continued to have faith in politics, especially when there was a possibility that he would be called to high office. He and the members of his circle believed that an opportunity presented itself in the depths of Britain's misery and defeat in war. The latter was the key point. Britain lost the thirteen colonies in North America, which formed themselves initially into separate republics. This first American Revolution could not have occurred without the support of France, in addition to Spain and the Dutch Republic. American and French troops united to defeat Britain militarily at Yorktown in 1781.

For Shelburne, the American experience showed that the empire had been corrupt, unstable and incapable of being maintained. If future crises were to be averted then immediate transformative medicine was vital, and Shelburne tried practically to solve the problems that Hume had identified. His motivation was patriotic. He considered himself to be capable of altering the nature of the British polity, being in a singularly fortunate position and beyond party:

> Men of independent fortune should be trustees between King and people, and contrive to think in whatever they do to be occupied in actions of service to both, without being slaves to either.[4]

In conditions of commercial crisis, war and the prevalence of the jealousy of trade, he concluded that a new politics of peace and social unity based on a scientifically articulated politics of the public good had to be formulated. Shelburne had a vision of laws and policies embodying the public good sufficient to establish a moderate consensus capable of preventing fanaticism. The solutions canvassed by Shelburne had to go beyond national boundaries if they were to have any chance of success; this led to a remarkable union with like-minded reformers in France. Shelburne was not a Commonwealthman. Solving the problem of lost liberty by turning to the people, creating a new religion or promoting the godly and virtuous would not work in the present, just as they had failed in the previous century. Shelburne's Circle accepted Hume's criticism of the various traditions of radical political argument, that they were utopian speculators presuming that historic states which they called 'free' could be replicated in a present of altogether different circumstances. Ancient or seventeenth-century political models were no longer applicable to an altered Britain. New philosophies were required to prevent the state widely praised as the most free in human history from descending into slavery and despotism.

The group around Shelburne tended to be associated in the public mind with the Whigs, although they were critical of party affiliation. The debt to Hume, however, was evident and widely commented upon. This led Shelburne himself to be branded an enemy of enlightenment. Many felt Hume's works to be especially dangerous: he was accused of being an enemy of established religion and of laying the foundations for the radical presbyterian philosophies of such men as the Dissenting minister and natural philosopher Joseph Priestley.[5] It was said that 'present rebellions against his majesty' could be traced to Hume and on to his friends.[6] The link was in part correct. Shelburne and his friends were much more critical of George III than Hume. But Hume unquestionably made the following generation think differently about Britain's politics and prospects. An illustration of this can be seen in the work of Richard Price, the Dissenting minister, moral philosopher and statistician, and Shelburne's closest collaborator in the 1770s and 1780s. Price's *Two Tracts on Civil Liberty* of 1778 examined Hume's final additions to the *History of England* 'written by him a little before his death' – Price described them as sending a 'dying warning to this kingdom'. One passage of Hume's analysis that Price drew particular attention to was that the supplies granted to Elizabeth I in her entire reign of forty-five years had been three million pounds, whereas in the late 1750s Chatham at war had expended such a sum in two months. The condition of Britain being suffocated by debt had become shocking and was getting ever worse with the progress of the American Revolution. Indeed, Price cited Hume writing that 'our late delusions have much exceeded anything known in history, not even excepting those of the Crusades.' As Hume put it, 'I suppose there is no mathematical, still less an arithmetical demonstration, that the road to the Holy Land was not the road to Paradise, as there is, that the endless increase of national debts is the direct road to national ruin.' It was incontrovertibly the case that 'numberless calamities' were 'waiting for us'.[7]

Hume was further cited by Price on the right to resist tyranny, on debt being the likely euthanasia of the constitution and on free governments being far worse to their provinces than despotic ones.[8] He asserted that the loss of liberty across Britain through ministerial policy and the excessive powers of the crown needed to be traced to their ultimate cause: the existence of a mercantile system addicted to war and empire. The Whig party, led by Charles Watson-Wentworth, 2nd Marquess of Rockingham, and generally supported by Shelburne, had assaulted the pensions, loans, sinecures and contracts circulating around the crown and North's ministry, which they blamed for the disaster in North America in the 1770s and intensifying problems in India.[9] Increasingly, and especially after Rockingham's unexpected death in 1782, the lynchpin of this movement was Shelburne, whose schemes were infinitely more expansive. Shelburne and his circle saw both Hume and Smith as being in accord with the view of the French reformers called the physiocrats or *économistes*, who argued that Britain's power and wealth rested upon insecure foundations, could not be maintained, and was being undermined by debt generated during ceaseless wars.[10] The Shelburne project for the reorientation and reform of Britain was therefore backed by what they saw to be the greatest minds of the time. It might entail a Britain reduced by the loss of empire and lesser as an international power, but enjoying the growth of wealth in a pacific world. Confidence about what needed to be undertaken and achieved was singular, although, like Hume's optimism, it did not last.

II

The reason Shelburne dedicated himself to creating a circle of the best and brightest was in part due to his belief that he had been inadequately educated – privately in Dublin and among his Irish relations.[11] Shelburne at first lived at Lixnaw House in Kerry under the care of his grandfather Thomas Fitzmaurice. He would later suggest that this did not offer him a 'great chance at a liberal education'[12] – as in the case of Scotland, Shelburne felt Ireland's social relations were servile, and marked by violence and by ignorance.[13] This was a nation, he believed, that had been held back economically by England, and so lacked the middle ranks necessary for wealth creation. It was a place that required root-and-branch reform if it was ever to surpass this condition. Shelburne's verdict upon the country of his birth was vitriolic:

> [I had] no great example before [me], no information in my way . . . good-breeding in my own family, which made part of the feudal system, but out of it nothing but those uncultivated, undisciplined manners and that vulgarity, which make all Irish society so justly odious all over Europe.[14]

Ireland was in his mind proof of the evils of empire, leading to a largely ignorant populace that embraced corruption to survive. The Irish lacked liberty and the opportunity to foster their own economic development, relying rather upon a class of landed aristocrats, many of whom lived abroad, often termed the Protestant Ascendency.[15] Shelburne, largely living in England but owning lands in Ireland, was aware that he too was part of the problem.[16] Although critical of Scottish culture, he was a fervent supporter of the union of 1707, believing that it had facilitated the spreading of wealth and the growth of towns.[17] He later favoured the Scottish solution to the Irish problem in the form of the creation of the United Kingdom by union with Ireland in 1801.

Alone among those who had educated him Shelburne praised his eccentric, independent and forceful aunt Lady Arabella Denny, well known in Dublin for projects to help the poor, especially women and children.[18] But he later made the point that his ignorance only began to be truly remedied once he enrolled at Christ Church, Oxford. Shelburne studied natural law and the law of nations, Livy, Demosthenes and Machiavelli. He attended William Blackstone's lectures on English law that commenced in 1753, just as Shelburne arrived in Oxford.[19]

It is fair to suppose that Shelburne's feelings of inadequacy were related to an illustrious heritage. On his father's side Shelburne was a scion of the Irish earl Thomas Fitzmaurice, 21st Baron of Kerry, but his maternal lineage mattered far more to him personally. He was named after his great-grandfather on his mother's side, William Petty (1623–87), who was Surveyor General of Ireland, fellow of the Royal Society, inventor, natural philosopher and pathbreaking social statistician, studying what his contemporaries called 'political arithmetic'. There is evidence that Shelburne especially identified with his namesake great-grandfather, but he was convinced his own talent was different. He believed his aptitude lay in politics and, most of all, patronage – in identifying the genius of others and putting it into practice. This was his mission, to take power in politics and do good, armed by the brilliance of the circle surrounding and supporting him.

Having damned feudal relations that he perceived to be so dominant in Ireland and Scotland, Shelburne believed the only route to reform was by using his own prominence in such a social structure. Marriage helped. His first, to Sophia Carteret, provided links with the powerful Granville family. His second, to Louisa Fitzpatrick in the 1770s, gave Shelburne strong connections to the earls of Ossory of Bedfordshire, and set him near the centre of Whig politics at Holland House in Kensington – Louisa's sister Mary was married to Stephen, 2nd Lord Holland, who was the brother of Charles James Fox, a prominent Whig politician.[20]

Like those of many who have experienced it, Shelburne's beliefs were greatly affected by his direct involvement in war: he concluded that almost all conflicts were entered into for foolish reasons, that they were badly executed and often led to far greater chaos. In addition, wars, he argued, were frequently ended too rashly, without solving any of the issues purported to have been their cause. The War of the Austrian Succession (1740–48), involving a large number of European states, was typical, Shelburne said, in being 'terminated by a peace which paid no regard whatever to the commercial grievances which were the subject of so much clamour'.[21] The Seven Years' War was similar, he felt, in being inspired by the typical domestic intrigues of power-hungry politicians: the French did not want it, the British were not ready for it, and those appointed to command were pitifully prepared, their positions based exclusively on their social standing.[22] Disaster was the anticipated outcome until Chatham worked out a way of taking advantage of France's and Spain's lack of leadership.

Shelburne considered himself to have been fortunate in being commissioned into the 20th Regiment of Foot in 1757 before exchanging into the 3rd Regiment of Foot Guards (later the Scots Guards) in 1758. For the first year at least he was commanded by James Wolfe, soon to be renowned for his exploits at Québec, and who 'made me read not only military books, but philosophy' and 'gave me liberal notions of every kind'.[23] Shelburne followed Wolfe in the expedition to take the port of Rochefort in south-western France in 1757, an attack intended to divert French arms from Hanover and Prussia; the abject failure of the invasion confirmed in Shelburne the view that, despite his good opinion of his commander, in Britain major political or military decisions were made for reasons entirely removed from qualification, suitability or competence.[24] Furthermore, he became sure that what he called 'private and bye motives, which men scarcely dare to own to themselves' were crucial to the creation and outcome of any conflict.[25]

Shelburne hated war, but it was in fact war that made him a public figure. He ultimately distinguished himself in the Seven Years' War, at the battles of Minden in August 1759 and Kloster

Kampen in October 1760, after which he was raised to the rank of colonel and appointed aide-de-camp to the then new king, George III. Returning to court as a war hero, Shelburne quickly became an associate of the prime minister, John Stuart, 3rd Earl of Bute, too, and worked as Bute's spokesman, liaising with prominent political noblemen to maintain Bute's rule.[26] Shelburne observed many of the leading politicians of the day demonstrate the worst impulses of human nature while in office: they would sell themselves for peerages or profitable positions and more generally refuse to take any action unless they received some sort of honour. Shelburne recognized that he was part of the hierarchy of aristocrats who ruled Britain alongside the monarch, and accepted that he too, and his own retinue, had to be rewarded until an alternative system replaced present practice. Shelburne's group was significant from the mid-1760s, beginning with the orators Isaac Barré and John Dunning, who were members of the House of Commons for seats Shelburne controlled (meaning that he chose the member of parliament himself), Chipping Wycombe in Buckinghamshire and Calne in Wiltshire.

In 1762, before he could take up one of these seats in the Commons for himself, Shelburne succeeded his father as Earl of Shelburne in the Irish peerage, and as Baron Wycombe in that of Britain.[27] His friend Isaac Barré took the seat of Chipping Wycombe. Of an Irish Huguenot merchant family, Barré had become a soldier and acquainted with Shelburne during the Rochefort expedition. Afterwards, however, he remained with Wolfe, fighting with distinction at Québec and being beside the major general when he died at the Plains of Abraham. Barré lost his left eye in the conflict and a musket ball could not be removed from his skull. He soon became disenchanted with Chatham and the government when lesser figures were promoted above him; Shelburne gave him the opportunity to fight corruption instead of the French. It was said that Barré had been so brilliant as a young actor when a student at Trinity College Dublin that David Garrick, the actor and theatre director, offered him a fortune to continue. Such skills were retained as Barré shone as an orator from the time of his maiden speech of 10 December 1761.[28] It was a vicious indictment of Chatham as war minister and a resounding demand for peace. Barré later popularized the description of the rebels in North America as 'sons of liberty'.[29]

If Barré was an early member of Shelburne's Circle, the prominent lawyer John Dunning soon followed. Dunning had defended Wilkes after the prosecution of *North Briton* and when he was refused entry to the House of Commons despite winning successive elections. Later, when MP for the other seat Shelburne controlled, Calne, Dunning became infamous for successfully spearheading the resolution in the Commons on 6 April 1780 that 'the influence of the crown has increased, is increasing and ought to be diminished'.[30] In the speech Dunning underlined the influence of Hume. Dunning declared that it was Hume who 'foresaw the increasing influence so early as the year 1742', before citing 'a passage from Hume's *Essays*, to shew that that able writer had prophesied, that arbitrary monarchy would one day or other be the euthanasia of the British constitution'.[31] The point for the three members of Shelburne's Circle was that George III was ruling like Charles I. Without having to worry about the threat of Jacobite rebellion, as his grandfather George II and great-grandfather George I had done, the new monarch was interested in ensuring that he governed personally. Victory in war in the first years of his reign had increased George III's confidence. The king began to use the Commons to maintain his control over government, mainly through bribes and patronage which made members of parliament loyal.[32] For Shelburne, 'governing by the House of Commons is in fact converting the Legislature into a false Executive.'[33] This was a reference to the king's expansion of his patronage networks throughout the Commons to the point, for Shelburne, that the House passively applauded government action rather than challenging the executive for the public good. Factions and parties dominated politics in such circumstances, overseen by the controlling personal rule of the king and the selfish ambition of ministers. Such polarization could, in Shelburne's view, only lead to one thing: fanaticism.

Among the most subservient members of the king's party were those whose wealth, often gargantuan, was derived from the empire and war profiteering. Hence under George III, further war and empire-building became national policy as, in the short term at least, it made courtiers and placemen richer. For Shelburne, it intensified the ongoing national crisis. In November 1763, after Shelburne and Barré voted against the king's prosecution of Wilkes for seditious libel, they were stripped of their military offices. Barré wrote to Shelburne that 'if things go much further, the Court will get beyond redemption.'[34] Believing that the seventeenth-century crisis of the Stuart monarchy was being returned to, the Shelburne Circle set their minds to the task of avoiding the descent into civil war caused either by the crown or by the rise of popular fanatics akin to Puritans, plotting social reformation in the name of liberty.

III

Despite his pessimism about the political world in which he was rising, in the early 1760s Shelburne was identified as a rising star. Bute stated in a memorandum of March 1763 that he expected Shelburne to soon be a leader of the country.[35] Contemporaries believed that Shelburne could cure national ills. John Hawkesworth noted in 1768, when dedicating his new translation of Fénelon's *Telemachus* to Shelburne, that he had manifested 'early virtue and noble views', was a 'friend of man, jealous of public liberty' and altogether a 'citizen from whom . . . your country may expect yet more important service'.[36] The natural philosopher and Dissenting minister Joseph Priestley in 1772 wrote that he considered Shelburne 'to be, for ability and integrity together, the very first character in this kingdom'.[37] Decades later Priestley made this remarkable statement, 'Had [Shelburne] continued [Prime Minister] to this day, his liberal and enlightened policy would have saved England, and all Europe, the horrors of the present most ruinous and impolitic war [with revolutionary France].'[38] From his position of relative powerlessness, Shelburne rarely expounded his critiques in public, except through his speeches in the House of Lords, but he was forever preparing policy either in the anticipation of office or in order to pressure those in power.

The desire to formulate policy meant that Shelburne was perpetually working to maintain and to broaden a network of prominent writers and philosophers. Through Bute he met Samuel Johnson, the prominent poet and playwright, and through Johnson both the poet Oliver Goldsmith and Joshua Reynolds, who painted Shelburne in 1764 and 1766. Attending through his friend Barré a group of young reformers at Hill Street, Mayfair, in London in the mid-1760s, Shelburne came to know Lawrence Sulivan, who opposed Robert Clive's strategy of empire-building in Bengal, and also James Townsend, then a friend of Wilkes, who became alderman for the City of London and Lord Mayor in 1772. His former tutor the jurist Blackstone, then writing his *Commentaries on the Laws of England* (1765–69), also had regular meetings with Shelburne in the early 1760s.[39] Shelburne was evidently seeking guidance, but Blackstone was not the man. Benjamin Franklin was of greater influence and after discussing the national crisis together, Shelburne soon pestered him for solutions. Shelburne recalled their earlier times together in 1782 – when Franklin was breaking up Britain's Empire as a leader of the new republics in North America – simultaneously providing a sense of what was expected from contributors to Shelburne's Circle and what it meant to promote 'the happiness of Mankind':

I find myself return'd nearly to the same Situation, which you remember me to have occupied nineteen years ago, and should be very glad to talk to you as I did then, and afterwards in 1767, upon the means of promoting the Happiness of Mankind, a Subject much more agreeable to my Nature, than the best concerted Plans for spreading Misery and Devastation. I have had a high Opinion of the Compass of your Mind and of your Foresight. I have often been beholden to both and shall be glad to be so again, as far as is Compatible with your Situation.[40]

Franklin, in concluding that Britain was doomed and that a new land of moderation and liberty had to be created in North America by separating from the mother country, did not prove Shelburne's inspiration either.[41] Shelburne refused to give up on Britain.

It was at Hill Street too that Shelburne made Hume's acquaintance. Shelburne had found finally his sage. As early as 1761 he invited Hume to join his circle. Refusing to move to England, Hume turned him down on the grounds that he had decided never again to live away from Scotland:

> Your Lordship may judge, by this specimen of my character, how unfit I am to mingle in such an active and sprightly society as that of which your Lordship invited me to partake, and that in reality a book and a fireside, are the only scenes for which I am now qualified. But I should be unfit to live among human creatures could I ever forget the obligations which I owe to your Lordship's goodness, or could ever lose the firm resolution of expressing my sense of them on all occasions. And when I shall see your Lordship making a figure in the active scenes of life, I shall always consider your progress with a peculiar pleasure, though perhaps accompanied with the regret that I partake of it at so great a distance.[42]

In Hume's case, Shelburne refused to take no for an answer. He maintained a correspondence with Hume, passing on information about national life in return for Hume's view of the state of Britain and its prospects internationally. Indeed, Shelburne's wife, Sophia Carteret, noted in her diary that Hume dined with them on 28 February 1766, where he revealed that he had enjoyed access to manuscripts at the University of Paris that described in detail Charles II's treaty with Louis XIV to restore Catholicism to England.[43]

Membership of Shelburne's Circle could be long distance, at one remove, or immediate and personal, by spending a few days or several months at Bowood House in Wiltshire. Adam Smith was also sought after as a member of the circle, and he took Shelburne's younger brother into his own house as a student. Smith followed Hume in refusing direct membership. Again, Shelburne refused rejection – he was convinced that Hume and Smith were diagnosing imperial ills with more perspicuity than anyone else. Shelburne had travelled in a coach with Smith from Edinburgh to London in the mid-1760s and frequently recalled their conversation.[44] He presented friends with copies of Smith's *Theory of Moral Sentiments*.

In the case of the French *philosophe* André Morellet, who was close to the political economist and sometime government minister Anne-Robert-Jacques Turgot, but also linked with the physiocrats and the minister for foreign affairs Charles Gravier, comte de Vergennes, the relationship was largely epistolary. Shelburne had met Morellet in Paris in 1771 and encouraged him to visit his country seat at Bowood in 1772 and again in 1782.[45] Morellet became increasingly important to Shelburne because his ultimate vision was for enlightenment to be restored in Britain and in France together, creating an axis capable of combating imperial impulses from Europe's autocracies, including Russia, Prussia and the Holy Roman Empire.

In addition to luminaries from Scotland and France, Shelburne and his acolytes in parliament, Barré and Dunning, took action to support a number of then lesser-known figures. They included young philosophers such as Jeremy Bentham, who later recalled spending the happiest months of his entire life staying with Shelburne at Bowood House.[46] Bentham's editor John Bowring reported Bentham saying of Shelburne ' "He raised me," I have heard him say, "from the bottomless pit of humiliation – he made me feel I was something." ' Bentham was equally attached to Louisa Fitzpatrick, Shelburne's second wife, stating 'She had the best, highest aristocratical education possible. She was as gentle as a lamb; she talked French and understood Latin extremely well.'[47] He was devastated by her death in 1789.

Relationships within the circle were open, in the sense of abandoning rank and hierarchy. As Dunning put it, 'I am happy in classing myself among that noble lord's dependants. I will assure those who have alluded to what they call dependence, that it is a state of dependence, accompanied with perfect freedom.'[48] The position of Shelburne's Circle was recognized by contemporaries. John Burnby, in a book dedicated to Shelburne in 1780, made the point that 'the constitution of this kingdom seems in a galloping consumption, and unless an able physician is called in I fear it will dissolve, and leave not a wreck behind.'[49] Shelburne spent decades positioning himself as the physician ready to cure these ills of the state and even the globe. He believed he had discerned the disease and had great faith that new strategies to bolster enlightenment were ready and waiting to be implemented in the form of a concretely defined public good enshrined in law, and policies to expand rights to Dissenters in England and Catholics in Ireland.[50] Shelburne wanted the groups within society that had not been granted full civil and political liberties to be trusted to be free. This was why he was sometimes accused of being a subversive follower of Locke, and of favouring both the excess of political liberty and popular rebellion that was then associated with the philosopher.[51] What was distinctive was that Shelburne believed that liberties could only be extended in conditions where the mercantile system was abolished. He therefore advocated for a transformation in the very nature of Britain's Empire.

IV

It was when he became a minister under Chatham that Shelburne perceived himself to be battling against fanaticism. After serving Bute in 1763 Shelburne briefly laboured as First Lord of Trade on behalf of Bute's successor, George Granville. During this time, in 1763 and 1764, he was becoming closer to Chatham and resigned from office on the latter's exclusion from Cabinet. When Chatham was restored to the premiership in 1766 Shelburne, at the age of twenty-nine, became Secretary of State for the Southern Department, a role that lasted until 1768. The post was one of the most significant in government, with responsibility for home affairs and

British relations with Ireland, the colonies and the western states of Europe. The lesser office of Northern Secretary dealt with other European relationships and the division lasted until the creation of the Foreign Office in 1782. As Southern Secretary Shelburne was faced with multiple threats, especially from a reinvigorated France under the foreign minister Étienne François, Marquis de Stainville, duc de Choiseul. Choiseul closely allied France both to the Holy Roman Empire and to Spain. He was planning for a return to war against a weakened Britain by 1770. In the interim, a policy of false pacification was pursued, entailing the pretence that war and conflict were to be avoided at all costs, offering to negotiate in disagreements between Britain and other powers, while all the time building up fortifications, and an army and a navy capable of invading Britain. Choiseul's policy suited Shelburne because, as the French minister was aware, however patriotic and vigorous the young minister was, he was desirous of maintaining a peace whose negotiation he had contributed to in 1763.[52] Shelburne in turn may have been aware of Choiseul's true intentions but felt that peace brought so many benefits that it was worth maintenance whatever the circumstances.

At this stage of his life Shelburne perceived himself to be someone who could conjoin the fractious, discussing issues flexibly with each party until compromise was reached. In other words, his sense was that personality alone could be relied upon to improve politics; rogues existed but, as in the case of Henry Fox, the influential Whig, paymaster general of the armed forces and the father of Shelburne's later rival Charles James Fox, they could be bribed with money and with appointments. Achieving peace might be grubby or even sordid due to the nature of human ambition – but the end justified the means. In this Shelburne was also following Hume, who justified corruption in greasing the wheels of free governments, so long as the public good was ultimately reinforced.[53] Being Chatham's favourite minister undoubtedly lay behind Shelburne's initial confidence, even though he was already out of favour with George III because of his stance on Wilkes. At a time of crisis, of evils likely incurable, as Chatham put it, when 'faction shakes and corruption saps the country to its foundations', Shelburne was sure that steps could be taken to reverse Britain's decline and put an end to what he termed 'the anarchy' of present politics.[54] There was, then, a period when he thought Chatham could be trusted to restore enlightenment by limiting George III's despotic impulses and by making a lasting international peace. His faith was soon to be shattered. The reason lay with the failure of the British government to pacify the unhappy colonists in North America, instead fanning the flames that led from discontent to separation.

Shelburne was initially involved in efforts to resolve the conflict arising from the taxing of the colonies to reduce Britain's national debt. He negotiated with the expectation that his efforts would be respected and would be perceived as effective once those around the table realized that he worked without any project or agenda other than peace. Once the boundaries of practical policy had been determined, Shelburne was willing to conciliate wherever possible, establishing through this process both trust and a framework for the resolution of future conflicts. In the case of North America, Shelburne for a long time believed the cause of ongoing union was not yet lost. Once all parties accepted that the purpose of Britain's colonies was trade benefits for all, rather than an extension of national power for one country, then hostile relations could be repaired. Shelburne's opinion rested on the work of his private secretary, the Shakespeare scholar Maurice Morgann, who stated in a memorandum that the colonies were 'obedient from habit, and from that reverence with which they considered their mother-country'. In its snatching away of the colonial assemblies' powers regarding the regulation of trade, the Stamp Act of March 1765 ruined everything. The Mutiny Act that followed, pushing onto the colonies the costs of quartering troops, gave every indication of confirming Britain's desire for despotic control rather than commercial union.[55] But if British authority was reaffirmed while promoting trade and respecting colonial powers and institutions, the threat of civil war would abate. As always, Shelburne had

England's post-union relationship with Scotland in mind when considering positive futures.

Shelburne was successful in pacifying New York for a time by such a policy, but he was soon made weak within government by Chatham's incapacitation by illness. Charles Townshend as chancellor refused conciliation and was given full backing by the king in the passing of what became the Townshend Acts in June and July 1767, asserting control over trade while penalizing colonial authorities who refused to enact laws issued from London.[56] Such measures were madness in Shelburne's eyes. Yet beyond the ministry, Shelburne was assaulted by Burke and the Rockingham group for not sufficiently pacifying the North Americans. Shelburne's sole success was in sending his secretary Morgann to Québec. They worked together to turn the formerly Catholic French subjects into newly loyal Britons, a strategy that resulted in the Catholic emancipation enshrined in the Québec Act of 1774.[57] Shelburne rejected the common prejudice that Catholics could never be loyal to George III and were incapable of being subjects in a free state.

Shelburne abhorred the turning of populations into slaves for economic profit. Despite his seeking to pacify the unhappy colonial governors across North America, Shelburne nevertheless sought to end what he identified as the grotesque exploitation of native peoples. In 1758 he wrote to Francis Fauquier, lieutenant governor of the colony of Virginia, that reports were being received in London of violence against tribes such as the Creeks of West Florida in order to expel them from their land.[58] Shelburne warned Fauquier that selfish merchants had 'too much succeeded in inculcating into the Minds of these poor People, that nothing will satisfy the Colonies but their Extirpation'. War was the outcome in circumstances where existing treaties were every day being violated by the colonial powers. Shelburne argued that the prosperity of the colonies, 'especially their back settlers, depends so much on maintaining Peace and Friendship with the Indians'. Given this fact, it was 'amazing, that such Enormities [violence against the Native Americans] can remain any time undiscovered'. Action had to be taken,

Shelburne insisted, by Fauquier against 'the Inhabitants of Augusta and Bedford Counties, in your Province' in the name of the crown to end abuse of Native American tribes.[59] Negotiating with Franklin and Phineas Lyman, the renowned soldier seeking to settle western Florida, Shelburne sought to establish trading settlements on the Ohio and Illinois rivers respectful of the hunting grounds and settlements of the Native Americans.[60]

Shelburne gained a reputation as a peacemaker when he was minister, someone who was willing to act to prevent stronger authorities from dominating the lesser. This was one reason why the smaller powers of Europe started to make diplomatic appeals to him directly, in the hope that he would intervene to prevent the loss of their sovereignty. On such grounds he was approached by the Corsicans and the Genevans among many other parties who perceived themselves to be being unjustly oppressed by France. In practice, despite warm words to the weak, Shelburne did little. Like his friend William Henry Nassau de Zuylestein, 4th Earl of Rochford, then in Paris as Britain's ambassador, Shelburne moved to the view that divisions in London, the weakness of Chatham's ministry, were translating into perceptions of decline abroad. The French, as Shelburne put it, through 'several secret intelligences' were taking steps to 'keep alive in every part of His Majesty's dominions every principle of division'.[61] Direct evidence of Britain's new frailty came from the fact that Spain was threatening the Falkland Islands while refusing to pay the ransom agreed at Manilla in 1762.[62] Corsica was secretly annexed by France in return for cancelling debts owed by the Genoese while Choiseul deceived the British.[63] Shelburne had little faith in popular leaders such as Pasquale Paoli, whom he knew via Rochford to have been negotiating with the French while he was appealing to the British as alone capable of protecting Corsican liberty. Shelburne saw Paoli, despite the plaudits of Boswell and the popularity of his cause in the British press, to be a fraud in the manner of Wilkes; each man was ultimately self-serving rather than acting for the public good.[64] This view was supported by Shelburne's friend John Stuart, known as Lord Mount Stuart while his father

Bute was alive, who travelled to Corsica and derided Paoli as a false prophet. According to Mount Stuart, Paoli was a would-be tyrant himself, seeking to govern 'weak and uncultivated minds' by means of 'visions, revelations and dreams to strengthen his power' like 'Numa and Mahomet'.[65] This was later to prove important to Shelburne when he considered the effects of popular liberty, leading him closer to Hume's view that greater political liberty merely allowed demagogues to thrive, setting themselves up to be tyrants far worse than George III was ever likely to be.

V

Shelburne's expressed intention of helping the weaker states of Europe against the great came to nought in 1766 and 1767 because he could not carry the Cabinet while Chatham was absent, something that was happening with ever-more frequency due to gout and a mental instability that led him to isolate himself for prolonged periods. Shelburne had higher hopes that he could act alone in another domain he was responsible for, British India. Here he found infinitely more grotesque injustices than in North America and sought to address them. When Adam Smith first used the term 'mercantile system' as a description of the British Empire, Shelburne considered that singular proof lay in British India – and more particularly in the personality and ambition of Robert Clive. Clive had greatly expanded British possessions in India, for many turning the East India Company into a state serving neither the people of India nor Britain, but shareholders alone. The connections of the governors and the social distinction of the wealthy shareholders, including Shelburne himself, meant that the necessary division between markets and politics had been lost. Rather, the wealth and power of the British state was being used to establish monopoly markets for the Company, destroying indigenous commerce, extracting natural resources and maintaining a system brutally exploitative of native peoples.

Shelburne in office tried to put an end to Clive's Company strategy of expanding the Empire to fund ever-increasing dividends for shareholders.[66] A rationale was being formed for a British Empire as a mercantile system by virtue of the link between the monetary rewards for those who owned shares and their identity as significant politicians and legislators directing Indian policy from London. This fact alone explained the failure of successive governments to challenge Clive. As Shelburne made clear in a private memorandum, the public were the first losers in the East India Company as then constituted. The Company by its measures had become 'an object of public policy' whose trade 'greatly depends upon the future support' of the British state. It was accurate to say that the Company 'existed by aid of Government'. It was evident that 'a particular set of proprietors' had been 'led astray by the hopes of present profit'. In such circumstances parliamentary control over dividends had to be asserted, cutting the link between war for profit and direct reward for the politicians and directors.[67]

Shelburne wanted free trade without empire and sought to use a parliamentary veto upon the actions of the Company to end the rule of 'factious sets of men' lusting for gain.[68] Once the capacity of the Company to own land and act as a state was forbidden, Shelburne expected a different economic relationship with India to be established. Shelburne was advised by his friend, and Clive's bitter enemy, Laurence Sulivan. Sulivan had battled Clive in the early 1760s for directorship of the Company and their two factions continued to be engaged in an internal company war.[69] When questions were raised about the accounts of the Company, leading to a parliamentary inquiry in 1766–67, Sulivan and Shelburne were given an opportunity together to formulate strategies for Chatham that sought to limit the power of the directors and to increase parliamentary scrutiny. Their shared goal was to return the Company to its original charter, the purpose of which had solely been trade. Shelburne and his associates wanted to forbid the Company from the acquisition of territories, which had characterized its actions from the time of the retaking of Calcutta by Clive in January 1757.

In every case Shelburne investigated the issue and sought to act to prevent war, intolerance, injustice and violence. On every front he failed. The combination of glory and profit promoted by pro-Company accounts of the British in India made economic sense to too many. Oppression and violence were ubiquitous in times during which war had become a means to lucrative empire. However much Shelburne asserted that the benefits of this system – whatever they were – would be temporary, as inevitable war would always be the ruin of all, assertion and personality in the context of a divided Cabinet and an imperially minded monarch amounted to nought. In the instances of both India and North America, Charles Townshend outmanoeuvred Shelburne because of Chatham's illness and because of the king's antagonism towards him. In the case of Ireland too Shelburne was faced with an entrenched body of Protestant landowners who refused to countenance the kinds of reform he wanted to initiate. Even simple legislation augmenting the army stationed in Ireland in the event of open rebellion proved an uphill struggle.[70]

Shelburne left office in 1768 exhausted and frustrated. A great deal of his time had been spent seeking an audience with the ill Chatham or seeking Chatham's opinion through the medium of his wife. Shelburne could not forgive Chatham's failure to use his position in the 1760s to alter the constitution and politics to make them less reliant upon the power of individuals and that of the monarch. It has often been claimed that Shelburne was at heart always a follower of his master Chatham.[71] Yet Shelburne's political vision was far grander, and in retrospect far less realistic, than that of his sometime mentor. In autobiographical fragments published by his descendant Edmond George Petty-Fitzmaurice in 1876, Shelburne called Chatham a false patriot who used bribes and court mistresses 'to please the King in his ruling passion and that of the Hanover family, viz. German measures and personal avarice'.[72]

If the first grave weakness of the British constitution was for Shelburne the excessive power of the crown, the second was the corruption of the populace, leading them to follow demagogues and potentially tyrants in their projects, and in the acceptance of injustice. Shelburne later reported that 'Lord Chatham told me that he could never be sure of the public passions, that all that he could do was to watch, and be the first to follow them.'[73] Shelburne found the populace to be inconstant and irrational. He confessed to being 'sorry to say upon an experience of forty years, that the public is incapable of embracing two objects at a time, or of extending their views beyond the object immediately before them'.[74] The people were also showing signs of addiction to a fanatic love of authority in some cases and of liberty in others, which was likely to add to the sense of societal turbulence.

The experience of governing changed Shelburne. He became less self-confident with regard to individual negotiation, less willing to play the middleman, and much more sceptical about individuals solving problems through parley. His vocation as he came to see it was to act as a statesman or legislator, proposing laws based on the most advanced and practical contemporary philosophy. Hence the necessity for a circle who would provide him with policies that could only be challenged with difficulty, cutting through the deceptions of cabal and propaganda. A second significant conclusion emerged from the direct experience of politics in the 1760s. Those who supported the crown in return for venal offices and favours were known as the 'King's Friends'. Shelburne came to perceive these men more concretely as the locus of corruption in Britain and saw much truth in the accusation that many had purchased rotten boroughs using funds illicitly gained in India. Shelburne was certain that this mercantile system was the source of Britain's wars for empire, supplying interest and rationale for the benefit of a malign but immensely powerful group. The mercantile system had the potential to destroy Britain because France, in his opinion the naturally superior power, would sooner or later be victorious in military conflict. Like the feudal household he saw himself to have been scarred by as a youth, the mercantile system for Shelburne made tyrants of men. Seeking to bring nations together, above all Britain and France, stimulating commerce and dismantling empire through an alliance of military powerful states was an objective that began to define membership of Shelburne's Circle.

Shelburne's first fascination with Hume was the latter's aspiration of creating a government of laws rather than of men, being the very embodiment of a public good and general interest beyond factional challenge or refutation. Shelburne from the end of the 1760s pursued Smith more forcefully because he thought that Hume's friend was more likely to define systematically such laws. Shelburne held fast to the Smithian view that a comparison could be discerned between a beneficial path of economic development that was pacific and the reality embodied by century after century of European history. An 'unnatural and retrograde' order had been created by feudalism, establishing foundations for the emergence of mercantilism that, like feudal social relations, benefited the eminent few and kept the rest in poverty.[75] The urbanization of Europe, beginning with those Italian city states that had survived the fall of the Roman Empire, had proceeded apace across the continent without any concomitant commercialization of agriculture. Forms of commerce had thereby emerged that facilitated war. The promotion of what Smith and Shelburne called 'natural liberty' was one solution, entailing the breaking down of merchant monopolies and limiting the control of markets by self-interested corporations willing to employ violence against those in their way. Natural liberty had to be restored carefully, however, because an abruptly introduced project was always worse than the disease it was intended to remedy.

Ultimately, however, combating the mercantile system relied upon the articulation of general moral principles 'as may embrace the Turk or the Gentoo (Hindu) equally with the Christian'.[76] Shelburne was in consequence smitten – the term he used was 'captivated' – by a notion derived from Hume, ascribed to Turgot and embodied by many of Price's projects, the idea of fundamental principles of law, commerce, morality and politics sufficiently comprehensive to embrace all countries.[77] Such laws – alas never specified – were unlikely to entail the replication of political systems or constitutional forms. They were envisaged rather to establish laws that prevented criminal behaviour or violence, as well as the formation of corrupt aristocracies. Bentham's aspiration when describing his panopticon prison, to build 'a mill for grinding rogues honest, and idle men industrious', gives a sense of the ambition of the legislative science.[78] Such goals made Bentham a natural member of Shelburne's Circle from the time that he was promising a rational system of law in his *Fragment on Government* of the early 1780s.

VI

It is significant that on leaving office Shelburne showed every sign of expecting to return. On 6 November 1768, after his early October resignation, Shelburne was trying and failing to see Chatham at Hayes before returning home with Barré. All three men were then involved from the following February in attacking George III and his administration for their treatment of Wilkes. As we have seen, Wilkes had originally been indicted for publishing No. 45 of the *North Briton*, which was heavily critical of the king, as well as for planning to publish a scandalous reworking of Pope's *Essay on Man* entitled *Essay on Woman* in December 1763. When the House of Lords found the essay guilty of libel and lewdness, he fled to France. On returning at the end of April 1768 he was arrested as an outlaw, and yet subsequently elected as MP for Middlesex on 10 May. In early June, Lord Mansfield cancelled the charge of being an outlaw but imprisoned Wilkes for libel. He was then expelled from the House of Commons on 3 February 1769, but re-elected thirteen days later. Parliament declared his election void on 17 February, but Wilkes was returned once more on 16 March. Again, the election was annulled the following day. Once more Wilkes was victorious in a further election on 13 April. This time, however, Colonel Henry Luttrell, Wilkes's defeated opponent, entered the Commons as member for Middlesex (on 15 April) – in defiance of the electorate's will. In the Commons, Barré verbally assaulted the king, accusing him of turning ministers and servants into slaves.[79] Chatham and Shelburne in the Lords on 9 January 1770 drew parallels with the times of the Stuarts and demanded a response to the many grievances of the people. Grafton, ridiculed in the wildly popular *Letters of Junius* and accused of being weak on the international stage, fell as prime minister. He was replaced by Lord North.[80]

The parallel between the 1770s and the actions of Charles I in the 1630s was evident to every member of the opposition. George III had refused to respond to the Remonstrance of the City of London complaining about the treatment of Wilkes, having failed to recognize an earlier petition on the Middlesex election. To Shelburne the monarch was behaving like a Stuart: 'the answer lately given to the City Address is similar to the answers given by Charles I, Charles II, James II and Queen Anne to similar applications of their subjects for redress of grievances.' Shelburne asked in the Lords on 4 May 1770, 'is there no instance upon record which suits the present occasion but instances from the reign of the Stuarts?' There was only one answer: Shelburne traced the source of the malaise to the same cause of the English Civil War. It was the 'secret influence' at work among the King's Friends who 'have directed their attention more to intrigues and their own emoluments than the good of the public'. A cabal was corrupting the state, Shelburne stated, a fact he said had been brilliantly analysed by Burke in his pamphlet *Thoughts on the Causes of the Present Discontents*.[81]

At the beginning of the 1770s, amid the fallout of the scandal, there was a widespread expectation that war with Spain or France would recommence and that Chatham would be recalled to office, uniting Britons and healing national ailments in the process, just as he had at the end of the 1750s. Chatham recognized Shelburne's qualities and saw him as sitting at his right hand whenever power beckoned.[82] Shelburne argued that a royal despotism had been created in Britain and in North America and called for the impeachment of North and threatened that the opposition would stop attending parliament.[83] The opponents of the administration might then gather their forces in the country. Chatham wrote to Shelburne on 29 September arguing that remonstrance was vital. By November 1770 Shelburne was asserting that 'the reputation of the kingdom is hourly given up' because ministers with interests at odds with those of the people could not recognize the public good. This explained the parlous state of the navy and the likelihood that when war next occurred 'the glory of the British Crown will be eclipsed and the queen of nations made an object of ridicule to every potentate in Europe.'[84] Chatham, on seeing what he called the 'omnipotence and imbecility' of the government, came to the conclusion that 'matters are hastening to some crisis', that 'all is ruined' and that 'the times are pollution in the very quintessence.'[85] Meanwhile, George III was seen to support private legislation to help his favourites, such as that to facilitate the Adams family of architects purchasing land in the City of London to erect the Adelphi theatre. Another instance was the Durham Yard Embankment Bill. Shelburne and Chatham were sure the present crisis would see a new ministry – their own.

That Shelburne and Chatham's expectations came to nought was due in part to Lord North's fortune in avoiding war with France and Spain: court politics at Versailles entailed Choiseul's departure from office and with him the likelihood of conflict. Civil war in America was popular with the British people on the mainland, with a patriotic press lauding the suppression of the rebels.[86] Chatham was also not the orator or leader he once had been. Furthermore, the party of Chatham and Shelburne disagreed with Whig leaders about the means of collapsing the mercantile system. Burke and Rockingham favoured austerity regarding the public purse, an end to places and corrupt forms of patronage. They rejected parliamentary reform, something which Shelburne saw as a tool to reduce the crown's control. As Shelburne put it to Chatham, 'I have never heard a reflecting man doubt on the country representation being the greatest restorative possible of the constitution.'[87] Shelburne did advocate shorter parliaments but when John Sawbridge proposed triennial parliaments in 1770 the bill was rejected by 105 to 54.[88] With the king and North in the ascendency, support for Wilkes falling and any parliamentary challenge lacking teeth in the early 1770s, office for Shelburne was as far away as ever.

VII

On 5 January 1771, Shelburne was shattered by the sudden death of his wife, Sophia Carteret. She was just twenty-five. They had married when she was nineteen and the second of their two children was born in 1768. By May, Shelburne commenced a trip abroad with Barré, feeling a need to escape Britain. The two men travelled to Milan, where they became acquainted with the reforming jurist Cesare Beccaria. Shelburne and Barré spent months, however, in Paris, becoming regulars at the salons of Madame Geoffrin, Madame Helvétius and the Baron d'Holbach. Through such gatherings Shelburne and Barré met Turgot and the abbé Morellet. A fast friendship soon developed between Shelburne and Morellet, who visited Bowood the following year.[89] In his long stay of 1772, Morellet underscored the vibrancy of Shelburne's Circle, where he met David Garrick, the playwright, and Price and Franklin, among many other luminaries. When major works of analysis and reform appeared, such as Smith's *Wealth of Nations*, Morellet took notice and discussed them with Shelburne.[90] Shelburne clearly made an impression upon the reform circles in Paris, who, like so many at the time, were certain that he would play a major role in the governance of Britain for years to come. For Shelburne, discovering so many like-minded critics of Britain who were also advocates of long-term peace between the great powers led to the end of his personal grief and the beginning of intellectual reinvigoration.

On his return to Britain, Shelburne once again took the role of a leading figure in opposition to the king and his ministers. Shelburne was convinced that India, now a neglected part of the British Empire because of American affairs, might soon contribute even more directly to national disaster. Famine had occurred across Bengal in 1770. The policy of extracting riches by directors and dividends for shareholders of the East India Company had proceeded apace, in conditions of higher costs for maintaining British rule, to the point that the Company itself had become heavily indebted. Shelburne wrote to Chatham in April 1772 that 'every man of every party acknowledges a blow to be impending in that part of the world which must shake to its foundations the revenue, commerce and manufactures of this.'[91] It was the case, he maintained, that the 'crimes and frauds of the servants [of the Company] in India' were so great they defied description. They were protected from public indictment because they were friends of the king; as Shelburne put it, 'the Directors [are] occupied in domestic pursuits equally fraudulent.'[92]

It was also after the death of his wife that Shelburne became closer to Richard Price. Shelburne had met Price through the London salon of Elizabeth Montagu, a noted intellectual and author of *Essays on Shakespeare* (1769). Montagu advised Shelburne to read Price's defence of Christianity, the *Four Dissertations*, in 1767 and after doing so Shelburne asked to meet their author.[93] Price had been writing about the foundations of morality since the late 1750s, but came to notice through well-publicized demands to pay off the national debt in 1769 and 1772.[94] Shelburne was so impressed with Price that he sent copies of his books to figures such as Chatham in the hope that they would be convinced by the reforms Price was suggesting. It was Price who introduced Shelburne to Joseph Priestley, then minister at the Unitarian Chapel at Mill Hill in Leeds. On 16 May 1772, Priestley became Shelburne's secretary and librarian and moved to Calne. For the next seven years he would spend the summer months there, and the remainder of the year at Lansdowne House in London on a salary of £250 per annum.

Both Priestley and Price were behind the Toleration bill of 18 March 1772, which allowed Dissenters to hold office municipally or under the crown without having to subscribe to the doctrines of the Church of England, under the condition that they first took an Oath of Allegiance and openly rejected the Pope's influence. The bill was rejected in the Lords and met the same fate the following year.

Despite such reverses, Shelburne was more prominent than ever as an opposition figure in the Lords. As the new session began on 31 October 1776, he likened the North Americans to the Whigs of 1688.[95] The Whigs of the present were united in their opposition to any income of the monarch independent of parliamentary control. Shelburne was especially vocal on national degeneracy. He blamed the lack of civic feeling and commitment to the national interest of lawyers and Anglican clergymen especially. The former in their selfishness were 'state Quixotes' and the latter 'the drones of society'.[96]

The true source of the malaise was the corrupt body of the King's Friends; Shelburne likened Lord North to a court spaniel.[97] Defeat at Saratoga at the hands of the Continental Army led to calls for a war government under Chatham. Divisions over the extent of conciliation called for by the Rockingham and Chatham factions prevented Shelburne's return as a minister. Instead, France embraced the American cause with an alliance with the new republics in 1778 and was followed by Spain. Shelburne made plans to marry Louisa Fitzpatrick, whose family were linked to Fox, thereby broadening his political orbit. Chatham died in May 1778 at a national low, the invasion of England being a real possibility. If this occurred, Barré advised Shelburne that collapse would likely be speedy in the face of French and Spanish forces. Plans ought to be made, Barré said, for leading a coup against the government in this moment of 'crisis when the balance of England stands trembling on its beam', as 'some bold and daring measure' of opposition to the invaders would 'stun the Court, awake the People, and then take the reins of Government into their own hands.'[98] The navy's victory against the Spanish fleet at Cape St Vincent in 1780 reduced such pressure, but an era of crisis unparalleled since the 1640s was acknowledged.

Ireland might, Shelburne argued, be the next seat of rebellion. On a visit to Valentia, the island off the coast of County Kerry, Shelburne wrote to Price that 'I found the land in a state of nature, the people worse: the result of poverty, and the Popery laws, which are subversive of all morality, public or private confidence and industry.'[99] In the Lords in June 1779, Shelburne declared that Ireland had more legitimate reasons for rebellion against Britain than the colonists in North America ever had.[100] Ireland was in a state of calamity and distress akin to countries visited by war or famine.

As there was no prospect of justice or relief, the people of Ireland were arming themselves 'to upwards of 40,000 men and were daily augmenting' with the government having largely 'abdicated'. In such circumstances, 'the people had resumed the powers vested in it; and in so doing were fully authorized by every principle of the constitution and every motive of self-preservation.'[101] Shelburne used Ireland to describe the likely future of mainland Britain because the dependent kingdom was only slightly ahead in the experience of the effects of corrupt crown patronage, economic decline due to the American Revolution and the more general oppression of Catholics and Dissenters.[102] However certain Shelburne was that his circle had discovered solutions to national and global ills he was aware that their schemes remained purposeless without power. The pursuit of office obsessed Shelburne as the North American crisis intensified, war recommenced with France and the widespread prediction that the mercantile system would ruin Britain appeared to be coming to pass.

VIII

By the late 1770s Shelburne's star could be seen to be rising again, after France joined the colonial war against Britain in 1778 and as Lord North's ministry faltered. With Chatham dead, Shelburne became the leading opposition figure alongside Rockingham. Shelburne and Price's perspectives upon contemporary politics were ever-more pertinent as the crisis they had predicted intensified. Equally, Shelburne was the beneficiary of a remarkable dovetailing of elements within British and French opinion. Figures within the Shelburne Circle could be matched by prominent French commentators who had come to similar conclusions, in part because they too were influenced by Hume.[103] The most significant was the second generation of physiocrats who laboured alongside Turgot when he was a minister in Paris between 1774 and 1776. Turgot had translated Josiah Tucker's work on the naturalization of Protestants and Jews in the 1750s, associated with the *philosophes* around Voltaire, and become close to the economic reformers who were friends of the government official Jacques-Claude-Marie Vincent de Gournay. De Gournay was credited with coining the terms 'laissez-faire, laissez-passer' and 'bureaucratie', the latter meaning, as we might imagine, government from desks. De Gournay called for the extension of commerce and industry across France.[104] Stimulating commerce and manufactures also became Turgot's goal as *intendant* (senior administrator) of the Limoges region between 1761 and 1774. During this period Turgot addressed economic problems, improved transport across the rural Limousin and combated inefficiency and corruption. The detested *corvée,* the process by which local nobles could insist upon feudal labour, was abolished, and schools were established to train pupils in veterinary medicine and agriculture. Turgot published a series of works to popularize his views including a defence of the liberty of the grain trade published in 1770 and an economic treatise, the *Réflexions sur la formation et la distribution des richesses,* written in the mid-1760s.[105]

Turgot's *Réflexions* was published by the physiocratic evangelist Pierre-Samuel Dupont de Nemours in his journal *Ephémérides du citoyen ou bibliothèque raisonnée des sciences morales et politiques* between 1769 and 1770. In 1774, Turgot was appointed controller- general, the equivalent of the British chancellor, by the new monarch Louis XVI. He plotted the economic transformation of France through free trade and the development of agriculture and commerce. Experiments in physiocratic legislation followed, including a bonfire of grain-trade controls. However, this policy fell foul of a poor harvest, soon followed by riots demanding a reduction in the price of bread. Turgot also introduced measures to give Protestants greater toleration and abolished guilds. Turgot weathered the storm of opposition but fell from grace due to court intrigues in 1776.[106]

Shelburne was fascinated by Turgot and had his work translated into English. Unquestionably encouraged by Shelburne, Price entered into what became a famous correspondence with Turgot about the American Revolution and the state of the world before the latter's death in 1781. It was Franklin who initiated the contact with Price after sending Turgot copies of Price's work.[107]

Turgot's most prominent acolytes, Morellet, Dupont de Nemours and condorcet, shared his view that before long Britain would be defeated by France. This began to be welcomed by Shelburne and his circle too because it would present an opportunity for the dismemberment of the Empire and a restoration of more natural economic relationships with Ireland, India and Canada. The relative economic health of Britain and France had long obsessed Morellet and was a key part of his *Nouveau dictionnaire de commerce*, on which he laboured for ten years from 1766. Morellet was educated at the Sorbonne between 1748 and 1752; he became a close friend of Turgot. In 1755, Turgot introduced him to another administrator/reformer, Vincent de Gournay, and ever after Morellet devoted himself to comparative political economy. This subject facilitated more accurate predictions about the future course of states and Vincent de Gournay encouraged the study and translation of English language works including those by Shelburne's grandfather William Petty, Charles Davenant, Josiah Child and especially the Irish writer Richard Cantillon.[108] Meeting Hume in Paris in the early 1760s, Morellet became a friend and correspondent. Like Hume, Morellet was increasingly optimistic about French prospects and negative about those of Britain. A *philosophe* and enemy of autocracy, he spent time in the Bastille from April to August 1760 for libelling a former mistress of Choiseul, Madame de Rebecq, in the pamphlet *La préface de la comédie des philosophes*.

If Morellet was closer from his youth to Turgot and the Gournay circle, Dupont joined the group later, following patronage from Quesnay and the other founding father of physiocracy, Victor Riqueti de Mirabeau. Like the two masters of the physiocratic sect, Dupont had always been sceptical of the purported British economic miracle.[109] In the 1760s, Dupont argued in a series of articles that the mercantile system in Britain was spreading a culture of idleness and debauchery, overconcentrating population in urban centres while neglecting agriculture. The British strategy of universal monarchy by empire-building was, he argued, bound to fail because their economy was increasingly unproductive.[110] Finding a different route to economic development, Turgot, by contrast, prodigiously stimulated productivity in France, mainly by creating a national market for French-produced goods. According to Dupont, Britain would never be able to make war upon France in future. Indeed, he claimed that Turgot expected France to defeat Britain so roundly in the American war that free trade at sea would be established while Britain's mercantile system lost its naval lynchpin.[111]

Dupont's Turgot was a part invention since Turgot had serious misgivings about any war, in this respect being closer to Shelburne himself. Writing to the foreign minister Vergennes in 1776, Turgot advised staying out of the war between Britain and its colonies, arguing that it was in the interest of France to allow its enemy to exhaust itself. Turgot's memoir was subsequently published by the wine merchant and arms trader Filippo Mazzei. Mazzei was a close friend of Franklin, Jefferson and Condorcet; it was the latter who probably passed on Turgot's memoir to Mazzei.[112] Mazzei was another physiocratic observer convinced 'as to the pretended flourishing trade of England nothing can be more false.'[113] Britain was a state on the verge of bankruptcy, with deluded ministers who 'think solely of the present and care little or not at all about the future' because they desired only to cling on to office. Population was falling, France had a superior 'economic system' and even the French navy would soon dominate a British navy whose fate was, Mazzei said, 'decadence'.[114] Significantly, Turgot's memoir to Vergennes was translated by Benjamin Vaughan for Shelburne as part of the broader campaign to end war. Vaughan translated other significant Turgot texts for Shelburne as his views were seen to be at one with those of the Shelburne Circle.[115]

The verdict upon Britain and its economy articulated by the

neo-physiocrats greatly influenced French policy even after Turgot's fall. An alternative to Britain's constitutional and economic model existed and had to be followed to avoid the British disease of debt, war, exploitative empire, political division and chaos. Such views were, as we have seen, akin to those of Shelburne and his associates. Parties on both sides of the Channel gradually came to the radical conclusion that defeat in war would in fact be an eventual boon to Britain. Loss would help move Britain away from the mercantile system. At such a moment, politics could be realistic and effective for the first time in decades, as ministerial or court propaganda would have little purchase in circumstances of national crisis. The process of turning Britain away from mercantile empire would happen naturally – the fanatic lust for gain that lay behind the country's actions was, they believed, always going to result in vocal and ultimately violent opposition to oppression. The recent history of Ireland, Bengal and above all North America provided all the evidence the members of Shelburne's Circle required.

In parliamentary opposition from 1768, Shelburne gradually came to accept the loss of the North American colonies and with his circle to formulate the measures deemed vital to push Britain onto an alternative future path. Shelburne became an advocate of federation and hoped that he could persuade the Americans to remain British while ruling themselves along the lines speculated about at the end of Adam Smith's *Wealth of Nations*.[116] He worried too that without access to North American markets the British economy would nosedive, and he argued in parliament that the sun would set upon Britain unless union was maintained.[117] Typically this kind of point led Shelburne to be branded a hypocrite anew, given that before long, in the 1780s, he acknowledged the necessity of complete separation. For Shelburne there was no inconsistency. While political interconnection was to be preferred, it was entirely possible to configure healthy economic relations between Britain and North America as independent states. Yet Shelburne's plans required power because he was certain that he alone, now backed with the greatest political minds of the day, could save Britain.

IX

But the American Revolution had not done enough to reduce the British Empire. Further steps had to be taken to combat the lust for war and conquest. The British state had to be made smaller still, ensuring that it existed in accordance with the vision of a natural and pacific economy. For a period, theory became reality when Shelburne himself became prime minister, after North's ministry collapsed through defeat in the American War of Independence and after the Whig leader Rockingham died suddenly in office. While unexpected and unwanted by George III and Shelburne's political enemies, the man himself was ready and took full advantage. A great experiment was initiated by Shelburne in office, composed of a series of inter-linked policies.

Shelburne's first goal was to put an end to war. Almost all of them he believed were now undertaken in pursuit of mercantile profit. He wrote to Price that he wanted him to make a reality of Turgot's vision of perpetual peace, outlined in letters to Price that were published in the 1780s but written in 1778. Turgot had said that national pride was an especially British sin, leading to imperial adventures and an excessive role for the unstable voice of the people in national cabinets. Turgot warned the North Americans that he was worried that both ideas played too great a role in their new republican politics. Against imperialism, Turgot stated that 'one nation can never have a right to govern another', and against democracy that 'a tyranny exercised by a people is, of all known tyrannies, the most cruel and insupportable, and that which leaves the fewest resources to the wretches it oppresses.' Turgot's were among the most important contemporary statements of the dangers of mercantile empire, and of the need for free trade and peace between Britain and France.[118] For Britain, Turgot advised the 'necessary amputation' of existing colonies. Trade would decrease and national power would decline, but the result would be a nation more united and more peaceful, having seen off 'the canker of luxury and corruption'.[119]

Price, in his *Observations on the Importance of The American Revolution*, reiterated the indictment of the mercantile system for causing wars that had 'converted Europe into a theatre of devastation and murder'. Fortunately, Price claimed, 'the time, thank heaven! is now arrived when patriotism will cease to be a hatred of mankind; when the purpose of a free state will cease to be founded upon the lust of empire, as it was at Rome, or on the love of war, as it was at Sparta.'[120] Shelburne agreed with Price that the basis of any reform was 'to cry down war throughout the whole world, which nothing can ever justify, and to prove the advantages of peace, and the right which all countries have to require it of their sovereigns'.[121] Shelburne's plan for peace entailed developing measures to link nations together to an extent that they would ideally no longer see any point in taking to arms, so irrational would war be from an economic perspective.

Morellet's letters to Shelburne confirm the linkage between British and French philosophies attempting to bring peace to the world by destroying the mercantile system. Morellet saw the counterpart to the liberalization of the French grain trade attempted by Turgot to be what he termed 'cosmopolitan politics'. These amounted to realizing the project for perpetual peace of Charles Irénée Castel, abbé de Saint-Pierre.[122] With respect to North America, Morellet constantly reminded Shelburne that 'if Britain wants to restore relations with its former colony, it can easily do so, and, through the liberty [of commerce], would quickly recover all of the advantages enjoyed under monopoly [trade], which cost Britain so dear.'[123] Morellet went to London in 1782 to negotiate with Shelburne on behalf of the French foreign minister Vergennes. In the aftermath of the protracted negotiations Morellet believed that he had helped to establish a new international order that rested upon mutual benevolence, itself founded upon enlightened self-interest, rather than upon egoism.[124] Although Parliament was in recess for five months of this period, it gave Shelburne time to become directly involved in the diplomatic negotiations to end the North American war aided by his emissary Richard Oswald and his private secretary Benjamin Vaughan.

Vaughan was vital in the negotiations because of his strong connection with Franklin and his friendship with American commissioners such as John Jay and John Adams. When a crisis point was reached because the Americans feared that France might see benefit in the continuation of the war or would want to carve up mercantile rights across North America between themselves, Spain and Britain, it was Vaughan who was sent to Shelburne with messages urging him to accept American demands immediately. Shelburne had offered the North Americans a federal union with full legislative autonomy.[125] He quickly now recognized that independence was necessary, but the opposition of George III to giving away too much, especially fishing rights and rights to navigate the Mississippi among other issues, remained a barrier to the conclusion of negotiations.[126] In practice Vaughan, Shelburne and Franklin, in particular, united about the necessity of collapsing the mercantile system. The desire to put an end to war motivated Shelburne to negotiate a peace deemed so generous that he was quickly thrown out of office.

A sense of the extent of the possibilities canvassed by those involved who were members of the Shelburne Circle is evident from the correspondence between Vaughan and Franklin; the latter's views were always passed on to Shelburne in detail. Franklin too shared the desire of abolishing violence among nations and suggested to Vaughan that particular groups in societies should be forbidden from being involved in war; only mercenaries should be allowed to be soldiers.[127] Once impulses to war from what Franklin called the 'Spirit of Rapine' were removed, he hoped that peace would be 'more likely to continue & be lasting'. Vaughan went so far as to advise Shelburne to give up Gibraltar, arguing that he and Franklin agreed that the reorientation of British trade towards a general liberty entailed removing likely future causes of war.[128]

Vaughan summarized the settlement agreed upon by underlining the extent to which the American negotiators were seeking to live, 'without future wars, unless of their own choosing, that they be spared the expense and mutual punishment of revengeful prohibitory laws in trade, that English rather than French ideas and manners may prevail in America . . . [and that] England should make an intimate union of some sort, rather than an alliance with them, as being both the surest and the least dangerous means for obtaining the above ends'.[129] Sacrifices were necessary in both countries to embrace peace. Franklin, Vaughan reported, appreciated Shelburne's position because the British people were 'ignorant or misinformed, and the great reason of all which seemed to be that the nation's strength was misrepresented to them'. Franklin ultimately blamed the royal power to create powerful stooges in a society where politicians were forever battling for prominence and pensions.[130]

The new international order was inaugurated after a provisional treaty of peace was signed between Britain and the United States in Paris on 13 November 1782 and when on 20 January 1783 preliminary articles were signed with France and with Spain.[131] The diplomatic work was deemed so significant that Shelburne persuaded Vergennes to give Morellet an annual pension after peace had been restored.[132] From Morellet's perspective, the Treaty of Paris of 1783 put right the diplomatic wrongs of the Treaty of Paris (1763) that had ended the Seven Years' War and the Treaty of Aix-La-Chapelle (1748) that had put an end to the War of the Austrian Succession. For Shelburne and his circle, in restoring peace between France and Britain they were working to end the post-1763 era of domestic crisis. In underlining the costs and dangers of an expansive empire, now plain in the light of the war's outcome, it was hoped this would remind the British that it was better to rely on trade rather than arms to sustain the state. Equally, the benefits of trade without empire represented a warning against future colonization. Above all, the Treaty of Paris was a chance for Europe to return to the natural progress of opulence by dealing a heavy blow against the mercantile system of controlled trade.[133]

In the House of Lords, Shelburne identified what he termed 'the era of Protestantism in trade'; the argument being that the new principle of commercial liberty, akin to the days when Protestantism had brought religious liberty to Europe, would bring all states together, however much antagonism and war had characterized their relationships in the past. He believed that free commerce with North America was the best future for Britain and, indeed, for the world. If states chose to abandon rather than protect monopoly, peace would follow.[134]

The tragedy was that Shelburne was forced to resign as soon as the peace was signed, on being defeated in the House of Commons on a motion censuring him for giving too much to the North Americans. But the Treaty of Paris of 1783 remained the culmination of Shelburne's work, including as it did a commercial treaty between Britain and France, and providing a vision of a cosmopolitan world of peace and trade. Shelburne wrote to Morellet that 'the great principle which pervades the whole [of the peace treaty] is a general freedom of commerce.'[135] Shelburne wanted to put an end to the close link between merchants and politicians. He sought to stop statesmen from seeing commercial companies as branches of the state and under their influence. Ultimately, he wanted to persuade politicians and monarchs to abandon empire and to reject associations between glorious war and the acquisition of territory.

X

Shelburne had genuine faith in the early 1780s that through peace with North America, Spain, the Dutch Republic and France, and by signing commercial treaties to establish free trade between these and other nations, means had been discovered through which to return European states to Smith's natural progress of opulence through natural liberty. He later argued that 'the general system of the late peace' had extinguished 'all mistaken ideas of rivalship'. Looking back from the perspective of a more adversarial stance towards France, which he saw developing in Britain and across Europe in the aftermath of the death of Frederick the Great of Prussia, he claimed that 'never was there a period when animosity so soon subsided, when so few subjects of discussion, much less of dispute, had occurred with France as subsequent to 1782.'[136] He also claimed at the end of his life, writing to Morellet, 'I have not changed an atom of the principles I first imbibed from you and Adam Smith. They make a woeful slow progress, but I cannot look upon them as extinct; on the contrary, they must prevail in the end like the sea. What they lose in one play they gain in another.'[137] Elsewhere, more realistically, he noted that Smith's principles 'have remained unanswered for above thirty years, and yet when it is attempted to act upon any of them, what a clamour'.[138]

What went wrong with Shelburne's programme, which he remained confident of despite his fall from office? The first challenge to the pacific system of international relations established in 1783 was the action by Joseph II the Holy Roman Emperor, in October 1784 to force the Dutch to open the river Scheldt, the closure of which since 1585 had prevented ships from reaching the ports of Antwerp and Ghent in the Austrian Netherlands. The vitriolic attacks on Joseph II by Jacques-Pierre Brissot, in two short works, were due to the latter's membership of Shelburne's Circle. Brissot followed Shelburne's line in warning Joseph II that commerce could only be developed where civil liberties had been established and where commerce was free.[139] Honoré-Gabriel Riqueti de Mirabeau also attacked the opening of the Scheldt in a pamphlet which praised Shelburne to the skies as the model modern legislator, and more especially the system of commercial treaties he had established between Britain and France as a means to 'banish forever [sic] all national jealousies'.[140] Mirabeau's pamphlet was, the 'English editor' stated in a preface, 'calculated to promote universal concord and harmony amongst the nations of Europe' on the basis of the rational philosophy to 'love all men without distinction of nations.'[141] In practice the war over the opening of the Scheldt resulted in only a single shot being fired, from an Austrian ship that travelled down the river. The French negotiated a settlement without the intervention of other European powers and without further war being risked. France appeared to be acting in accordance with the principles of the new system.

When the Anglo-French Commercial Treaty was signed by William Eden for the British government and Gérard de Rayneval for the French, at Paris on 26 September 1786, the expressed intention was peace through commerce.[142] Dupont de Nemours declared that the treaty 'is alone the guarantor of peace between the great empires', essential if Europe was to maintain itself as a home to civilized life.[143] Shelburne was publicly fully in favour of the treaty, being in many respects its real author. That Britain and France were now both adhering to the principle of armed neutrality, following the example of the commercial treaty between Prussia and North America of 1785, was especially pleasing to him. Shelburne was realistic, however, and wondered if the alliances he had fostered would last in the face of self-interested mercantile empire and xenophobic nationalism.[144] The forces ranged against the treaty were powerful. Charles James Fox, who so often presented himself as a cosmopolitan, opposed the treaty in the House of Commons on the grounds that France was Britain's natural enemy.[145] William Eden faced enormous difficulties convincing fellow ministers. John Holroyd, Lord Sheffield, an opponent of free trade and adviser to Eden, recognized that the treaty was so favourable to British interests that France might soon be inundated with British goods, an outcome that would not prove long acceptable to any French ministry.

The Treaty of Paris and the Anglo-French Commercial Treaty together for Shelburne had transformed international relations. But the problem, from the perspective of the Shelburne Circle, was that commercial treaties and a general peace could not be maintained without fully dismantling the mercantile system. Evidence that military battle was being replaced by commercial Machiavellianism arose with an Order in Council supported by William Pitt and George III in 1784 which excluded all North American citizens from Britain's West Indies trade.[146] Vaughan, who was a member of the Committee of West India Merchants and Planters, attempted and then failed to have the Order in Council rescinded. He was warned by Franklin that 'England will get as little by the Commercial War she has begun with us as she did by the Military.'[147] Shelburne's

Circle had long anticipated the growth of French power, and that the end of the American revolutionary war would likely see Britain's economic defeat follow on the heels of military loss. As Price put it to Franklin: 'we may lose the trade and friendship of an increasing world and throw it into the scale of France.'[148] What Shelburne identified as a 'disposition universally gaining ground to dissipation and corruption' would further weaken Britain.[149] Price was open with Eden that future war might result from other powers recognizing how pitiful Britain had become as a polity.[150] To Thomas Jefferson he underlined his sense that Britain was on the brink of ruin.[151]

There was therefore little surprise when the Anglo-French alliance went up in flames. The Dutch Patriot's Revolt (Patriottentijd) provided the spark. The French controller-general, Charles Alexandre de Calonne, established a French East India Company from 1785.[152] France was itself creating a mercantile system on the British model. When in September 1787 Prussia invaded the Dutch Republic to maintain the House of Orange, a general European war became likely once again due to French support for the Dutch patriots. Price asserted to Shelburne that 'France was likely to take measures to regain her weight which would open a new scene in Europe', such that war would occur between Britain, Prussia and the Dutch Republic against France, Russia and the Holy Roman Empire.[153] William Pitt the Younger, now prime minister, appeared to be hastening such an end in promising arms for Prussia and expressing a willingness to fight France. France was already swallowing up Dutch trading posts in the Far East. A direct challenge was perceived to British interests across India.[154]

Although war was avoided, détente based on the long-term benefits of trade and peace had clearly not been established. The politics of principle appeared to have disappeared in a world governed by short-term interests and the domestic struggle for power. As Vaughan wrote to Franklin, 'These late struggles have unhappily shown however, how little any of these people [new or recent ministers] are capable of grand political ideas or plans. They understand faction, and even that often but ill, but seem to know nothing of the new systems of general politics.'[155] The mercantile system remained intact. The cultures it fostered explained the break-down of Shelburne's grand projects for peace and economic development.[156]

By 1789, Jeremy Bentham had added his voice to the jeremiad chorus emanating from the Shelburne Circle. In a series of letters to the *Public Advertiser* written pseudonymously as 'Anti-Machiavel', Bentham assaulted 'Pitt's Machiavellian System', intended to destabilize Russia by encouraging war with Sweden, as establishing a 'confederacy of tyrants' with Denmark and Prussia. Bentham warned that if the mercantile system was not dismantled 'a war of all against all would be the consequence, and the race of man would be swept from off the earth.' He was labouring to 'prevent the miseries of war' and combat 'that chimerical love of glory which has so frequently and so unnecessarily stained Europe with blood'.[157] By the miracle of a late-arranged peace, Britain had survived the turmoil of the American Revolution and domestic crisis, rampant debt and defeat in war. No member of Shelburne's Circle believed that Britain was going to be so fortunate in the final decade of the century. By 1788 it appeared that George III would not recover from his most recent descent into madness. The Regency Crisis followed. The mercantile system remained intact, war loomed and the national debt continued to be high. The only genuine surprise for politicians of Shelburne's ilk was that revolution occurred not in London, but rather in Paris.

XI

When the French Revolution began to be associated with violence and massacre, mapped out by Burke's *Reflections* in November 1790 with the accompanying prediction that there was far more ferocity to come, Shelburne and his associates began to be represented by many as crazed republicans, a theme in attacks dating back to the 1770s. Shelburne saw himself to be an advocate of moderation and worried about the extremes he saw in the world around him, and yet he and his friends were typically portrayed as fanatics, whose actions would lead to anarchy and savagery. This is clear from a William Dent print entitled 'Revolution Anniversary or, Patriotic Incantations', dated 12 July 1791. The print had Joseph Priestley, Fox, Joseph Towers the Unitarian and Richard Brinsley Sheridan the playwright dancing together around a cauldron spewing 'French Spirits' from itself, all celebrating the second anniversary of the Fall of the Bastille. The cauldron has the motif of an anchor upon it, a symbol of hope, but its true nature is revealed by the accompanying pikes, swords and weapons, all beside a flag of liberty. Tiny demons either side of the cauldron blow pipes and beat drums, again underlining the message that war was imminent.

This print and others like it reveal the ease by which thinkers who had argued against mercantile systems on the grounds that they fuelled international conflict and state collapse, were now contorted into figures who had not only seen their dearest hopes realized in the upheavals of France, but who were also anxious for Britain to follow the same road towards national ruin. A case in point is Benjamin Vaughan, who had spent the early years of the French Revolution travelling between London and France. In 1792, Shelburne gave him one of the seats he controlled, and Vaughan became the Member of Parliament for Calne. Like so many others he embraced events in Paris, seeing them as an opportunity to transform the world. He published tracts in favour of reform, including demands for the civil equality of Dissenters, Catholics and Jews in addition to the disestablishment of the Church of England.[158] Vaughan sent Shelburne a memorable account of the Fête de la Fédération of 14 July 1790 at which he had observed the French king, 'bulky and look[ing] broken' and the bemused queen amid the leaders of the Revolution.[159] Through membership of the Shelburne Circle many of the latter he knew, naturally including Mirabeau.

Shelburne liked to have people like Vaughan and the Genevan pastor Étienne Dumont reporting to him from Paris so that he received first-hand information; it may be the case that he retained some hope that in time of crisis he would be recalled to office. As time passed Vaughan's reports became bleaker. He did not, however, turn against the Revolution. Ultimately, he blamed the increasing extremism at Paris upon the actions of Britain and Europe's monarchies against the French Revolution. He accused them of seeking to carve up both France and Poland, waging a crusade against revolution and reform. This was the verdict of Vaughan in the 'Calm Observer', a series of works calling for the restoration of peace, originally appearing as letters in the *Morning Chronicle* newspaper.[160] He maintained that xenophobic nationalism fuelled by the demands of the mercantile system for the expansion of markets remained the source of war. Vaughan continued to identify Burke and his allies as deluded crusaders, reminding readers of the verdict of William Robertson, in his *History of Charles V*, that crusade was 'the only common enterprise in which the European nations ever engaged which all undertook with equal ardour' and 'remains a singular monument of human folly'.[161]

Disappointment and disaffection intensified for Vaughan after the church and king mobs at Birmingham in 1791 attacked the Unitarian meeting house, the Dissenting merchant William Russell's house and Priestley's laboratories. Rather than offering the victims compensation, Vaughan was concerned that the authorities would take action against reformers on the grounds that they were turning treacherous, undertaking correspondence with French radicals and seeking to initiate revolution at home. By 1794, Vaughan was willing to attack the war that had broken out between Britain and France but avoided membership of radical societies, in part because he evidently felt he could do more in Parliament without an extremist tag earned outside. Gradually, however, he became sure his person was in danger, with accusations of sedition abounding and treason trials commencing.[162] In April 1794, he fled to France and lived under the name of 'Citizen John Martin'. The reason was that he had been approached by a spy sent to foster the rebellion of the United Irishmen and became certain he would be implicated in the Irish republican movement. His departure was swift but avoided public notice until personal attacks upon him as a fanatic and revolutionary in 1796, at which time his friend Bentham stepped in to defend him.[163]

Joseph Priestley had departed before Vaughan, arriving in the United States in July 1794. One of Priestley's reasons was 'a violent spirit . . . in many of the lower orders'.[164] Shelburne appealed to Vaughan to return quietly and rely upon his personal connections and Vaughan's many friends. In the meantime, Thomas Hardy, of the London Corresponding Society, Vaughan and Shelburne's old friend John Horne Tooke were among those taken to the Tower of London for treason in May. Habeas corpus was suspended on 22 May. Vaughan's father Samuel agreed with his decision to leave the country, writing that 'The *Calm Observer* and your general conduct rendered you the most obnoxious man in the kingdom to ministry. Therefore, you had nothing to expect but the most severe persecution.'[165] Vaughan arrived at Passy at the beginning of May, was arrested as a British subject and interrogated by a delegate of the Committee of Public Safety. Satisfied that he was not a spy or enemy to the Revolution he was allowed to proceed to Switzerland with a warrant signed by the leading figures in the French Republic: Maximilien Robespierre, Bertrand Barère and Jacques-Nicolas Billaud-Varenne among others.[166] From Switzerland he wrote to Robespierre advising him not to turn France into a warlike republic for increase, reminding him of the glory associated with small states like Sparta and Geneva.[167] As his letter arrived on the day Robespierre fell from power, the ninth Thermidor, it was opened by Billaud-Varenne and Barère and used by them to accuse Robespierre of involvement with an English spy who envisaged a new and smaller federal France. Fortunately for Vaughan, he had arrived at Geneva on 14 July 1794 and was saved from further harassment by friends in Paris.[168] Vaughan went on to Bern and Basle, where he remained a year, deciding with his wife Sarah that they should emigrate to North America. Sarah Vaughan left with her seven children in August 1795, arriving in New York at the end of September. Vaughan did not join them until the spring of 1797, as he was involved in projects to make a success of the French Directory. Attempts to persuade Pitt to embrace peace had failed and he no longer thought positively about Britain.[169] Pitt signalled to Vaughan in 1797 that he would not be arrested if he chose to return, but Vaughan had had enough of the struggle to defeat the mercantile system and bring peace to the globe; he retired to Hallowell, Maine.

That the reformers like Vaughan who had ardently opposed fanaticism and enthusiasm were now being identified as the apotheosis of such passions is significant. In the 1790s no one could deny that the great achievement of the Enlightenment, the ending of the kinds of civil warfare that had characterized the period of the wars of religion in Europe, had fallen to pieces. In previous decades, the mercantile system of merchants and politicians seeking their own profit had been blamed for unleashing turbulence upon the world. From the early 1790s, the critics were themselves accused of putting an end to enlightenment by unleashing revolutionary and republican fury and enthusiasm. The sense of the reality, that enlightenment was ending, was increasingly widespread for the British. A vision of Europe, of the world, built upon the natural development of treaty and trade without empire, was dead. The division and destruction that had characterized religious antagonisms in previous centuries were being faced once again.

Shelburne, while hounding Pitt's ministry when he could for their assault upon civil liberties, while demanding peace with France, recognized that care had suddenly to be taken, especially with foreign contacts – one of the defining features of his circle. Bentham, furious at not having been given one of Shelburne's parliamentary seats, was brutally honest with his eminent friend. There had been a Shelburne party 'which by mere weight *of* reputation told in the ballance against the great aristocracy *of* the country: it was as they say *at* Cricket, *Shelburne against England*'. Yet it had failed; Bentham described Shelburne's residual Circle as being 'like the figure I have seen *of* Mr. Nobody *at* the puppet-show:—*a* great head without any *body* to sustain it.'[170]

4.

Catharine Macaulay and the End of Liberty

I

Rather than being a prophet of counter-revolution, Hume predicted rebellion by the people, exactly as it came to pass in the French Revolution, although he supposed it most likely to occur in Britain. His writings therefore played a major role in shaping perceptions of politics in the 1770s and 1780s. Hume was convinced towards the end of his life that political superstition had been unleashed in the form of patriotism desirous of war with the French. Yet Hume continued to be attractive to Whigs, regardless of his claims about the potential need for the violent suppression of popular liberties. Despite his criticisms, Hume always believed in the importance of the people's role within a mixed state. The Whigs agreed with many of his arguments about the roots of popular corruption – they too claimed to hate war and disorder. If the dying Hume articulated an end of enlightenment in Britain because political enthusiasm was likely to result in disorder and revolution, he provided ammunition, especially for members of the Shelburne Circle, to circumvent such an outcome, and to put the genie of superstition back in its bottle. Hume's reflections on a potential revolution could be deployed to avoid disorder and prevent the subsequent rise of tyrants.

Drawing upon Hume, the Shelburne Circle, as we have seen, was in the vanguard of those asserting that Britain had become addicted to war and empire, being a mercantile system increasingly controlled by a corrupt nexus of merchants and politicians. In the eyes of those around Shelburne, a mercantile elite profited from the riches that accompanied commercial and military dominion and cared little for justice or the peoples from whom they drew their wealth. Yet they were so influential in politics that they could be portrayed as having propelled Britain onto a path that saw the national debt expand exponentially, wars being fought for commercial dominion across the globe and British society ever-more divided between those whose lives depended upon the mercantile system and those who were its victims. The sense of crisis was acute. Few observers of political affairs were optimistic about the future. This was especially the case after the successive failures of opponents of the mercantile system to establish governments that ruled in accordance with laws for the good of all, rather than those expressive of the interests of a tiny minority of rich and well-connected men. For many, the ills of Britain were so great that they could only be righted if a more natural path of societal progress was returned to, one that might entail accepting France as the dominant European state, since it had the most resources and population.

The Shelburne Circle, which as we have seen included numerous physiocrats in France, Founding Fathers in North America and small-state republicans across Europe, tended to see Britain as being turned into a tyranny after the Seven Years' War. Ministers and the monarch were subverting the constitution – Economic collapse, national bankruptcy or the outbreak of civil turbulence was likely to bring the crisis to a head. The Shelburne Circle expounded the view that new forms of enthusiasm and superstition were abroad, in the form of ideas about the mercantile system, and Reformation-style tempests were anticipated.

In response to such accusations, critics of Shelburne frequently argued that he and his friends were radical republicans, themselves the kinds of fanatics who fomented disorder everywhere. Shelburne was in print frequently presented talking to Cromwell or acting like a mad iconoclast and anti-patriot. In the early James Gillray print dated 14 August 1782 entitled 'Guy-Vaux & Judas-Iscariot', Charles James Fox became Guy Fawkes conspiring with Shelburne, as Judas, for self-enrichment. Both men were portrayed as dangerous extremists willing to contemplate any action to obtain their ends, such as arming the people or involving the church in politics. They were deemed capable of sinking the ship of state. The fact that Fox and Shelburne were themselves divided underlined the pathetic nature of their rebellion against the state.[1]

But it is a mistake to label either Shelburne, Fox, Hume or any member of the Shelburne Circle a follower of the Commonwealthmen, those who looked back to Cromwell's times and the 'Good Old Cause' of the English Republic, seeing the restoration of enlightenment and liberty in a return to the politics of the past.[2] Neither Hume, Shelburne nor anyone associated with them had faith in allowing the people to take up arms. Such a strategy itself entailed the fomentation of extremism, using fire to put out fire. Nor did they believe in the restoration of public virtue, the great hope of seventeenth-century reformers associated with Milton and a host of Commonwealth heroes, who argued that enlightenment entailed living a life in accordance with the word of God, based on self-sacrifice and selflessness for the public good, as well as the rejection of luxury, office and the pursuit of money. For Hume and Shelburne, such strategies were pipe dreams. They had failed in the past but were more dangerous still in the present because commercial society, once established, could never be reformed around virtue alone.

It is important to relate the history of Commonwealth ideas at the end of enlightenment because if they failed to convince Hume and Shelburne, they nevertheless attracted large numbers of followers. The greatest Commonwealth author of the period, Catharine Macaulay, had at first a total faith in the possibility of the restoration of public virtue. For Macaulay, virtue and morality went hand in hand. She traced the problems of Britain to an excess of selfishness, deepened by the progress of commerce. Her solution was a moral reformation of manners that would spread selflessness, restore manliness and find the proper social place for the action of all people. History showed the benefits of virtue. If restored in the body of the people and in their ruling ministers, the future of Britain, liberty and enlightenment would be secured.[3] The story of

Macaulay's gradual but ultimately complete loss of faith in a free Britain is another way of charting the end of enlightenment, with the failure of strategies that first convinced utterly, before finally being rejected. Macaulay is all the more important to this story because while she considered the Commonwealth cause to be extinct in Britain by the late 1780s, she saw it alive and flourishing in the new American republics. Yet at the very end of her life, the French Revolution provided fresh hope that it might be reborn in Europe. Her message to Britons was to flee their country and seek enlightenment in other parts of the world, in nations more capable of nurturing republican virtue.

II

When the widowed Catharine Macaulay married a humble surgeon's mate named William Graham in 1778, then aged twenty-one and twenty-six years her junior, the scandal sheets and gossipmongers ran wild. As a figure renowned as a Stoic, a woman many believed to be wary of the baser passions, she was accused of suddenly giving in to lust now she was in her late forties. Macaulay's patron and admirer Thomas Wilson went as far as to cast her out of the home where she had lived with her daughter for the previous two years. Furious, Wilson portrayed her as a thief and threatened further scandal through the publication of scurrilous letters.[4] Only a year before he had celebrated her forty-sixth birthday with a public event where he named her 'The genius bold, of Liberty, array'd in Roman vest'.[5] If her reputation was sullied – her notorious liaison was whispered about still when she visited North America years later in 1784 – the marriage to Graham was both long-lasting and a boon to her productivity. During the scandal Macaulay published the sixth and seventh volumes of her *History of England*, and the final eighth volume followed in 1783. Her continued output cemented Macaulay as one of the most renowned historians of her time and one of the most prominent advocates of republican principles writing in Britain.[6] The impact of public notoriety upon Macaulay is unclear. Her politics by 1783 had, however, altered profoundly. The key issue by then was where the republican seed, the liberty tree, might be planted. It was no longer England or Britain. Macaulay believed that the Enlightenment in Britain had been in decline since the 1690s, a downturn that had become precipitous since the end of the Seven Years' War and terminal by the final days of the American Revolution.

Macaulay became well known because of the acclaim accompanying the first volume in 1763 of *A History of England from the Accession of James I to that of the Brunswick Line*.[7] She had been born in 1731 at Olantigh in the parish of Wye in Kent to the landowner John Sawbridge and Dorothy Wanley, the daughter of a London banker. She was married late for the times at thirty to the physician George Macaulay; her husband and his friend Thomas Hollis encouraged her to publish her writing. Its popularity and impact derived from the fact that her subject was broadly that of liberty, allowing readers to draw direct parallels from the contemporary world to the past. As she put it at the beginning of her first volume, in her youth she had immersed herself in 'the annals of the Roman and the Greek republics' and such histories exhibited 'Liberty in its most exalted state'. The natural response of any rational being on reading these works, she thought, was to experience 'that natural love of Freedom which lies latent in the breast'.[8] This was unquestionably the feeling of her numerous readers, explaining why Mirabeau translated her work into French in the 1780s, why editions flooded the new republics of the United States and were popular in revolutionary France in the 1790s.[9] Her history frequently amounted to commentary upon the present state of the nation through comparisons with former periods of national crisis and, in particular, the experience of monarchical tyranny. How far Britain remained a free state or could maintain itself as a polity were burning issues amid contemporary accusations that the treatment of Wilkes underlined the loss of freedom, while schemes for oppressive taxes were plotted to pay the growing national debt, which caused ructions in the colonies especially. Further volumes of Macaulay's work followed in succession in 1765, 1767 and 1768, quickly establishing her as an influential political writer, a position she would maintain until her death in 1791.

Macaulay was unquestionably a republican author, the most significant of latter-day Commonwealthmen. The fourth volume of her *History* in 1768 justified the execution of Charles I. The fifth, in 1771, called the period of the English Republic 'the brightest age that ever adorned the page of history'.[10] The Commonwealthmen, laid low for much of the preceding decades, were becoming vocal once again in national life in the 1760s. Macaulay's friends Thomas Brand Hollis and Richard Baron, both nonconformists, played a significant role alongside Brand Hollis's patron Thomas Hollis, who deployed his riches to publish and widely distribute new editions of the classical canon of Commonwealth literature – the works of John Milton, John Toland, Algernon Sidney, Henry Neville, Marchamont Nedham and John Locke. With Commonwealth ideas being popularized for new generations, Macaulay and her brother John Sawbridge joined Brand Hollis and Hollis to establish a movement arguing that liberty had been lost and that the long-established rights of freeborn Britons, for which so many had died in the previous century, had of necessity to be restored. As Macaulay put it, 'the works of Nevil[le], Sidney and Harrington are performances which excel even the ancient classics on the science of policy.'[11] In other words, the Commonwealthmen were sending messages to the present concerning the means of restoring liberty and toleration under threat.

Macaulay can be interpreted as an archetypal Commonwealthman, in that she staked out again arguments made since the final years of the seventeenth century. It was then that John Toland, an Irish freethinker and Commonwealthman, published his life of Milton as a preface to *A Complete Collection of the Historical, Political and Miscellaneous Works of John Milton* (1698), an edition of Algernon Sidney's *Discourses Concerning Government* (1698), the *Memoirs of Lieutenant General Ludlow* (1698–99) and a life of Harrington within a new edition of *The Oceana of James Harrington* (1700).[12] Toland argued through these publications that although the English believed themselves to have obtained freedom in 1688–89, this liberty was in fact not sustainable as it did not rest upon the entrenchment of popular liberties and the activity of the people as agents in politics, directly able to defend their sovereignty. John Trenchard and Walter Moyle in 1697 lamented the 'unhappy age, when an universal Deluge of Tyranny has overspread the face of the whole Earth'; England was the 'Ark out of which if the Dove be sent forth, she will find no resting place till her Return'.[13] This was why standing armies, undermining 'the Institution of this Gothick ballance' between the crown and the people, were so dangerous. Professional armies had been instruments of Stuart tyranny and had then been embraced by William III in his wars, expanding the national debt in consequence. The following decades saw the appearance of John Trenchard and Thomas Gordon's *The Independent Whig* (1720–21) and *Cato's Letters* (1720–23) in addition to Gordon's own *Political Discourses on Tacitus* (1728), *Political Discourses on Sallust* (1744) and editions of Tacitus and Sallust.[14]

All of these figures were associated with the Irish MP Robert Molesworth, formerly William of Orange's ambassador to Denmark. Molesworth had composed an account of a state in crisis collapsing into tyranny in his *An account of Denmark as it was in the year 1692* (1694). His preface to a translation of François Hotman's *Franco-Gallia* was written in 1705 then published in 1711 for the publisher Timothy Goodwin and in a second edition in 1721, then again with the title *The Principles of a Real Whig* in 1775.[15] Molesworth warned in his writings of the relative weakness of Britain, the need for broader parliamentary representation and more regular parliaments, the danger of electoral corruption and the overweening power of the executive. That the Glorious Revolution of 1688–89 had not been the fount of liberty united those of a Commonwealth persuasion. So too did a singular fear of the effects of commercial society upon the capacity of Britons to sustain a free community. An excess of passion pervading all forms of life accompanied the spread of trade; it was followed in turn by ever-greater corruption and luxury. Such evils, Commonwealthmen argued, led directly from the neglect of liberty and its ever-deepening loss.

III

It has been argued that in considering Macaulay's legacy, a mistake has been made in associating her too directly with Commonwealth arguments: her republican idea, it is supposed, was as much a Christian state as it was a secular republic. But the latter term would have made no sense to Macaulay. In the eighteenth century, religious belief was inseparable from politics. Macaulay associated with Dissenters but remained outwardly an Anglican, admitting her devotion to Christianity while privately rejecting the Trinity.[16] Such a stance was not lightly taken. It is therefore right to see religious commitment behind all of her calls for the restoration of community in the face of the threats posed by the excessive growth of commercial society towards luxury, debt, war and empire-building.[17] And it was obvious to the eighteenth-century mind that calls for the restoration of religion and the creation of a republic went together: both were demands for stronger forms of sociability at the base of human associations and both rested on a belief that a shared sensibility was necessary to ameliorate the more destructive and selfish passions of a trading age. Those who lacked belief could not be trusted to be members of any community.

Macaulay was equally an enemy to Catholicism as she considered it to be a faith supportive of tyranny. Catholics had always opposed the Commonwealthmen, and a republican polity could therefore never be Catholic. This was why she could not countenance the acceptance of Catholicism in Québec when it became part of the British Empire after the Seven Years' War, ceded to Britain by France.[18] The toleration of Catholicism, she believed, was a step on the road to despotism. The Catholic faith was intolerant and incapable of accepting rival religions within a faith community. Such a community could not last, being incompatible with the merest of liberties, and therefore the British in Canada were sowing the seeds of their own demise. Right religion, being a form of Protestantism, had to be the foundation stone of any Commonwealth. This had been obvious to Macaulay's hero Milton, just as it was to her. She called Milton a 'sublime genius . . . in whose comprehensive powers were united the highest excellencies of poetry, the acuteness of rational logic, and the deep sagacity of politic science'.[19] Macaulay worried that the people of Britain were becoming attracted to false idols once more, just as they had Catholic popes and the line of Tudor and Stuart monarchs who had destroyed English liberties historically. George III, if he turned himself into a papal or a Caesar figure, was, she believed, likely to be exactly such a false idol in her own time.

The challenge for Macaulay was to explain what had gone wrong with the great attempt to turn England into a Commonwealth in the seventeenth century in the aftermath of the victorious war against the tyrant king Charles I. Macaulay's answer was that one despot had ultimately been replaced by another: a monarchical head of state had been replaced by Cromwell as the head of the English Republic. The fourth volume of her *History* called Cromwell and his supporters 'wrong-headed fanatics' who stole power from Parliament and 're-subjected the nation to the yoke of an individual and again involved it in discord, faction and their attendant evils, tumults, conspiracies and general discontent'.[20] Cromwell was the monster usurper who had created another court sustained by taxing the people at the very time when the wisdom and virtuous conduct of 'illustrious patriots' had 'raised the glory and the felicity of the nation to an unrivalled height'.[21] Under Cromwell, she maintained, 'Morals, the great supporter of Liberty, declined.' Those who had served the English Republic lost faith or became selfish. Puritanism, a religion Macaulay believed to be fanatic, by 'profane jargon', managed to battle 'those religious principles in the people which had been so sedulously cultivated by the Parliament'. In a memorable passage Macaulay wrote that 'Cromwell's reign, though short, was sufficiently long to make a perpetual entail of those evils his wicked ambition had occasioned.' Dictators and tyrants ruined liberty directly by taking it from the people, but they also, she believed, poisoned the wellspring of future liberty by ruining manners, by familiarizing people with despotism to the point that they might even support it. So extensive was this national corruption, Macaulay argued, that the Stuart line was restored, questioning the very point of the 'long and bloody war' to establish liberty and the republic.[22]

Liberty had failed in the seventeenth century for Macaulay because Cromwell, the Stuarts, the Cavaliers and the Puritan Presbyterians had corrupted the morals of the people, causing them to turn away from the Commonwealth cause. The people had then fallen for false idols, but Macaulay hoped that present generations, informed by her about the lessons of history, would be more circumspect. Macaulay was equally attuned to another historical parallel she held to be directly pertinent to Britain in the 1760s, the loss of liberty in another republic, that of Rome in 27 BCE. In 1767, Macaulay published an attack on Thomas Hobbes, portraying him as the great enemy of natural sociability, and holding that society was the product of natural impulses, rather than being Hobbes's artificial schema of an all-powerful legislature founded upon fear. Macaulay, always holding firm to a sense of goodness and virtue, argued against Hobbes that the Golden Rule – 'do unto others as you would have them do unto you' – was the basis of a universally shared law of nature, from which proper conduct could be developed, as well as a politics that best defended such a moral edifice. She appended a letter to the Corsican general Pasquale Paoli, then ensconced in a battle against the French to maintain the independence of the small republic as it was transferred from Genoa to France.[23] Macaulay's recommendations to Paoli were intended to facilitate the maintenance of Corsican liberty and included the standard fare of Commonwealth politics, being the separation in two chambers of the proposing of laws from assenting to laws and the regular and strict rotation of every office. Macaulay added comments on the decline of the Roman Republic, which she ascribed to excessive inequality between the rich and the poor. If this had been prevented at Rome by the imposition of an agrarian law limiting the acquisition of land and wealth by an oligarchic elite, or redistributing the land on a regular basis, Macaulay argued that it would have 'prevented that extreme disproportion in the circumstances of her citizens' which in turn 'gave such weight of power to the aristocratical party' that they were gradually able 'to subvert the fundamental principles of the government, and introduce those innovations which ended in anarchy'. After anarchy, absolute monarchy always followed, being 'its natural effect'.[24]

If Macaulay felt that contemporary Britain was characterized by the rise of an aristocratic faction and a potentially despotic monarch in conditions of the general depravity of manners, she nevertheless had faith in the people to reassert their liberties. Her brother John Sawbridge had become member of parliament for Hythe in 1768 and in 1769 founded with John Horne Tooke the Society of the Gentleman Supporters of the Bill of Rights.[25] This became the Constitutional Society in 1770 and then the Society of Supporters of the Bill of Rights, which was prominent in demanding parliamentary reform and in petitioning against the rejection of John Wilkes's successive election to the Middlesex seat for the House of Commons.

Macaulay and Sawbridge were painted in Roman garb by prominent artists in these years, perceiving calls to expand voting rights to be replicating the Social War (91–87 BCE) in Rome, when client states across Italy rebelled against Roman authority because they were neglected by the metropole, with equal citizenship for all being the outcome.[26] Hope that Roman-style societal conflicts might spark the kind of conflagration that returned the people to power was the transmission mechanism then envisaged by Macaulay. The people in arms led by virtuous men in parliament, acting to restore liberty and purge corruption from the body politic, was Macaulay's ideal route to the preservation of Britain as a free state. For Macaulay, as for Hume and Shelburne, the parallel between the late 1760s and the 1630s was indubitable. She was distinctive, however, in advocating Roman republican solutions to the problem of the renewal of political fanaticism, threatening liberty, toleration and enlightenment.

IV

When Burke published his *Thoughts on the Cause of the Present Discontents* in 1770, it proved influential because it detailed Britain's decline since the accession of George III and traced the source to the fall from power of the Whig party. Macaulay's response to Burke, entitled *Observations*, equally went through numerous editions and attracted substantial public attention. Both authors agreed that contemporary Britain was in a desperate condition. Burke's pamphlet identified a faction among George III's courtiers that had set themselves on destroying traditional constitutional liberties on behalf of a monarch who sought power only for himself and his friends. Burke criticized the growth of prerogative power in Britain – the power of the monarch that was not reliant upon the consent of Parliament – against the background of the development of court influence in significant offices across the land. This was Burke sounding very much like a member of Shelburne's Circle. Macaulay, however, was altogether distinctive in her diagnosis of the ills of state. She agreed with Burke about George III, but nevertheless stated that the danger he represented was underplayed by the Whigs, who carried 'a poison sufficient to destroy all the little virtue and understanding of sound policy which is left in the nation'.[27]

Burke, as a leading Whig, was portrayed by Macaulay as an advocate for an aristocratic faction motivated by pleonastic self-regard. Burke became a cipher for the Whig nobility in general, including Shelburne and the so-called Whig radicals. These aristocrats, Macaulay held, were as much responsible for the decline of liberty in Britain as George III, a fact proven by their refusal to give more power to the people. They were afraid of a fanatical populace, whereas they should have acknowledged instead that the people in arms were a source of liberty and virtue. This was a significant point of difference. Macaulay saw the English Civil War as a period when the people had risen gloriously – only to be betrayed by their leaders. What she called 'vigorous and enlightened zeal in the great body of the people' was key to the establishment of a free society. Yet the Whigs, she argued, feared the people as much as they feared a tyrant king. The Whigs and George III represented two sides of the anti-liberty coin, battling against each other for supremacy and accusing one another of destroying the constitution when either group prevailed in controlling the ship of state.

To Macaulay, Burke's arguments amounted to rank hypocrisy, just a pitiful lament that the Whigs were no longer in charge and a self-interested cry for the return of normal times – meaning their own rule and nothing more. Burke's politics had nothing to do with liberty, as Whigs had always sought to prevent the people from asserting their rights and what she called 'true reformation' to take place:

> In all the great struggles for liberty, true reformation was never by the ruling party either effected or even intended. The flaws in the Revolution system left full opportunity for private interest to exclude public good, and for a faction, who by their struggles against former tyrannies had gained the confidence of the people, to create, against the liberties and the virtue of their trusting countrymen, the under-mining and irresistible hydra, court influence, in the room of a more terrifying, yet less formidable monster, prerogative.[28]

According to Macaulay, a 'system of corruption' and 'wicked system of policy' had commenced at the time of the Glorious Revolution and 'growing from its nature with increasing vigour, was the policy of every succeeding administration.' Parliament became debased, ceasing to defend the people, because of a cabal formed between ministers of the crown and the representatives of the people in Parliament. Dividing up the plunder derived from 'a credulous people' became their goal. Parliament was no longer the houses of the people. It had been taken over by a monstrous oligarchic faction, with men like Burke and Shelburne, ultimately in cahoots with George III, turned instruments of oppression rather than of liberty.[29]

Governments in Britain failed to secure what Macaulay called 'the full and impartial security of the rights of nature'. They went to war because this too brought profit personally. The result was an enormous national debt, a standing army, a mass of placemen and pensioners drawing income from offices granted by the Whigs and the court, irregular parliaments, with elections held only once in seven years, and ever-more burdensome taxes upon the generality of the people.[30] Macaulay stated that 'the nation, instead of being the paymasters, were to become the creditors of government.' Burke had turned himself into 'the mouth of faction', the voice of a selfish and misinformed nobility, rather than a statesman offering his service in the name and interests of the sovereign populace.[31] Macaulay argued that there were republican institutions that could ameliorate the cancer at the heart of Britain's politics if adopted by her peers, these included more frequent elections – she suggested once every three years – and the rotation of public office. As she put it, 'democratical power never can be preserved from anarchy without representation, so representation never can be kept free from tyrannical exertions on the rights of the people, without rotation.'[32] Although Macaulay's pamphlet was sorrowful about Britain in 1770, and despite admitting that the people could easily be corrupted, she argued that hope was not lost. There was, because of philosophers like Hobbes and Burke, 'a false mistaken notion of a non-existing virtue in mankind'. If Parliament could be made free and restored as the true voice of the people by virtuous men, then the people would enjoy liberty and embrace virtue.[33]

Over the following years, Macaulay, observing closely the development of the American Revolution and supporting the rebel cause from the outbreak of conflict, concluded that the British had lost their liberty and indeed were no longer deserving of the enjoyment of it. The cause of Wilkes and that of the Americans, she stated in a pamphlet that appeared in 1775, had shown the Britons how to save themselves from 'the dark cloud that hangs over the empire'.[34] Revolution in America had been anticipated because of the reassertion in the colonies of the Norman Yoke, being 'that barbarous system of despotism imposed by the Norman tyrant on the inhabitants of this island'.[35] Contemporary British ministers, she argued, were behaving like latter-day Normans and liberty-hating Stuarts. Being lovers of liberty and retaining residual virtue in their culture, the North Americans had naturally taken to arms rather than continue to experience what Macaulay called 'the lowest abyss of national misery', with commerce declining for 'once-opulent traders', 'starving mechanics' and 'the numerous half-famished poor which we meet at every turn in our streets'.[36] Yet the difference between the Americans and the English, Scots and Irish – Macaulay did not mention the Welsh – was that all bar the former had become supine. One of the root causes was the lust for empire, which had a corrosive effect upon national manners and ruined states, causing them to decline. Empire amounted to a pot of gold for tyrants or would-be despots to corrupt their people and sustain their brutal regimes. Macaulay held that if Charles V had remained monarch of Spain alone, rather than seeking to expand the domains over which he ruled to the point of being a universal monarch, the Spanish might have ended up being the freest people in Europe. Instead, the pursuit of empire had run its course and contemporary Spain was in a dreadful state, with no liberty left, leading Macaulay to conclude that empire was as bad for the oppressors as it was for the oppressed:

> The conquest of foreign nations are dangerous triumphs, even to the liberty of republican states; but in limited monarchies, when on the conquered are imposed laws, opposite and hostile to the limitations of power in these governments, it never fails of subjecting the conquerors to the same measure of slavery which they have imposed on the conquered.[37]

Macaulay held that the route to liberty was clear. It had been mapped out by her friend the educationalist James Burgh's *Political Disquisitions*, which had appeared in 1775, just as their author, the founder of the Dissenting academy at Newington Green, died in Islington. Burgh had damned the power of the king and the Whig aristocracy in national life, calling for a reduction in expenditure upon pension, place and the army and taxes on luxury and gaming, as well as more regular elections.[38] As the tax burden fell with reduced expenditure on armaments and corrupt officeholders, there would be no need to tax colonies or the people in general to support ruinous empire. The abolition of taxes in North America would be a basis for ongoing union, Macaulay claimed. If the British government refused to embrace reform, however, a civil war would continue to the point that even if defeated they would 'effect your slavery in their ruin'.[39] Macaulay argued that the union created in America by British oppression was so strong that it would break Britain, collapsing the mother country by bankruptcy or war with the European powers, Spain and France, who were ready to take advantage of any weakness shown by their northern neighbour.[40] Macaulay was right, as France joined in the revolutionary war against Britain in 1778, followed by Spain in 1779.

V

By 1778, Macaulay was still more despondent about Britain. In *A History of England, from the Revolution to the Present Time,* completed while she was still living in Wilson's house at Bath, Macaulay repeated the argument that the Glorious Revolution had been an opportunity to vanquish prerogative power, being the product of a revolution by Parliament against a corrupt throne. Her history was full of lament at this failure because the new monarch, William III, and the aristocratic elite supporting him, drawn from England and the Dutch Republic, kept the people at bay while enriching themselves. The story she recounted was parallel to Cromwell's great betrayal of the people two generations before. The constitutional model established in 1688–89 was far away from what Macaulay named the Saxon ideal of clear rules and a contract between monarch and people. She called it Saxon because she believed this paradigm had been first established when the people gathered in the woods with their rulers in Anglo-Saxon times. The Saxons had firmly limited the power of government, only to see all limits abandoned by the Norman invaders. Macaulay described William III and Mary as new Normans, with monarchical authority becoming ever stronger and more dangerous as the eighteenth century progressed.[41] The point had been reached, she argued, that corruption had become a system of government. Macaulay's history of England, in its reach into recent memory, charted the growth of grotesque and self-serving rule by successive monarchs and aristocratic factions. A sometime virtuous figure such as William Pulteney, who was praised for his opposition in the Commons to the corrupt prime minister Walpole in the 1730s, was archetypal in accepting the title of Earl of Bath by George II in 1742, thereby becoming an object of Macaulay's contempt by descending from patriot to courtier.[42]

Whigs in her own time, Macaulay argued, had stooped lower still by accepting standing armies, refusing to bring to justice perfidious ministers, ending toleration and rejecting any idea of parliamentary reform.[43] The establishment of a seven-year gap between elections, the Septennial Act of 1716, replacing the Triennial Act of 1694, was described as an injury fatal to the constitution.[44] According to Macaulay, ministers were addicted to dividing up the spoils of state rather than maintaining public welfare. The people, made lethargic by commerce and poverty, and ignorant through the long-term loss of liberty, were abject and lacking virtue, being asleep amid oppression.[45]

One way of tracking Britain's decline, Macaulay asserted, was to mark the acceptance of wars for trade by the rulers of Britain and the prevalence of such wars as British policy. For Macaulay, in line with many of her contemporaries, including, as we have seen,

Hume, Burke and Shelburne, commerce was naturally among the arts of peace. Commerce could, in the right conditions, become a force for bringing peoples in different nations together. Societies flourished, Macaulay argued, not by conquest and rapine, but in conditions of peace. James I, when monarch, had, Macaulay claimed, put forward such a view of trade and encouraged it in consequence. Yet this fact had been abandoned altogether in contemporary Britain. When she studied the present state of the national debt, 'with all its baneful consequences', Macaulay confessed that 'I cannot help wishing that the successors of this Solomon of the English nation [James I] had possessed the pacific disposition of their great founder.'[46] James had been a special monarch because, she believed, he had not betrayed the people, as his son Charles I and Cromwell and then all the monarchs after had done. The reason for the history of decline since James I, at least in terms of liberty, was the increasing addiction to ruinous wars for trade.

At the same time, Macaulay made it clear that she was not necessarily averse to war. On occasion Britain had entered into a just war and had been foolish to make peace too early. Her prototypical example was the Seven Years' War. Macaulay had only praise for Chatham, the leader who prosecuted that war. His conquests over the French when prime minister had, she held, been altogether worthy. Had they been maintained, a permanent peace with France from a position of strength might have been established. Instead, Chatham's successors had agreed to peace far too soon and given too much back to France in 1763. The nation had been about to emerge from 'the poverty which war produces'. Yet, because of the situation in America and the stupidly unjust taxation of the colonies, another war had commenced, corrupting the people anew with anti-American 'paroxysms of Quixote rage'.[47]

The final volume of Macaulay's *History* was repetitive.[48] But she was more precise than hitherto about the date at which Britain's decline had turned terminal. Britons had believed that victory in war during the 1760s showed their vitality. They were altogether mistaken: it had, she held, been a resurgence before death. The Seven Years' War had led Britain to 'the brink of political mortality', expanding the national debt while spreading trade, each confirming the utter corruption of contemporary morals.[49] Macaulay's friend and fellow Commonwealthman James Burgh said in 1769 that there was a good chance of 'the British Empire's being enslaved by a designing Ministry'. The suppression of popular liberties would be enacted by soldiers who 'are slaves and they are detached from the people. They look on the people with an invidious eye.'[50] Reiterating traditional concern about standing armies leading to tyranny, Macaulay agreed with Burgh's view that the 'mad' government might well use troops against the people, resulting in 'general destruction'.[51] The conclusion was that liberty had died when Chatham fell from power.

One of the problems for Macaulay was the trouble in identifying true patriots, the great men involved in public debate who could act as the vessels of the people, who would restore liberties and lead the populace through a political reformation, removing corruption and excessive power while rejuvenating virtue. Macaulay believed Chatham was exactly such a figure. His great war ministry up to October 1761 'makes a capital figure in the annals of this country'. Macaulay was acquainted with Chatham through their mutual friend David Steuart Erskine, Earl Buchan, who served as his secretary.[52] As mentioned, Macaulay was not an opponent of war. Violence was, she believed, necessary in the battle for liberty. Popular war which strengthened the state while revealing the extent of corruption was accepted as a means by which liberties might be restored. Macaulay was sure that the Seven Years' War as it was fought by Chatham saw exactly the kind of purgative conflict required to save Britain. The war had brought the populace together, and they had shown great affection for their leader. Unquestionably for Macaulay her view of Catholicism as the religion of tyrants was showing itself. The fact that the Seven Years' War was largely conducted against Catholic powers, especially France and Spain, mattered to Macaulay. This was another reason why Chatham was portrayed as the patriotic ideal, uniting the people in a war against despotism and Catholicism conjoined.

Macaulay was certain that Chatham ought to have been acclaimed by the king in accordance with 'the voice of a free people, either in their collective or representative capacity'.[53] In other words, he ought to have been trusted by George III, remained in office and given full reign to reform domestic politics and the workings of the state. As we have seen, this was also Shelburne's view when serving Chatham. Instead, Chatham was obliged to compromise and, finally, resign. Chatham had been prime minister at the death of George II. The final year of the monarch's reign, 1759, was called the *annus mirabilis*, seeing British forces invade the French colonies of Martinique and Guadalupe, defeat the French at Québec, avoid the invasion of Britain and prevent the French from conquering Germany. George III, rather than supporting Chatham, meddled in his policies and refused to allow him to conduct the war to a glorious end. Macaulay would have been aware that Chatham had wanted to carry the war to Spain and continue to battle the French on all fronts with the goal of permanently limiting French power. But the new king had been more concerned with establishing his own party rather than the public good. That Chatham was replaced by the king's friend and counsellor John Stuart, 3rd Earl of Bute, had appalling consequences for Britain.

Macaulay recognized that she risked being accused of hypocrisy – she attacked war in general while praising Chatham's execution of it. She acknowledged that Chatham had created large armies on the continent and given substantial subsidies to German princes, with corruption prevailing through the whole system of administration. Military victory came at the cost of filling the pockets of suppliers at enormous expense, an increase in the price of positions in government and the administration, called by Macaulay 'the lucrative appendages to office', and the oppression of the nation 'with such an additional burthen of taxes and debt, as to forbid any hopes of salvation'.[54] Yet, according to Macaulay, Chatham's conduct had been extraordinary, since, despite the compromises needed to prosecute the war, she believed he continued to have the public good and liberty at the forefront of his mind. Why she was so certain that Chatham was ever a friend of the people remained unclear, but that he was venerated and beloved by the populace at large was unquestionable.[55] Accordingly, Macaulay's presentation of Chatham was very much in line with popular perceptions. He had been prominent in his opposition to corruption within Robert Walpole's administrations from the 1720s into the 1740s. This was when Macaulay was sure that Chatham had become a true patriot, a term associated with the works of Viscount Bolingbroke, the author of *The Idea of a Patriot King* (1738).[56] Bolingbroke had described an ideal of leadership focused on the public good and altogether selfless. True patriots were lovers of virtue, enemies of excessive commerce and luxury, stoic and devoted to improving the lives of the populace.

Macaulay went so far as to assert that Chatham's leadership amounted to 'a perfect miracle in political history'.[57] The miracle was that a patriot king – she meant George II, rather than George III – and a patriot ministry were co-operating with the body of the people to remove septennial parliaments, reinstate the people in their constitutional right of election, and pay off the debt.[58] Chatham, being an experienced political actor, had been fully aware of the extent of monarchical corruption in government. He had, after all, criticized George II for an excessive concern for the interests of Hanover, the north-west German state which he ruled in a personal union, rather than exclusive devotion to Britain. But Chatham had focused on military operations and enjoyed 'brilliant successes'. Rather than being allowed 'to crown the expectations of the public by a peace adequate to the expensive exertions of Great Britain', taking advantage of the military victory he had inspired, he was removed from office. His successor, Bute, was an enemy of the people and concluded 'an inadequate destructive peace'.

There was some irony in Macaulay's call for the beggaring of Britain's enemies and the use of their resources to cover Britain's debt. It flew entirely in the face of Macaulay's critique of wars for trade and her worries about the effects of commerce. Yet she was supportive of Chatham's grand plans for the expansion of Britain's empire, had he remained as minister in the final years of the war. This was a controversial stand given the general pressure upon all states involved in the conflict.[59] But, in the person of Chatham, Macaulay found someone who epitomized good rulership from a Commonwealth perspective while at the same time showing none of the drawbacks of a Cromwell. Chatham came across as a man of the people who would genuinely rule for the public rather than for his own purse or person. Equally, although supportive of the Church of England, Pitt was a moderate on religious questions, lacking any hint of wild belief or fanaticism.

Macaulay's view was that Chatham represented the last chance for the political system erected in 1688–89. With Chatham's fall, liberty was gone and the only option for the people was to take up arms. In 1788, she ceaselessly drew parallels between contemporary evils and the catastrophes of the seventeenth century. The history of the English Republic and Commonwealth authors was mined for messages from past to present. The main one was that Britain in the late eighteenth century was in a far worse condition than ever before; as she put it, 'England from the earliest period of its empire to the present moment never was in so perilous, so Desperate a state.' When another one of her heroes, the republican martyr Algernon Sidney, who was beheaded in 1683 for treason, had identified the ills of the country after the restoration of the Stuarts he had given a moving description of liberty lost:

> . . . the Liberty which we hoped to establish oppressed, Luxury and Lewdness set up in its height instead of the piety virtue sobriety and modesty which we hoped God by our hands would have introduced, the best of our nation made a prey to the worst, the Parliament, the Court, the Army corrupted, the people enslaved, all things vendible, no man safe but by such evil and infamous means as flattery and Bribery.[60]

For Macaulay, Britain in 1788 was in a position more parlous. Sidney's corruption had been 'confined to the Parliament, the Court, and the Army'. Her own times were worse because 'the Empire of corruption has no bounds'. To the Parliament, the Court, and the Army she added 'every Corporation through the whole Dominions, to every Corporation we may add all the inhabitants which possess the Country at large'. Macaulay could see no latter-day Sidney, or Milton or Locke. There was no virtue, no light and no enlightenment.

The very 'vitals of the Commonwealth' were, she believed, putrefying. Self-interest was the 'leaven which destroys the power of every good tendency in the human character'. It existed with ever 'more malignant force' in 'the merciless Statesman, the needy Placeman, the Opulent Landholder, the rapacious monopoliser [and] the extortionate retailer'. Trade was collapsing and national bankruptcy imminent.[61] Liberty had to be restored to the people. If necessary, they needed to take up arms and replace the current government with new men. This was not a call for republican revolution across Britain because there were no Commonwealth leaders in evidence. It was rather a scream of anguish against the policies of current ministers and the king, along with a lament for Chatham's fall. He too was gone, having died in 1778.

VI

Macaulay traced the contemporary crisis of the British polity to the growth of luxury and wars for trade, to the decline of morals and the loss of old republican virtues and to the policies of the new tyrant George III. The Commonwealth strategy of the people taking up arms to restore their liberty was no longer possible since the populace was corrupted and lethargic because of the growth of commercial society. The people had last revealed vital signs in their enthusiasm for Chatham. That they were reliant entirely upon Chatham, however, was another sign of their lethargy. The extent of the corruption of the nation was then underscored by the failure of that great minister to return to office. There had been no popular uprising for Chatham, no sense that his demise marked a turning point in national history, that with him the Commonwealth cause had collapsed.

And so, Macaulay's eyes turned elsewhere. Republicanism in the United States, by contrast with Britain or other parts of Europe, made sense because it was less urbanized, and the people were more in tune with nature and not yet addicted to commerce and luxury. At numerous occasions up to her death in June 1791, Macaulay explained that the new republic of the United States offered a ready and easy way into a healthy political future. As she wrote in 1774, 'the situation of England and her Colonies is grown very alarmingly critical.' It was now the case that 'no degree of public virtue exists in the generality of Englishmen.' At the same time, 'some few among us yet retain sentiments worthy of a Roman Breast, and those few wait with all the anxiety which the passions of fear and hope occasion the determinations of America.' The outcome of the American Revolution would 'either establish the power of our Despots on a permanent [basis] or lead to the recovery of our almost lost liberties'.[62] By the 1780s, Macaulay was no longer making such statements because the war for British liberty had been lost.

The North American republics had initially embraced the small state model of a republican confederation like the Dutch, as embodied in the Articles of Confederation composed in 1776–77. As the American Commissioners, led by Franklin, wrote to their secret agent in the Dutch Republic, Charles-Guillaume-Frédéric Dumas, 'The Netherlands have been our great example of defending liberty; our similar situations and constitutions may bring us together, while commercial intercourse erases the bad impression made on some Americans by the Dutch refusing them military supplies in their distress.'[63] Executive and judicial branches were lacking for the American confederation as a whole, powers to raise revenue or force individual states to adhere to international treaties. By the

1780s, the confederation was showing all the signs of weakness experienced by the Dutch. Throughout the seventeenth century, fragilities such as these were used as evidence of republicanism's structural deficiencies; Samuel Pufendorf's criticisms of chaotic, irrational and self-defeating republics were perhaps the most influential.[64]

Macaulay was not initially concerned with the stresses that would likely be faced by a republic in the new world. She believed the people in arms in North America were exhibiting virtue in the same manner as the English in the previous century, by which she meant a selfless devotion to a patriotic cause embodying both the public good and the reformation of morals. This was one of the reasons why she welcomed correspondence with leading Americans,[65] and it was no surprise that they in turn praised the platform she had promoted for Britain. They were her Puritan saints reborn.[66] John Adams, at the time a member of the First Continental Congress, informed Macaulay that he agreed with the reforms being proposed in the House of Commons by her brother John Sawbridge.[67] These ranged from the reduction of the national debt, the extinction of luxury, the end of the standing army and the creation of a more popularly elected parliament. Despite his regard for such a programme, Adams had no faith in its realization and was convinced that both Sawbridge and Macaulay would fail: there was no example in history, he argued, of radical reform being realized in a country whose culture was already so debauched. As he put it, 'A Nation is easily corrupted but not so easily reformed.' Adams concluded that 'the present Reign may be that of Augustus, but upon my Honour, I expect twelve Caesars will succeed it.'[68] Adams was foreshadowing Macaulay's conclusion about Britain.

The bicameral constitution of the United States with its powerful executive, legislative and judiciary, controlled by means of a system of checks and balances, emerged after the constitutional convention held at Philadelphia between May and September 1787.[69] Yet from an eighteenth-century perspective, even the federal union established at Philadelphia still bore a strong resemblance to the vulnerable republican confederations in Europe. The relatively weak executive and relatively strong individual states with their powerful local governments smacked of the Dutch and Swiss, associated in recent history with military weakness and a lack of international status. But the history of both republics had been glorious. Macaulay's conclusion was that North America had become in its politics altogether different to Europe, being a throwback to a better age of the defence of liberty; this fitted with the popular diagnosis of Montesquieu, with his emphasis upon the impossibility of political change in one place working out in the same way as in another context. At the same time Macaulay rejected the degeneracy thesis made popular by Georges-Louis Leclerc, comte de Buffon, in his *Histoire naturelle* (1749–88), which asserted that transporting plants, animals or people from one climate to another altered their character, the fundamental assumption being that movement from Europe to the west made all things weaker.[70] For Macaulay this was nonsense – North America looked to her to be in ancient rather than modern circumstances, retaining slavery and a surfeit of land while being relatively undeveloped commercially and not having an entrenched landed aristocracy or mercantile elite.

Such conditions meant that the political options were far more diverse than they were for Europeans, including the possibility of returning to or establishing fresh a Commonwealth polity. Samuel Adams in 1780 had hopes that Boston might become 'a Christian Sparta', although he could not but be disappointed at seeing 'more Pomp & Parade than is consistent with those sober Republican Principles'.[71] It was of obvious political importance to someone such as Adam Smith that America was different because 'No oppressive aristocracy has ever prevailed in the colonies.'[72] One worry was that for all the colonists' republican pronouncements and rhetoric in favour of the rights of all, British politics could readily be seen to be guiding North American practice, so that while the Americans thought they were doing something new, they were in fact recreating the corrupt political cultures of the mother country without realizing it.[73] This view was commonplace in French commentary in the circles around Turgot.[74]

For those who emphasized the differences between Europe and America, the latter had since the seventeenth century been an 'exotic dream' for Europeans, in Gilbert Chinard's memorable phrase, where men of the woods lived close to the state of nature and where, lacking civilization, people were happier and more moral.[75] North America was distinctive because of the combination of abundant land with limited transport, technology and trade. Widespread prejudices inherited from Fénelon meant that for the French especially inhabitants of North America lived more naturally than the populations of Europe.[76] Macaulay said as much, writing to George Washington in 1790, noting that France 'has undergone the fiery trial of temptation and come out purified'. An example had been set to the world, she said, 'unparalleled in the annals of humanity'. It was possible to move from 'the depths of frivolous dissipation to the most exalted height of National conduct'.[77] The population of the United States, by contrast, had not faced a time when 'commerce pours in'. This meant that they had yet to face the trials of luxury and 'the deceitful pleasures of a vicious dissipation'. Macaulay worried, by 1790, that it was more than likely that the new republics in North America would, like Britain, fail the test and that because of the progress of commerce all virtue in the country would be overturned. In other words, America too would face a time when the populace lost their virtue and their commitment to liberty, just as the English had before them. The message was to avoid following the European model of state behaviour, by avoiding war, rejecting empire and refusing to seek to control the markets of other states for your own economic gain.

A similar point was made around the same date to the poet and pamphleteer Mercy Otis Warren. Macaulay wrote that it was vital for the United States to remain largely concerned with agricultural production. Liberty would thereby be preserved. If, however, the United States became a large commercial state and rich through trade from South America, there was no reason to see why the path of Spain into decline would be avoided. Mercantile profits would ensure that the power and pageantry of government would grow at the same time as the people were overtaxed and lost their commitment to liberty. Ultimately, Macaulay warned, 'the invidious distinctions of Aristocracy will be easily introduced.'[78] Like so many at the time, in recommending the pursuit of agriculture in the United States she was oblivious to the aristocratic structure of American chattel slave ownership. For her, slavery meant the denial of civil liberty rather than literal enslavement, with the horror of which she was unconcerned.

VII

The London Baptist minister William Winterbotham asserted in the early 1790s that the true rationale for the large armies of Europe was the need to discipline domestic populations:

> The governments of Europe, for the most part, though they in many things differ materially from each other, agree in keeping up a large military force, the excuses for which, are the jealousies they entertain of each other, and the necessity of preserving a balance of power . . . But if the policy of keeping standing armies was fully investigated, it would be found to have its origin, not in the jealousies of one nation with respect to another, but in the tyrannic principles and fears of different governments, with respect to their subjects at home. The fact is notorious, that the origin of most of the old governments, has been in conquest and usurpation.[79]

For Winterbotham, who composed his book while in prison for supporting the French Revolution, the United States was perceived to be in circumstances altogether divorced from Europe: it was singularly fortunate in not having to prepare for invasion by neighbours with modern armies. Rather than having to call upon professional forces, it could defend itself by means of a popular militia. This gave it a great advantage over the states of Europe. In Europe, it made sense to create permanent professional armies, termed standing armies, because the threat of conflict was constant. For many, such forces, created to maintain states, amounted to a permanent threat to liberty because a monarch or would-be Caesar or Cromwell could turn the army against the people. Winterbotham concluded that this was, at its root, incompatible with republican government. It was a miracle that America did not need them, and Winterbotham concluded that a purer form of republican politics was therefore possible across the Atlantic.

The supreme court judge and Founding Father James Wilson agreed. Writing in 1792, Wilson noted that other than a few troops for the western frontier there was no need of an army in the United States: 'our enemies finding us invulnerable, will not attack us, and we shall thus prevent the occasion for larger standing armies.'[80] Politicians in the early United States did not have to be constrained by the imperative of constant preparation for and expenditure upon war. A more expansive politics resulted. The abolitionist Thomas Branagan demanded the liberation of all the enslaved on the grounds that they could be given land to own and become citizens. This was possible in North America, unlike any other place, where land was already owned or in productive use. As Branagan put it, 'one industrious farmer is of more benefit to a nation than a standing army of one hundred thousand strong.'[81] It was an example of the gulf in conditions that existed between Europe and America.

North America was perceived to be following the classic 'four stages' progress of natural economic development outlined by Smith, from hunter-gatherer to pastoral farming, arable farming and then commercial society. Most significantly, lacking sovereignty while being governed from London, it had not suffered the kind of derailment that Smith and the physiocrats were certain that Europe's commercial states had experienced by seeking empire, creating the dreadful lust for luxury and economic dominion in Europe's monarchies.[82] It was significant too that the United States lacked the urban pull of overweening cities. The particularities of European circumstances had to be accepted, and this in turn meant that in North America a republican monarchy, with its non-noble executive president, rather than a monarchical republic led by the aristocrat-in-chief like Britain, was the dominant political form.

Such differences fostered an increasingly common original position in many thinkers of the time, that it was Europe's aristocracy that was sustaining the mercantile system. Noblemen owned the land but also tended to have substantial investments in national bonds and shares in commercial companies. Interested in profit and luxury for themselves, they pushed politicians to encourage war-mongering and empire-building as the quickest routes to short term gain. These opinions led European writers to seemingly radical conclusions about the means of reforming their world in the 1780s. One was that the best way to abolish the mercantile system was to abolish aristocracy itself, on the grounds that less corrupt forms of trade would be the outcome.

Another major reason why Commonwealthmen across Europe could only with difficulty draw direct lessons from the United States was that it did not see itself to be an empire in the European sense. It had indeed been founded upon the denunciation of Britain's imperial relationships with its colonies, the mission of dismembering an 'over-grown empire'.[83] This meant that it could hardly operate as a model for states that accepted empire as necessary for their survival, as a vital supply of resources, revenues and markets. At the same time, the new republic of 1787, established after the failure of the original confederation of 1776, was seen to be replicating the union between England, Scotland and Wales that was deemed to be the key to the strength of Britain, and which differentiated it from other popular states where the form of union was irregular. If the United States could establish a centre like England alongside strong states on the periphery like Scotland, which maintained their own identity while developing economically, the best of the British model would be emulated. This point was made by the Irish MP Edward Cooke when arguing in favour of a union between Britain and Ireland:

All writers have agreed in condemning what is called *imperium in imperio* [state within a state]. It is this vice of constitution which has annihilated Poland, where every senator was a sovereign; and has enslaved the Seven United Provinces, where each province was a Sovereign. Franklin and Washington, the founders of the American Empire, had not courage in their first project of a constitution for the American states, to exclude this radical evil, but left each state independent. So soon as the pressure of necessity, which had confederated the states, ceased in consequence of peace, the fault of such a constitution became evident: it was clear to men of common capacity, that an empire, consisting of Thirteen independent societies, without one common Imperial control, would soon divide into Thirteen independent empires. To obviate this necessary, though possibly distant consequence, the wisdom of the Americans projected a new constitution, in which this original vice was remedied; the separate independency of each state was wisely relinquished; a general legislative, and a general executive were formed for the government of the Union in every imperial concern; and each respective state was confined to local and municipal objects . . . To the wisdom of this plan of Union the strength and happiness of the United States may be attributed.[84]

It was widely held that politics in the United States was without parallel, that an entirely different kind of empire had been created. As the popular novelist of the early American republic Charles Brockden Brown put it, 'the foundation of this republic affords a splendid spectacle to the eye of the universe.' Historical empires, Brown said, 'arose from conquest'. This was the case with 'the Assyrian, Persian, Macedonian, and Roman empires, the dominions of Charlemagne, and the Saracens'. By contrast, the 'American empire' was 'formed by commerce, and the arts of peace; by people arising from the same stock, emigrating from the same country, possessing the same language, religion, laws, manners, and pursuits'.[85/86]

Brown could have added the British to his list of empires founded on war. John Adams and Alexander Hamilton might appear to be

Anglophiles to their critical fellow citizens, dedicated to replicating the commerce and empire of the mother country on foreign shores, very much a republic armed for expansion rather than a pacific agricultural polity.[87] Yet the North American union of states with a federal centre was ultimately very different to the union of England and Scotland, or indeed that of England and Wales. The United States saw much more power being granted to the component states, with their legislatures and their senators, and the local and national forms of democracy in urban centres. It was the latter that Alexis de Tocqueville admired so much in the 1830s and compared with the centralized politics he found in Paris.[88] Macaulay would have made the point that enlightenment had failed in Britain when the battle to restore liberty became futile. The circumstances of North America presented an opportunity to save liberty and enlightenment together. Drawing upon the Commonwealth tradition had been Macaulay's grand strategy for the salvation of Britain. She and her Commonwealth friends saw the dark forces corrupting Britain, the mercantile system of war and empire, intensify to the point of killing hope for the future. This was why the turn to North America was so significant. It was the last place on Earth where the Commonwealth of liberty might live again. The United States was a city on a hill, a product of unique circumstances. The message to Britons was to flee if they could to the promised land rather than remain in a place where the light had already expired.

VIII

The gap between Hume's and Macaulay's perceptions of the end of enlightenment narrowed as Macaulay aged. She soon too arrived at the opinion that a pure and virtuous republican populace would never emerge through the process of being given arms and turned into a patriotic militia. Change had to deal with an entrenched aristocracy, the desire for war, the vast national debt and the likelihood of invasion if the state became weak, none of which could be overcome in a British context. The people, as she now perceived them, were too corrupted by luxury. Macaulay repeated her view time after time in letters that the citizens of the United States had escaped European conditions and their politics would be distinctive so long as the problems they faced diverged. There had always been overlap between their respective positions on contemporary politics. Hume declared his agreement with the view that in ancient times the republics had been much superior to monarchies, accepting 'that the Republican Form of [Government] is by far the best. The ancient Republics were somewhat ferocious and torn [internally] by bloody Factions; but they were still much preferable to the Monarchies or [Aristocracies] which seem to have been quite intolerable.'[89] Macaulay, too, followed Hume, for example in identifying public credit as 'this diabolical engine, which has too long threatened to put a final end to the prosperity of our country'.[90]

Hume had always felt, however, that Macaulay's political prescriptions were far weaker than she perceived. Indeed, without Macaulay realizing it, he believed she was fostering the very end of enlightenment that she wished to avoid. In 1764, having read the first volume of the *History*, Hume wrote to Macaulay about her work. Characteristically, he made a number of telling points that advocates of any commonwealth had to face up to. The first was that the Commonwealth itself had failed in the previous century and had, ultimately, not been worth the blood spilt in its creation. Hume was blunt about this deficiency in referring to heroes of the English Republic, such as the leading parliamentarians of the 1640s John Pym and John Hampden, both of whom could ultimately be said to have failed to turn England into a free state:

> I grant, that the cause of liberty, which you, Madam, with the Pyms and Hampdens have adopted, is noble and generous; but most of the partisans of that cause, in the last century disgraced it, by their violence, and also by their cant, hypocrisy, and bigotry, which, more than the principles of civil liberty, seem to have been the motive of all their actions.[91]

Hume's point was that the vaunted virtue and self-sacrifice that Macaulay lauded had not been much in evidence in practice, especially over longer periods of time. This meant that any contemporary advocate of commonwealth ideas had to explain why the present was different, and why ideas that had failed in the past would now succeed. In addition, Hume asked, who could be trusted to be virtuous in the first instance and who could be relied upon to remain virtuous in the most challenging circumstances of crisis politics, such as transforming government from a despotic monarchy to a free republic? Macaulay might have replied to Hume that if the seventeenth-century republican experiment had failed so too had the eighteenth-century experiment in maintaining liberty in Britain, meaning that Hume too had to explain how to maintain liberty in modern, commercial and imperial societies.[92]

Hume underlined to Macaulay his belief that there was nothing special about republican principles in establishing legitimacy, virtue or liberty because, as he put it, 'I look upon all kinds of subdivision of power, from the monarchy of France to the freest *democracy* of some Swiss cantons, to be equally legal, if established by custom and authority; I cannot but think, that the mixed monarchy of England, such as it was left by Queen Elizabeth, was a lawful form of government, and carried obligations to obedience and allegiance.' There was no reason, he argued, why armed people would better be able to discern the common good than those currently in power. Indeed, they were very likely to be as mistaken as the most self-serving minister, becoming frenzied in the pursuit of their enemies, over-obsessed with establishing liberty while being uncertain about what the conditions of liberty actually entailed. Hume, as we have seen, defined the end of enlightenment as the people taking arms in the name of liberty, acting in the same way that religious fanatics had in previous centuries and likely with the same deleterious consequences.[93]

In Hume's view pure republicanism was irrelevant to Britain, unless a way could be found of turning the polity into a union of small states – republicanism, he was certain, only made sense as a political doctrine in small states, where cultures were relatively homogeneous and stable over time, where the people knew one another and could observe themselves at close quarters, all the better to maintain their virtue. It was also irresponsible, Hume said, because advocates of republican ideas were playing with fire in their talk about arming the people:

> . . . an establishd Government [cannot] without the most criminal Imputation, be disjointed from any Speculation . . . any Attempt towards [republicanism] can in our [Country], produce only Anarchy, which is the immediate Forerunner of Despotism.

If the nature of Macaulay's republican alternative was vague, then the transition mechanism that would establish a republic was inexplicable. Calling the people to arms risked causing the polity to fall back into civil war, repeating the dreadful cycle of the previous century. As Britain was so often on the verge of war with France, the outcome of domestic revolution would be certain invasion. Republicans like Macaulay were therefore abetting Britain's enemies and weakening the very polity they considered themselves to be patriotically devoted to.

What concerned Hume most was that no republican guidebook existed for the circumstances of modern Britain, and no republican author had mapped the road regarding republicanism in large commercial polities. Hume was dismissive of those who, like Macaulay in her letter to Paoli, thought that Harrington's *Oceana* might be a republican bible. In Hume's view Harrington was an 'Author of Genius; but chimerical'. His idea of an agrarian law to redistribute property was impractical and his senatorial class would, Hume was certain, end up being like the aristocratic Whigs in having excessive political power.[94] Hume made a final point which was characteristic of his brilliant irony: perhaps there was an advantage in republican revolution, and it lay in the fact that republics were a sure way of limiting popular liberty, because, however much they praised liberty as an ideal, republics demanded an extent of cultural homogeneity and social union that quickly defined enemies, turning any republic into a place where critics were unlikely to be tolerated: 'One great Advantage of a Commonwealth over our mixt Monarchy is, that it [would consid]erably abridge our Liberty, which is growing to such an Extreme, as to be incom[patible wi]th all Government. Such Fools are they, who perpetually cry out Liberty: [and think to] augment it, by shaking off the Monarchy.' This was why republics so often experienced civil war and so often sought war with foreign states. The bottom line was that Hume thought of republican movements as following processes akin to the establishment of Churches, with inevitable moments of oppression to establish the 'true' faith and as time passed likely division into further sects or factions.

Such light-hearted facetiousness aside, Hume stressed to Macaulay that there were conceptual mountains to climb if she wanted republicanism to contribute seriously to modern politics. The doctrine made little sense in contemporary Europe, he believed, and supplied no solutions to the crises of the end of enlightenment. In the final work she completed before her death, an attack on Burke's *Reflections on the Revolution in France*, Macaulay confirmed that she had moved to Hume's position on republicanism in Britain. She argued that the pessimism of the old aristocratic Whig, who had never trusted the people, was being refuted by the progress of events at Paris.[95] Macaulay had of course become infatuated with the French Revolution. The people, in taking arms against despotism, had turned themselves virtuous, she believed, meaning selfless, devoted to the cause of liberty and showing every sign of changing their natures towards the pursuit of morality and community. Macaulay saw no reason at all why the French would not remain united and devoted to the republican cause. As she put it in one of her final letters, 'that wonderful event the French Revolution fills all our thoughts and occupies the whole mind. We desire its permanence and prosperity, with more than paternal solicitude.' It would, she claimed, 'necessarily bring after it the final emancipation of every other society in Europe, from those Monarchic and Aristocratic chains imposed by the violence of arms and rivetted on mankind by ignorance, credulity, and priestcraft.'[96]

Everything changed with the French Revolution, which was unexpected in the sense that it was Britain rather than France that had hitherto been perceived to be further along the road to crisis, because the mercantile system was believed by many to have captured the state. This viewpoint was so widely held that republican constitutional architects, such the former priest Emmanuel-Joseph Sieyès in Paris, were able successfully to argue that whatever the revolutionaries did, they should never adopt British political or constitutional models. Those who did look to Britain, the so-called Monarchien group around Jean-Joseph Mounier in the National Assembly, were shouted down on the grounds that following Britain was to emulate a failed state.[97]

This was altogether Macaulay's opinion. No lessons beyond dark warnings could be drawn from Britain's history. Yet at this time Macaulay had returned to the optimism of her first writings: she had lived to see republican principles in action once again in a European state. France, both Catholic and despotic, had, she believed, secretly been experiencing a renaissance of virtue among the people. How it happened was beyond her. But her message was that liberty, even that in North America, depended on the progress of the revolution in France. European states were far stronger than the republic in the new world and might still wage war on American liberty. But a republican stronghold in Europe would make this a much less likely prospect. The devotion to the cause of the revolution and the willingness to die for liberty manifesting itself in France meant that a far greater commonwealth ideology was being forged. For a follower of Hume, such as Burke, the lesson was exactly the opposite, republican liberty in France amounted to a return to the kinds of fanaticism last seen during the wars of religion, and division, violence, chaos and war would inevitably follow. Burke proved the prophet, but by the time he was being praised for anticipating bloody consequences of the French Revolution, Macaulay was dead. She had died near Reading 'after a long and very painful illness' on 22 June 1791, lamented by her husband William Graham.[98] It was before the dawn of Terror in France, especially intense between March 1794 and the fall of Robespierre, inquisitor-in-chief of the ruling Jacobin Club, on 29 July. The descent of the Revolution into war and civil violence posed still more challenges to those who saw the creation of a moral commonwealth as the best way of restoring enlightenment.

5.

Edward Gibbon and the End of the Republics

I

One particular worry for Britons who called themselves friends of liberty, like Shelburne and Macaulay, was that liberty had been proved to be a fragile plant elsewhere. Yet free states did exist across Europe, especially in the variety of republics that had either survived since the Middle Ages, such as those across Italy and Switzerland, or which had been established by war in early modern times, such as the Dutch Republic. Seeing the decline of such states during the eighteenth century, while they were acknowledged to be in a different position to Britain, signalled to many that there was something grievously amiss in the enlightenment project.

The renowned historian Edward Gibbon, whose six volumes of *The Decline and Fall of the Roman Empire* appeared between 1776 and 1789, was devastated at the collapse and ultimate death of Europe's diversity of state forms.[1] Gibbon's view of the Enlightenment was exactly that of his friends Hume and Smith – its singular achievement lay in ending the wars of religion.[2] But he perceived its end differently. The reason was his personal experience of living in threatened polities beyond Britain. The irony Gibbon underlined was that while absolute monarchies seeking to expand their territories had traditionally been identified as the key threat to the liberties of weaker states and republics, evinced by the carve-up of Poland from 1772, in the final decade of the century it was a putative free state, revolutionary France, that was responsible for putting an end to the independent polities Gibbon venerated.

II

Although born in Putney and educated at Westminster School and Oxford, Gibbon spent sixteen years of his life in Switzerland. He was first sent by his father in June 1753 in horror at his son's youthful conversion to Catholicism while a student at Magdalene College. Gibbon spent the following five years at Lausanne, reconverting to Protestantism on Christmas Day 1754 under threat of being dis-owned, and only departed in April 1758. He returned from May 1763 to April 1764 as part of a Grand Tour that would eventually take him to Italy; and, finally, would visit again from September 1783 to May 1793, after abandoning his parliamentary career as the member for Liskeard (1774–80) and Lymington (1781–84). In Switzerland, Gibbon began to speak and write in French. Indeed, he embraced the local culture to such a point that at times he considered himself to be no longer primarily English, but rather Swiss.[3] A great deal of Gibbon's engagement with classical rhetoric, writing and literature, his inter-est in Protestantism and its history, and above all the history of Switzerland and the smaller states of Europe, can be traced back to his time living in the town of Lausanne in the mountainous Pays de Vaud, which had been annexed by the republic of Bern in 1536, during the Reformation.[4] In his subsequent *Memoirs* Gibbon wrote that, 'such as I am in Genius or learning or in manners, I owe my creation to Lausanne; it was in that school, that the statue was dis-covered in the block of marble.'[5]

It was at Lausanne in 1757 that Gibbon fell in love with Suzanne Curchod, the impoverished daughter of a pastor; his father stepped into his life once again and forbade marriage to someone so lowly. Gibbon would never marry, but remained friends with Curchod, who went on to wed Jacques Necker, one of Europe's richest bank-ers and a French politician, despite his Genevan origins. It was in Lausanne that Gibbon met two lifelong friends, Jacques Georges Deyverdun, whose house Gibbon shared during his third stay, and John Holroyd, later titled Lord Sheffield, who was to become

Gibbon's literary executor. And it was there too that he first became acquainted with the French literary genius Voltaire, and where he himself became a writer, completing much of his first publication, the *Essai sur l'étude de la littérature* (1761), in addition to his last, the two final volumes of *The Decline and Fall*.[6] His house in Lausanne became a place of pilgrimage, especially for would-be literary giants, who could read in his *Memoirs* Gibbon's description of putting down his pen after completing the final book of his *History*.[7] Gibbon never forgot the happiness he had enjoyed in Lausanne, when he had lived a relatively impoverished and altogether studious existence, in the company of people he loved dearly. He said that if his life had continued at Lausanne in such circumstances, he would have been for ever content.[8] When Gibbon returned to Lausanne in 1783 he was lionized as an incomparable historian, continuing to be at the centre of society until he departed in 1793.[9]

The Pays de Vaud, the canton home to Lausanne, was culturally close to France, although Switzerland was a focal point for European culture more generally, its toleration and cosmopolitanism attracting visitors from across the continent. Eighteenth-century Geneva, the republic to the south along the north bank of Lac Léman, was a destination for many British travellers, some of whom ended up living there, often for reasons of health due to the quality of both the air and the expertise of the available physicians.[10] Young English noblemen, like Philip Stanhope, the son of Lord Chesterfield, or Lord John Sackville, travelled for their education or arrived on their Grand Tour through Europe. The city Gibbon was sent to by his worried father in 1753 was renowned as a bastion of Protestantism; the Swiss cantons were also famous for their republican union, surviving into modern times while so many lesser republics had disappeared. Liberty survived in the cantons because of the bitter and continued struggle for independence against the military and economic threats emanating from the monarchies that surrounded them. During the fourteenth century, the old Swiss cantons had won significant battles against the Holy Roman Emperor's larger armies at Sempach and at Morgarten and, in 1474 and 1476, against Charles the Bold, the Duke of Burgundy, at Grandson and Murten. The latter victories, together with their exploits in the Italian Wars, supplied the Swiss with a reputation for invincibility. Their example served republican thinkers in Europe with the most important example of the superiority of militias over standing armies. But by the eighteenth century Swiss militias were widely held to be in decline. As the English envoy Abraham Stanyan reported in 1714, 'a disuse of war, during so long a tract of time, has given rise to an opinion, that the Switzers are much fallen from their ancient valour.'[11] At the same time the Swiss were still regularly described as the most heavily armed people in Europe.[12] The standard account of Swiss valour and virtuousness was summarized by the British author John Campbell, who in 1750 stated that the Swiss were 'naturally of a martial disposition' and 'never at a loss for as large and well-disciplined an army as any government in Europe can rise'.[13]

Gibbon became obsessed by the contemporary predicament of small states, especially the Swiss cantons and that of Bern most especially. The history of republics and republicanism fascinated him. The impression is sometimes given that the eighteenth-century republican experience was broadly similar to that found in the Renaissance. In other words, the republican defence of liberty in the face of persistent crisis at the hand of monarchs, generals, aristocrats and mercenary captains was something of a shared European heritage.[14] Eighteenth-century republicans concerned about the capacity of their state to maintain itself could recall that the republic of Pisa lost its independent status in 1399, Novgorod in 1478, Florence in 1537 and Siena, like Florence after many ups and downs, finally in 1555. Every small state and republic was under threat, some disappeared and some miraculously survived, all tied into the eternal cycle of rise, corruption, decline and, ideally, resurrection. There seemed to be nothing new under the sun.

Republicans tended to live in fraught political universes where danger was everywhere and crisis ever present.[15] This made for powerful civic cultures often associated with morality and manliness, the illustrious defence of the polity against fearful odds and magnificent rhetorical laudations for the liberty enjoyed within particular city states or republics.[16] Gasparo Contarini's work in praise of Venice, for example, was reprinted time after time through the seventeenth century and into the eighteenth, often appearing alongside additional orations.[17] Monuments to past glories became objects of civic pride. For many republicans, as for Gibbon, in discussions of republics the classical past spoke directly to the present.[18]

Gibbon's first occasion to observe the constitutional, economic and cultural specificities of the different cantons presented itself in 1775 when his tutor Pavillard and his wife took Gibbon on a month-long tour across northern Switzerland. From Gibbon's travel journal, submitted to his father, we have a record of the exact itinerary of the tour. At Grandson on Lake Neuchâtel, for example, he found in the castle walls the cannon balls fired during the battle against Charles the Bold, the Duke of Burgundy. Victory over the mighty Burgundians at Grandson, Gibbon reported, was for the Swiss what Marathon, Salamis, Plataea and Mycale were to the Greeks.[19] Further evidence of Swiss military glory was found in Solothurn and in Zürich where Gibbon was able to see the Burgundian tapestries and weapons purloined in victory. The Swiss cultural emphasis upon their past military greatness for Gibbon translated into an equal focus upon the need for similar preparedness in the present.

III

In 1765, after he had resided in England once more for a year, Gibbon returned to the subject of the history of liberty. At first, he could not decide between writing the history of the defence and decline of the Florentine republic or the establishment of liberty in the Swiss cantons. After his friend Deyverdun arrived from Lausanne the decision was taken in favour of the history of the Swiss, to be composed up to the defeat of Charles the Bold.[20] Gibbon proposed to encompass a 'parallel between the revolutions of Florence and Switzerland' covering the period 'of two hundred years, from the association of the three peasants of the Alps to the plenitude and prosperity of the Helvetic body in the sixteenth century'. He made clear in his *Memoirs*, however, that the Swiss attracted him because of their combination of a society based on liberty and the capacity to defend it by armed force:

> I should have described the deliverance and victory of the Swiss, who have never shed the blood of their tyrants but in a field of battle; the laws and manners of the confederate states; the splendid trophies of the Austrian, Burgundian, and Italian wars; and the wisdom of a nation, which, after some sallies of martial adventure, has been content to guard the blessings of peace with the sword of freedom. *Manus haec inimica tyrannis Einse petit placidam cum libertate quietem.*[21]

Gibbon's Latin read 'This hand, an enemy to tyrants, seeks with the sword calm peacefulness in liberty.' The phrase was derived from Algernon Sidney, who was said to have written it in a visitor's book on arrival at the University of Copenhagen.[22] Despite his friend Hume's positive response to the first two chapters, though, Gibbon abandoned the work because of criticism from others.[23]

Holroyd included Gibbon's surviving first chapters, entitled 'Introduction à l'histoire générale de la République des Suisses', in the 1814 five-volume *Miscellaneous Works of Edward Gibbon* he edited and published.[24] There was more than an echo of Commonwealth argument in this text, identifying the source of Swiss liberty in the lives of toil lived in the mountains, away from luxury and the corruptions of commerce. Challenging conditions translated into a fierce independence sufficient to defeat the feudal oppression of the Holy Roman Emperor, whose mercenaries could not stand against the free warrior militias of the Swiss, fighting like ancient Goths against latter-day Romans. If the Swiss were independent and proud as individuals, they were nevertheless fully aware of the necessity of a strong form of community, willing to carry out any duty for the public good. As such, a love of both equality and liberty was nurtured, the basis of a free state able to maintain itself in the midst of tyrants.[25] This mattered to Gibbon because the cantons, when Confederation was established with the joining together of Zürich, Bern, Lucerne and Glarus, offered a 'rare sight, and one more worthy of human nature', of free states that served the interests of every member of their community rather than the privileged few, including courtiers.[26] Once such republican communities were secure, forms of trade commenced which spread wealth more generally, because trade was fully compatible with free government as long as it was carried out under the rule of law.[27]

Gibbon was, however, clear-eyed – the history of Bern revealed the excessive powers of republican military leaders such as Rudolf von Erlach after the victory of Laupen in 1339, underlining the danger of republics becoming nurseries for tyrants, especially in time of war. Bern, which Gibbon turned to in his manuscript, was a fascinating case because it told the story of republican greatness and decline, which was worrying for fellow republics in modern Europe. Bernese rule extended from the eastern tip of the Aargau down to the western end of Lac Léman, covering over a third of the Swiss Confederation's territory. It had, Gibbon argued, gradually become an oligarchy, limiting the privileges of foreigners and adopting the Venetian republican model regarding the election of magistrates, meaning that they began to be selected from a small number of leading families, generation after generation. But, crucially for many commentators, the members of these families did not turn themselves into a commercial elite but rather tended to develop their land or pursue military careers in one of the foreign regiments in France or the Dutch Republic. Lacking direct taxation and with a focus on the pursuit of agriculture and arms, Bern looked like the commonwealth ideal – an agrarian military republic in Europe.[28]

For these reasons, Bern was seen to be escaping the hellish dilemmas dominating the politics of other states across the continent. Above all, Bern had no public credit, being in the happy position of having a fiscal surplus, even generating substantial revenues from investing in the bonds of other states. Major public investments followed, ranging from a hospital, orphanage and new roads to a vast national granary, ready to feed the people in time of shortage. When the last European war of religion between Protestants and Catholics had broken out in 1711, after the subjects of Toggenburg rebelled against their Catholic prince-abbot of St Gall, the Protestant cantons of Bern and Zürich battled against the Catholic cantons of Uri, Zug, Unterwalden, Schwyz and Lucerne.[29] Bernese military prowess was reaffirmed with victory by 1712, the defeat of the Catholic cantons and the restoration of toleration, although the resulting peace of Aarau was denounced by the pope. The blending of private frugality, public luxury and militarism caused Montesquieu to call Bern a potential new Rome for the modern world in *Considérations sur les causes de la grandeur des Romains* (1734).[30] Gibbon was less convinced. He did note that Bernese magistrates with their standing and equipage looked like Roman consuls.[31] But he felt that the republic was suffering a relative decline because of the growth in modern times of corruption in the oligarchy, a self-interestedness among the patrician families.[32] The process, he worried, could weaken the state, making it potential prey to the larger monarchies seeking empire.

Gibbon wrote another essay on the Swiss, the *Lettre sur le gouvernement de Berne*, probably composed at Lausanne in 1763 or 1764.[33] At the time the Bernese Œconomic Society, founded in 1759, was offering prize essay competitions on significant issues of the day. The main objective of the Œconomic Society was to foster both patriotism and economic development, the latter in the form of practices compatible with the public virtues associated with the agrarian household economy, rather than individualistic self-interested money-grubbing of commercial societies like Britain. To promote such patriotism, the Œconomic Society established local branches in municipal towns, including Lausanne, and Gibbon attended at least one of their meetings in 1763.[34] A major question of the time was Bern's control over its 'empire', the Pays de Vaud taken from Savoy during the Reformation. Many rural areas were suffering depopulation as people moved to the towns, making the future uncertain for rural hinterlands like the Vaud.[35] Gibbon was interested in such issues because Lausanne was the largest town in the area, and outlined his position in *Lettre sur le gouvernement de Berne*. Here he said Bern had indeed become an oligarchy in the worst sense, and that the public good was being neglected, while its Calvinism had become calcified and doctrinaire. But Gibbon was much more positive about life under Bernese rule, praising the climate, the fertility of the soil, and the wealth of the ordinary subjects to the point that in the Vaud 'one dares to think and one knows how to live.'[36] Taxes were low, laws were fair, toleration manifest and property secure. These were the benefits, he held, of a genuine enlightenment.

Gibbon worried, however, that the Vaudois region in general and the rural cantons like Bern were falling economically behind the commercial nations of Europe. As Gibbon put it, in reference to Britain, France, the Dutch Republic and parts of Germany, 'From being barbarians they have become civilized, from being ignorant they have become enlightened, and from being poor they have become rich. I see towns where there were deserts and where forests have been cleared and transformed into fertile fields.'[37] Although the Vaudois enjoyed peace and relative wealth, they risked being overtaken by their neighbours before too long. Gibbon worried that Bern, when it turned itself into an empire ruled from within the Great Council, was renouncing the Gothic heritage of Europe that went back to the barbarian invasions of the fifth century, the equivalent of Macaulay's free Saxons. The Holy Roman Emperor Charlemagne's Gothic constitution had not prevented social and military conflict, but it had granted small communities and cities a share in the political and legislative process: 'The foundation of this Constitution has remained throughout all the revolutions, and nothing is better than this foundation. These states, their members and their rights were maintained always and by everyone, and everywhere were the same.'[38] Although the Scots had lost their parliament in 1707, they were still involved in the legislative process at London, and such an example of the protection of lesser polities within a greater union was recognized to be a Gothic legacy.

The Gothic framework had facilitated the development of modern liberty in certain states, in line with the modernization of Europe's feudal monarchies and the growth of their economies. The question facing the Vaud region, for Gibbon, was neither their current circumstances nor that they were ruled by Bern. Even if they considered themselves to be slaves, Gibbon argued, the Vaudois were as happy as any Bernese citizen. The real question was about the future, how far Bern could embrace a path of economic development that would enable it to maintain its wealth in the midst of that of its monarchical neighbours. If it fell behind because it was a backwards-looking empire ruled by an oligarchic republic, then it was likely to lose its independence.

Even if Bern's generosity towards its subjects in the territories it ruled could be interpreted as proof of the sovereign's goodwill, the mere fact that all powers were held by a single body meant that the sovereign's current disposition could never be anything more than a temporary phenomenon. It could not be relied upon over time. For a condition of liberty to be permanent, 'each order of citizens, and each part of the state has to have representatives dedicated to opposing any law destructive of their rights, or destructive of their happiness, since they themselves would be the first to recognize the negative consequences of the law.'[39] Gibbon argued that it was through exactly such a separation of powers and representation that many European nations had managed to shed the last vestiges of barbarism and become rich and civilized. From this perspective, any attempt to modernize Bern's republican household, without rectifying the underlying political structure, was bound to fail.

Gibbon's worries were not specific to Switzerland and nor did he believe that old Gothic constitutionalism, however successful it had been historically, would be sufficient to maintain liberty and toleration in modern times. It was indubitable, Gibbon argued, that commerce and public credit had changed the world to such a degree that the smaller and weaker polities, including the republics, would find it increasingly difficult to maintain themselves. The markets they offered would be too tempting to empire-builders jealous of wealth and economic potential. Traditional survival strategies, from diplomatic endeavour and the balance of power, economic specialization and reliance upon the manliness or virtue of the citizenry, were no longer sufficient, because a gulf had grown in the power gap between the states across Europe, with France and Britain by far the most powerful, being followed by states which could construct vast armies, such as Austria, Russia and Prussia. In the Swiss case, France was becoming more and more influential in the councils of the republics, as they sought to ensure that French interests in politics and economics were pursued. These areas were increasingly falling under French dominion, but as a result of soft power, rather than by direct military force.

Gibbon's critique of Bern mellowed as he aged and by returning to the canton over time. As he became famous as a historian his social status was elevated, and he became close friends with leading magistrates, especially Gabriel Albert von Erlach. More importantly, however, after 1789 Gibbon was faced with the rise of a very different kind of state, one that turned itself into a republic in 1792, and one that he saw as being far more menacing to its neighbours and far more brutal towards a substantial proportion of its own citizens. Compared to revolutionary France, Bern now seemed a haven, a place where tranquillity was the norm, where the rulers followed the public good, being prudent rather than rash or radical. Yet Gibbon's reappraisal never quite went as far as that of Edmund Burke, who described Bern as 'one of the happiest, the most prosperous, and the best governed countries upon earth'.[40]

In his *Memoirs* Gibbon, writing in July 1789, accepted that 'while the Aristocracy of Bern protects the happiness, it is superfluous to enquire whether it be founded in the rights, of man: the economy of the state is liberally supplied without the aid of taxes; and the magistrates *must* reign with prudence and equity, since they are unarmed in the midst of an armed nation.'[41] Gibbon's great friend Deyverdun had recently died when he wrote these words, and he was concerned that he would increasingly be 'alone in paradise [Lausanne]'. What Gibbon called 'the revolution or rather the dissolution of the [French] Kingdom' had led to a 'swarm of emigrants' escaping from 'the public ruin'. His central worry, however, was that the 'triumphant democrats' of Paris had such extensive local support. As he put it, 'the fanatic missionaries of sedition have scattered the seeds of discontent in our cities and villages, which had flourished above two hundred and fifty years without fearing the approach of war, or feeling the weight of government.' He feared that a 'French disease' might well infect the Swiss republics. It amounted to a new and more deadly enemy than any hitherto contemplated. The ideas of the revolutionaries, he thought, were altogether foolish and were historically without foundation, being 'wild theories of equal and boundless freedom'.

In 1789, Gibbon was still sure that the Swiss would be 'faithful to their sovereign and themselves'. He was also convinced that domestic rebellion would 'terminate in the ruin of the country', declaring that 'the first stroke of a rebel drum would be the signal of my immediate departure.'[42] Three years later he was much less confident. By the time of his final return to England and death a year later, Gibbon had become convinced that the Swiss republics he had known now belonged to a different epoch. A new task had been set for historians like himself, that of understanding how the new French form of republican empire could be made compatible with the existence of a Europe of small independent sovereignties, proud of their history and distinctiveness.

IV

According to John Holroyd, his closest English friend, Gibbon was confident about contemporary politics and largely unaffected by them late into the 1780s. Enlightenment, as far as Gibbon was concerned, could still be identified at least in the two countries he loved best: England and Switzerland. Writing to their mutual friend

William Eden, 1st Baron Auckland, Holroyd noted that 'the Gibbon' remained largely uninterested in politics, to the extent that 'I have not yet succeeded in infusing a proper political zeal into him.'[43] This was exaggerated. Gibbon had, like Hume, marked the progress of enthusiasm in British politics. He had been present in London at the time of the anti-Catholic riots, which lasted for several days in June 1780. This rebellion, known as the Gordon Riots because they were led by the Scottish Lord George Gordon, head of the Protestant Association, were launched to press Parliament to repeal the 1778 Papists Act, which allowed Catholics to inherit property, purchase land and serve in the army, as long as they gave an oath of allegiance to the crown. Gibbon had noted to his stepmother, Dorothea Gibbon, that 'the old story of religion has raised most formidable tumults in this town.'[44] In another letter he gave a description of the rioters which became famous with the appearance of Holroyd's edition of Gibbon's *Miscellaneous Works* in 1796: he likened Gordon and his acolytes to 'forty thousand Puritans such as they might be in the time of Cromwell'.[45]

Fortunately, Gibbon reported, 'government, with 15,000 regulars in town and every gentleman (but one [Gordon]) on their side' managed to 'extinguish the flame'.[46] Fortunately too other cities lacked 'that scum which has boiled up to the surface of this huge cauldron'. Gibbon was sanguine in his assessment of the riots because of the capacity of the landowning classes to retain the loyalty of the armed forces. Foreboding came, however, with the French Revolution. Gibbon was widely accused of being a dangerous religious sceptic and historian of unbelief because of the fifteenth chapter of the first volume of *Decline and Fall* in 1776, which implied that barbarism and religion had risen together with the fall of Rome. Gibbon adopted a more moderate tone in subsequent volumes when dealing with the history of the church.[47] When the French Revolution commenced, he followed events closely, aware that as the French assaulted their own church establishments Gibbon himself would be blamed as an ideological source for their actions. As events within France became bloodier, and more still as the turmoil of revolution spilled over the borders of France into Switzerland, Gibbon gradually arrived at the conclusion in his final years that the Enlightenment had ended; the Switzerland of his youth had gone and with it the toleration and diversity of Europe. Abstract reason, in the form of French Revolution principles, had been unleashed upon the world and had led to catastrophe. In coming to this view Gibbon was following Burke. Gibbon had known Burke from his time as a member of parliament for Liskeard between 1774 and 1784. Their closeness, however, stemmed from the publication in 1790 of Burke's *Reflections on the Revolution in France*, a book that Gibbon had a 'thirst' for, asking his publisher Thomas Cadell to send a copy to him at high speed.[48] Gibbon then identified Burke's work as the most insightful guide to contemporary events:

> . . . a most admirable medicine against the French disease, which has made too much progress even in this happy country [Switzerland]. I admire his eloquence, I approve his politics, I adore his chivalry, and I can even forgive his superstition.[49]

Before long Gibbon was stating that despite Burke being 'the most eloquent and rational madman that I ever knew', regarding 'that cursed Revolution', he was 'as high an Aristocrate [sic] as Burke himself'.[50]

Gibbon's open conversion to Burke's politics meant that he opposed revolutionary anticlericalism, as the French took away the wealth and lands of the Catholic Church and ended its control over education. Gibbon, despite his personal opposition to Catholicism, supported Burke's view that the attack on throne and altar in France had had terrible consequences for long-established cultures and institutions. Without the church to guide them, Gibbon feared that individuals would cease to follow traditional rules of morality. Gibbon was so worried by events in France that he set aside late works such as the *Antiquities of the House of Brunswick* because he was afraid that they might be used by radicals to challenge the crown. Any criticism of traditional forms of authority might, at this crucial juncture in history, add fuel to the revolutionary flames.[51]

Burke believed initially that the French Revolution had weakened France because of exactly this undermining of traditional institutions: if war came it would end quickly in the nation's defeat. Gibbon agreed, and in 1790–91 believed France to be 'in a state of dissolution'.[52] Gibbon was similarly optimistic that French chaos wouldn't spread to Switzerland; as he put it, 'the popular madness of France and Flanders has not reached these tranquil regions, and . . . the Swiss have sense enough to feel and maintain their own happiness, which is endeared to them by the disorders of the neighbouring Countries.'[53] So convinced was Gibbon at this stage that the French revolutionary idea of liberty would not spread, that his optimism was not challenged by his spending four days at the house of Jacques Necker at Coppet near Geneva in February 1791. Necker had until recently been the French *directeur général des finances*, effectively chancellor of the exchequer, until he lost his post amid the turmoil in Paris. Gibbon called him 'the Minister and perhaps the Legislator of the French Monarchy'.[54] Necker was also the father of Anne Louise Germaine de Staël, already writing popular works, and the husband of Suzanne Curchod, to whom Gibbon remained dedicated.

Gibbon described Necker as an archetypal victim of the French Revolution. Necker was now 'abused by all parties' and no French person dared set foot in his house. Seeing Necker at close quarters, Gibbon declared, 'I have really a much higher idea than I ever had before' of Necker and of his opinions. Necker had recently published *Du pouvoir exécutif dans les grands états* (1791), which justified his conduct as a minister in the early stages of the French Revolution with the claim that he had always been seeking a British-style constitutional settlement. Gibbon praised the book to Lord Loughborough as an antidote to domestic radicalism.[55] He said the book presented 'a valuable testimony of his esteem for our Constitution'. The lesson was that 'the testimony of a sagacious and impartial stranger may have taught some of our countrymen to value the political blessings which they have been tempted to despise.'[56] Gibbon wrote of Necker that 'he was overwhelmed by the hurricane, he mistook his way in the fog, but in such a perilous situation, I much doubt whether any mortal could have seen or stood.'[57] Even though Necker was despondent, Gibbon drew from him support for Burke's view of the French Revolution: that France was becoming weaker as a state. Gibbon asserted that 'the master-movers in France, (I know it most certainly)' were of the opinion 'that their troops will not fight, that the people have lost all sense of patriotism and that on the first discharge of an Austrian canon, the game is up'.[58]

Gibbon was therefore sure that the Revolution was likely to be crushed. What he termed 'the prosperity of England' formed 'a proud contrast with the disorders of France', which was on the verge of ruin: 'In the moving picture of this World, you cannot be indifferent to the strange Revolution which has humbled all that was high and exalted all that was low in France. The irregular and lively spirit of the Nation has disgraced their liberty, and instead of building a free constitution they have only exchanged Despotism for Anarchy.'[59]

V

There was still a danger from the Revolution, even if Gibbon thought that France had ceased militarily to be of consequence. If civil disturbance by revolutionary malcontents occurred elsewhere across Europe, it might very well lead to the fall of governments, the change of culture and the collapse of toleration and peace. Gibbon soon realized that revolutionary doctrines were attracting adherents across Switzerland, and he became obsessed with the possibility of their attracting Britons. This goes some way to explaining Gibbon's move from a self-described 'citizen of the world' to being vociferous about his patriotic Englishness. English national character for Gibbon in 1792–93 necessitated devotion to the constitution as currently constructed. At the end of 1792, he wrote that he was delighted to hear that Holroyd had 'crushed the daring subverters of the Constitution'; this was a reference to the rejection of Charles James Fox's motion of 15 December 1792 to recognize the French Republic, a debate in which Holroyd, since 1790 a member of parliament for Bristol, had spoken against Fox.[60]

Gibbon was so fearful about the danger of revolutionary France that he wanted the government of William Pitt the Younger to go much further. Even 'the moderate well-meaning reformers', the old Whig supporters of Rockingham who considered themselves to be friends of liberty, needed to be prevented from political action because 'the slightest innovation' could launch the country 'without rudder or compass on a dark and dangerous ocean of Theoretical experiment'.[61] Gibbon went so far as to chastise his friend Holroyd for failing to pronounce himself opposed to *any* species of reform:

> Will you not take some active measures to declare your sound opinions and separate yourselves from your rotten members [the reformers]? If you allow them to perplex government, if you trifle with this solemn business, if you do not resist the spirit of innovation in the first attempt, if you admit the smallest and most specious change in our parliamentary system, you are lost . . . Do not suffer yourselves to be lulled into a false security. Remember the proud fabric of the French Monarchy. Not four years ago it stood founded as it might seem on the rock of time, force and opinion, supported by the triple Aristocracy of Church, the Nobility, and the Parliaments. They are crumbled into dust, they are vanished from the earth.[62]

Gibbon had 'shuddered' at the young parliamentarian Charles Grey's motion on 30 April 1792 for the reform of the franchise – forty years later in 1832, Grey would be the prime minister who successfully implemented the Reform Act. Gibbon worried that the reformers, who he perceived to be led by Grey, the playwright and satirist Richard Brinsley Sheridan and the lawyer Thomas Erskine, might 'heat the minds of the people'. Gibbon asked Holroyd, 'will the bulk of your party stand firm to their own interest and that of their country?' In the same letter, marked 'most private', Gibbon stated that when thinking about current politics 'I feel myself an Englishman.' Gibbon perceived himself to have recognized the necessity of public order against would-be revolutionaries and advocates of societal reform.

Gibbon suddenly regretted the criticisms of Christianity that he had penned in the first volume of *The Decline and Fall*.[63] Did he go further and blame himself for contributing to forms of unbelief and irreligion that were widely perceived to have led in turn to political extremism? It was soon commonly held that the extremism of the French Revolution was the outcome of a conspiracy of unbelief. In part this occurred through the popularity of the Catholic priest Augustin Barruel's *Memoirs Illustrating the History of Jacobinism* and the sometime professor of natural philosophy at Edinburgh John Robison's *Proofs of a Conspiracy against all the Religions and Governments of Europe*, both of which first appeared in 1797.[64] It was even claimed that the French were ploughing a furrow set down by the Romans, whose republican liberty was lost with the progress of irreligious Epicurean philosophy:

> It was late before the atheism of Epicurus gained footing at Rome, but its prevalence was soon followed by such scenes of proscription, confiscation, and blood, as were *then* unparalleled in the history of the world; from which the republic being never able to recover itself, after many unsuccessful struggles, exchanged liberty for repose, by submission to absolute power. Such were the effects of atheism at Rome. An attempt has been recently made to establish a similar system in France, the consequences of which are too well known.[65]

The question was posed whether 'the barbarities which have stained the revolution in that unhappy country are justly chargeable on the prevalence of atheism'. The clear proof, for any who doubted, was to 'recollect that the men, who, by their activity and talents, prepared the minds of the people for that great change [the French Revolution]; Voltaire, d'Alembert, Diderot, Rousseau, and others, were avowed enemies of revelation.' These men promoted together 'the diffusion of scepticism and of revolutionary principles'. Their condemnations of 'the Christian priesthood and religious institutions' were vitriolic and led directly to the collapse of France into Terror:

> [The *philosophes*] . . . atrocities were committed with a wanton levity and brutal merriment; . . . the reign of atheism was avowedly and expressly the reign of terror; in the full madness of their career, in the highest climax of their horrors, they shut up the temples of God, abolished his worship, and proclaimed death to be an eternal sleep . . . As the heathens fabled that Minerva issued full armed from the head of Jupiter; so no sooner were the speculations of atheistical philosophy matured, than they gave birth to a ferocity which converted the most polished people in Europe into a horde of assassins; the seat of voluptuous refinement, of pleasure and of arts, into a theatre of blood.[66]

In the work of Barruel and Robison, as well as many others, religion was portrayed as a moderating force for peace and order, opposed against the true enthusiasts, fanatics and terrorists: the exponents of unbelief, heterodoxy and atheism. Their discourse turned the tables on those who, as we have seen, drew a direct line between religious fanaticism and enthusiasm for liberty. In short, the very exponents of enlightenment, who were most concerned about its end, were themselves accused of abetting a descent into superstition in politics, and hence into the kinds of terror that became commonplace in revolutionary France and across Europe. Hume and Gibbon were each named and censured for causing the present discontents.[67]

Claims became widespread that the miserable deaths of revolutionary martyrs by guillotine or suicide was punishment by Christ for their attacks upon organized religion. Gibbon was cited by the self-appointed defenders of religion as someone who always 'sneer[ed] at Christianity' and endeavoured 'to bring it into contempt'.[68] It was clear from his letters that before he died Gibbon accepted that opposition to the Christian religion had contributed to the societal collapse manifesting itself in France. Contemporary evidence of Gibbon regretting his supposed infidelity, his criticism of Christian belief and institutions, was the answer reportedly given by Burke himself, when discussing Holroyd's edition of Gibbon's *Miscellaneous Works* on 1 May 1796 with Arthur Young:

> On my observing that Mr. Gibbon declares himself of the same opinion with him [Burke] on the French Revolution, he said that Gibbon was an old friend of his, and he knew well before he died, that he heartily repented of the anti-religious part of his work for contributing to free mankind from all restraint on their vices and profligacy, and thereby aiding so much the spirit which produced the horrors that blackened the most detestable of all revolutions.[69]

It is equally worth recalling Burke's own response to Barruel's *Mémoires,* which he read on its appearance in 1797, that 'the tendency of the whole is admirable in every point of view, political, religious, and, let me make use of the abused word, philosophical.' Burke went so far as to confirm Barruel's suspicions in stating that a plot by the irreligious against the institutions of society had existed since the 1770s:

> I forgot to say, that I have known myself, personally, five of your principal Conspirators; and I can undertake to say from my certain knowledge, that as far back as the year 1773, they were busy in the Plot you have so well described, and in the manner, and on the Principle you have so truly presented. To this I can speak as a Witness.[70]

Burke did not name Gibbon and would not have numbered Gibbon among those plotting in 1773.

The debate about the relationship between criticism of Christianity by freethinkers and enemies of Christian orthodoxy, such as Hume and Gibbon, and the outbreak of the French Revolution, caused Holroyd to be careful about the publication of Gibbon's posthumous works, particularly his autobiography.[71] Holroyd played down Gibbon's heterodoxy and also his relationship with Burke. Holroyd considered Burke an inconsistent figure in politics and philosophy, having become an opponent of radical change late in his life and always having espoused or flirted with the dangerous opinions of radical Whiggism, risking thereby the collapse of trade and empire. According to the anti-Catholic Holroyd, Burke had also been too supportive of the Catholics in Ireland, risking the very revolution he opposed in France.[72]

Such arguments aside, the fact is that both Gibbon and Holroyd followed Burke. They did so, first, in arguing that the French Revolution had made France militarily debilitated. They then came to the conclusion, again with Burke but against the argument of his *Reflections on the Revolution*, that France was being transformed into a different kind of polity, one whose power, founded on the union of a republican populace, was destroying enlightenment and restoring religious war to Europe. Gibbon did not, however, ever express the view that his own work or opinions were in any way responsible for the progress of revolution and terror, and the fact remains that, regardless of the worries of the time, the French Revolution was not a plot by enemies of religion to destroy Christian churches by reordering society.

VI

As late as August 1792, Gibbon was convinced that the progress of events at Paris was tarnishing radical ideology. As he put it, 'the last revolution of Paris appears to have convinced almost everybody of the fatal consequences of Democratical principles, which lead by a path of flowers into the Abyss of Hell.'[73] In the summer and autumn of 1792, Gibbon anticipated the end of the

French Revolution by military means. His hopes rested with Charles William Ferdinand, Duke of Brunswick-Lüneburg and Prince of Brunswick-Wolfenbüttel, commander of the combined armies of Austria and Prussia, who invaded France at the end of July 1792. Of Brunswick, Gibbon said, 'On every rational principle of calculation he must succeed.'[74] A professional and highly trained force fighting against an undisciplined mob devoid of so many of its officers would surely, Gibbon and many observers believed, have one outcome only. The defeat of Brunswick at the Battle of Valmy on 20 September shocked all of the opponents of the French Revolution. It went against military logic. The battle was speedily followed by the French invasion of Savoy. Gibbon wrote to Holroyd that with French troops in the immediate vicinity, 'it is possible that you may have some trifling apprehensions of my being killed and eaten by those [French] Cannibals.' This was a joke about Gibbon's own corpulence, yet it underlined his real fear of French savagery.

After Valmy, Gibbon radically altered his view of the prospects for France and for Europe towards the end of 1792. The Revolution had created a state that was better at making war than any other. This fact troubled Gibbon's final years and coloured particularly his view of the Swiss states, his 'home by adoption' for more than a third of his adult life, just as he left them for the last time. Gibbon said of his beloved Lausanne in 1792, 'I never knew any place so much changed.'[75] Toleration and peace, Gibbon's vital sense of a Swiss Enlightenment, had ended, replaced by revolutionary fervour for liberty and equality. He began to plan an escape to Bern or to Britain, because the 'Gallic wolves' were roaming, advocates of detested democratic principles and 'wild ideas of the rights and natural equality of man'.[76]

The French, Gibbon was sure, were republicans of a different stamp to the Romans, the Florentines or the Swiss. Gibbon became certain that he was experiencing the decline and fall of old Europe at first hand. He increasingly saw the French as being on the brink of tearing up the existing map of independent states in perpetuity and establishing in its place an imperial democracy. Holroyd shared this view, writing to Gibbon that, 'I consider the French affairs so far out of the line of common Politicks, that I wish the whole world to declare against them.'[77] Common politics for Gibbon, as for Holroyd, meant the views he had expressed throughout his life – supportive always of law and generally existing political establishments, opposition to violence and intolerance everywhere and support for civil liberties wherever they could be expected to flourish. Gibbon did not consider himself to have contributed to the revolutionary ferment. Things went from bad to worse for Gibbon as a French army led by General Anne-Pierre, marquis de Montesquiou-Fézensac, came to the gates of Geneva in October 1792. Gibbon was certain that the little republic could not withstand a siege. Although the fortifications 'were not contemptible', the number of supporters of the French Revolution in the city meant that the spirit of the defenders was not sufficient to hold fast against the invaders: 'the malcontents are numerous within the walls, and I question whether the spirit of the citizens would hold out against a bombardment.'[78]

Feeling that he was in 'hurricane latitudes', Gibbon's mood became increasingly negative. At Geneva he anticipated 'a Democratical revolution, which would probably renew the horrid scenes [September massacres] of Paris and Avignon'.[79] He wrote to Holroyd that he was increasingly concerned about 'the Leviathan France'. Swiss troops were pouring into the region of Coppet and Nyon, north of Geneva and on the north-east bank of the Lake, and there were Swiss men in arms from Schaffhausen to the Pays de Vaud, Gibbon's own 'little paradise'. For Gibbon, however, the Swiss cantons, despite their great military reputation, were 'not equal to a long and expensive war, and as most of our Militia have families and trades, the country already sighs for their return'. His conclusion was that 'the smaller powers may acquiesce without dishonour.' The French were 'new Romans' and could not be stopped.

Gibbon was naturally more concerned than ever in the final months of 1792 that French notions of democracy and equality would spread to Britain; if revolutionary doctrines had proved too potent for the Swiss, how would Britons not be similarly swayed? He asked Holroyd for 'a full and confidential account of your views concerning England, Ireland, and France'. He saw the revolutionary disease spreading across Europe with the progress of French arms. They had, by the beginning of 1793, defeated Prussia, conquered Savoy, pillaged Germany, invaded the Dutch Republic, and were threatening Spain and all of the states of Italy. Gibbon concluded that 'the whole horizon is so black, that I begin to feel some anxiety for England, the last refuge of liberty and law.' As 'the Gallic dogs' were enjoying the 'most insolent prosperity', it was conceivable that the British would succumb to the general revolutionary ardour and 'eat the apple of false freedom'.[80]

At the same time, Gibbon feared a British war with France. The British could easily justify such an engagement as the French had violated existing treaties in their invasion of the Austrian Netherlands and Savoy. Yet France, which he now termed the 'new Sparta', was proven to be so deadly in battle that to fight would entail 'plunging headlong into an Abyss, whose bottom no man can discover'.[81] When war was eventually declared on 1 February 1793, Gibbon opposed it. To Holroyd he stated that he wished 'it could have been avoided and . . . we might still have continued to enjoy our safe and prosperous neutrality'.[82] The reason was that he was unsure whether Britain could defeat revolutionary France, even with 'a confederacy such as was never opposed to the ambition of Louis XIV'.[83] This, Gibbon reported, was the conclusion 'after the experience of last year' after which he distrusted 'reason, and confess myself fearful for the event [war]':

> The French are strong in numbers, activity, enthusiasm; they are rich in rapine, and although their strength may be only that of a frenzy-fever they may do infinite mischief to their neighbours before they can be reduced to a straight waistcoat. I dread the effects that may be produced upon the minds of the people by the increase of our debts and taxes, probable losses, and possible mismanagement. Our trade must suffer, and though projects of invasion have been always

abortive, I cannot forget, that the fleets and armies of Europe have failed before the towns in America which have been taken by a handful of Buccaneers.[84]

Gibbon left Lausanne on his fifty-sixth birthday, 9 May 1793, travelling to Basle, Frankfurt, Cologne, Brussels, Ostend and then finally London.[85] He no longer felt safe on mainland Europe, although the specified reason for his departure was to be with Holroyd, after the sudden death of his wife, Maria. For Gibbon, it was evident that established ideas about politics were dead and that, with the French Revolution, the republics of the old world, and especially the Swiss Confederacy, were locked into a process that would soon see their extinction. Evidence came from Lausanne itself, where French migrants preaching revolution, called by Gibbon 'the fanatic missionaries of sedition', had been the beneficiaries of such extensive local support. He had seen them scatter 'the seeds of discontent in our cities and villages, which had flourished above two hundred and fifty years without fearing the approach of war or feeling the weight of government'.[86] There could be no better description of the end of enlightenment.

In this he agreed with Burke; yet at the same time there was a sense that this analysis was no more than diagnosis of the world's ills. No antidote to the poison was in evidence. Gibbon speculated about the response that might be given by moderate men faced by the proliferation of fraudulent ideas about liberty in the general population: 'I have sometimes thought of writing a dialogue of the dead, in which Lucian, Erasmus, and Voltaire should mutually acknowledge the danger of exposing an old superstition to the contempt of the blind and fanatic multitude.'[87] What solutions they might express in the dialogue remained unspecified. Gibbon died in England in January 1794 from the effects of gout and peritonitis, depressed in consequence about Europe, full of lament at seeing the enlightened world in which he had flourished destroyed – especially so in the case of the small states which he had loved. A new doctrine of republican egalitarianism was, he believed, addicted to war and more suited to waging and sustaining unlimited patriotic war than any other doctrine in history. The motivation of the promise of universal liberty was singularly potent. The notion of making all states free and all states the same was being put about with a zeal unseen since the Reformation. For Gibbon, the new religion of revolution was more frightening, and potentially deadlier, than any experienced hitherto. Gibbon could see no reason why the British people would avoid being seduced by promises of liberty and equality. He did not see how France could be fought or any prospect of ultimate British victory.

6.

Edmund Burke and the End of Europe

I

From the time of Hume's death numerous philosophers and politicians believed the world they saw as enlightened to have altered for the worse, to have ruptured, or to be in danger of imploding. For these generations, looking at their own times, the figures of Fortuna and Fantasia were everywhere, the inconstant and irrational Roman goddesses associated with the vicissitudes of commercial life and especially paper credit, who plotted the erosion of virtue through commercial passion and an inevitable descent into corruption.[1] Doubts about the loss of fortune or the implications of blind chance could be found everywhere in speculation about the future in eighteenth-century life and letters. It especially accompanied the uncertainty that followed commerce and the risk that the rule of money and the lust for gold translated into injustice, oppression and corruption. To the prevalent cultural force of Fantasia and Fortuna we need to add Folly, the goddess Atë (ἄτη), whom Homer identified as the eldest daughter of Zeus, associated with ruin, delusion and mischief. Folly, widely held to be akin to madness, was the goddess who had snared humanity. Fantasia, Fortuna and Folly were deemed to be prevailing over enlightenment. David Hume was aghast at the end of his life that a form of patriotism had emerged in British politics associated with war, empire and an excess of liberty. In circumstances of national debt and social division, Hume anticipated a revolution by bankruptcy, defeat in war or popular uprising in the name of liberty. His hope was that the monarch, nobility and gentry would come together to restore order.

Rebellion was expected to be violent, and Hume accepted that crushing it would be still more bloody.

Edward Gibbon's was a different end of enlightenment, because he perceived enthusiasm in the form of French revolutionary republicanism sweeping away the diverse Europe of small and large states and cultures that he loved, and especially those across Switzerland. Gibbon admitted the attractiveness of French republicanism, especially to the poor, as revolutionary liberty promised to change their world, upend hierarchies and cease social injustice. Sceptic that Gibbon was, the price of the transmission mechanism to a better world, entailing violence and civil war, and the homogeneous revolutionary culture that he perceived to be on the horizon, was not worth paying. Seeing the Europe he valued overrun by French republican armies led to Gibbon dying despondent. Edmund Burke perceived the French Revolution just as Gibbon did, feeling its force in just the same way. Burke hoped, however, that a new Britain might emerge, entirely dedicated to war on revolution. The patriotism generated in the process would put an end at least to strife within Britain, and possibly in Ireland too. It would, he hoped, restore men to power in politics and the church who he believed would be true defenders of liberty and the public good in the face of fanatical opposition. The advocacy of the creation of states which saw their first function as war upon a deadly competing ideology was an important response to the end of enlightenment. We tend not to associate the justification of war to the death with political authors within Whig/Liberal or Tory/Conservative traditions identifiable in British or European history, but such claims were made in response to the end of enlightenment crises. They were especially important in shaping the politics of the next century.

II

If the end of enlightenment that Burke sensed overlapped with that which Gibbon perceived, it was also distinctive. Burke was an outsider and self-made figure, as he reminded lordly critics in his final years when Francis Russell, the 5th Duke of Bedford, and James Maitland, the 8th Earl of Lauderdale, attacked him for being a placeman with a pension who was nevertheless living beyond his means.[2] In his excoriating reply, the *Letter to a Noble Lord* of February 1796, Burke described himself as an 'old man with very young pensions' replying to a 'young man with very old pensions' and ridiculed the stupidity of lords who welcomed the French Revolution before considering what it would do, if implemented in Britain, to their own wealth and possibly their lives.[3] The outsider status was acknowledged by all, leading to his being caricatured in numerous political cartoons as a Jesuit in the establishment, wearing black and bespectacled, his long nose always up to no good; it also meant that he was recognized to be independent with regards to his distinctive opinions, derived from long and deep philosophic labour.[4] Nevertheless, when he rose to be a figure of status in politics, he explained it as not an accident of his singular genius, but as a positive characteristic of the British system.

Burke was an outsider in part because of religious prejudice. His mother was Mary Nagle, of a prominent Catholic family from Cork fallen upon hard times, like so many such families. His sister Juliana was brought up a Catholic and remained in the faith. Burke's father, however, was a Protestant lawyer in the capital, where Burke was born, and he was a strong adherent to his father's religion, and a staunch defender of the Church of England and the Church of Ireland as key to the maintenance of liberty and as bulwarks against fanaticism. Burke's Irishness was the second reason for his outsider status. This would have mattered far less if Burke had been heir to substantial lands across the nations, as Shelburne was, or had married into such property. Yet Burke married Mary Jane Nugent, a daughter of the physician Christopher Nugent. They were wed on 12 March 1757 and had one son, the beloved Richard, who survived into adulthood.[5]

Burke made his own way. After being educated at schools in Cork and Kildare and graduating from Trinity College Dublin he went to London in 1750, with the intention of becoming a lawyer at the

Middle Temple. Eventually deciding against a career in law, he became editor of the Annual Register, writing much of the content himself from 1758 until the mid-1760s, before serving politicians as secretary, confidant, public defender and accompanying office holder. The first was the MP William Gerard Hamilton in 1759, who became chief secretary in Ireland in 1761 and chancellor of the Irish exchequer in 1763. In serving Hamilton as private secretary, Burke secured a pension of £300 per annum and in time observed the injustices suffered especially by the Catholic peasants, oppressed because of their position in society, their religion and the law which in Burke's view very rarely came to their aid.

After quarrelling with Hamilton at the end of 1764, which meant the loss of his pension, Burke was employed as private secretary to Rockingham, the new prime minister and leading Whig, from July 1765. In January 1766, he entered the House of Commons as an MP for Wendover. By July the ministry had been replaced by that of Chatham. Burke had little time for Chatham, whom he considered an actor and a demagogue, and soon went into opposition with Rockingham. It was an ideal match. There was trust and high regard between the men, and serving Rockingham turned Burke into a political notable. Rockingham considered Burke to be vital to the justification of Whiggism and the ultimate restoration of the Whigs to power through altered times of opposition and despite their lack of one of George III's support. For his part, Burke considered Rockingham the ideal Whig grandee, a defender of the public good fully attuned to the dangers of radical change and enthusiasm.[6] Burke lived his creed while working with Rockingham, the very definition of what Burke called 'the great oaks', the men whose landed wealth made them independent of the court and distinct from the people, the moderating force for liberty and enlightenment and the protectors of the constitution established in 1688–89.[7]

The period after the Glorious Revolution of 1688–89 was crucial for Burke. The contrast with the Wars of the Three Kingdoms, from 1639–52, seeing civil and religious conflict continued across England, Scotland and Ireland, could not have been starker. William of Orange, the Dutch Stadtholder, landed at Torbay in Devon in November 1688 while King James II fled to France, allowing William and Mary to be crowned the following February. The Convention Parliament declared that the crown was being passed to James's daughter because of his abdication, and a Bill of Rights enshrined the liberties of the people. Although war lay ahead in Ireland, the Highlands of Scotland and then across Europe against Louis XIV's France, there was no renewal of civil war. Nor did the religious establishment shudder. The people were not given an opportunity to turn fanatic. Whig grandees subsequently developed an approach to politics validated by the creation of the post-Glorious Revolution free state. The Whig party, defending Protestantism and the Revolution Settlement, had stood fast against Jacobitism and had seen Britain commercialize and be successful in war without losing liberty in the manner of the Danes or Swedes. One of the opinions that marked Burke was his defence of the laws of primogeniture (that the first-born male inherited the estate) and entail (limiting the inheritance of property to a single line), which guaranteed the continuity of intact landed estates through the generations, maintaining the wealth and status of figures like Rockingham and other Whig families, the Bedfords, Pelhams and Grenvilles.[8]

In Burke's mind, landed property, by which he meant substantial territorial possessions, made all property secure by linking the interests of land and commerce together.[9] Those who held land could not liquidize their assets and flee in crisis. They had an interest in peace and toleration, the loss of which might threaten the security of their land ownership. The kind of commerce favoured by the landed was likely to be equally respectful of property, and therefore supportive of Britain as a free state. Rank and wealth translated into prudence, recognizing the dangers accompanying change but also the role played by the institutions of church and state in guaranteeing the Revolution Settlement, preventing the return of fanatic religion and being combative when it arose in the form of Jacobitism. Burke asserted that Britain had been successful under the first two Georges because of the land-owning Whig oligarchs in parliament who, together with the established Church and the monarch, guaranteed the possession, occupation, accession and succession of rights to property. Property was defended in accordance with the Common Law doctrines of precedent, justifying the origin of such rights, and prescription, the long-term enjoyment of the rights of possession.

The role of the Common Law in politics in turn signalled the importance of manners, the conventions and habits that formed codes of justice and morality, responsible for stability and enjoining deference in the face of social rank. For Burke, Rockingham embodied politeness, gallantry and fealty, honour and chivalry. The exercise of such virtues, Burke was convinced, translated into the generation of respect from the people below and sufficient power to be able to act as a moderating force upon executive action when necessary.[10] But the virtues were nothing without piety, and one of the major differences between Burke and his friends Smith and Hume was his absolute repudiation of their infidelity, as he termed it, and scepticism.[11] For Burke, religion, as much as any other force in society, prevented the descent into barbarism and fanaticism, anchoring modern civility. It was the noble and clerical ranks together, Burke argued, that maintained not only learning in a society, and therefore political wisdom, but also commerce and manufactures, because they flourished 'under the same shade in which learning flourished'.[12] Whigs like Rockingham in tandem with the established church could be relied upon to promote trade, while preventing a repeat of the seventeenth century when violent enthusiasms caused turmoil in religion and politics. And they were a bulwark against absolute monarchy.

In return for the articulation of Whig principles, embodying what Burke was later to call a 'manly, moral, regulated liberty', Rockingham paid Burke a salary in the form of loans to be cancelled on the latter's death, and from 1771 to 1776 he held the office of agent to the provincial assembly of New York for £500 per year.[13] Borrowing from friends allowed Burke to purchase the estate called Gregories in Buckinghamshire, owned in the previous century by the Civil War poet Edmund Waller. Such status made Burke a figure in society. But he also developed close friendships with literary men and women such as Samuel Johnson, Oliver Goldsmith and Elizabeth Montagu, as well as famous painters, including Joshua Reynolds and James Barry. Together in 1764 they founded the Club that met once a week for supper, conversation and drink at the Turk's Head in Soho. It was through Rockingham, too, that in March 1782 Burke was elected a member of the greatest Whig club, Brooks's on Pall Mall.

In questioning the policy of successive administrations through speeches in the Commons and in published writings, Burke pressed for causes he believed in with a passion and aggressiveness that could be matched by few others. Yet Burke was never a negative-voiced Jeremiah. For him there was no natural step concerning current politics and society from criticism to lamentation. Indeed, from his first work, *A Vindication of Natural Society* (1756), he ridiculed Bolingbroke's arguments that the Anglican establishment was intolerant and misguided.[14] According to Burke, Bolingbroke was overly pessimistic, foolishly damning the present state of Britain. Burke's early writings were marked by the influence of Hume's defence of civilized monarchy, accepting that enlightenment had put an end to wars of religion and that Britain had become a free state in 1688–89 and continued to be a bastion for liberty. This was the message of the work Burke co-authored with William Burke, a close friend rather than a relative, the *Account of the European Settlements in America*, which was published on 1 April 1757. The Burkes advised the commercial development of the Empire following the successful model of the French, with moderate tax regimes for the colonies and prudent governance, facilitating the growth of industry and wealth in all imperial areas as a salve to political disquiet.[15] The point about Jeremiahs was that in asserting the existence of crisis they demanded political innovations that would likely be worse than the disease, threatening the Whig ascendency that was responsible for the liberties enjoyed by Britons.

Despite Burke's protestations the literature of jeremiad reached a peak in the aftermath of the Seven Years' War, having been fired by

John Brown's *Estimate of Manners*, and stoked by William Knox, the spokesman of the prime minister George Grenville, who argued in a pamphlet on *The Present State of the Nation* in 1769 that Britain was in danger of becoming a tributary to France because the decay of trade had translated into national weakness.[16] Burke took it upon himself to assault such politics as dangerous and delusory. Knox's arguments were 'common-place lamentations' which had been 'ten times repeated' and 'a thousand times answered before'.[17] Rather than Britain's predicament being 'piteously doleful', evidence of national power had been displayed in the last war, 'the most prosperous we ever carried on, by sea and by land, and in every part of the globe', resulting in the substantial increase of both trade and revenue.[18] While France remained a dangerous rival, and while Britain ought to have expanded its commercial possessions when it had the chance during the war, especially by taking Guadeloupe and Martinique from the French, it was nevertheless a fact that France was in a far worse position. He argued that French national finances were so parlous and the economic crisis across the country so intense as to expect 'some extraordinary convulsion in that whole system'.[19]

Britain, by contrast, as a free state founded on law and constitution, was in good health. As Burke put it, 'The old building stands well enough, though part Gothic, part Grecian, and part Chinese' – meaning that the British system was a happy product of accidental accretion, alternative traditions and history – 'until an attempt is made to square it into uniformity.' He warned against innovators who would cause a 'uniformity of ruin' on the grounds that 'great will be the fall thereof.' Following Hume and Smith, Burke warned against speculators, projectors and men of system, whose uniform and utopian solutions to the problems of the day forever had to be castigated – Britain had experienced these ideas before, and it had led to anarchy.[20]

Burke repeated himself concerning the naysayers about the health of Britain in a further pamphlet, *Thoughts on the Cause of the Present Discontents*, which appeared in 1770. Yet Burke's analysis was changed, with arguments that marked his work for the rest of his life. He now identified a basic fact as key to British politics: the loss of Whig power since the accession of George III in 1760. He still condemned those who complained about the age they lived in, about those in authority and who conceived 'extravagant hopes of the future'. The latter were fools, Burke said, expressing opinions characteristic of 'the ignorance and levity of the vulgar'.[21] Britain remained both stable and powerful. A young monarch had ascended the throne in 1760 who did not have to worry about the threat from the now-vanquished Jacobites and who was soon victorious across 'every part of the globe' in 'a mighty war' underlining his military strength, influence and capacity for conquest.[22] But Burke admitted that 'a great change has taken place in the affairs of this country.' It had been largely silent but unquestionably substantial, being at least as extensive 'as those which have been marked by the tumult of public revolutions'.[23]

Burke was referring to the economic and social change that could be seen around him, in addition to the fact that Britain, as a world empire in his eyes, had become a polity akin to ancient Rome, divided between plebs and patricians, something manifest in the popularity of John Wilkes amid the Middlesex election scandal. But he was also talking about the way that George III had altered British politics through his rejection of the Whigs and his embrace of his particular friend Bute, creating a court party dependent upon the whim of the monarch, and therefore, for Burke, lacking substance in the form of connection to land and history.

Burke argued that Bute's rule had been such a break with tradition, and the legislation of successive ministries in the 1760s so error-strewn, that the prophets of doom suddenly had material to work with; threats to Britain which in normal times could be dealt with were being addressed by false prophets and innovators who could not be trusted. In short, government itself was at once 'dreaded and contemned', the laws were 'despoiled of all their respected and salutary terrors', rank, office and title had ceased to be revered, foreign policy was 'as much deranged as our domestic economy' to the extent that 'our dependencies are slackened in their affection, and loosened from their obedience.' It was a fact 'universally admitted and lamented' that a time had arrived of confusion and division, 'in families, in Parliament, in the nation', so great as to be 'beyond the disorders of any former time'.[24] One of those Burke portrayed as a dangerous speculator and projector was Shelburne.

Burke argued that the consequence of the collapse of the Whig party and the rise of a cabal of King's Friends, enjoying 'all the gross lucre and fat emoluments of servitude', was that court patronage and money threatened to terminate Parliament as an independent arm of government. Burke recognized that parallels were being drawn with the times of Charles I, but he held them to be false; the weakness of Parliament in the present meant that there would be little opposition as long as the state remained strong. It was the case that 'the increase of the power of the State has often been urged by artful men, as a pretext for some abridgement of the public liberty.'[25] Conflict with the colonies was popular for patriotic Britons living in England, Scotland or Wales. Even as Britain became weaker, the army and navy would remain loyal and the King's Friends, whom Burke called a 'double cabinet', being outside government but of such influence, could further extend their domain. A real danger would then arise because figures such as Brown or Knox would be listened to and gain legions of adherents. Burke particularly worried about Brown, believing that he detested aristocracy and saw the role of an aristocratic class to be a fault in the British constitution. Burke saw himself to be playing a major role in drawing the sting from such critics, warning of the dangers of radical Wilkite policies including triennial parliaments and secret ballots. At the same time, it was vital to constrain monarchical power and patronage.[26]

Burke in the 1770s did not accept the diagnosis that the Enlightenment had ended, but was aware that new conflicts had arisen and that new steps had to be taken to restore the defences of liberty and moderation that had been effective in the past. He was certain, nevertheless, that Britain was less free than it had been, and that manners were being corrupted. As he put it to Rockingham, 'We seem no longer that eager, inquisitive, jealous, fiery people, which we have been formerly, and which we have been a very short time ago. The people look back, without pleasure or indignation; and forward, without hope or fear.'[27] Another consequence was that Britain was weaker internationally and less capable of playing a role maintaining peace in Europe. This was evident, Burke argued in a letter to a Prussian correspondent in 1774, in the lamentable events in Poland, which had been partitioned by Prussia, Russia and Austria in 1772. Burke called Poland 'but a breakfast', worrying that future war across Europe was to be expected because of the armed might of such states, incentivized by pitiful Britain.[28] When the North American crisis turned into another international war Burke declared himself to be astonished at the economic strength of France, which appeared to have learned from Britain and created a stable system of public credit guaranteed by a fierce patriotism.[29] He was equally worried that 'war, indeed, is become a sort of substitute for commerce', because mercantile schemes for supplying means of war were flourishing, while commerce in domestic necessities appeared to flounder.[30]

III

At the beginning of the 1770s and throughout that turbulent decade of imperial crisis and defeat, Burke argued that the loss of Whig influence was translating into disastrous policy characterized by the lack of moderation and a capacity for extreme measures, especially in America, India and Ireland. Regarding Ireland, the ongoing refusal to introduce Catholic emancipation and free trade with England, Scotland and Wales infuriated Burke, who considered assertions that cheap Irish labour would undercut prices on the mainland to be 'nugatory'.[31] Burke watched Ireland suffer economically as the imperial relationship with the North American colonies broke down. As the Irish armed themselves in preparation for a possible French invasion, Burke's advice was conciliatory. It was the same policy he advised for America.

From the time of his 'Speech on Declaratory Resolution of 1766', and subsequently in the notable speeches on 'American Taxation', of 19 April 1774, and then on 'Conciliation', of 22 March 1775, Burke prescribed a strategy of minimal taxes, the repeal of every piece of legislation that had angered the Americans and an appeal to fellow Britons for ongoing union in conditions of self-government.[32] When such a strategy was rejected, Burke was horrified at the upsurge both of xenophobic patriotism and warmongering, neither of which he felt had any role to play in normal politics. Indeed, he portrayed the use of German mercenaries in the British army in North America as not only unwise, but evidence that Britain was changing for the worse, encouraging strategies and tactics that would ultimately be a threat to liberty at home as well as in the Empire – but this was to be expected when George III and his friends ran amok. That there was no natural – Burke would have used the term Whig – limit upon policy was signified by rumours of the purchase of Russian troops from Catherine II in September 1775. In a letter Burke feigned to credit that the British would unleash what he termed 'Russian Barbarism' upon America.[33] Burke felt the same about the employment in British ranks of Native Americans, whom he accused of being cannibals and torturers.[34]

When military defeat arrived at Saratoga in 1777, Burke considered it to be a vindication of the stance he and the Rockingham Whigs had taken, warning of the direct link between the abandonment of traditional political practice, the worsening of relations between government and people and the decline of Britain abroad. When Cornwallis surrendered at Yorktown in 1781, British authority in the thirteen colonies ceased. While pleased at the fall of North's government in consequence, Burke was clear about Britain's decline, which had been rapid and marked, because of the turn against the Whigs in the 1760s.

Burke's initial approach to India was similar: he attempted to dissuade the government from further complicating existing relationships. This changed when he became involved in the situation in Tanjore, where his friend William Burke was serving its raja.

He informed Burke that lands had been illegitimately stolen by the East India Company and its ally, the nawab of Arcot. Their return to the raja of Tanjore was favoured by Lord Pigot, Rockingham's supporter and then governor of Madras, but he was deposed in a Company coup. The abuse and loss of property of Britain's allies was occurring apace in India and North America. Burke was becoming much more involved in affairs in India as the leading member of a select committee overseeing the supreme court at Calcutta, which North's Regulating Act had established in 1773. Such work led Burke to accuse Lord North of acting in a manner that would ensure that he lost not just one empire, that of the west, but another in the east.[35]

A series of reports emanating from Burke's committee, especially the Ninth Report of June 1783, damned the situation in India as a product of rapacious merchants turning governors. The fundamental mistake being made in India was the same as that at Westminster – traditional leaders, wise and connected to the soil through their ownership of land, were being replaced by men seeking profit alone or the pleasure of their masters, including ultimately the king. The loss of the Whigs and their replacement by stooges or traders was destroying Britain's Empire, and thereby undermining the capacity of the state to preserve itself against France and other jealous powers.

Whether it was through William Burke, direct evidence to Parliament and its committees or via another of his friends, Philip Francis, who served on the East India Company council at Calcutta, Burke became convinced that a significant root of the evil was Warren Hastings, the first person appointed governor-general of Fort William in Bengal in 1773. Hastings, it was reported, had become ludicrously wealthy from his Indian offices.[36] Burke described him as the apotheosis of British decline. While he had overseen the East India Company, British possessions had been threatened by Hyder Ali, the ruler of Mysore. In the second Anglo-Mysore war, Company forces were defeated at the Battle of Pollilur and Madras was threatened. That war came to an end in 1784 with the Treaty of

Mangalore, and Hastings's supporters considered him to have saved British India. He returned to Britain in June 1785, to be portrayed by Burke as self-serving and treacherous, an agent of the mercantile system and corrupt empire, which had lost Britain America and, if Hastings had his way, would do the same in India.

Burke's reasoning in Hastings's case was that debts, such as those of the nawab of Arcot, were being passed on to the taxpayers of Britain, who were forced to step in to save the Company from bankruptcy, while those who had caused the debts to be created were filling their pockets with ill-gotten profit. In a speech of 28 February 1785 to Parliament, Burke condemned Hastings and North as self-serving monsters responsible for ruining Britain by their neglect of the public good.[37] Becoming obsessed with Hastings and accusing him of the dreadful treatment of native peoples, including the Rohilla tribes of Oudh, and of existing rulers, such as Chet Singh, the ruler of Benares, whom Hastings deposed, Burke called for his impeachment, charging him in the House of Commons on 4 April 1786. Through the support of Fox and William Pitt the Younger, then prime minister, Burke's indictment succeeded on 13 June.[38]

It took two full sessions to secure Commons agreement on the charges, and the trial before the Lords did not begin until 13 February 1788. Burke then became concerned that the evils he had identified in Britain were replicating themselves – the presiding judge had to be the lord chancellor, Edward, Lord Thurlow, who was a school friend of Hastings. Burke's worries were brilliantly captured by William Dent in a popular print which appeared on 28 February 1788, entitled 'Alexander the Great Conquering all the World'.[39] The message was clear: Britain might literally burst if it continued on its current path. Edward Thurlow represents Britain, with his grotesquely inflated stomach, the globe. He faces Hastings, who pours into an aperture in the globe guineas from the end of his turban which expands into a cornucopia. Thurlow's legs are marked 'Bengal' and 'Ireland', supporting the world through the wealth they generated while being the victim states of Britain's mercantile system.

In addition to bringing Hastings to justice, Burke supported what he termed 'economical reform' to limit government expenditure, especially on places and pensions which he believed the King's Friends could not live without. Hopes were raised when, in March 1782, Rockingham became prime minister after sixteen years in opposition, with his two leading Whig lieutenants Fox and Shelburne at the foreign office and the home department, respectively. Burke became paymaster general for the army. Disaster soon struck, however, with Rockingham's unexpected death on 1 July. Both Fox and Burke resigned rather than serve under Shelburne. Trust did not exist between the men, although Fox was to prove at least as complicated and far less consistent than Shelburne. After the latter fell in 1783, attacked in Parliament for bringing peace to North America, the Fox–North coalition saw Burke return to his role of paymaster general while drafting legislation for the reform of the East India Company.

One element of Burke's plan was to put politicians in charge of the activities of the Company when it came to matters of Indian politics. Although this was entirely in line with his philosophy, because Whigs could be trusted to pursue the public good while avoiding the temptation to act with enthusiasm or autocratically, Burke was accused of seeking to turn Fox into an Oriental despot. Satirical prints had Fox riding an elephant dressed as a pasha led by Burke, who had replaced the description 'friend of the people' with 'king of kings'.[40]

George III was furious, as the appointments Burke had in mind to oversee the Company were beyond the influence of the monarch. After the king warned that anyone who supported the bill would no longer be considered his friend, the legislation failed along with the government. William Pitt was brought into office and the resulting general election of March 1784 confirmed him in power.

Burke went into opposition once again, lamenting that the power of the Commons was 'worse than extinguished', that the people and the court together had pulled it down and 'demolition is very complete'.[41] There were minor victories, such as the prevention in

Parliament of Pitt's plan to alter the commercial relationship between Britain and Ireland, giving the Irish a modicum of free trade within the Empire. A sign of Burke's desperation concerning British politics came after November 1788, when he supported Fox in demanding the transfer of monarchical authority from George III to the prince regent when the former had descended into the depths of madness. That the Whigs were so unpopular with the public and incapable of forming a government except through such measures underlined Burke's dilemma; creating a popular party was something Burke always opposed because it risked becoming populist, meaning yielding authority to self-serving and ungrounded fanatics, hence the only route to the restoration of Whig power was through becoming new King's Friends themselves. A further factor was the lack of progress in Hastings's trial, which crawled on to April 1795, when the Lords found him not guilty. One of the key facts about Burke's life is his perception of having failed. He did not blame himself, though, but rather the altered times. As a leading Whig, Burke believed he should have seen office more regularly but instead, due to the king and the turbulence of the people, he watched Britain decline and risk chaos from the sidelines.

IV

Burke's political genius was in part a result of his frequent reflection on the possibility of times worse than the present. Rather than lamenting recent history, Burke's response was to work out what policy might prevent further decline. Britain, for example, remained a free state in which property was secure, however much the Whigs had been neglected in recent decades. Such a perspective gave him tools, he believed, to analyse ideas that were presented as curing the ills of a state, but which in fact risked doing more damage. This was clear in the case of the French Revolution, in a series of innovative and radical laws that transformed politics and the social order rapidly in 1789, enacted during popular rebellion against despotism. Rather than their being a solution to the problem of the end of enlightenment, though, Burke quickly concluded that the revolutionaries were less original than they believed and far, far more deadly. In November 1789 he called them slaves on the grounds that they were creating a polity in which the popular will of the people, always difficult to harness or control, was set above reason and justice, creating what Burke termed the 'worst of all slavery – that is, the despotism of their own blind and brutal passions'.[42] The French had 'made a revolution but not a reformation'. They had 'subverted monarchy, but not recovered freedom'. As such they were like the Romans under Sulla and Caesar, giving a check to patrician power but risking the collapse of liberty through the imperial rule of an Augustus, or giving power to the wild renegades Marius and Saturninus who did whatever they wanted in the name of the people when serving as tribunes.

Having warned against jeremiad literature throughout his career, Burke embraced the genre he knew so well in 1790 with the publication of his most famous work, the *Reflections on the Revolution in France*. In this moment, it was a book akin to *1984*. It used the recent history of France to warn against a likely future for Britain, if British politicians, as Burke feared, fully abandoned Rockingham Whiggery – which he was soon to call the principles 'Old Whigs' – for a populist strategy of radical reform associated with the 'New Whigs'.[43]

The French revolutionaries in their actions since early 1789 had rejected every element of Burke's philosophical credo, from the necessity of a landed aristocracy and established Church, to limits upon the power of the people and the countenancing of the populace as direct political agents. The American Revolution for Burke had been altogether different, having a multitude of sometime Whigs defending liberty, social hierarchy, property and religion. France, instead, was putting into practice a strategy that Burke personally associated with Shelburne and the Dissenters. While they saw themselves to be battling for enlightenment, Burke's view was that their remedies were far worse than the disease, because they would break the existing social order. When the limits upon political action embodied by rank and church were replaced by equality and a secular civil religion, Burke held that power came to be separated from property, so that legislators became furious and extravagant republicans.[44]

Burke held that democratic doctrines everywhere fostered ignorance and cruelty, being akin to the fanaticism of extreme religious belief. Democratic government generated tyranny for the same reason.[45] In these arguments, Burke was sure that his longstanding philosophy was being vindicated by events in France and that the crisis, being so substantial, might well see a return of the Whigs and the rule of a Rockingham-type figure in conditions of support from the monarch and the people, very different to the long period of opposition they had in fact suffered.

In a letter to his friend Philip Francis of 20 February 1790, Burke drew a parallel between reformers in France and in Britain, linked by the 'coffee-houses of Paris and the Dissenting meeting houses of London'. He had been infuriated by Price's sermon at the Revolution Society second anniversary meeting, drawing a direct parallel between events in France and the Glorious Revolution, arguing that both events a hundred years apart had seen the people take power to defend their rights. For Burke, such a claim was fatuous to the point of insanity. He declared that his intention in writing the *Reflections* was not 'controversy with Dr Price, or Lord Shelburne, or any other of their set', but rather a complete refutation of their politics: '. . . to set in full view the danger from their wicked principles and their black hearts'.[46] Burke saw in France a combination of Price's and Shelburne's 'sordid and degenerate philosophy' and a new monied interest seeking to benefit from the confiscation and sale of Church lands. That 'speculations of finance' were justifying the Revolution made it all the more likely to descend into civil war.

A reader called Captain Thomas Mercer wrote to Burke to say that he must be contradicting himself and foolishly turning his back upon a Whiggish battle for liberty in Paris, since the representative government replacing despotism in France was alone 'fit for rational beings to live under and submit to'.[47] Burke's reply was that the French Revolution represented a new species of assault upon liberty since 'The *tyranny* of a multitude is but a multiplied *tyranny*.' In a few months the French democrats, as Burke called them, had done more damage to freedom than 'all the arbitrary monarchs in Europe'.[48] Burke presented the evidence in the *Reflections* in the form of the shabby treatment of Marie-Antoinette when the mob invaded her apartments at Versailles on 6 October 1789. The near assassination of France's queen at the hands of a murderous mob signified the loss of 'that generous loyalty to sex and rank, that dignified submission'. Burke lamented the abrupt termination of a culture characterized by 'noble equality', in which the practice of honour and respect for status created an ethical code by which the eminent served those beneath them and the people venerated the great for their justice and generosity. He detested the female furies who were marching in Paris.[49] In the past, nobility, church and monarch together prevented the kinds of violence and upheaval that were commonplace in revolutionary France.[50] Burke concluded that the 'age of chivalry' had been replaced in France by another dominated by 'œconomists, and calculators'.

That a monied interest might well unite with philosophers in Britain to pursue the same course as France was Burke's admonishment. The commercial rich might see the collapse of the landed aristocracy as an opportunity to make profits and add to their own wealth, just as the English gentry did when Henry VIII closed the monasteries. The mechanism would be the coming to power of the Dissenters, such as Joseph Priestley and Price, for whom Christ was anticipated to restore man's God-given gift of reason. Burke feared their Unitarianism – a belief in a single God rather than in the Trinity – was at the point where it could turn apocalyptic and revolutionary, presaging the return of Christ by political turbulence.

As early as the 1770s Burke had stated that these thinkers were closet republicans and had indicted the Dissenting interest for working to divide and weaken Britain.[51] At the same time he had supported reform which would have seen the removal of civil restrictions upon Dissenters and Catholics. Yet in May 1789 Burke had absented himself from a debate about the repeal of the Test and Corporation Acts of 1661, 1673 and 1678 – the restriction of the civil liberties of those who refused to assent to the sacraments of the Church of England – while claiming continued sympathy with the Dissenting cause.[52] The real reason was his manifest suspicion of the growing radicalism of the group and their advocacy of a politics based upon the rights of man.[53] Burke was sure that there was something natural in Dissent aligning itself with the French revolutionary cause. Dissenters and Jacobins, as the 1790s progressed, could be lumped together. As he wrote in September 1791, 'the body of the Dissenters' formed a dangerous 'Phalanx of party' that was 'a more active, a more spirited and a more united body, than the Jacobites ever were'.[54] When discussing the Dissenters Burke tended to employ metaphors about fire. He saw the group he termed 'English Jacobins' to be akin to the embers of a blaze, 'still alive under the Ashes', such that 'Every encouragement direct or indirect, given to their Brethren in France, stirs and animates the Embers.'

The problem for Burke was that the British people were more than likely to follow the New Whigs rather than the Old. There was a hint of Catharine Macaulay in Burke's analysis of the corruption of the people and their willingness to take the poison of innovative doctrine, although Burke was certain the revolutionary draughts had in fact been brewed by Macaulay herself. The New Whigs had fallen for 'a general evil' whose 'spirit lies deep in the corruptions of our common nature'. Terrifyingly, 'it exists in every country in Europe.'[55] They had been seduced by the siren song of French legislators, themselves drawing on the Commonwealthmen:

It seems, we have put wax into our ears, to shut them up against the tender, soothing strains, in the *affettuoso* of humanity, warbled from the throats of Reubel, Carnot, Tallien, and the whole chorus of Confiscators, domiciliary Visitors, Committee-men of Research, Jurors and Presidents of Revolutionary Tribunals, Regicides, Assassins, Massacrers and Septembrizers. It is not difficult to discern what sort of humanity our Government is to learn from these syren [sic] singers.[56]

Still worse for Burke was that his own Whig colleagues increasingly shared the views of Price and Shelburne. In the Commons in February 1790, Burke called the French declaration of the rights of man a 'digest of anarchy' causing the state to be torn to pieces. This led his long-term Whig associate the playwright Richard Brinsley Sheridan to declare himself friend no more. Fox was ever-more critical of Burke, whom he considered to have turned a Tory and a hypocrite, and the final termination of their political alliance came on 6 May 1791 in the Commons, after which, despite Fox's tears and appeals, Burke sat with Pitt and the government.[57] On Burke's deathbed six years later, Fox was refused an entrance; reconciliation was unimaginable.

Although he had been so critical of the king and the actions of the King's Friends in politics for such an extended period, Burke now saw the court party and Pitt's administration as the defenders of the old order, re-describing them as latter-day Rockinghams. After attending a royal levee early in 1791, Burke was praised for his defence of 'the cause of the Gentlemen'.[58] In a political somersault, those Burke had long damned for causing Britain's decline were now identified as having been Whigs all along sustaining the polity. Such reimagining of history and the contemporary political land-scape were the direct effect of the French Revolution. Burke was looking for allies and desperate because of the power of France and of the republican ideology sustaining the new state.

Burke's new friendships did not prevent him from attacking the House of Lords as committing a grave mistake in not convicting Hastings in 1795. The failure to serve out justice to abuse and cor-ruption, Burke said, did more than anything else to encourage domestic revolutionaries. The mercantile system he identified in India and which Hastings embodied, he now perceived to have taken root in Ireland, where Catholic Emancipation continued to be impeded. He went so far as to relate directly together the mercantile system that he found across the British Empire and the related system of republicanism then rampant in Paris, through which politicians were serving themselves in the name of the people, being the product of fanatic belief and resulting in tyranny:

> I think I can hardly overrate the malignity of the principles of Prot-
> estant ascendancy, as they affect Ireland; or of Indianism, as they
> affect these countries, and as they affect Asia; or of Jacobinism, as
> they affect all Europe, and the state of human society itself.[59]

This was very much the playbook of Hume and Smith or indeed Shelburne.

The predictions presented in his *Reflections on the Revolution in France* about the damage being done to France by events in Paris speedily became reality. Burke began, by many, to be venerated as something of a prophet.[60] Revolutionaries, who for some had been sympathetic figures, were now, for most, violent barbarians and rude savages.[61] The Revolution now amounted to the worst kind of civil war, uprooting rank and religion, dividing families and fostering a vast emigration. By collapsing the social and religious orders of society France had been irredeemably weakened, just as Britain had been weakened by similar experimentation since the 1760s. Government was in a parlous state and moderation had made an exit from the public arena. Ill-bred brutes were taking control of the state. Property was no longer being respected. What Burke called 'the ruin of their country' would necessarily follow.[62] Rulers had taken charge who were unqualified for their roles, many of them being 'of the lowest condition'.[63]

V

Many still see Burke as the defender of a conservative ideology in the sense that he sought to maintain those institutions he believed upheld a free state in a condition of liberty: the crown, the church and the aristocracy, in the case of Britain's mixed polity, in circumstances of the rule of law, and political liberty in the form of the representation of the commons.[64] It is certainly the case that Burke had this view of Britain, but most readers of Burke have failed to examine the final works of his life, when he had to adapt to a world which he saw, like Gibbon, to have been destroyed by republican military power of unparalleled historical force. Like Gibbon and Hume, Burke was of the view that enlightenment politics had failed along with the Whig ascendency, although it was only in the 1790s that the full effects of the end of enlightenment were experienced. New forms of superstition had been unleashed, more transformative of society than the most fanatic Puritanism. New political doctrines were necessary if elements of the old world were to be salvaged for the new. Moderates, as Burke saw himself to be, had suddenly to cope with revolutionaries selling an addictive moonshine, being 'the projectors of deception'.[65]

For Burke, as for Gibbon, the key event was the defeat of the Duke of Brunswick at Valmy in September 1792. Burke had already identified Brunswick's progress as 'the most important crisis that ever existed in the world'.[66] In a letter he wrote that 'The Duke of Brunswick is as much fighting the Battle of the Crown of England as the Duke of Cumberland did at Culloden.'[67] The outcome was devastating. Burke could not understand how Brunswick's professional soldiers had been defeated by 'a troop of strolling players with a buffoon [Charles-François du Périer Dumouriez] at their head'. Burke blamed Brunswick and praised the French commander François-Christophe de Kellermann: 'vigour and decision, though joined with crime, folly and madness, have triumphed.' Burke became concerned that all of Europe would fall to the revolutionary horde. He went so far as to write that 'their mountains will not protect the Swiss.'[68] Burke's mood became blacker still as Dumouriez's forces overran the Austrian Netherlands after another victory at Jemappes on 6 November.

Burke was convinced that the power balance between Europe's

states had been drastically altered. When the First French Republic was proclaimed in September 1792, a new focus had been given to revolutionary ideology. Burke called the new republic 'a vast, tremendous, unformed spectre, in a far more terrific guise than any which ever yet have overpowered the imagination and subdued the fortitude of man.'[69] Everywhere Burke believed he saw effusive speeches and tracts written in favour of republican liberty as the basis of a new world being created. Wild patriotic devotion to a republican motherland translated into military supremacy: the larger the number of citizens who would be willing to lay down their lives, the larger the potential armies of France.

The certainties of the *Reflections* were gone, and Burke was a prophet no more – he had evidently been mistaken that revolution would translate into decline. He had never been a circumspect author or politician, yet for the first time in his life he expressed doubt and apprehension. The feeling never left him. Two months before his death in July 1797 he wrote to French Laurence, his friend and an MP, that 'the times are so deplorable, that I do not know how to write about them.'[70] Burke could not account for the popularity and spread of the revolutionary contagion. A new force had been created in politics and the acknowledged rules of political life were being torn up. Revolutionary movements in the past seeking to upend social ranks and mores, bodies of Levellers and Epicureans, Burke said had been an 'unenterprising race'. The French revolutionaries, however, were 'grown active, designing, turbulent and seditious'. They were 'sworn enemies to Kings, Nobility and Priesthood'. Burke was not surprised that one of the most prominent leaders was the philosopher Condorcet, 'the friend and correspondent of Priestley', who had become 'the most furious of the extravagant Republicans'.[71]

For Burke, the invasion of the states of Europe by French soldiers should have been fought by the populace, but instead the newly subject peoples welcomed the armies. A bankrupt state whose economy was in tatters should not have been able to wage war effectively, let alone mount bold new campaigns across numerous theatres. The monarchs, noble ranks and clerical orders of the continent should have been able to combat the revolutionaries rather than crumbling, as if accepting that they were indeed outdated and illegitimate. For the first time in the history of Europe an imperial power bent on dominion was being called liberator and friend to mankind:

> The poison of other States is the food of the new Republick. That bankruptcy, the very apprehension of which is one of the causes assigned for the fall of the Monarchy, was the capital on which she opened her traffick with the world. The Republick of Regicide, with an annihilated revenue, with defaced manufactures, with a ruined commerce, with an uncultivated and half depopulated country, with a discontented, distressed, enslaved, and famished people, passing with a rapid, eccentrick, incalculable course from the wildest anarchy to the sternest despotism, has actually conquered the finest parts of Europe, has distressed, disunited, deranged, and broke to pieces all the rest; and so subdued the minds of the rulers in every nation.[72]

Burke was worried that Britain, increasingly exhausted by war and concerned about bankruptcy, would soon be conquered too. He was worried that forces within domestic British politics had already sold out to republican France. Powerful figures in British life, including Charles James Fox, Shelburne, Sheridan, Price, Charles Stanhope (Mahon) and John Horne Tooke had all, Burke believed, been seduced. They were forming a party of New Whigs, supportive of revolutionary enthusiasm and fanaticism. Burke was sure that they represented a fifth column that wanted to shift British politics away from its historic foundations and to create a constitution anew in accordance with the principles of enthusiastic reason. These men were, Burke's son Richard wrote, 'wading on, step by step, 'till they are out of the depth of all morality'.[73] Burke himself added 'Paine, Priestley, Price, [George] Rouse [Rous], [James] Mackintosh, [Thomas] Christie &ca &ca &ca'.[74] Any supporter of the French

Revolution, even if their assessment of events at Paris was nuanced, was dangerous and deluded according to Burke.

When peace initiatives were being considered by William Pitt the Younger in 1795, Burke was altogether horrified. The British, he argued, had to acknowledge that they were 'at war with a system, which, by its essence, is inimical to all other Governments, and which makes peace or war, as peace and war may best contribute to their subversion'. The great danger was that the French Republic had 'a faction of opinion, and of interest, and of enthusiasm, in every country'. It amounted to 'a Colossus which bestrides our channel. It has one foot on a foreign shore, the other upon the British soil.'[75] Peace with such a state amounted to surrender. Burke was not surprised in April 1797 at news of the Spithead mutiny, when sailors of the Royal Navy created a miniature republic on the Solent off Portsmouth Harbour. He called it 'the first nidus and hotbed of their [French] infection'. It might well be a prelude to a French invading force 'convoyed by a British Navy to an attack upon this kingdom'.[76]

VI

In Burke's eye there was, however, a small ray of hope. It amounted to the identification of a possible 'after enlightenment' that might be able to cope with the problems raised by the end of enlightenment. If British patriotism, commercial power and military strength could be fully mobilized, then French revolutionary enthusiasm and fanaticism might yet be defeated. This was the message of Burke's last great work, *Letters on a Regicide Peace*, published in October 1796, directed against signs of dangerous appeasement on the part of Pitt's government. Burke drew a parallel between those who advocated peace with the French Republic – on the grounds that Britain could never defeat the revolutionary state – and those who had prophesised defeat for Britain on the eve of the Seven Years' War. In the latter camp, Burke held up John Brown's *Estimate of*

Manners, just as he had in the late 1760s. Brown's work had, he recalled, been received rapturously as a work of Pythagorean certainty – selling out edition after edition.

Brown had asserted that the corruption of manners in the form of an addiction to luxury and resulting effeminacy in Britain would lead to military defeat – but he was wrong. Equally, Burke argued that the jeremiad voices of the 1790s might be proved false because 'the heart of the citizen', being 'a perennial spring of energy to the state', could bring the British to victory. Burke wrote that although Britain's 'pulse seems to intermit, we must not presume that it will cease instantly to beat'. The public 'must never be regarded as incurable'. Equally, modern Europe had been in a more flourishing state than any historic continent and enjoyed more liberty even than the ancient republics. So, Europe had to be protected at all costs against the revolutionary virus and contagion.[77] This was the goal of Burke's final publications and private letters: to fortify that heart, to convince the British people of what was at stake, of the importance of making every possible sacrifice to defeat France and save Europe, and that death in the cause of ruining the French Revolution was the ultimate moral act.

It is significant that in his vision of a Britain newly enthused with a patriotism capable of defeating France, Burke turned to the Saxon jurist Emer de Vattel. This has been noted by numerous interpreters.[78] Like Vattel writing in the aftermath of the War of the Austrian Succession at the end of the 1740s, Burke argued that Europe amounted to a moral entity, being composed of Christian states that had embraced an identifiable moral code and defended one another when necessary, particularly against attempts at universal monarchy. As Burke put it, 'no citizen of Europe could be altogether an exile in any part of it', having had their sense of self and national culture shaped by the forces of Germanic law building on the foundations of Roman Law:

The writers on public law have often called this aggregate of nations a Commonwealth. They had reason. It is virtually one great state having the same basis of general law; with some diversity of provincial customs and local establishments. The nations of Europe have had the very same Christian religion, agreeing in the fundamental parts, varying a little in the ceremonies and in the subordinate doctrines. The whole of the polity and economy of every country in Europe has been derived from the same sources. It was drawn from the old Germanic or Gothic customary; from the feudal institutions which must be considered as an emanation from that customary; and the whole has been improved and digested into system and discipline by the Roman law. From hence arose the several orders, with or without a Monarch, which are called States, in every European country.[79]

Burke's distinctive assertions made no mention of the Catholic Church. The radical conclusion was that France rather than Britain was now the most unnatural of states. The French Republic was erected upon a legal foundation 'contrary to that of the wise Legislators of all countries, who aimed at improving instincts into morals, and at grafting the virtues on the stock of the natural affections'.[80] The Revolution had broken the ties of human associations, replacing a code based on honourable manners and morals with one in which the most violent and fanatic demagogue was the most likely to enjoy the support of a deluded populace.[81] This meant that the attempt at creating a universal republic was far more pernicious than any of Louis XIV's imperial dreams. It had to be fought to the death.

Burke had always seen France as a threat to the 'system of Europe, taking in laws, manners, religion, and politics, in which I delighted so much'.[82] In the past, however, Burke had not considered it to be necessary for Britain to combat France directly on mainland Europe, to invade France itself, or to become involved in mainland European politics in the sense of directing international relations between fellow states. The French Revolution altered everything. Burke began to argue that it was necessary to restore the French monarchy, its civil and ecclesiastical orders and their property. The only means to such an end was a revolution in British foreign policy, entailing intervention in Europe in order to keep the peace, to protect the old world, and maintain it for the economic development of all those states who favoured trade, morals and religion.[83] Britain had to become, he argued, 'the great resource of Europe'. Britain could no longer be 'detached from the rest of the world, and amusing herself with the puppet-shew of a naval power'. Rather, Britain had to be 'embodied with Europe'. The resulting war was 'just, necessary, manly, pious'. Its goal was to 'preserve political independence and civil freedom to nations . . . national independence, property, liberty, life, and honour, from certain universal havoc'.[84] In short, it was 'a war for . . . and of all nations'.[85] Defeat would entail for Europe another decline and fall.

There was a further parallel with Vattel. Like the Saxon jurist, Burke was under no illusion about the trend of the times. However vocal the claim might be that Christian morality was a shared continental heritage, it could not be relied upon to overcome domestic or international divisions. The countries of Europe were also divided into rich and poor, weak and strong, due in part to the commercial dominion of the British and the effects of their mercantile system. Christianity could not, therefore, be relied upon to do the work of papering over social cracks or gluing broken social fragments together to make a unified whole. In other words, Burke seemed to be arguing against his former self. He had damned Britain as an unnatural empire promoting immorality and corruption, not only in North America but also across India. Burke had been, to his critics, an arch-advocate of the end of enlightenment in Britain, arguing in accordance with the works of his friends Hume and Smith. Yet he was now lauding Britain as a state with an unblemished record of liberty and union.

For Burke, however, Ireland remained a particularly weak point for Britain, because in Ireland the British could straightforwardly be presented as tyrannical brutes. The philosophy of *Liberté, égalité, fraternité* being expounded in France straightforwardly made sense to oppressed and impoverished Irish Catholics. It might well present the means to a better life in terms of freedom and wealth. Burke called Ireland 'a melancholy infirmary', meaning a madhouse full of people so ill at ease with their predicament that no obvious solution offered itself, given the refusal to emancipate the Catholic majority.[86] Burke believed that the refusal to embrace the people of Ireland risked the end of Europe, because the funds being spent upon the maintenance of British control would have been sufficient to pay a Russian army to combat directly the French.[87]

In his *Letters on a Regicide Peace,* Burke was now representing the same politicians he had vilified in 1786 as contributors to a wondrous political system that alone could save European liberty. It was deemed by many to be going too far. That a man who had condemned the partition of Poland now advised subsidizing the armies of Europe's imperially minded autocracies was condemned as hypocritical. Even radical Whigs who turned towards Burke, such as James Mackintosh, because they too were horrified by the progress of the French Revolution, could not accept that such an advocate of liberty, someone who detested like Gibbon the loss of the small states, was now accepting of Europe's absolute monarchies.[88] The French revolutionaries, by contrast, were effectively creating a new world and in doing so saw themselves to be moving towards what ought to be termed 'after enlightenment', having accepted the failure of the eighteenth-century political doctrines they had inherited. Restoring the world to a state of perfect justice was seen by many to be on the cusp of realization, so great was the social union that had been established in France on the ruins of monarchy, aristocracy and the established Church.

This was the reason that, just like his friend Gibbon, Burke died depressed, expecting the French Revolution to make further conquests and to perhaps destroy Britain itself. Rather than defending that which existed, the only way of combating revolutionary ferocity and enthusiasm was to create a Britain dedicated to the pursuit of war, a government for war, rather than a government of laws or of men. Ironically, for altogether opposed reasons, French revolutionary republicans, including Thomas Paine and Mary Wollstonecraft, came to similar conclusions, just as their own attempts to move beyond the end of enlightenment failed.

7.

Jacques-Pierre Brissot and the End of Empire

I

On 31 October 1793, in the first moments of the Reign of Terror, Jacques-Pierre Brissot went to meet his death by guillotine. On his way to the scaffold, he sang the 'Marseillaise', the battle hymn of the Revolution. Despite ultimately being consumed by the radical change he had helped to bring about, his hatred had not waned for the international enemies of this new French republic.[1] But Brissot perceived the Revolution to be threatened by domestic bodies too, above all the Paris Commune and the Montagnard group led by Robespierre, in addition to the national guard of *sans-culottes* led by François Hanriot.[2] He believed that such factions, exactly in the manner of a mercantile system, were controlling state action for their own ends, rather than for the public good.

With Hanriot's men armed with cannon and pikes stationed outside the Convention, Montagnard deputies led by the president, Marie-Jean Hérault de Séchelles, had moved for the arrest of Brissot and other members of his Girondin group on 2 June 1793, after which they were rounded up, convicted of treason in October and executed. Before Brissot met his fate, in a personal justification, he called for the massacre of barbarous Montagnards and the leaders of the mob of *sans-culottes* using precisely the same justification as his enemies, the necessity of saving the Revolution. Anarchists, Brissot claimed, had betrayed the principles of 1789 by domestic terrorism and international piracy. The invasion of Belgium, for example, ought to have been a war of liberation, but in fact entailed pillage and despoliation, often for the benefit of powerful Montagnard politicians.[3] However vibrant and glorious the songs might be, the process of establishing and spreading liberty had not gone as planned.

Looking back on his life from prison, Brissot composed his memoirs. He presented himself as a consistent advocate of 'the true principles of liberty and equality' and a perpetual warrior for liberty, having waged 'war, with unshaken fortitude, against all the prejudices which form a rampart around the privileged tribes, and all the abuses of despotism'.[4] Many contemporaries, not least the enemies who were on the verge of judicially murdering him, would have disagreed with Brissot's self-assessment. So would his critics across Britain who considered him a fanatic, a peddler of a corrosive revolutionary religion. Historians have been similarly divided. Their views are worth brief consideration because they underline how difficult it is to explain what Brissot was doing, reflecting in turn the problem of understanding the Revolution and the response to its failure.

The leading historian Robert Darnton has portrayed Brissot as learning revolution from Rousseau's *Contrat social* of 1762, which railed against the injustice of peoples being born free but living in chains. Darnton has described Brissot living from hand to mouth, becoming a 'gutter Rousseau', to the point of being forced by bankruptcy into the life of a police spy after a spell in the Bastille, between 12 July and September 1784, for spreading copies of a *libelle* critical of Queen Marie Antoinette.[5] According to Darnton, Brissot became supportive of radical action after this experience through his horror at a regime which forced its *philosophes* to corrupt themselves in order to survive.[6] It was Brissot's adoration of Rousseau that inspired his passionate commitment to an alternative political culture in 1789, one that was democratic, popular, radical and passionate, one that mobilized Grub Street against the elite writers, the followers of Voltaire, who stood for satire, moderation and enlightened reform.[7]

Darnton has long argued that Brissot found Rousseau's vision of a free society realized in Michel-Guillaume-Jean de Crèvecoeur's *Letters from an American Farmer*, a popular book of 1782 venerating

Soldiers pillaging and massacring innocent civilians, using religion to justify murder and torture, is a central theme of Jacques Callot's prints *The Miseries of War* (*Les Grandes Misères de la guerre*), first published in 1633 during the horrors of the Thirty Year's War (1618–48).

The Dutch Republic in the seventeenth century demonstrated the wealth and power attainable by societies underpinned by international trade, with ships and merchants able to seek out and exploit markets across the globe. (Ludolf Bakhuizen, *Nederlandse schepen op de rede van Texel* [*Dutch ships in the Texel roadsted*], 1671).

Fierce speculation on Spain's colonies in South America caused the South Sea Bubble and subsequent collapse. This is lampooned in William Hogarth's *Emblematical Print on the South Sea Scheme*, 1721: an excessive lust for commerce leads to social collapse, the end of morality and the erection of monuments to greed and excess that dwarf St Paul's Cathedral.

The serene philosopher David Hume in 1766, just as he was coming to the conclusion that strategies to sustain enlightenment were failing. (Allan Ramsay, 'David Hume, 1711–1776. Historian and philosopher').

William Petty, Lord Shelburne in 1766, serving under William Pitt the Elder as Secretary of State for the Southern Department. Shelburne had already started to gather the best and brightest to combat enlightenment's demise. (Sir Joshua Reynolds, William Petty, 1st Marquess of Lansdowne (Lord Shelburne).

The purpose of history is to guide the politics of the present. Catharine Macaulay in Roman garb, wearing the purple sash of a senator, showing her support for reform in general and the American Revolution in particular. Mary Wollstonecraft called her 'a woman of the greatest ability, undoubtedly, this country has ever produced.' (Robert Edge Pine, 'Catharine Macaulay (née Sawbridge)', c. 1775).

The simple garb of a committed republican. Mary Wollstonecraft, pregnant in 1797 with Mary Shelley, had dedicated herself to the cause of revolutionary France. Her husband, William Godwin, hung this picture above his fireplace after his wife's death. (John Opie, 'Mary Wollstonecraft', 1797).

The message of James Gillray's *The tree of liberty must be planted immediately!* (1797) is clear: supporting the French Revolution leads to terror and execution. It imagines the decapitation of the leader of the Whig party, Charles James Fox, wearing the red hat of liberty, and fellow supporters of the First French Republic.

In William Dent's 'Revolution Anniversary or, Patriotic Incantations', 1971, modern witches – Joseph Priestley, Charles James Fox, Joseph Towers and Richard Sheridan – are portrayed dancing around their French cauldron, fostering devilry, fanaticism, violence and the burning of priests.

By 1805, mercantile systems were the norm. Seeking global empire, Britain, led by William Pitt the Younger, and France, led by Napoleon Bonaparte, were the dominant powers doing the carving. (James Gillray, 'The Plumb-pudding in danger – or – State Epicures taking un Petit Souper', 1805).

the morals and labours accompanying a life devoted to agriculture. Darnton's Brissot saw agricultural toil as described by Crèvecoeur as the ideal schooling for future citizens, or *Émiles* as he would have put it in accordance with the title of Rousseau's novel of 1762.[8] Other scholars have emphasized the influence of American revolutionary works more generally as the key to Brissot's republicanism, the claim being that it was not Rousseau who created revolutionaries but rather Franklin, Jefferson and other Founding Fathers – the difference being that Brissot believed the seed of rebellion could in fact germinate in France.[9] Initially, however, Brissot lost faith in the possibility of toleration and peace being maintained in Europe. In the late 1780s, Brissot, seeing the turmoil of Europe and the lack of liberty within both commercial and non-commercial empires, seemed dedicated to abandoning the old world for the new. He arrived in Boston towards the end of July 1788, and it was only the shock of the French Revolution that brought him back.[10]

An alternative reading of Brissot has him as a more consistent republican follower of the Commonwealth Tradition in the manner of Catharine Macaulay, rejecting priestcraft and the tyranny of popes and kings. Here too, the impact upon Brissot of reading Rousseau has been seen to be crucial, with particular emphasis upon the statement of his own faith, in Rousseau's profession of the Savoyard vicar in the novel *Émile*. From Rousseau, in short, Brissot learned to hate priests in all established religions as would-be tyrants and to love the core commonwealth principles advocating lives dedicated to the public good. Brissot's *Mémoires* recounted that his deep reading in the *philosophes* when he was young – and he lumped Rousseau together with Voltaire and Diderot – led him to compose pamphlets critical of established Christianity, with Saint Paul, canon law and the papacy his principal adversaries.[11] Brissot's *Rome jugée* and *Lettres philosophiques sur Saint Paul*, written in the late 1770s but published in the early 1780s, sought, like Rousseau, to 'identify religion with straightforward rational truth'.[12] A debt to Voltaire was signalled in the title of the *Lettres philosophiques sur Saint Paul*, which were stated to have been translated from the English 'by the *philosophe* of Ferney', a reference to Voltaire's residence outside Geneva. Brissot's vitriolic opposition to priestcraft generally, his praise for the Commonwealth authors Algernon Sidney and for John Toland, for the Quakers, and for the '*démocrat*' Jesus Christ, has led the historian Leonore Loft to describe Brissot's anticlerical tracts as the root of his republican ideology, dovetailing with the republicanism of the Commonwealthmen which then burgeoned at revolutionary Paris.[13]

Brissot's remarkable intellectual trajectory derived from his fervent belief that enlightenment was ending, that fanaticism and tyranny were spreading and that the cultures and institutions he found around him were set for change. He dedicated himself to preventing the end of enlightenment and this led him to embrace alternative and incompatible strategies at different times. When the French Revolution commenced, Brissot thought that his views were being confirmed by events and that a utopia of peace and prosperity was going to be realized on Earth. On returning from America, he began to dress plainly, in the manner of the Quakers, and saw the Revolution as a secular apocalypse. Yet Brissot ultimately moved from friend of humanity to terrorist between 1789 and 1791. The people, he came to realize, had to be violently forced to be free.

Brissot had, from the time he came to prominence as a leading figure in the Legislative Assembly at Paris from October 1791 until September 1792, consistently advocated the seeking of national unity by violence. In the Legislative Assembly and through his journalism, the latter through the *Patriote François*, the newspaper he edited and largely composed between 2 June 1789 and 28 July 1793, he promoted the policy of defending the revolution by taking arms against its enemies, even to the point of creating an empire for liberty. Brissot's hope, shared by fellow Girondins such as Thomas Paine, was that people across Europe would rise and foment revolution themselves if they were aided by France. Brissot increasingly felt that the peoples of Europe living under corrupt and tyrannical imperial governments needed help from invading French forces to manage the transition from despotism to liberty. Brissot's journey to the guillotine marked a movement from identifying himself as a cosmopolitan enemy of nationalism and empire, a republican who envisaged a world of perpetual peace and thought it could be realized, to being an advocate of ceaseless war against the enemies of France abroad and terror towards domestic opposition.[14] He had begun feeling certain that empires established by a republic/commonwealth like France were by nature empires of liberty. As he died he was less sure, recognizing that nationalists had hijacked the project and that he himself would be branded as a cosmopolitan turned terrorist.

It was from a remarkably early age that Brissot sensed that the Enlightenment was under threat, even from those who considered themselves to be its defenders. As a young man his voluminous works amounted to a mishmash of commonwealth and anticlerical speculations within a broader framework of demands for legal reform through the defence of natural rights. It was no surprise, then, that he became close to Catharine Macaulay when he first visited Britain, having views akin to her own, commencing a correspondence that continued to her death. Even into the early 1780s Brissot, with his support for the American Revolution and defence of liberty across Europe, would not have considered himself to have been far from the views of Burke or Gibbon. All shared a love of the free states of Europe and a deep concern about the threats they faced through the imperialism fostered by jealousy of trade.

But Brissot underwent a political conversion between 1782 and 1785, as related by his *Mémoires*, and the writings, private letters and manuscripts which survived him. By 1783, he had written tracts and books amounting to a reform programme for the French state inspired by Rousseau, Voltaire and prominent philosophers such as Cesare Beccaria, focused on creating laws capable of pushing human behaviour towards practising the public good. In this, as we have seen, he was similar to Shelburne in the 1770s and Richard Price or, indeed, the young Hume. Yet Brissot abandoned his initial approach to reform because of a burgeoning friendship with the Genevan republican Étienne Clavière, who provided Brissot with what he was later to call 'a second education', becoming his mentor in the process. As Brissot wrote in his *Mémoires*, until 1782 he had been 'rather a slave to existing prejudices than an apostle of truth'.[15] Brissot's conversion to a different set of political tactics was confirmed by his involvement, also mainly through Clavière, with the Shelburne Circle. Brissot became obsessed, as all members of the Shelburne Circle were, with getting rid of empire and the systems of commerce and war they sustained. Above all he wanted to take advantage of the opportunities presented to the world following the perceived collapse of Britain's mercantile system in North America at the end of the American revolutionary war.

Creating independent political communities that could defend themselves, maintain peace and espouse the public good, and at the same time avoid a descent into fanaticism, became the grand goal of politics for Brissot from the time he met Clavière. Both men battled to combat the end of enlightenment. Brissot's ultimate reliance upon a national rebirth, by arming the citizens and making them choose between liberty or death, was a further and final tactic he controversially arrived at in the hope, odd though it may sound, of moralizing politics and creating a community that would be independent, ultimately tolerant and immune to war and empire. Turning from a cosmopolitan to a terrorist was less abrupt a change than it might seem: it was the ultimate gamble, one designed to prevent the failure of enlightenment, to stop the world descending into a new dark age. Brissot thereby moved from the Shelburne Circle to being the apotheosis of the fanatic extremes Burke had always discerned to be lurking in the philosophies of Shelburne, Price and their Dissenting friends. The irony was that in Brissot's final calls for all-out war on his enemies, the strategies for saving what he called liberty and enlightenment were akin to those enunciated in Burke's *Regicide Peace* letters.

II

Brissot was born on 15 January 1754 at Chartres, the cathedral city south-west of Paris. His father was a master chef in the catering trade and his mother a devout Catholic devoted to her many children. Brissot was educated at the Collège de Chartres, where he was marked out by his ability to learn languages and by voracious reading. He loved especially the travels of Ferdinand Magellan, George Anson, Francis Drake and Engelbert Kaempfer, the history of China and the works of Plutarch and Fénelon. Choosing to enter the legal profession, Brissot was employed by a local lawyer named Horeau; his studies of civil, canon and criminal law were the basis of ambitious essays on the rights of property. Brissot's studies, especially into Voltaire and Diderot, led eventually to a crisis of faith. Brissot later reported that Rousseau's *La profession de foi du vicaire savoyard* spurred him towards heterodoxy.[16] He described himself as a sceptic and Brissot's attacks upon Catholicism soon became zealous. In 1774, at the age of nineteen, Brissot left Chartres, and a mother disconsolate about the fate of her son's soul, for Paris and the role of clerk to a lawyer named Nolleau. It was at this time too that Brissot added to his name 'de Warville', the anglicized form of Ouarville, a little village where his father owned some property to the east of Chartres. Writing later to the woman who became his wife, Félicité Dupont, Brissot despaired of the people of Chartres, calling them submissive and fanatic imbeciles 'who believe only the oracles of their priests'.[17]

In Paris, Brissot soon gave up law for philosophy, dreaming of becoming a Voltaire or a Beccaria.[18] He wrote to his heroes pressing them for succour and sought patronage everywhere, while trying to make a living from his pen.[19] One of those he appealed to, the polemicist and exponent of paradox Simon-Nicolas-Henri Linguet, advised Brissot against becoming a man of letters, because of the difficulty of consistently obtaining an income.[20] Yet Brissot, ever the passionate and committed activist, obsessively campaigned throughout his twenties for the reform of the penal law in particular and laws in general by precisely defining the public good and the legal procedures and tactics that ensured that, once defined, such a good could be practically embodied in law and legal institutions. He completed a two-volume *Théorie des lois criminelles* in 1778, which Voltaire praised and advised Brissot to send to the Œconomic Society of

Bern.[21] The work was published in 1781 with an oddly inconsistent preface describing the laws and constitution of Britain as a model, while affirming that Brissot was a devoted patriot and loyal to the monarch of France.[22]

The basis of legislation was morality, and Brissot's plans were as much to do with a reformation of morals and education, as well as planning the amelioration of poverty, as they were with law. This was clear from attempts to win prize essay competitions, so popular in these years, such as one on the deadly effects of egotism (*Des funestes effets de l'égoîsme*), which received an honourable mention from the Academy of Besançon, and another essay in defence of a humane legal code abjuring capital punishment, which was crowned by the Academy of Châlons-sur-Marne.[23] Brissot's calls for education and reform led to further work, including an attack on the legal profession in France for its corruption and decadence, *Un indépendant à l'ordre des avocats: sur la décadence du barreau en France* (Berlin, 1781) and the giant compendium that Brissot hoped would be the basis of a new legal education, the ten-volume *Bibliothèque philosophique, du législateur, du politique, du jurisconsulte*, published from 1782, popularized in a further work, the *Correspondance sur ce qui intéresse le bonheur de l'homme et de la société*.

Such large projects dovetailed with Brissot's second obsession, the maintenance of enlightenment. He aimed to do so by identifying and combating the forms of knowledge that kept humanity in darkness, defined by him as the ignorance and superstition he found to be ever-more prevalent across Europe in churches, which then spread across society through the influence of priests. He spent the final months of 1777 writing a book on scepticism. Brissot's position was not that of an Academic Sceptic of the ancient Greek school – he did not argue that it was impossible to have knowledge or that everyone who claimed to have knowledge was dogmatic. Nor was he a follower of Pyrrhonism because he did not advocate suspending judgement. Yet Brissot argued in a Pyrrhonist manner: if studies of God, man and nature were examined, he believed, and academic disciplines from metaphysics to natural philosophy and political economy scrutinized, a farrago of falsehood would emerge. In the 92-page unpublished manuscript of a planned book, entitled the *Plan Raisoné*, Brissot attacked those he termed spiritualists, devout philosophers such as Descartes, Locke, Newton and Clarke, in addition to materialist philosophers such as Spinoza, La Mettrie and d'Holbach. Knowledge existed but was rarely in evidence. Brissot asserted that people believed they were living in the midst of enlightenment (*'au milieu de la lumière'*), but in fact ignorance and stupidity abounded while errors of the past had yet to be vanquished and new errors threatened humanity.[24]

Brissot sought to move from the identification of false knowledge to dangerous religious beliefs, envisaging a table of idolatry covering all cults and superstitions. Although Brissot's *Plan* was never published, it did serve as a basis for several claims in his 1782 book *De la verité*, where he continued to argue that steps had to be taken to combat contemporary enthusiastic beliefs (*'interrogez l'enthousiasme'*), where he warned against taking enlightenment for granted and called for a new science of morality (*'la morale, ou la science de l'homme'*) for the benefit of all of humanity.[25] The generation before him, Brissot believed, had laid the foundation of a new science of positive law by attacking the irrationality and obfuscatory nature of legal systems based on Roman, canon and provincial customary law. Voltaire and Beccaria were seen to be in the vanguard of this movement, perceived by Brissot to be building on Rousseau's call for a return to natural law in his *Discours sur l'inégalité*.[26] In this regard, Brissot believed that the important labour had been undertaken by Helvétius, who had attempted to reconcile moral progress with science and civilization.[27] In *De l'esprit,* Helvétius had revealed the power of *analyse*, the scientific interrogation of ideas to ensure their clarity and certainty by relating them to the experience of sensation, the source of all objective, unassailable knowledge. In skilled hands, sensationalism would allow human beings to restore laws and institutions to their original purity; core ideas derived from sense experience represented a return to the voice of nature, the common goodness implanted in men by God at the Creation. Brissot described himself, following Helvétius, as a modern sceptic, someone who had abandoned the Aristotelian and Christian scholastic fallacies that continued to mislead otherwise enlightened luminaries, such as the brilliant but foolishly devout Locke.

De la verité also contained a sketch of a religion for sceptical philosophers, the end point of Brissot's goal of creating true defences for enlightenment.[28] He continued to seek to prevent religion from turning fanatic, as he was convinced it had been at Chartres during his childhood, embodied by his mother. As a self-described foot soldier in the war against grotesque intolerance, legal injustice and religious prejudice, Brissot formulated his own civil religion. This, grandiosely, entailed specifying the nature of morality and promoting legislation for the good of all while at the same time returning contemporary Christianity to a 'reasonable simplicity', intended to negate and then outlaw the dangerously superstitious effects of the confessional state and priestcraft, whether Catholic or Protestant. In relation to the church, Brissot's programme was indeed radical, condemning original sin, the Calvinist denial of free will and all millenarian movements.[29] It was directly inspired by Rousseau's precisely delineated reformation in his 1764 book *Letters Written from the Mountain* (*Lettres écrites de la montagne*). Religion had been corrupted by politics, leading to false and tyrannical ideas about social morality, particularly polygamy and prostitution, both of which Brissot defended. Religious strife was to be vanquished by uniting the two heads of the church and state eagle, returning to a more personal morality and theology, independent of contentious liturgy and dogma.[30]

Yet while he defended the right of the people to depose and replace their priests, and the right of civil authorities to control churches, it is a mistake to relate Brissot's ideas about the church to republican politics. The *Lettres philosophiques* and *Rome jugée* were critical of church councils and 'democratic' attempts to govern religious belief. Brissot's right to resist tyrants was nowhere synonymous with opposition to kings. Patriotic kings, such as Henri IV of

France, received great praise.[31] The Brissot who emerged from the pamphlets had grand philosophic ambition. He wanted to refute existing materialism (Spinoza and d'Holbach) and quietism (Féne-lon).[32] He believed the supposedly enlightened philosophers of reform, whose works were greedily devoured by new generations of readers, were in fact fostering violence and intolerance. In the *Bibliothèque philosophique* he made the point that d'Holbach's popular *Système de la nature* was too widely read and that d'Holbach, rather than being a friend of liberty, was teaching kings 'to burn their capital and slay their subjects for personal pleasure'.[33]

In steering a middle course between atheism and orthodoxy, Brissot failed to make a name for himself. He could not match d'Holbach's intemperance of language and consequent notoriety. But he did join the swollen ranks of anti-Gallican, anti-Jesuit and anti-Jansenist polemicists. Without the genius of Turgot, and lacking both a mentor and a patron, Brissot remained an impecunious member of Grub Street. But he refused to give up.

III

Brissot would not have described himself as a revolutionary in the late 1770s and early 1780s. He was a minor contributor to a movement within France focused on making law more enlightened, following Montesquieu, but very much within the framework of the 'royal thesis' (*thèse royale*), meaning that he accepted the authority of the monarch in France, the longstanding system of government, and saw reform as possible only through the person of the king. French kings could be patriots, defenders of their people and instruments of social peace. Brissot also accepted that France ought to be the dominant European power and that Britain's rise had been unnatural, explicable only because of the vicissitudes of commerce. The challenge of the times was to restore France to primacy without risking a descent into tyranny and war. This was the goal of France's ministers under the widely praised new monarch Louis XVI, who ascended to the throne aged twenty in 1774. And Brissot had high hopes for official patronage. He began to follow Linguet, whose lackey he was sometimes seen to be, partly because of the latter's links with French ministers.[34]

Brissot was soon contributing to Linguet's *Annales politiques, civiles, et littéraires*, first published in April 1777.[35] The *Annales* was founded because of censorship of Linguet's earlier *Journal de politique et de littérature*. Although the *Annales*, initially published from London, contained attacks on French ministers, and was accompanied by Linguet's *libelles* against them, it is significant that the court was content to allow the journal to circulate openly in France.[36] Linguet's defence of a popular monarch standing above the *parlements*, and also above Britain, was at one with the vision of the future enunciated by Emmanuel Marie Louis, marquis de Noailles, the French ambassador to London, and by Vergennes. As minister for foreign affairs, and a leading contender for the role of patriotic reformer, Vergennes was concerned with the image of France being propagated in journals across Europe.[37] Vergennes gave tacit support to the *Annales* and was in regular contact with Linguet concerning its readership and content.[38]

Brissot's *Testament politique de l'angleterre*, also written in the late 1770s and published in 1780, was intended to attract Vergennes's patronage, a parallel case to the planned book on scepticism intended to impress Diderot. The *Testament* amounted to French propaganda against Britain, and Chatham in particular, arguing that Britain had never been a free state, that since 1688 Britons had been addicted to wars for commercial empire, and that the best outcome for the benefit of Europe and the peoples of the world would be for Britain to collapse. Precisely this was occurring with the disastrous war upon the American colonies which was likely to grow Britain's debt to the point of ruin.[39] According to Brissot, Britons had always been fanatics. The difference in modern times was that a lust for trade had replaced religious motivation as the basis of their fanaticism.

Although Vergennes was always on the lookout for propagandists, he was said to consider Brissot's *Testament* too incendiary, and it was published anonymously outside France. It did succeed in getting Brissot employment, however, as the owner of the *Courier de l'Europe*, Samuel Swinton, liked it and gave Brissot a role in editing the edition published at Boulogne, between the spring of 1778 and the autumn of 1780. Vergennes enjoyed significant influence over Swinton's *Courier de l'Europe*, and the editor was paid to promote the views of the court. The *Courier* was used, Brissot later claimed, by Vergennes to attack his ministerial rival Jacques Necker.[40] When the French censor insisted that the *Courier* ignore French politics altogether Brissot lost his post. At Boulogne, however, he did meet his future wife, Félicité Dupont.

Remarkably, given his subsequent trajectory, Brissot warned against excessive engagement in politics. Man was, he argued, not a political animal by nature: mobs or representatives of the people were to be feared as irrational constraints upon reforming legislators. As long as despotism was avoided, and certain liberties established, individuals could seek happiness and experience tranquillity under a monarch, which Brissot described as the natural form of government for a large state.[41] In *De la verité* he described republicanism and the defence of mixed governments like Britain as dangerous doctrines.[42] Nor was Brissot converted to republicanism by his observance of events in North America. While praising the Pennsylvanian constitutional code, he argued that it was unwise to follow the North Americans, because democracy was not suited to monarchical states.[43] He was pessimistic about North America's prospects because of the lack of proper criminal laws. In following English civil law too closely, they risked creating a state that would see the kind of civil unrest then being experienced in the Dutch Republic.[44]

Brissot's work (hilariously, given what came after) identified enlightened despots as the most capable contemporary rulers, including Joseph II, Frederick II and above all the tsarina Catherine, 'whose name alone is a perfect eulogy'.[45] Brissot hoped to enlighten the Bourbon king Louis XVI, whom he advised to build on the French chancellor René Nicolas Charles Augustin de Maupeou's reforms reducing the power of the regional *parlements* between 1770 and 1774.[46] Brissot's ideal was 'a nation united, well-governed, and by a good king'.[47] Brissot was therefore being misleading in his *Mémoires* when he described his early life as one of consistent opposition to kings and aristocrats, of continued defence of the rights of the people. Between 1776 and the early 1780s he believed the common good to be compatible with rule by enlightened despots who respected the law. He was enunciating a messy and inarticulate vision of Hume's civilized monarchies.

The reason Brissot sought patronage so assiduously was his poverty. His family refused him sustenance unless he returned to the Catholic faith, although the death of his father at the end of 1779 led to him receiving a legacy of 4,000 livres, the equivalent of just over £50,000 today. A desire to satisfy Félicité Dupont's parents regarding his prospects led Brissot to return briefly to law. After his distaste for lawyers was confirmed, Brissot determined to leave France for London. He proposed to establish what he called the *Lycée de Londres*, combining a club to unite *philosophes* who felt themselves to be the 'party of humanity', a school and a corresponding society for defending enlightenment.[48] The idea may have been borrowed from the prospectus published in 1777 by Pahin de Champlain de La Blancherie.[49] Brissot gained financial support from figures such as Jean-Baptiste-Jacques Élie de Beaumont, a lawyer who had written in favour of the persecuted Calais family made notorious by Voltaire. A move to London offered an opportunity to continue to serve Vergennes, who would have appreciated reports from the enemy capital.[50] A *Journal du Lycée de Londres* was also envisaged as a means of spreading pro-French propaganda. It is significant that Brissot initially received a *privilège*, granting official permission to publish this journal for the substantial term of ten years. In early 1784 he was writing to Vergennes seeking similar support for another publication on the state of British science, the *Tableau de l'état des sciences en Angleterre*.[51] There was a further reason: Brissot married in secret in September 1782 because Félicité Dupont, then serving Madame de Genlis in the family of the duc d'Orléans as governess, was worried about losing her position. London offered a different life for them both.

When he moved to London, Brissot courted opposition figures, including Catharine Macaulay but also Priestley, Price and David Williams, the Dissenting minister and educationalist.[52] For Vergennes, Brissot was useful because the pessimism about Britain he espoused was exactly the message that Versailles sought to foster among the French reading public. The fact that it could be transmitted from domestic critics of Britain to Brissot and then to France was better still. When Félicité Dupont translated a summary of Catharine Macaulay's *History of England* in 1783 it was officially sanctioned and then published in Paris.[53]

Like his projects in France, Brissot's London *Lycée* failed. The reason was unquestionably financial, although Brissot later claimed that Vergennes had both ordered the closure and offered to cover the costs.[54] Brissot must have fallen foul of the minister because a government order (*arrêt du conseil*) terminated the *privilège* of the *Lycée* journal in April 1784. At this time Brissot was entering a debtors' prison in London. On his release he returned to France but was arrested in Paris on 12 July 1784 and sent to the Bastille as the author of *Le diable dans un bénitier*, a mistake because it was composed by Anne-Gédeon Lafitte, marquis de Pelleport.[55] In his *Mémoires*, Brissot claimed that the Bastille confirmed him in his republican political philosophy. This was not the case. Clavière, the person who saved him from bankruptcy when he was released on 10 September 1784, led him to different strategies to prevent the end of enlightenment.

IV

Brissot had travelled to Geneva in the early 1780s in order to arrange for the publication of his books. At Geneva he met the young lawyer François d'Ivernois, who was producing a new edition of Rousseau's works, including those in manuscript at his death, such as the autobiographical *Confessions*. A critic of the ruling magistrates in Geneva, d'Ivernois belonged to the *représentants*, a party led by Clavière. At the time, the *représentants* were in crisis, despite being the most popular political movement in the small republic. The government was controlled by the Council of Twenty-Five, a body dominated by families who had come to be seen as a noble class within the city. The *représentants* wanted to remake the constitution of the republic, broadening the citizen body, reaffirming Calvinism and reorienting the economy. The view of the *représentants* was that the governing class, who called themselves *constitutionnaires* or *négatifs*, were too close to Catholic France, and had become neglectful of their religious duties while being too focused on the large profits they made from their investments in French industries, especially the production of luxury goods. According to the *représentants*, the *constitutionnaires* were selling their city to France and in the process had abandoned Calvinist and republican values. After a revolution in the city which brought the *représentants* to power in April 1782, France invaded Geneva and, with 12,000 troops before the city gates, the leaders of the movement, including Clavière and d'Ivernois, fled to Neufchâtel. They were then invited by Shelburne, as prime minister, to recreate the republic of Geneva at Waterford in Ireland.

While the project of Irish emigration was ongoing, Clavière became associated with Brissot in London, where the young Frenchman had opened his *Lycée* establishment.[56] Clavière thereafter used Brissot as a hired pen, promoting, for example, the Waterford experiment in new work and justifying the actions of the Genevan *représentants* after they left the city.[57] It was probably through Clavière that Brissot came to be associated with other members of the Shelburne Circle, although it may equally have been through Price or d'Ivernois. The bottom line for Clavière and his fellow Genevan *représentants* was that small republics like Geneva were being incorporated into modern empires. French ministers, either directly or clandestinely through their control over the elite families who had substantial investments in France and in the French national debt, were reducing Genevan independence to zero. This was a threat to Calvinism but more directly to the capacity of small states to maintain themselves in a world where large states were going to war for commerce.

Rousseau was a hero to the *représentants* because he had attacked the growth of modern empires and their ever-greater dominion over small states, which he believed were becoming endangered species. As he put it in his reflections upon contemporary Poland in 1772, 'Greatness of nations! Size of states! The first and principal source of the miseries of humankind, and above all of the countless calamities that sap and destroy politically organized peoples.'[58] For many, Rousseau's words were immediately prescient given the first partition of Poland. Brissot, before he came into Clavière's orbit, had shown little interest in the condition of the existing republics across Europe and the crises they faced because of the imperial appetites of the great powers. Getting rid of corrupt empires dedicated to the jealousy of trade by war became an obsession as Brissot embraced the cause of republics and free states, which in turn led him to focus on the lessons for Europe that could be derived from the experience of the United States, the only recent successful experiment in the creation of a republic since the Dutch Revolt.

The Waterford experiment combined many of the causes Shelburne favoured, entailing the movement of the productive classes of the republic of Geneva to Ireland. The plan was to scotch the French, who had led the armies that put down popular revolution within the city republic at the end of June 1782, and to revivify the Irish economy by introducing into the largely Catholic population entrepreneurial Calvinist artisans.[59] Shelburne probably imagined an Ireland that was more tolerant and enlightened, in which new towns of industry challenged the rule of the Protestant Ascendency. Equally, events in Waterford allowed Shelburne to take action to support existing republics, an area where the British had failed in the past, as in the case of Corsica when Shelburne had been a minister under Chatham in the 1760s.[60]

Clavière worked ceaselessly for two years to make a success of the Waterford experiment. He became an Irish subject of the British

crown at Dublin at the end of 1782, sponsored by Shelburne. Traditionally he had been sceptical of British politics and shared the view
that Britain was a state on the decline because of its foolish imperial
adventures and mercantile system. Arriving at the view that Britain
might act as a saviour of European republics in crisis, like Geneva,
had been a long and difficult process. When the Waterford project
failed, because of Shelburne's fall from power, Clavière was confirmed in his earlier view of Britain's corruption and weakness. One
influence over him was Adam Smith – Clavière was an avid reader
and considered himself to be Smith's disciple. He was certain that
Smith's identification of the mercantile system explained contemporary politics and the contagious lust for war and empire that was
infecting the continent. Clavière also followed Turgot, Shelburne
and Price in believing that the future was likely to see an increase in
French power at the expense of that of Britain.[61] Britain had let
down the republic of Geneva and small states more generally. It had
proven itself to be a friend of tyranny rather than liberty, a verdict
that shaped Clavière's subsequent politics. This meant that the outcome of the Waterford experiment had a significant impact upon
Brissot as well.

Brissot wrote in his *Mémoires* that Clavière transformed his own
view of modern politics. Brissot recalled that when he had first visited Geneva in 1782 his political ideas had been naive, or, as he put it,
'very French'.[62] In Geneva he was intellectually seduced by a man
who quickly became his 'friend and Mentor' who 'had an inexhaust-
ible stock of new ideas, of great ideas capable of captivating minds'.
Since Clavière found it difficult to express his thoughts in written
form, and in any case was involved in so many commercial ventures, he turned to Brissot as a professional writer. The partnership,
as Brissot described it, operated with Clavière's genius being translated into forms of communication explicable to all: 'His [mind]
was a limitless mine of brute diamonds: it required a craftsman to
fashion them.'[63] Brissot admitted that Clavière 'knew more about
mankind, his country and his century than I did'. He had 'sacrificed
his fortune, his time and his life to the people'.[64] Above all, he had

'an invincible momentum which carried [him] towards revolutions and towards those who were able to influence them'.[65] The last point was problematic – Clavière acknowledged the likelihood of the populace being corrupted in a commercial society and was suspicious of the people in arms turning fanatic. Revolutions in conditions of crisis were likely to break out, but it was necessary to shepherd them away from violence and prevent them from turning enthusiastic. It was vital to consider the future of liberty in the long term because it could so easily be lost, as had happened in contemporary Britain and Geneva, in Poland and in Denmark.

While Brissot served Clavière in writing about what had happened at Geneva and at Waterford in the *Philadelphien* and the *Bibliothèque*, he began to write for the Shelburne Circle more generally and launch attacks on tyrannical empires in the mid-1780s. The Holy Roman Emperor Joseph II's assertion of October 1784 that he would open the river Scheldt to merchant traffic was defended by Brissot's old friend Linguet.[66] Brissot attacked both Linguet and the emperor as dangerous fanatics hell bent on fostering a general European war.[67] Brissot declared his detestation of nationalism and the jealousy between nations. He went so far as to predict that 'cosmopolitanism will replace this ridiculous patriotism or national honour, words invented by despots to keep their slaves loyal.'[68] Brissot did not say when the cosmopolitan moment would arrive. Brissot's membership of the Shelburne Circle was signalled by the appearance of his works as having been published at Dublin, still at the time a centre for Shelburne's friends critical of empire from Geneva.[69]

It was through the Shelburne Circle too that Brissot encountered Bentham.[70] The two men began a friendship that lasted until Brissot's death. The association played a significant role in Bentham's being given French citizenship by the National Convention in 1793, and in his presentation of the book *Emancipate your Colonies!* to the revolutionaries at Paris.[71] It was Clavière, however, who did the most to reorient Brissot's thinking towards the call for an end to war and empire. Clavière too was full of praise for the work of

Price and Franklin. Hume equally was a source of inspiration, especially concerning the natural death of states through public credit and the anarchic condition of international relations.[72] Clavière also employed Mirabeau as part of a stable of writers.[73] Drawing on Brissot's ceaseless capacity for composition, Clavière increasingly demanded the transformation of France rather than the far-too-corrupted Britain as a means of re-enlightening the world by putting an end to the mercantile system of war and empire.

The pivot to France was a step of profound importance. If Britain was to be sidelined, being too corrupt to be reformed and near collapse, other states had to become the focus of cosmopolitan zeal to restore enlightenment and bolster both liberty and toleration in perpetuity. Clavière was rich, had large investments in the French economy and ultimately turned himself into a Shelburne at Paris, patronizing a growing group of writers, including Bentham's soon-to-be editor and translator Étienne Dumont, who also worked for Shelburne. Clavière's workshop was, for example, responsible for drafting the declaration of the rights of man and the citizen at Paris.

V

The abandonment of the Waterford experiment signalled Clavière's conversion to a more aggressive republican stance regarding the possible future of Europe. He was one of the very few individuals in Europe who believed, before the French Revolution, that France should and could be turned into a republic. His vision of a republic had very little to do with ancient or contemporary examples, in part because he had lived through the destruction of his own republic. Clavière thought that there was no purpose in creating small republics. The military insignificance of Geneva and the consequences for domestic politics, and the invasion by France of Savoy and Bern in 1782, greatly shaped his thinking. It was Clavière whom Brissot followed in calling for a new kind of French republic, as the only means of making a reality of the Shelburne Circle's reform project of putting an end to the mercantile system.

In the final years of the 1780s Clavière and Brissot, together in their books *Observations of a Republican on the Different Systems of Provincial Administration* (*Observations d'un républicain sur les différents systèmes d'administrations provinciales*) and *France and the United States of America* (*De la France et des États-Unis*), sought to create a different kind of commercial society.[74] One of the more complicated strategies they formulated was intended to turn highly inegalitarian societies into societies where everyone enjoyed moderate wealth, which they termed 'ease' (*aisance*). In such visions they were influenced by Price in particular, who argued similarly, and Franklin, whose *Poor Richard's Almanack*, published from 1732, described a functional society where moderate wealth held sway.[75] In Price's case insurance schemes and taxation would prevent men from emerging whose gargantuan wealth allowed them to dominate political landscapes. Clavière and Brissot believed that the new society they imagined was incompatible with slavery. In consequence they created the *Société des amis des noirs* in February 1788 in France, seeking the abolition of slavery across the globe. Clavière was the first president, and other figures who were subsequently to become prominent in French politics became members.[76]

Clavière and Brissot believed that the recent war with the French, the Spanish and the Dutch had put an end to Britain's mercantile ambitions. Taking advantage of anti-British sentiment in North America would, they were sure, establish an international axis of mutually beneficial and pacific trade between the largely agrarian United States and industrializing France. If the two economies were linked together, and British trade rejected, a powerful alliance would be established that might lead Europe and the world to a more pacific and prosperous commercial future. This was the goal of another society, the *Société gallo-américaine*, established in November 1787 by Brissot, Clavière and Crèvecoeur, the advocate of the benefits of agrarian living in a new world.[77] The goal was to spread knowledge across France of the opportunities presented by North America, and to foster industry, a commercial treaty and ever-stronger ties between the countries for the benefit of humanity.[78] A new politics was the counterpart of the economic vision, necessary in order to remove mercantile crooks from being dominant in national legislatures. For the politics to work, elites had to be replaced, including the monarch as constituted in contemporary France, because royal influence was one of the surest means of replicating the mercantile system in France.

Clavière and Brissot declared themselves to have been inspired by Turgot, who they took to be a republican from comments in Condorcet's *Life of Turgot* (*Vie de Turgot*) (1786). Turgot had made a mistake, however, in having faith in landed proprietors as the wise men who could be relied upon to steer the ship of state towards liberty and prosperity. The landed interest would, in practice, act as an aristocratic caste in cahoots with monarchs and rich merchants. Rather, it was the industrious people, those of moderate wealth, who lived laborious lives full of hardship but also fulfilment, who could be trusted in the political arena. They were the economic backbone of the country. It was such people, they argued, who should gradually be made sovereign, electing representatives drawn from their own class to pass laws for the common good.

'Gradually' was among the most important words in Clavière's and Brissot's lexicon. Steeped in republican history as they were, and more especially Rousseau's reassertion of Machiavelli's argument that reform projects lived or died by the state of the culture (*moeurs*) of a community, they did not underestimate the extent of the corruption of the people. France, they had learned equally from Rousseau and their own experience, was the country whose political culture was at odds with nature in the same manner as commercializing Britain.[79] Addiction to luxury was rife, a force that would sooner or later corrode cultures supportive of the public good. The court represented a centrifugal force for mercantile politics, creating courtiers and controlling patronage, impeding honest industry and promoting profligacy and war. The present generation in power, having been educated in a society at war with itself through the institutions of monarchy, nobility and church, and because commerce had been allowed to grow in every direction, could not be trusted to enact the necessary reforms to restore France to a natural growth path. Laws, however good they were, had to be adhered to and accepted by the general population. Otherwise they would quickly fail. This was the reason why Clavière's and Brissot's reform schemes were always coupled with plans for civic education, for the freedom of the press, and for short terms of political office. They advised a wait of twenty years before the time would be ripe for an uncorrupted republican generation of the young to take power. In other places they recommended a wait of three years, while the industrious figures who were elected to an estates general would debate, gain political education and then formulate a new constitution for France.

VI

Both Clavière and Brissot were surprised by the commencement of the French Revolution. Indeed, as the economic links between France and the United States had not developed as anticipated, both men had been looking towards the new world as a possible future home, as they contrasted it with moribund Europe. Brissot was travelling across the new republics of North America when news came from France.[80] It was obvious that the Revolution, however turbulent and unpredictable it might be, magnified options for would-be reformers. Clavière was already living in Paris among his coterie of brilliant pamphleteers. He soon had access to power as Mirabeau rose quickly to become the leading popular orator of the new National Assembly. Clavière's main initial goal seems to have been to reverse French policy at Geneva. He also combated Jacques Necker, then Louis XVI's chief finance minister and an arch-advocate of the mercantile system. Clavière had never forgiven Necker for standing aside when the French invasion of Geneva occurred in 1782, a high crime according to Clavière because Necker, although he held office in France, was a Genevan citizen. Necker had put the economic interest of France before the liberty of his homeland.

Shelburne sent Dumont, now Shelburne's secretary, to Paris to experience the Revolution at first hand. Dumont sent back detailed reports, which became the basis of the best insider history of the early events of the Revolution, composed in 1799, but posthumously published in 1832, *Souvenirs sur Mirabeau et sur les deux premières assemblées législatives*.[81] Dumont too became a member of Clavière's group and authored several of Mirabeau's speeches in the National Assembly. Dumont's insightful first-hand account of the collapse of revolutionary ardour from the end of 1789 to 1791 cast Louis XVI as a weak and ineffectual figure. The fundamental contradiction of the system erected in 1789–91 was that Louis XVI could not bring himself to support the transition from a French system of absolute royal authority to a version of the British mixed monarchy. Dumont blamed bad ministers like Necker for not adjusting to the revolutionary crisis. Necker was a fool and a failure because he could so easily have taken advantage of the love of the people for their monarch, combating extremism and fanaticism in the process. Instead, he dithered, termed by Dumont 'a watch that is forever slow'.[82]

Necker justified himself after he fled Paris in September 1792 and returned to his mansion at Coppet where, as has been noted, he enjoyed the company of Gibbon. Until the end of his life in 1804, Necker claimed that he had tried to turn France into Britain.[83] This won him many friends. Those who knew him would have been aware that he sidestepped the problem of the mercantile system. He could not explain why his expressed goal had been to turn France into a state seemingly in terminal decline, whose politics were dominated by the very corrupt aristocracy held responsible for destroying the French economy and causing the Revolution. Such a narrative became plausible in part because Britain, in challenging revolutionary France at war, suddenly appeared a stronger and more stable polity. Necker's arguments naturally made no sense at all to Dumont or Clavière, because they knew how nonsensical the strategy of turning France into Britain was in the early 1790s. All of the Shelburne Circle thought Britain to be diminished; the notion of emulating Britain as a free state was farcical.

Brissot, Clavière and Dumont were still more dismissive of the person deemed by many to have plotted the course of the Revolution, Emmanuel-Joseph Sieyès. Sieyès, they argued, had unleashed the forces of popular liberty without having a plan for moderating them.[84] All of the members of the Shelburne Circle at Paris took pains to prevent the people from becoming enthusiastic and fanatic. They were aware of Hume's predictions and of the thin line between popular liberty and chaos. The tragedy of the French Revolution was that a popular war against tyranny was squandered because it turned into mob rule. That Sieyès lacked knowledge of Hume and failed to anticipate the turbulence of the enthusiastic forces released into the world amounted, so the Circle held, to a combination of arrogance and ignorance.[85]

Long after Sieyès had exited the political scene, only to re-emerge during the Directory, the Girondin/Brissotin group, including Clavière and Brissot, found themselves developing political tactics capable of creating a stable and moderate republic in a large state at high speed. The inauguration of the First French Republic in September 1792 presented another opportunity, because it solved the problem of Louis XVI's being an obstacle to reform. It was dangerous, however, because the constitution had to be created anew via national convention in circumstances where the armed people in action, deemed the embodiment of patriotic virtue, could turn for one party or another. Clavière and Brissot found themselves in power with the institution of a Girondin ministry before the fall of the monarchy. Clavière's personal victory was to serve as Louis XVI's last finance minister from March 1792. The Girondins were encouraged by the fact that aristocracy had been abolished and the Bourbon monarch's power of patronage made history. The church too could no longer act as a body pushing its own mercantile interests. France was declared to no longer be an empire. A law was passed abolishing offensive war. A new kind of economy was promoted, one founded on landownership for all, through the paper currency derived from the sale of national land called *assignats*. The vision of a truly free state and economy, the commerce of which could be described as pacific, moral and cosmopolitan appeared to be being realized. There was singular overlap between Shelburne's programme and that of the Girondins.

On the surface the situation for Clavière and Brissot looked straightforward. Europe should be restored to peace, France to pre-eminence, and all states to a natural growth path of economic development. Clavière and Brissot were, however, realistic – in practice the situation was the opposite of ideal. The first problem was the realization of the vast number of legislative measures being enacted. One of the contradictions of a time of perceived liberty was that the new government was being asked to change the world, which in turn necessitated more intervention in the lives of the people. The form of this government was also unclear, with the clubs of Paris and the national guard operating as a shadow power.

Clavière and Brissot's strategy in 1790 and 1791 was to ask the French to look towards North America for lessons in how to maintain their new liberty. Brissot published an account of his travels to the new republics in 1788 that appeared in April 1791, intended for French readers mired in revolution. Brissot, citing Clavière throughout, emphasized that revolutions only succeeded if manners were virtuous. He sketched out a series of educational projects aimed at preventing fanaticism, ranging from lectures to teach politicians, to the encouragement of landownership and artisan labours, and the maintenance of moderate wealth and independence.[86] The *New Travels (Nouveau voyage)*, as the book was termed, included letters from Clavière asking Brissot to examine especially closely the working of the new federal constitution in the United States. Brissot was aware that recommending the Quakers – a Protestant sect with a fanatic history – as a model of how to live was going to meet resistance in France. Equally, Brissot knew that the American republics had the advantage of being largely agrarian, so that the transition to a free state where most citizens owned land was possible.

Nevertheless, Brissot argued that France could remain free if the gradual reformation of manners to make the populace more republican was attempted. One way of doing this was to link the economies and politics of France and the United States together; Brissot republished his and Clavière's book *France and America* of 1787 as part of the *Nouveau voyage*. There were plans, Brissot said in the preface, to publish a further volume showing how the French could create a federal republican constitution, although the work never appeared.

The irony was not lost upon Brissot, however, that the revolutionary leaders were following the rule book of the most violent of mercantile systems in dealing with perceived enemies. Above all, membership of and obedience to both government and state was defined by individual manifestation of republican patriotism. This was accepted as being the unifying force which gave the Revolution its strength and vigour. In these circumstances, those most dedicated to the Republic were the best and most valuable citizens, and death in its service became the most significant political action. Although the Girondins went along with the rhetoric of republican patriotism, they were aware that erecting a political system based on such passions was likely to result in the spread of fanatic enthusiasm.[87] Another problem was that the specifics of republican dedication were defined by whatever government held sway. The price of falling from power was likely to be the guillotine, and politics became a matter of compromised living, martyred dying, running away to a hidden domestic bolt-hole or emigrating abroad.[88]

Enthusiastic politics derived from passionate causes could readily, Hume had taught, turn both fanatic and factional. Precisely this happened in France as the celebrated national unity that characterized the early days of the Revolution fell apart in 1792/1793. Politicians were forced to focus upon the maintenance of constituencies of support rather than legislative programmes. In addition to domestic division a growing sense emerged that the positive initiatives being canvassed at Paris were being thwarted by foreign powers. And indeed, external states were using their wealth to foster division in France. Associated especially with émigré nobles or churchmen, the claim was made that fifth columns of opposition were active across France in attempts to impede the Revolution.

Such feelings were intensified with the grave threat presented by Austria and Prussia's invasion in mid-1792. At a time when vitriol thrown towards every revolutionary actor was especially intense, and when Clavière was facing opposition to his redistributive paper money, Brissot took a step which horrified many members of the Shelburne Circle. It was presented as the product of necessity, a last chance to prevent the excesses of the Revolution from overwhelming all the good that had been achieved. Extremism was employed against fanaticism in the hope of keeping hold of power. Brissot's strategy was international war. After Kellerman's victory over the Austrians and Prussians at Valmy on 20 September 1792, the spirit of national unity that manifested itself became a force that Brissot sought to harness. The invaders had been chased from France by 2 November, but love of country demanded the expansion of France by force of arms. The cosmopolitan had become a warmonger.

VII

At the beginning of 1792, Brissot realized that a crusade in the name of universal liberty might maintain the unity of the people – unity necessary to make a success of the Revolution.[89] War was proclaimed as a vital battle against the enemies of humanity, those who viewed a nation of many millions to be equivalent only to the person of a single king. Wars of national liberation were intended to bring independence to peoples who would become brothers to the French. The Holy Roman Empire, and the 'Austrian committee' around Marie Antoinette, were soon held up as the greatest enemy, calling for a sacred war upon tyranny.[90] Brissot argued that the French were bringing liberty to any territories their soldiers trespassed upon. Inaugurating revolution abroad would ensure economic development and fuller lives for individuals in communities hitherto oppressed by aristocrats, priests and kings.

Brissot had visions of a republican empire stretching from Italy to Switzerland, and from the southern Netherlands to the borders of Prussia and England. He was confident that the large republic could maintain itself because the patriotism of the people, now deemed an essential ingredient of the modern polity, was mightier than the resources of its opponents. Whereas the goal of Brissot and Clavière had been to save the small republics of Europe, the plan was now to create a vast republic of free peoples. The new state would be militarily impregnable. The reversal of traditional politics and tactics was evident in the order given to General Anne-Pierre de Montesquiou-Fézensac in October 1792 to enter with his troops the gates of the republic of Geneva. When he refused, he was removed from office.[91]

Brissot's project was deemed a near-complete success by the end of 1792. On 19 November, the representatives of the nation in the republican Convention decreed that France would actively support the campaign of any populace seeking liberty. Savoy and Nice were annexed. The river Scheldt in the Austrian Netherlands was opened to trade, something no longer opposed by Clavière and Brissot. On 15 December, the Convention decreed that wherever French troops were to be found the sovereignty of the people was to be proclaimed and revolutionary institutions introduced. Brissot called it 'war to the castle and peace to the cottage'.[92] He was accused of having the intention to 'set fire to four quarters of the globe'.[93] People everywhere had a natural right to liberty, he believed; the French were facilitating this worthy goal.

The logical end point of Brissot's war for revolution was to fight Britain, which against expectation had yet to collapse. The British were described by Brissot as Machiavellian monarchists. The French republicans, by contrast, espoused true political morality and natural law, being the rights of the people to justice and liberty.[94] As brothers to all, the French were enemies to 'the politics of those who believe in the old balance of Europe, and enemies to merchants, who seek the monopolistic control of markets'. They were neither destroyers of Europe, nor atheist sceptics concerning morality, nor imperialists seeking to 'turn the Low Countries into Bengal'.[95]

Brissot's message was that advocates of liberty had to decide what a free Europe looked like. Britain controlled the foreign policy of Prussia, Portugal and the Dutch Republic through funds transferred to monarchs and ministers. For Brissot, Pitt's strategy was the very essence of the mercantile system in practice. The intensification of British commercial dominion was proceeding apace. An alternative was a new world of economic and political liberty, entailing the development of humanity to new heights of economic, intellectual and moral endeavour. Stopping Britain for a brighter and cosmopolitan future became a republican imperative. Never was there a more significant crusade.

By February 1793, Brissot was so convinced that Britain was doing to Europe's states what it had done to the Dutch Republic, turning them into satellites, that he called for war. The British had been using 'the perfidious mask of neutrality' to foster their own imperial designs upon the continent. George III had 'meditated secretly and for a long time a war against liberty'. False ruses were being employed to hide Britain's barbaric intentions. British ministers from Pitt downwards had, he believed, corrupted domestic public opinion against the French Republic. The British were speculating that war would destroy the *assignat* paper currency and that a national bankruptcy would end the French Republic by causing it to descend into civil war. The British were ignorant. North American experience revealed that nations could be free despite the death of the paper that facilitated economic exchange. Currency depreciation caused turmoil but did not destroy republics. In waging war against the French, Brissot argued that the British were waging 'a fratricidal war' against 'the liberty of all the peoples', which was 'a crime against humanity itself'.[96] The outcome was predicted to be the fall of the British monarchy and the turning of Britain into a republic when it went bankrupt itself or when the people opened their eyes and rebelled against malign rulers.

If the warmonger for liberty advocated a policy of violence against the enemies of the Revolution outside France, it translated into the justification of terror against the enemies of the Revolution within France, as defined by Brissot.[97] In 1792, he called for the closure of the Jacobin Club as the source of an anarchy that was preventing the National Convention from establishing a republican constitution. Brissot demanded that the Jacobins be 'annihilated'. Brissot had spent the early years of the French Revolution praising the unity and virtue that characterized the ever-more republican populace, by contrast with the corrupted monarchical and aristocratic manners to be found abroad. But assaults on foreigners for their lack of republican virtue were now redirected against fellow republicans hitherto deemed virtuous. This was a move that became part and parcel of revolutionary tactics, to turn from enemies abroad to former fellow travellers in the republican cause. Conspiracy theories abounded.[98] The Jacobins had greater support among the populace of Paris and were cunning in redirecting Brissot's accusations against himself and all the members of the Gironde. Brissot was thirty-nine when he was arrested and put to death, defining himself at the end as a terrorist for liberty.[99] His friend Clavière, arrested on 2 June, killed himself on 8 December 1793 in prison to avoid the guillotine.

8.

Thomas Paine and the End of Revolution

I

Thomas Paine was the most furious republican of the end of enlightenment era. He was throughout his life strident and unflinching in his demand for the abolition of social rank and the monarchy by popular revolution. He was also the most arrogant: only his republican project would restore peace and toleration on a global scale.[1] Paine insisted that he did not read any books at all except his own, all of which he knew by heart.[2] He presented his own ideas as altogether new and invariably rejected attempts to link them to other writers. As he put it in *The American Crisis* letters, 'what I write is pure nature', adding 'my pen and my soul have ever gone together.'[3] When the United Irishman and republican Wolfe Tone met Paine in Paris in 1797, he noted that Paine was 'vain beyond all belief' and 'drinks like a fish', 'a misfortune which I have known to befall other justly celebrated Patriots'.[4] Paine asserted that Burke had gone mad in his final years not because of the death of his son but because he had been refuted so completely by Paine's own *Rights of Man*. Yet Tone also held there to be excellent grounds for Paine's vanity since 'he has reason to be vain and for my part I forgive him. He has done wonders for the cause of liberty, both in America and Europe.'

Paine's achievements as the apostle of republican revolution to restore enlightenment led the journalist William Cobbett to dig up the corpse of Paine on the New York farm where it had been buried ten years before. The farm, at New Rochelle, was a war gift to Paine from the New York assembly in June 1784; it had been owned by

British loyalists and after being confiscated such property was distributed among supporters of the American Revolution. Taking possession of Paine's remains, Cobbett had them shipped from the United States to Surrey in England.[5] Cobbett had hopes that Paine's bones might stimulate reform across Britain, that they might kick-start a movement halted since Paine's own *Rights of Man* had been linked from June 1793 to the Terror in Paris. Paine called the Terror 'execrable' but also said that it was a passing phase of the journey to peace, liberty and enlightenment. The French Revolution remained 'the first burst of light that dispels the darkness'.[6] Attacks on Paine as an advocate of terrorism and anarchy, civil collapse and libertinism had then become standard fare for anti-revolutionaries across Europe.[7] More particularly, Paine was accused of hating Britain, of wanting to replace king, church and aristocracy with republican legislators preaching a heady deist religion of semi-Christian ethics indebted to Jesus, the Quakers, Confucius 'and some of the Greek philosophers'.[8]

Cobbett himself had been in the vanguard of the attack on Paine at the turn of the century, a paid agent of the war secretary William Windham, defending church and king with gusto.[9] Ironically too, given the extent of his devotion to the French Revolution, Paine was himself a victim of the Terror at Paris.[10] On the orders of Robespierre and fellow leaders of the Jacobin Club he was arrested on 28 December 1793 and imprisoned in the Luxembourg until the following November, during which time he witnessed what he called 'a continued scene of horror' in which 'no man could count upon life for twenty-four hours.'[11] Avoiding the guillotine was mainly down to luck.[12] Yet Paine remained in France and continued to defend the French Revolution, becoming a personal friend of Napoleon Bonaparte. He saw Britain as the pariah state, and accused it of continuing to infect the United States with its poisonous culture; for true liberty to thrive, he argued, Britain needed to stop seeking influence in global politics.[13] The American and French revolutions remained the hope of the human race for peace and enlightenment. Britain claimed to be a free state and to be defending enlightenment itself.[14] For Paine, it was the cancer at the heart of the end of enlightenment. The invasion of Britain by gunboats from France was, he informed Thomas Jefferson, his personal idea.[15]

Cobbett gradually concluded after the end of the Napoleonic Wars that Paine had been right about the lack of liberty enjoyed by Britons. Rather than being a source of solutions to the challenges of the new century, Britain was, he now believed, a major problem. Cobbett thereby moved from patriot to radical, from believing that Britain was the last bastion of earthly liberty battling against the evils of revolution to seeing Paine's ideology as the inspiration for a vital national transformation and rebirth.[16] Following Paine, Britain was redescribed by Cobbett as a mercantile system, where the monied interest controlled the politicians and where law served them rather than the common people. Paine's solution had been to seek the abolition of monarchy, the end to the rank of nobility, the establishment of limited government as a 'necessary evil' and the closure of all established churches.[17]

Such arguments had become popular during the French Revolution, but what marked out Cobbett's interest in Paine, as opposed to other republicans of the time, was Paine's conclusion that republicanism could only thrive as an ideology if it became a civil religion. It was only if republican morals became habitual, defining a dominant general culture, that they would have a chance of success. Cobbett was certain that the ills of Britain in the early nineteenth century, marked by the grotesque abuse of the poor and propertyless, could be traced to adopting the wrong form of Protestantism at the Reformation.[18] Equally, a new reformation was required to return Britain and Europe to a free and prosperous path. Despite widespread interest in such ideas among the populace, Cobbett's goal of using Paine's body to create a new republican religion for the betterment of the landless and exploited came to nothing. The failure paralleled the fate of Paine's own attempt to create a new deistic moral code for contemporary societies, sketched out in his attack on contemporary Christianity, *The Age of Reason*, subtitled 'an investigation of true and fabulous philosophy' in 1794, which he completed while in prison, rejecting both original sin and the Trinity.[19] A new religion, because republicanism proved insufficient, was going to create a new enlightenment.

The problem from the first was that Paine's call for a new religion of humanity bringing all souls together was derided as sectarian and enthusiastic. Paine became a pariah in the later 1790s in his adopted homeland of the United States because he was accused of blasphemy, and because the militant republicanism he was associated with was falling out of favour.[20] Even former members of the Shelburne Circle, such as Priestley, attacked him as a dangerous heretic and potential fanatic.[21] The publication of his *Letter to George Washington*, dated Paris, 30 July 1796, did not help. Paine had been wholly supportive of Washington hitherto, dedicating the first volume of *The Rights of Man* to him. But he became convinced that Washington had engineered Paine's imprisonment at Paris with Robespierre and the US representative, Gouverneur Morris; Paine had a paranoid streak and perceived himself to be the victim of the machinations of hidden enemies. In the case of Morris, he was correct. But Washington was also accused by Paine of being a British pawn and of fostering his own reign of terror across the new republic, and thereby betraying the American Revolution.[22] Such sentiments, coming from someone already branded an anti-Christian heretic living in France as a French citizen, further tarnished Paine's reputation. When he died in 1809, he was refused a Christian burial and only six mourners attended his funeral. Even a request to be buried among Quakers was turned down.[23] When his body was snatched by Cobbett the act was welcomed rather than condemned in the press on the grounds that the remains of such an unbeliever were better in corrupt Britain than in free America.[24]

The tragedies of Paine's later life were underlined by his assertion that enlightenment had ended even in North America. Enunciating such a claim would have had Catharine Macaulay spinning in her grave. It was all a far cry from 1776 when Paine's letters published as *The American Crisis* were widely held responsible for bolstering the spluttering cause of American independence. At the time Paine was serving as secretary to General Nathanael Greene in Washington's army and observed the retreat towards Philadelphia before British troops. It was at Trenton in New Jersey on 26 December 1776 that Washington was reputed to have had Paine's first *American Crisis* letter read to his troops to invigorate them before battle. Paine's language was distinctive, memorable and inspirational:

> These are the times that try men's souls. The summer soldier and the sun-shine patriot will, in this crisis, shrink from the service of his country: but he that stands it *now*, deserves the thanks of man and woman. Tyranny, like hell, is not easily conquered: yet we have this consolation with us, that the harder the conflict, the more glorious the triumph. What we obtain too cheap, we esteem too lightly; it is dearness only that gives everything its value.[25]

Just as in the pamphlet *Common Sense*, which had made him famous as the leading advocate of an American republic, Paine described the new America as a moral community to be contrasted with a corrupt and collapsing Britain. Washington's war was being carried on by devout patriots who could be relied upon to create a better world. Europe, and Britain more especially, was suffering the end of enlightenment. Paine was in the vanguard of those who believed that this was taking place because of the institutions, cultures and social and religious practices of the old world. North America, lacking such diseased limbs, could be relied upon to do things differently in perpetuity. Paine saw himself as a crusader, battling against infidels with the zeal of the first Protestants. Although he never lost his faith in a moralized politics within a republican community, Paine changed his mind about the foundations of such a community and its nature, just as his personality ill-fitted the communities he found himself within, illustrated by his little-lamented death and the undignified journey of his human remains afterwards.

II

Paine was the opposite of a consistent republican ideologue. Like all republicans in the final decades of the eighteenth century, his stance altered with the political options open to him. Today we tend to see him far too generally, as someone who ought to be lauded for his lofty rhetoric in support of human rights and liberty, for his actions in revolutionary North America and France and for his attempt to foment revolution in Britain. Paine understood both self-moralization, something he was addicted to in print, and the tactic of moralizing eminent individuals to sway an audience, but he would have recognized that such tactics distorted reality. From the perspective of his contemporaries, he was a changeling, someone who adapted his stance to the times just as he remained the most vocal preacher of contemporary crisis and the end of enlightenment. While he was a consistent painter of visions of peace and prosperity, the communities that he imagined would realize this dream tended to alter. Belief in the possibility of moral association between free and selfless individuals remained, traceable perhaps to Paine's rudimentary education among the Quakers after his birth in Thetford, Norfolk, in 1737.[26] In *Common Sense* and other early writings Paine sounded like someone describing an idealized Quaker community, self-sustaining, supporting every one of its members and altogether pacific in intention.

Yet Paine was baptized as a child into the Anglican church and was critical of Dissenters, including the Quakers, during his life. As a boy Paine initially sailed on privateers to make a living, before following his father into the corset-making trade. After working in London, he became a tax collector in Lewes, Sussex, before opening a tobacco and snuff mill at the end of the 1760s. Evident ability with a pen led Paine to be asked to author *The Case of the Officers of Excise* in 1772, a call for better pay and conditions for the tax collectors. He also wrote for the *Sussex Weekly Advertiser; or, Lewes Journal*, a newspaper that supported John Wilkes and called for the restoration of

English liberty. Paine debated politics with friends at the Head-strong Club at the White Horse public house in Lewes.[27] He was, according to his friend and sometime fellow Quaker Thomas Clio Rickman, a Whig.[28] Through such circles he was introduced to Benjamin Franklin.[29] By 1774, he had been become bankrupt, was dismissed from the excise service and then divorced his wife, Elizabeth Ollive, whose family had owned the failed mill.

Aged thirty-seven and armed with letters of introduction from Franklin, Paine arrived in Philadelphia on 30 November 1774. He found employment editing the *Pennsylvania* magazine owned by Robert Aitken, an émigré bookseller and printer from Scotland. Within a year Paine had turned republican and completed *Common Sense*, which became the most popular pamphlet of the American Revolution, turning Paine into a figure of international significance. *Common Sense* made a remarkable argument. In part it reiterated longstanding commonwealth and radical Whig arguments about the decline of Britain. The liberty of Britons, Paine argued, had been entirely dependent upon the republican element of the constitution, the independence of the House of Commons through free election. George III had destroyed this independence. Whigs such as Price or Shelburne were likely sources for Paine's assertion that enlightenment was being threatened by dire forces centring on the monarch. While they refused to give up on Britain, because they believed vestiges of liberty remained, Paine concluded otherwise.

How far Britain had ever been truly free was a real question for Paine, given the power of monarchy, aristocracy and church. Tyranny rather than liberty was the abiding theme of English history since the Tudors. As he put it in *Common Sense*, the British constitution amounted to 'the base remains of two ancient tyrannies, compounded with some new Republican materials', the latter being the control of Parliament over money.[30] Proof that the republican materials were no longer working lay in the horrific war being waged against would-be Britons in the colonies, the true lovers of liberty, whose towns were being burned and communities divided and then ruined. Americans who believed in liberty had to cease to be British. Quoting Milton, since 'deadly hate' marked relations between Britain and America independence became vital.[31]

In both *Common Sense* and the series of letters published consecutively as *The American Crisis*, Paine attacked Britain's monarchy as absurd and ridiculous. The greatness of Britain, Paine was certain, like so many of his contemporaries, was entirely historic rather than contemporary. North American independence amounted to the saving of a child while the mortally wounded parent could be left to die. Seed had been sown to create a new social body, while the British were doomed to further decay.[32] North Americans were advised to ready themselves to 'receive the fugitive and prepare an asylum for mankind.'[33] Paine in the 1770s was not advocating national conventions of the people across Britain. He was no exponent of a general theory of reform or revolution. Europe, from Paine's American perspective, was finished, having manners so corrupt that nothing could be done to restore virtue. There were no political tactics sufficient to maintain European states. Starting afresh in a new place with a people who deemed themselves to be a founding generation was the only sensible manoeuvre.

Paine was confident about the future of North America because he believed it to be self-sufficient in the provision of subsistence goods to the point of abundance. This meant that all the European powers would trade with America. Like Clavière and Brissot, he imagined America feeding the more industrial states of Europe. Having America as a free port, favouring commerce altogether without duty or restriction, meant that the economic future of the American republics was likely to be secure. Equally, there was evidence in *Common Sense* that Paine wanted to avoid extensive international trade in the manner of Britain because of the negative effects of luxury upon a community. America did not need such commerce because it could defend itself, being in the near-unique position of not having a mighty neighbour on its doorstep. It could grow naturally and pacifically in consequence, its natural endowments being singular, having land around it that could be further exploited. Such statements resonated with Christian and commonwealth critiques of luxury indicting the growth of selfishness and commerce together. Significantly, Paine was not interested in the issue of chattel slavery.[34] Nor was he interested in the position of women or the rights and liberties of Native Americans, supporting from the first the expansion of the new states west. He wanted men like himself to govern, secure in the knowledge that they could define the public good for those who lacked liberty or were excluded from politics altogether. In the case of chattel slavery, Paine's silence, a contrast with so many others obsessed with the end of enlightenment, including Price, Clavière and Brissot, may have been due to the ownership of slaves by so many of his patrons in America.[35]

Paine changed his perspective on politics during the 1780s. He came to the view that Europe too, led by France and Britain, could be reformed and that America might play a role as a model polity within a world characterized by commerce and peace. The reason for Paine's change of stance was his return to Europe and connections to members of the Shelburne Circle. In Philadelphia, Paine had been given the post of secretary to a newly created committee on foreign relations in March 1777. With the entry of France into the war, Paine advised the rejection of every British peace proposal.[36] Praise of France, no longer portrayed as an old-world tyranny, now littered Paine's prose. He accompanied Colonel John Laurens, from February to August 1781 on the ship *Alliance*, to obtain a loan from France to support the war, a mission that proved a success.[37] French money, Paine later said, admittedly in partisan mode due to his change of view of the president, did more than Washington's military activities to defeat the British.[38] While in France, Paine made contact with *philosophes* such as Shelburne's friend André Morellet who was serving Vergennes as part of the French diplomatic effort. Morellet acted as a link to the Whigs who shared Shelburne's view of Britain. Together they explored opportunities for permanent peace between nations following the collapse of Britain's empire in America. Returning to the United States, Paine, in need of funds, was paid to argue in favour of more substantial taxes for Congress.[39]

Paine was also paid by the French ministry for his work. *American Crisis No. 11* demanded a collective peace between the allies fighting the British rather than a separate peace, in accordance with the desires of France, Spain and the Dutch Republic.[40] The bottom line for Paine was that France was in a far better state than Britain. France's support for the new republics economically and militarily, in addition to the support of French ministers for Paine personally, signified the health and vitality of French politics. Such views accorded with those prominent in the Shelburne Circle – that France was naturally a stronger power than Britain. There was hope for the future of France and for Britain if the latter made peace. Paine's view of international politics was akin to that of Shelburne's Circle up to the French Revolution, when he changed his views again regarding the means of establishing peace. At this point in his life there was nothing universal about Paine's politics: unlike Brissot, he was not the kind of republican who dreamed of republics being established globally.

There was another reason for Paine's interest in France. In December 1782 he revealed to Franklin a model of the single-span iron bridge that he believed would make his name in natural philosophy in addition to his fortune. When the Pennsylvania assembly refused investment in the project, in part because of the lack of foundries capable of building an actual bridge, Paine was forced to turn abroad. He left for France in April 1787, landed in May, and soon became friendly again with Thomas Jefferson, who was the American envoy in Paris. He had high hopes of government funding for a bridge across the Seine after a presentation to the French Academy of Sciences. Progress was slow, however, and once more Paine turned elsewhere, to Britain, where he patented the plan for the bridge. In November 1788 he commissioned the Walker brothers at Rotherham to build an arch of 90 feet. By April 1789 it was ready and shipped to London, arriving in May 1790 and displayed from September near the Yorkshire Stingo public house in Marylebone, which attracted attention because of the adjoining pleasure gardens. With no further investment the bridge began to corrode and was returned to Rotherham by the end of November. As with the tobacco mill, Paine failed in business and returned to politics.

Links between Paine and Shelburne's Circle then became closer than ever before with Paine's publication of *Prospects on the Rubicon* in 1787. The text had been discussed with Morellet at Paris. Morellet was aghast, like his friend Shelburne, at the collapse of the peace projects established at the end of the American war and likely failure of the recent commercial treaty between France and Britain. Britain under William Pitt was rearming in anticipation of another war with France, this time over the Patriot's Revolt in the Dutch Republic. The British and Prussians were supporting the Stadtholder while the French, as in America, supported the popular party.[41] Paine's language was as abrasive as ever, accusing the British of 'resigning up the prerogative of thinking'.[42] Pitt was accused directly of ruining the opportunities for the restoration of enlightenment promoted by Shelburne and Morellet. The prime minister was destroying 'the harmony that appeared to be growing up between the two nations; to lessen, if not totally destroy, the advantages of the Commercial Treaty, and to lay the seeds of future wars, when there was a prospect of a long and uninterrupted peace'.[43] Pitt was a fool, in Paine's opinion, because France was proving to be in a healthier condition, having defeated Britain in war. Reform was imminent in France where 'a very extraordinary change is working itself in the minds of the people of that nation.'[44] National pride had been stoked across France through the defence of liberty in America and it could be drawn upon to vanquish Britain if the warmongering state sought future battle. He held that the latter was in a parlous condition because of the extent of its national debt. As we have seen, such arguments were drawn directly from the playbook of the Shelburne Circle. Paine was returning to his Whig roots now with linkages, because of Shelburne, across Europe. Brissot and Mirabeau, funded by Clavière, were singing from a similar hymn sheet. They had been recruited into Shelburne's army in a last-ditch attempt to save the world as it had existed after the peace of 1783. Paine readily described Shelburne's sentiment and those of his friends as, 'A silent wish on both sides was universally expanding itself, that wars, so fatal to the true interest and burthensome by taxes to the subjects of both countries, might exist no more, and that a long and lasting peace might take place.'[45]

When Paine travelled on to Britain, arriving on 3 September 1787, he made contact with Shelburne, expressing the view in a letter that 'I wish that this infamous business of perpetual wrangling between England and France might end' and adding that 'peace might be easily preferred were proper persons in the management of affairs.'[46] He would have known from Franklin, Morellet and others that such arguments had been favoured by Shelburne for many years and that a copy of *Prospects on the Rubicon* he had presented to Shelburne would be received with singular favour. Paine was impressed by members of Shelburne's entourage. Probably his favourite was Price; Paine later called Price 'one of the best-hearted men that exists' and 'a friend and republican'.[47] This was a different Paine from *Common Sense*, where Britain and Europe had been rejected as places incapable of restoring enlightenment and doomed to rapid decline and political irrelevance. He admitted he was 'in pretty close intimacy with the heads of the opposition', meaning the opposition to Pitt.[48]

III

Although the Patriot Revolt did not lead to a general European war, Paine's view of Pitt remained negative. Britain appeared to be in free fall as a polity – George III had succumbed further into mental illness, while Shelburne and his group had been reduced to carping from the sidelines about their projects of peace and prosperity. The outbreak of the French Revolution gave Paine great hope: it confirmed the view of France outlined in the *American Crisis* and *Prospects*, that it was a state capable of reform and learning from the American Revolution regarding the establishment and maintenance of an ordered liberty. While Price and Shelburne at first considered that the French were following the English in the Glorious Revolution of 1688–89, Paine was sure that something grander was afoot. Especially after he discovered Burke's negative view – something of a shock because he had previously enjoyed cordial relations with the fellow lover of American liberty – Paine felt compelled to turn himself into the advocate of 'common sense' in France just as he had been on the continent. The tactics he called for were more extreme than anything considered practical by the Shelburne Circle: ultimately, he advocated a national convention of the people to change politics and initiate the process of transforming society root and branch.[49]

Paine's response to Burke, the *Rights of Man*, was published in 1791.[50] In it, he outlined at the outset his broad project of turning Europe's monarchies into republican communities. As he put it in the dedication to President George Washington, Paine's prayer was that the new world would now regenerate the old.[51] In the preface to the English edition, Paine mentioned the affinity between his plans for peace in the late 1780s and those he found in France. Projects for peace and enlightenment were now being realized in France. But Paine had never hitherto advocated revolution by national convention as a transition mechanism. The point was now, he argued in the preface to the French edition, that the peoples of France, England and America were 'enlightened and enlightening' and together would be powerful enough to compel 'the practical enforcement' of what Paine called 'good government' everywhere.[52] Good government meant life in a republic dedicated to Paine's definition of the rights of man. Paine held that ancient superstitions were being identified and abandoned in France, shattering the idols of the divine right of kings, papal power both spiritual and temporal, and the identity of church and state. Regarding the latter Paine wrote that 'the key of St Peter and the key of the Treasury, became quartered on one another, and the wondering cheated multitude worshipped the invention.'[53] As in the American case, Paine focused upon the benefits of the new moral world by listing the ills being suffered by the people of France and of Britain under governments that ought to have been free but had in fact never been so.

Just like the radical Protestants of Reformation times, Paine moved from portraying existing horrors and injustices to the depiction of a world of peace, morality and justice beyond anything experienced before. When Horace Walpole called Paine a 'Leveller', meaning an opponent of social hierarchies in the manner of the seventeenth-century civil war sect, he was right with regard to Paine's doctrine and to his lineage, although Paine was ever a defender of property rights, except in instances such as the patriots in North America, whose property confiscation he had benefited from directly.[54] Paine's reply was that the only true doctrine in which levelling took place was hereditary monarchy, entailing 'mental levelling'.[55] Paine argued that the French revolutionaries had proved that a modern society did not need ranks, because every aristocracy was necessarily corrupt rather than wise. In what became a famous riposte to Burke, Paine stated that the Irishman 'pitied the plumage but forgets the dying bird'.[56] Nobles were, he contested, outdated in politics. So were kings in the sense of beings from whom law for the public good could be expected to emanate. The French had restricted the power of Louis XVI to ensure that his role was to enact the will of the people, turning him into an agent of the national will, rather than its source. Equally, France did not need a powerful Church establishment. It was the Church organized by and for the state that needed to be feared. Religions and religious people were naturally of benefit to any society; they turned evil when they served the state. Paine made this clear in a revealing passage about what he termed 'law-religions':

> Persecution is not an original feature in *any* religion; but it is always the strongly marked feature of all law-religions, or religions established by law. Take away the law-establishment, and every religion reassumes its original benignity. In America, a Catholic priest is a good citizen, a good character and a good neighbour; an Episcopal minister is of the same description: and

this proceeds, independently of the men, from there being no law-establishment in America.[57]

Paine stated that Spain had declined because of its tyrannical religious establishment, and so had France after the Revocation of the Edict of Nantes put an end to the toleration of Protestants in 1685. Equally, the manufactures of Manchester, Birmingham and Sheffield, Paine held, were thriving because they were an 'asylum' from the Church of England. Paine predicted that Dissenters 'who have carried English manufactures to the height they are now at' would soon flee to France.[58]

As Burke recognized, the transition mechanism to Paine's proposed universal republic was 'the abolition of monarchy, nobility, and church establishments . . . in each country', removing the very forces that Burke considered to be upholding society. Paine's was a 'seductive liberty' entailing a 'revolution of doctrine and theoretick dogma'.[59] To Burke it was evident that Paine was an arch-generalizer, setting aside the fact that the political options open to a European were altogether different to those of an American. Paine, in short, had abandoned Montesquieu, and particular circumstances or entrenched faiths, beliefs and mores were being ignored. Paine acknowledged this when he attacked Montesquieu, Voltaire, Rousseau, Quesnay and Turgot for having limited ideas about liberty because they had lived under a despotism.[60] For Paine, beliefs were dangerous when they became infected by tyrannical institutions and political structures. If the structures and institutions were abolished, people would respect one another and the rights of all. Paine was relying on forms of social cohesion and unity generated in the heat of revolution. He thought they would last into the future. He appeared unconcerned that such patriotic and republican fervour might turn enthusiastic. Rather, he expected the republican revolution to proceed apace, relying on the goodness and patriotism of a populace dedicated to the cultures that accompanied the worthy cause. As he put it, 'the human faculties act with boldness [under a republic] and acquire, under this form of government, a gigantic manliness.'[61] If Hume had been alive, he would have recognized Paine's falling into a standard trap for republicans. Just as Macaulay before him, Paine did not explain how to prevent the new republic/ church from falling prey to projectors, demagogues and prophets, or from breaking up into separate factions as republics and Reformation churches had done in the past. Hume would have been unsurprised by the break up of the Jacobin Club into groups seeking the annihilation of one another, at the brief rise of Robespierre or the longer reign of Bonaparte.

Paine's optimism about a republican future at this point in his life was complete, being zealous to the point of brooking no objection. He believed that the political representation of all men was the great discovery of modern times, and he was certain that open and free systems of representation would ensure that wise individuals would be elected.[62] The men who came to office were likely to be enlightened and genuine servants of the public. The problems of 'the old governments of Europe', Paine asserted, following Smith and Shelburne, derived from the mercantile system. This could be traced to 'distortedly exalting some men, so that others are debased, till the whole is out of nature'.[63] In future there would be no courtiers and no patronage. The term 'commons', which in earlier times Paine had praised, he now damned as degrading. He said it was 'unknown in free Countries'.[64]

Paine was sure that the consequences of the abolition of social ranks and hierarchies would be momentous. In future, there would be 'no riots, tumults, and disorders'. This was a peculiar argument to make because it seemed so naive, but Paine seems to have developed a near-religious faith in the capacity of a united republican humanity to join together and solve all problems in perpetuity. He was certain that the establishment of universal republican government would improve life for every inhabitant. An end would be seen to the 'class of poor and wretched people who are so numerously dispersed all over England'.[65] The only way to address the problem of poverty was to remove monarchs, noblemen and church establishments.

Paine took a step beyond the Shelburne Circle when he argued that the only means of abolishing war in the modern world, and of establishing perpetual peace, was to remove the causes of international conflict, which could be found in the ambition of kings, princes and nobles for glory, gold and land. War was a consequence of the need for revenue within monarchical polities. By contrast, republics were pacific 'because the nature of their Government does not admit of an interest distinct from that of the Nation'.[66] In discussing republics Paine was, naturally, discussing modern republics like the United States and now revolutionary France, despite its not being a formal republic until September 1792, rather than historic republics. From Paine's perspective, the existence of aristocracy in such republics would have been the cause of war. As such, his argument was highly specific and unproven. Indeed, there was more than a dash of enthusiasm in the absolute association of modern republics with peace, especially given the history of the newly independent North American republics and their mutual animosities even in the short period between the Declaration of Independence in 1776 and the creation of a federal republic in 1787.

Paine's goal in *Rights of Man* was to persuade the British to follow the French. Paine presented himself as following the logic of existing schemes of reform, proven by the experience of the American republics and now by France. He cited Shelburne, without reference and erroneously, as having said in Parliament that it was up to the British people whether they chose to be governed as a monarchy or a republic. Paine was correct, nevertheless, to acknowledge the inspiration of Smith, almost the only philosopher who received unstinting praise.[67] Smith, for Shelburne as for Paine, had described the mercantile system and Paine both blamed its existence for the state of the country and demanded revolution as the only practical solution. As Paine put it, the French had been bankrupted by their own mercantile system of war and empire while being superior to Britain in every respect economically. The French had enjoyed 'a revenue of nearly twenty-four million sterling, with an extent of rich and fertile land above four times larger than England, with a population of twenty-four millions of inhabitants to support taxation, with upwards of ninety millions of sterling of gold and silver in the nation, and with a debt less than the present debt of England'.[68] Revolution, Paine claimed, had solved the problem of the French national debt by making the nation sovereign rather than a monarch supported by 'the monied interest'.[69] The nation, being the might of the people united, could never go bankrupt and no longer had to fear debt.

The great question was whether Paine was right in depicting a largely peaceful revolution in France, where he underlined that the violence to date – he was writing in late 1790 and early 1791 – had been far less than that experienced by Americans in creating their republics. Equally, Paine asserted that the economy of France was now taking off, generating wealth for all rather than a corrupted few. It was the case, he said at the end of part one of *Rights of Man*, that 'what were formerly called revolutions were little more than a change of persons, or an alteration of local circumstances.'[70] The possibility of 'a general revolution in Europe' was a source of wonder. Paine saw peace ahead because 'it is an age of revolutions, in which everything may be looked for.'[71] He blamed the 'intrigue of courts' for keeping up 'the system of war' and anticipated, after republican revolutions had occurred, 'a confederation of nations' to abolish war.[72] Writing in 1791, Paine argued that 'a European Congress, to patronize the progress of free government and promote the civilization of nations with each' was an event 'nearer in probability than once were the revolutions and alliance of France and America'.[73]

IV

Such conviction and confidence for the future meant that Paine travelled to France in April 1791, soon after the appearance of *Rights of Man*, in euphoric mood. His optimism about the course of the French Revolution knew no bounds. Gouverneur Morris, the American envoy replacing Jefferson, who met Paine at a 4 July celebration, reported Paine to be 'inflated to the eyes and big with a litter of revolutions'.[74] To the Abbé Sieyès, who had mapped out the projects followed by revolutionaries at Paris in the first half of 1789, Paine boasted that he was an 'avowed, open, and intrepid enemy of what is called monarchy', likening such government to that by brutes in open opposition to the 'dignity and honour of the human race'.[75] Returning to London, Paine completed the second part of the *Rights of Man* while living with his friend Rickman and being visited by fellow friends of liberty including Wollstonecraft and Priestley.[76] Partly through the radical Whig John Horne Tooke, he became involved with the Society for Constitutional Information, which subsidized the printing of Paine's *Address and Declaration* to Britons in August 1791 calling for the popular seizure of power to establish a republic. At a meeting of the Revolution Society on 4 November 1791 called because of the visit from France of Jérôme Pétion de Villeneuve, the mayor of Paris, Paine proposed the toast 'the Revolution of the World'.[77]

The Rights of Man: Part the Second, Combining Principle and Practice appeared on 16 February 1792. By May, Paine's publisher Jordan was being prosecuted for sedition; Paine's prosecution for seditious libel followed. It took until December for a London jury to find Paine guilty of subverting the constitution, social order and peace.[78] Yet the popularity of Paine's works is difficult to question. The *Rights of Man*, Paine claimed, sold 500,000 copies in Britain in the decade following its appearance in 1791–92. While it would have been impossible to obtain precise figures, Paine became notorious. Paine himself claimed that, although the British government had 'honoured me with a thousand martyrdoms, by burning me in effigy in every town in that country', the *Rights of Man* 'had the greatest run of any work ever published in the English language'.[79] By the time he was found guilty Paine was back in France. The Legislative Assembly at Paris declared him an honorary citizen on 26 August. Four départements then elected him to the National Convention intended to revise the constitution. One of the four, Pas-de-Calais, sent Achille Audibert to England with the mission of bringing Paine back in order to contribute to French politics.[80] He was successful, taking Paine to Dover, where he departed before a hostile crowd on 13 September, naturally to be warmly welcomed at Calais.

Paine took the success of his writings across Britain, the manifest fear of the authorities, and his perception of the French Revolution as a success, to be proof of a national convention soon being formed in Britain. In the preface to the second part of *Rights of Man*, he was bombastic about the effects of the French Revolution: 'I do not believe that monarchy and aristocracy will continue seven years longer in any of the enlightened countries in Europe.'[81] Government founded on what he termed 'a moral theory, on a system of universal peace, on the indefeasible, hereditary rights of man' was now 'revolving from West to East'.[82] There was 'a morning of reason rising upon man' as the 'barbarism of the present old governments expires'.[83]

The main benefit to be gained for the world was peace. Paine repeated the argument of the first part of *Rights of Man* that wars could be blamed on the forms of government that had an interest in maintaining them. Contested succession within hereditary monarchy explained the civil wars of France, the Hundred Years' War in England and the War of the Spanish Succession. The rebellions of the people of the Dutch Republic in the 1780s against their stadtholder was entirely to do with the latter's hereditary office. Poland, by contrast, had seen fewer wars as an elective monarchy. Europe in recent decades had experienced 'a perpetual system of war and expense . . . [which] drains the country and defeats the general felicity of which civilization is capable'.[84] Paine stated that, 'All the monarchical governments are military. War is their trade, plunder and revenue their objects.'[85] He followed this with the argument that commerce in its natural form tended to peace, and would ultimately establish peace between nations, once the corrupt forms of politics had been eradicated, as had happened in France. He praised the new French republic as the ideal state.

Paine also reiterated a theme traceable back to his *Prospects on the Rubicon* that Pitt had come to be prime minister at a singularly propitious time, when 'everything was in his favour.' If Pitt had followed Shelburne's policy and maintained peace in Europe, 'commerce and prosperity would rise of itself.'[86] Instead, Pitt had turned to wars for empire, turning himself into the 'knight-errant of modern times' as he 'ransacked Europe and India for adventures'.[87] Pitt had turned the British into the barbarians of the contemporary world. They were addicted to wars for empire with no thought for the spoliation and destruction that followed. Paine noted that the 'horrid scene that is now acting by the English Government in the East Indies, is fit only to be told of Goths and Vandals, who, destitute of principle, robbed and tortured the world they were incapable of enjoying'.[88] There was hope, however, that an opportunity existed to 'rescue the world from bondage'.[89] Furthermore, change might be accomplished by reason rather than by force – the will of the British people, he believed, was changing.

Paine wrote that of all the nations in Europe 'there is none so much interested in the French Revolution' as Britain.[90] If France and America were united with Britain and the Dutch Republic as free states, then a scheme of perpetual peace across the Earth could be realized. Paine held that his personal mission was to bring peoples together who knew little of each other and even hated one another because of xenophobia and ignorance: 'Nations, like individuals, who have long been enemies,' he wrote, 'become better friends when they discover the errors and impositions under which they had acted.'[91] Once a confederation of free states was established it would be possible to dismantle the navies of Europe, facilitating the reduction of taxes and reducing the capacity of states for war. What Paine termed 'court governments' would then be replaced in other states. Paine's favoured initial step was Spanish America, which, once independent after the end of empire, could be opened for commerce for the benefit of all.[92]

Paine's boundless optimism was based on the identical effects he discerned of the American and French Revolutions. American events meant 'freedom has a national champion in the Western world.'[93] With France the same could be said for Europe. Paine's rhetoric pronounced the restoration of enlightenment and peace, the introduction of rights across human societies and a better and more just future for all. All that was needed was for other significant powers to join with the republican league:

> When another nation shall join France despotism and bad govern-
> ment will scarcely dare to appear. To use a trite expression, the iron
> is becoming hot all over Europe. The insulted German and the
> enslaved Spaniard, the Russ and the Pole are beginning to think. The
> present age will hereafter merit to be called the Age of Reason, and
> the present generation will appear to the future as the Adam of a
> new world.[94]

The key to the arch was Britain. Paine wrote the *Rights of Man*, he said, to appeal to the people of Britain to change their state. Events in France amounted to the greatest of opportunities for Britain and then for all Europe. If all governments served free peoples, becoming part of the representative system, then nations would become much more interlinked, abandoning the 'animosities and prejudices by the intrigues and artifice of courts'.[95] In time, Paine predicted, sailors would be turned into merchants rather than agents of war. Confederated free states together could put an end to the actions of Algerine pirates so damaging to trade along the Barbary Coast.

Yet the tone of the second part of *Rights of Man* was also different to that of the first part. Paine now recognized that republican patriotism could not be relied on alone to make a success of the French Revolution. It needed specification and direction. Hence Paine sketched out a series of innovative laws and policies to destroy aristocracy in perpetuity by moving wealth from the rich to the poor. Paine's ideas were different from those of the Shelburne Circle. He no longer had faith in national alliances and commercial treaties. *Rights of Man* part two was much more a manifesto to be realized by a republican convention than a justification of republicanism in general.

This meant that the level of vitriol directed against established authorities in Britain was still greater than that of the first part of

Rights of Man. The people, Paine was arguing, were ripe for revolution and this could be done pacifically in a convention after a national uprising. The evils of the existing government, the lack of liberty and general poverty, demanded it. In England, the government acted against civility and civilization. All the 'improvements in agriculture, useful arts, manufactures and commerce' were 'made in opposition to the genius of [England's] government'.[96] Britain's people, because of their government, were increasingly wretched, with 'age going to the work-house and youth to the gallows'.[97] Charters and corporations controlling towns, the landed interest and aristocracy more generally were responsible for the impoverishment of the people, the weak economy and high taxes. Paine called primogeniture, the guarantee of the wealth of the landed interest, 'a law of brutal injustice'.[98] The British people were being 'governed like animals for the pleasure of their riders'.[99] Seventy million sterling per year was spent maintaining the Hanoverians, 'a family imported from abroad, of very inferior capacity' and ever seeking wealth for themselves.[100] It was no wonder that 'jails are crowded, and taxes and poor-rates increased'.[101] Concrete steps were necessary, including old-age pensions, life assurance schemes and the abolition of primogeniture, combined with abolition of the poor rates and poor laws, 'those instruments of civil torture', educational provision for children and a fairer distribution of taxation. Paine called for levies on luxuries and the profits from land with the goal of extirpating 'the unjust and unnatural law of primogeniture, and the vicious influence of the aristocratical system'.[102] Even aristocrats would see the benefits of change, Paine argued, as so many family members became beggars after the first-born son inherited everything.

V

Paine's sense of mission was evident. Although some saw his call for a national convention to be unprecedented in British politics, it underlined the extent to which Paine's politics were derived from the practice of religious reformation, founded on a belief that a community of the faithful existed, the task being simply to call it to action. Yet in demanding a convention Paine's timing could hardly have been worse. He arrived in France a few days after the commencement of the September massacres, entering French politics at a time of renewed uncertainty, upheaval and popular violence that ultimately created the First French Republic. The period leading up to the Terror saw the fracturing of the national unity perceived and lauded by Paine. It amounted to a second revolution, directly refuting Paine's claims about peaceful transitions and national reconstruction by reasoned debate. By 1793, it was Burke who looked like the seer rather than Paine. In such circumstances Paine's confidence might have been expected to lessen because of the violence, the manifest division of the republican community in France and the refusal of the British populace to embrace revolution. Yet Paine became more certain that he was right. His tactics did, however, change. Paine traced the failure of peaceful republicanism in France to the forces ranged against it. Paine blamed Britain, identifying this state as the epicentre of a mercantile system now globally defined, even capable of putting barriers to the progress of republicanism in France. Britain's aristocracy and monarch, promoting and tied together by profits from what Paine called 'the funding system', linked in turn with the monied interest of merchants and bankers, operated like a spider with legs reaching not only to India, the Caribbean and Canada but across Europe's states and their empires too.[103]

When the Austrians and Prussians invaded France in 1792, Paine published an appeal to the soldiers to join the French because theirs was the cause of the people against corrupt courts and despots: 'O, ye Austrians, ye Prussians! ye who now turn your bayonets against us, it is for you, it is for all Europe, it is for all mankind, and not for France alone, that she raises the standard of Liberty and Equality!'[104] The revolutionary armies defending France embodied the cause of all nations, against the forces of tyranny in the form of monarchs and nobles. Modern republics had an advantage because they waged a new kind of war, 'a war of the whole nation . . . When a whole nation acts as an army, the despot knows not the extent of the power against which he contends.' Should enemies successfully penetrate France, they would find themselves 'in the midst of a nation of armies'.[105] This became his view of Britain too after war broke out at the end of February 1793. Paine soon advocated war against the British as the only means of making the French Revolution safe into the future and as the only way of purging humanity of the ills that prevented true happiness, liberty and peace from being experienced by all.

Calling himself a citizen of the world, someone who 'regards the whole human race as his own family', Paine gradually became convinced that a general war upon Britain was the only way of removing monarchy and aristocracy.[106] Thoughts of the peaceable establishment of a national convention were abandoned in favour of the advocacy of two forms of war. First, the rising of an oppressed people who took arms in the name of liberty to challenge tyranny. The failure of the British people to create their own republic Paine blamed upon the power of monarchy and nobility to degrade national culture by making it servile and xenophobic. A spark was necessary, and Paine became interested in Ireland in consequence.[107] It was notable that Rickman named the United Irishman Edward Fitzgerald as a regular visitor to Paine in London. Fitzgerald had come to the same view of Britain as Paine. After being dismissed from the army for renouncing his titles of nobility, he advocated French invasion and was involved in planning Lazare Hoche's unsuccessful attempt upon Ireland of December 1796. Later, in May 1798, while in the process of organizing a national rising in Ireland, Fitzgerald died being arrested.[108] There is evidence that as early as November 1792 Paine was plotting civil uprising in Ireland supported by French money and arms, alongside Fitzgerald, passing on information to French ministers about the likelihood of Irish support for an invasion.[109] Paine's links with the United Irishmen continued with his association with another leader of the movement, James Napper Tandy, in addition to the Scottish republican Thomas Muir. It was said of the three that 'no Frenchman hated more than they did the present British government.'[110]

At some point, just as in the case of mainland Britain, Paine concluded that the forces ranged against domestic rebellion were so great that only an invasion by France would be sufficient to stir the people to action.[111] Paine remained certain that, if given the opportunity and if convinced of success, the British would rebel against their masters. Increasingly, however, they needed the French to act first, or even the Americans. He continued to contribute money to facilitate the abolition of the English government by French invasion, imagining Britain becoming a sister republic to the French in the manner of Italy.[112] French victory, spreading the revolution, was the only route to perpetual peace.

By 1797, Paine was vociferously justifying the invasion by France of other states to spread liberty, arguing that the French would break oppressive chains and teach others how to establish and enjoy liberty.[113] The invasion of Britain, however, was uppermost on his mind, being the vital step to protect France and ensure an alternative future for humanity. Paine sent detailed plans to members of the ruling Directory at Paris in 1797, also outlined in the newspaper the *Bien Informé*, explaining how the military defeat of Britain could be accomplished by over a thousand gunboats arriving on the shores carrying troops.[114] To his friend General Brune in 1799 he stated that there would be 'no safety on the ocean till that tyrannical power be reduced, or a revolution affected in that country'.[115] The same sentiments littered Paine's correspondence with American politicians including Jefferson and James Monroe.[116]

Paine always felt that the French Revolution was worth the cost. Political representation, what he believed to be the great discovery of his age, had led to the establishment of republican nations with cultures homogeneous and patriotic. Contested with America and France, the monarchies had been shown to be lesser militarily than such republics, meaning that a rebalancing had occurred in Europe. As had been the case at the time of the foundation of the Greek Commonwealth and of the Roman Republic, the freest states on Earth were the most formidable. That liberty made for stronger states, better able to maintain themselves against the tyrannies surrounding them, was the key fact of modern politics. Fervently patriotic citizen soldiers devoted to the representative system meant that 'America was enabled thereby totally to defeat and overthrow all the schemes and projects of the Hereditary Government of England against her.'[117] Even the troubled government of the new French Directory, the latest attempt to bring stability to the French republican experiment, was superior to any alternative. He remarked of the new constitution of 1795 that 'a better organized Constitution has never yet been devised by human wisdom.'[118] At the same time he acknowledged the necessity of a coup against the first Directors in his *The Eighteenth Fructidor* pamphlet on the grounds that they were acting too much in favour of the Catholic Church and the exiled nobility.

Paine continued to couple the French and American revolutions together as positive events in human history, even after he returned to the new world. The latter became possible when the peace of Amiens was agreed on 27 March 1802 by the French, British, Spanish and the Batavian Republic, putting an end to the War of the Second Coalition. For fourteen months travel became possible across to North America without fear of British naval vessels. Paine took advantage, departing on 1 September 1802.

Paine only became fearful for the Revolution when politics became acutely divisive, as had happened under Robespierre. Paine was of course a victim through his imprisonment and closeness to death. Before the Terror, however, Paine was signalling a concern about revolutionary culture. Significantly, he blamed religious beliefs. In *Rights of Man, Part the First* Paine had attacked the superstitions that could be associated historically with politics, linking priestcraft with statecraft. At the end of the second part of *Rights of Man* Paine warned against religion's becoming what he termed a 'political machine', giving the example of established churches which corrupted the state and were in turn infected by politics.[119] Avoiding both atheism and priestcraft, both of which he was certain led to division and violence, was the goal of *The Age of Reason*, which Paine composed between April and December 1793 while living in Saint-Denis.[120] While Paine was sure that Britain would ultimately implode through economic crisis or political chaos, he did, however, recognize that the French too had failed to create a stable republican community. Paine continued to predict the imminent demise of Britain in major pamphlets such as *The Decline and Fall of the English System of Finance* (1796) and *Agrarian Justice* (1797). But republicans too needed a culture that underpinned their institutions and that operated to prevent the kinds of instability and crisis that plagued revolutionary France before the rise of Bonaparte.

But if Paine felt let down by Washington and underwhelmed by the constitution of the United States ratified in 1788, he also acknowledged that the French experiment had been a failure. At the end of 1802, he wrote to his friend Jefferson, now president, that the French were bankrupt and exhausted. The time was right, Paine said, for the United States to purchase Louisiana.[121] The Louisiana purchase was justified on the grounds of preventing future wars, stopping France or Spain from establishing communities that might one day challenge the United States. For this generation, the belief that 'of all the despotisms in the world that of a mercantile monopolizing company is the worst' was commonplace.[122] To sceptics, the expansion of the United States set in train the process by which the new republic became a state just like those of Europe, recognizing that mercantile empire was the surest means of maintaining a state. Paine's contribution to this process might have underscored his realism. Small republics or republican unions had to defend themselves, and the best way was to become larger and stronger. It may also have reflected the longstanding lack of interest in the native peoples and chattel slaves affected by the expansion of the United States. Paine's citizens, following classical models, were male, pale and owned land.

VI

Both Paine and Burke identified the other as an advocate of terror. Two reasons were given. First, they considered the governments that each defended to be incompatible with liberty and order. Secondly, and more significantly, each concluded that their own view of human flourishing would be safe only if the other's vision was exterminated. With the progress of the French Revolution, Burke began to argue that it was necessary to restore the French monarchy, its civil and ecclesiastical orders, and all their sequestered property. The only means to such an end was the transformation of British foreign policy. International policy had to encompass intervention in Europe to keep the peace, to protect the old world of the continent, and to maintain it for the economic development of all those states which favoured trade, morality and religion. As Burke put it, Britain had become 'the great resource of Europe'. Britain could no longer be 'detached from the rest of the world and amusing herself with the puppet-show of a naval power'. Rather, Britain had to be 'embodied with Europe'. The resulting war was 'just, necessary, manly, pious'. Its goal was to preserve 'political independence and civil freedom to nations ... national independence, property, liberty, life, and honour, from certain havoc'. It was a 'war for all nations'.[123]

Burke's war on the Revolution had to be continued until Britain collapsed or the French Revolution itself was made history. The extent of the transformation of political thought in response to the perception of the end of enlightenment can be made plain. Three men, Brissot, Paine and Burke, all of whom saw themselves to be advocates of peace and liberty, became convinced that the destruction either of Britain or of republican France alone could secure a tolerant future. Each of them had embraced fully Hume's diagnosis of the ills of the time and the key danger posed by superstition and fanaticism. From pacific patriots, Brissot, Paine and Burke became warmongers, advocates of terror against the peoples and governments who espoused a different point of view. Deathly struggle between competing ideologies was the order of the day.

9.

Mary Wollstonecraft and the End of Equality

I

As we have seen, those who tried to avert the end of enlightenment were themselves often accused of being dangerously fanatical. Accusations of being subversive Protestants, friends to rebellious Catholics, regicides and parricides, supporters of republican anarchism or monarchical absolutism, of wanting to ignite wars of religion, or import the lascivious manners of the East into the West, were all employed again and again in the 1790s. In times of such political discord, the commonwealth tradition subsisted as myth, a monster to be evoked to tarnish and disparage. Paine, Macaulay and Brissot were tarred alongside Price, Shelburne and Priestley. Yet Mary Wollstonecraft's reputation was trounced more bitterly than that of anyone else. The main reason was that Wollstonecraft's vision of a true enlightenment and her projects to make it a reality were more radical than any other. This is because they entailed equality between the sexes. As we might suspect, such condemnation was gendered.[1] It was compounded too by the naivety of her devoted husband, the philosopher William Godwin. Godwin, through the publication of *Memoirs of the Author of a Vindication of the Rights of Woman*, written in grief to laud and commemorate his dead wife, revealed too much about their private life to his eighteenth-century audience. Wollstonecraft's critics were provided with all the ammunition they needed to deride her as a person and dismiss her work.[2] Although she always attracted devotees who were inspired by her writings, Wollstonecraft's reputation only fully recovered when she was adopted as a heroine by the suffragettes in the twentieth century.[3]

But in the time she lived and wrote, as today, Wollstonecraft was a visionary. Her idea of a new enlightenment restoring a lost and always partial tolerance was so grand. One of the consequences of seeing the collapse of trust and toleration, and of the descent into all the species of havoc Hume had foreseen, was the opening of the imagination to very different ways of living, an explicit rejection of tradition and history. Wollstonecraft was convinced, following Hume and the Dissenters who followed him, that the present condition of the world would not last much longer. In such circumstances, it was right, she felt, to speculate, to imagine better futures. Amid shifting ground, opportunities to move in new directions had arisen for the first time in centuries. Wollstonecraft concluded that much of the force that was destroying enlightenment derived from relations between men and women; these were sick, unnatural and decaying. She followed Shelburne and Price in arguing that the time was right to incorporate into the public realm those who were not trusted and tolerated, including Dissenters and Catholics, those excluded from the Revolution Settlement at the end of the seventeenth century. But Wollstonecraft had a more encompassing notion of liberty and of equality, one in which men and women lived in parity. If this happened, she argued, true enlightenment would be experienced for the first time.

Wollstonecraft was important too because although the change she imagined in society was far more extensive than that of her contemporaries, she believed it could be accomplished through the arts of peace. Even in the depths of the French Revolution, in a Europe torn by war and where ideological ferment in localities frequently turned violent, she refused to identify enemies whose guilt was so great that they needed to be expelled from politics or from life. This became a major dividing line among those who experienced the end of enlightenment. Shelburne, Price and Wollstonecraft deeply detested war, arguing always that human conflict, however justified it appeared to be, would only exacerbate problems rather than leading to a resolution through victory. Burke, Paine and Brissot, as we have seen, turned to war as a necessary purgative, an unavoidable evil that had to be carried to the end point of wiping from the face of the Earth the forces – either monarchy, nobility and established church on one hand, or revolutionaries on the other – preventing enlightenment from being restored.

Wollstonecraft and Godwin fully embraced the French Revolution as a glorious event unprecedented in history. They believed it was the moment most likely to realize the historic enlightenment defined and defended by *philosophes* such as Locke, Rousseau, Condillac and Voltaire. The French Revolution presented what they perceived to be the greatest opportunity yet seen to build a better world for all. The early successes of the Revolution were crucial to such a perception. The French people had come together, and their monarch and his ministers had embraced reform. Resistance, at least initially, was minimal. And it was lauded everywhere by those who called themselves cosmopolitans and friends of humanity. Evidence was being presented of better ways of living, leading to the conclusion that liberty and equality could be established and maintained while inaugurating breathtaking social and political improvement.

The Revolution was revealing, Godwin said, that humans were not perfect – but they were perfectible.[4] For Wollstonecraft and Godwin, men such as Burke were apologists for the end of enlightenment, accepting a world in decline, where liberty had been lost and where commerce was increasing luxury, immorality and inequality. To both, the mutual disgust and antagonism between opposing camps was incomprehensible. Why would someone as obviously able as Burke condemn the greatest experiment in creating a paradise on Earth? How could friends of liberty attack liberty abroad? Why would one free state, perceiving itself to be among the few that existed on Earth, question liberty newly planted in another, especially when the English journey to liberty had itself been bloody?

Wollstonecraft in particular could not understand why Burke could question events in Paris while being a critic of British politics and a friend of the American Revolution. For her, the only problem with the French Revolution was that it did not go far enough. It was necessary to assert the rights of woman alongside the rights of man and to seek the abolition of slavery and injustice everywhere. Wollstonecraft even abandoned Britain for France, so strong was her faith. If the abolition of slavery was contested and then passed into law on 4 February 1794, momentum appeared also to be building for equality between the sexes, with the appearance of Olympe de Gouges's *Declaration of the Rights of Woman and the Female Citizen* in 1791 and the foundation of the Society for Revolutionary Republican Women in May 1793.

Yet after observing, and in Wollstonecraft's case experiencing, Terror, instability, injustice and war, by 1797 the faith of every supporter of the French Revolution had been sorely tested. The rights of man had been erected at the root of successive constitutions in Paris, and then soon violated with abandon – resulting in poverty, massacre, frenzy and death. For Wollstonecraft the tragedy was personal: she was abandoned by the lover she met in Paris and was left with their child. For her, it was ever the case that the personal and the political were intertwined.

The French Revolution, ardent supporters were admitting by the late 1790s, was evidently not a ready and easy way into a higher level of enlightenment. Rather, every progressive philosophy associated with events in France had been tested and found wanting. But Wollstonecraft refused to question the goal of creating a tolerant and pacific world where women were equal to men, while acknowledging that the tactics necessary to meet such a goal had of necessity to change. Wollstonecraft too refused to turn from cosmopolitan to sectarian. At the same time, as for the entire end of enlightenment generation, she perceived herself to have failed in her mission. When she died of puerperal fever eleven days after giving birth on 30 August 1797 to Mary Wollstonecraft Godwin, later to become famous as the author of *Frankenstein*, she had reconciled herself to the failure of the French Revolution. Her disillusionment with events in France was the greatest wrench in a decade of political turmoil and personal trauma. Wollstonecraft knew what enlightenment meant and how to make a reality of it, but she ended up accepting that remedies both traditional and revolutionary had become worse than the disease.

II

The vision of enlightenment and a world of equality and toleration owed much for Wollstonecraft and Godwin to their reading of the *philosophes,* but more still to their membership of communities of Dissenters. The Dissenters directly experienced exclusion from public life and lived lives lacking civil liberties. They recognized the benefits of being tolerated in the sense of being allowed to practise their religion in conditions where an alternative and established church held sway. But they also battled to maintain Britain as a free state amid forces they perceived to be sustaining tyranny. Above all they knew that enlightenment, as it had been established in Britain and elsewhere, required further consolidation. They called to be let into civil life by being granted liberties equivalent to those of the Anglican community.[5]

In Wollstonecraft's case the Dissenters around Richard Price when he was minister at Newington Green in London became a second family in the 1780s – Price was a major source of personal support and intellectual inspiration.[6] He introduced her to Joseph Johnson, a favourite publisher for reformers, and Johnson became a second father to Wollstonecraft over the following years. She wrote to him in 1788 stating, 'You are my only friend—the only person I am *intimate* with.—I never had a father, or a brother.'[7] Godwin came from a family of Dissenting ministers and was educated at Hoxton Academy, run by Andrew Kippis, another member of Shelburne's Circle, and Abraham Rees.[8] After a spell as a minister himself, Godwin too turned to a literary career.[9] His religious views were always considered heterodox even among Dissenters, tending towards a Sandemanian defence of primitive Christianity entailing the absolute rejection of organized churches – faith for Godwin was spiritual and belief entirely personal.[10] Despite his heterodoxy, Kippis was instrumental in obtaining an income for Godwin as a contributor to the New Annual Register from 1784 and he remained close to prominent Dissenters. Wollstonecraft, while working with Dissenters and being inspired by them, refused ever to join any Dissenting sect. Hers was always an independent and personal religious belief, following Rousseau's *Émile,* while rejecting altogether his view of women.[11]

Wollstonecraft needed a new family because her own had been entirely dysfunctional. Her violent father, whom she termed a despot, wasted the family fortune built up by her grandfather through a silk weaving business in Spitalfields.[12] Seeking to turn himself into a gentleman farmer, Edward Wollstonecraft was a disaster as a tradesman and a monster as a drunk, especially abusive towards his submissive wife, Elizabeth. Mary Wollstonecraft, because of the familial descent into poverty, had a peripatetic existence as a child and meagre formal education. Of the numerous surviving Wollstonecraft children, only the oldest son Ned received support and, according to Mary, love in any form from their mother. This did not prevent Wollstonecraft educating herself to an astonishing degree, leading to the acquisition of numerous languages and unquestioned brilliance as an author, in addition to becoming an editor and translator. Due to her need for money, she initially served as a governess, seamstress, lady's companion and school mistress. Despising such work, she turned to literature, undertaking labours akin to those of Brissot, publishing in rapid succession a self-help manual in 1787, *Thoughts on the Education of Daughters*, her first book, and her first novel, *Mary: A Fiction*, in 1788, a collection of writings for women readers, *The Female Reader* (1789), and tales for children, *Original Stories from Real Life* (1788), while contributing a stream of book reviews to Johnson's *Analytical Review*.[13]

Wollstonecraft's work before the French Revolution detailed the injustices that were legion in contemporary society, describing the rising levels of intolerance and poverty. At the same, and very much in the manner of Dissenters like Price, she preached stoic self-control when surrounded by a sea of temptation in a commercial and urban society. Warnings were issued against excessive passions held to be wasteful, ranging from gambling and the theatre to frivolous dress and the enjoyment of luxury.[14] What made Wollstonecraft's works so appealing to readers was the acknowledgement and description of struggle and perpetual impediments in her search for a life of virtue and happiness. Her early letters reveal a complicated figure, singularly confident and yet self-effacing, often only ever seemingly happy in devotion to others, such as her friend the illustrator Fanny Blood. When Blood died in childbirth in 1785, Wollstonecraft was devastated.[15] She recognized that she was different to others in the extent of her condemnation of existing modes of life, especially for women. She was also distinctive in tirelessly campaigning against such treatment, refusing ever to be silenced.

III

As with Brissot, it was the French Revolution that made Wollstonecraft famous. Her reply to Burke's *Reflections*, entitled *A Vindication of the Rights of Men*, brought her widespread attention for lauding events in France as 'the most astonishing that has hitherto happened in the world'.[16] She became a fixture in radical gatherings supportive of events in France that occurred across London. This was how she came to know Godwin. They had first met at the house of her publisher Joseph Johnson at a dinner in honour of Paine in November 1791.[17] Paine had said little and Godwin reported that Wollstonecraft had dominated the conversation; neither liked the other at the time.[18] In the early 1790s both Godwin and Wollstonecraft were committed to a far more extensive enlightenment than had existed hitherto in human societies, entailing toleration and peace but also far greater equality between ranks and genders, all conversing together.[19] Godwin did not expect as speedy a victory for liberty in France as had happened in North America, but he was certain that

Paine's *Rights of Man* had sowed a seed of revolution that was unstoppable; it *would* lead to far-reaching political and social transformation.[20] Godwin called Paine 'the unalterable champion of liberty in America, in England & in France', declaring his personal objective, like Paine's, to be the erection of a republic in Britain.[21] Yet Godwin's vision and that of Wollstonecraft was even greater in scope than that of Paine, entailing a complete alteration of relations between persons and an altered world of human behaviour in conditions of what they termed civilization. Equality was the watchword, but the behaviour necessary to sustain equality was the substance of their philosophies.

If Wollstonecraft focused on the political, institutional and moral constraints upon equality, Godwin at this time was more interested in the power of the mind to change the individual self, creating a better society in the process of self-realization; he anticipated transformation even as far as the immortality of the body in his *Enquiry Concerning Political Justice* published in February 1793.[22] Wollstonecraft's *A Vindication of the Rights of Woman*, published in 1792, ploughed a related furrow in calling for a new moral world. In their focus on individual behaviour, their thought was closest to the Protestant reformers of Reformation times, figures they increasingly praised as the decade went on. Unsurprisingly, one of Wollstonecraft's favourite points of reference was John Milton. Like Milton, Wollstonecraft held that 'an immoderate fondness for dress, for pleasure, and for sway, are the passions of savages.'[23] Individuals had to harness and limit their own passionate natures, becoming better behaved for the common good. The parallels between the feminist and the Puritan went deep.

Wollstonecraft's strategy for enlightenment emerged through a deep engagement with and refutation of Burke. It was too early, she argued, to work out whether the French Revolution was going to be a success and therefore his attacks were based on little or no evidence. The deeper point, however, was that Burke was someone who had always acknowledged the limits of contemporary politics and the problems of the world and in rejecting events at Paris out of hand, at the same time as Price's reform programme for Britain, he had become an apologist for corruption and injustice. The French, in taking the evils of the modern world seriously and in trying to combat them, deserved support. To do otherwise was to justify a status quo of marked decline in wealth, morals and freedom.

Wollstonecraft's diagnosis of the evils identifiable across Britain defined an end of enlightenment indebted both to Price and to Macaulay.[24] Following Macaulay, Wollstonecraft's response to Burke was full of laments for the extent of contemporary poverty and the dreadful lives lived by the poor, especially in cities. There was in her writing a Commonwealth-inspired distaste for urban living and commercial society. It was in cities that misery 'lurks in pestilential corners', where unemployment was rife because of the ups and downs of commerce, called by Wollstonecraft the 'flux of trade or fashion', where idleness and vice were ubiquitous.[25] What she called 'the specious train of luxury' also ensured that the poor became brutish, lusting after unaffordable baubles, while the rich, mired in excess, became debauched, resulting in a general misery for all.[26] Rural life was superior, especially if large farms were divided into small farms. Wollstonecraft disliked enclosure and wanted common land to be given in parcels to those willing to undertake honest toil for their own betterment and that of their families. But Wollstonecraft was no environmentalist. She asked why 'huge forests [were] still allowed to stretch out with idle pomp and all the indolence of Eastern grandeur' and questioned the existence of 'the brown waste . . . when men want work'.[27] We must bear in mind, however, that the forests she disparaged were the preserve only of the nobles and of the court – as much a symbol of inequality as any palace.

Britain, Wollstonecraft argued, had once been a free state but the constitution had become tarnished over time. Burke knew this but was defending Britain as if it were freer than France. This made no sense to Wollstonecraft: in Britain, she argued, there was but 'a shadow of representation' and recent times had seen disaster after disaster in politics, with debt, war and crisis following each other.[28] Burke too was fully aware given his personal history in opposition,

raising the issue for Wollstonecraft of whether his was a real or artificial veneration for the constitution.[29] The truth, she said, had been
revealed by Hume in his *History of England*: under Edward III, the
monarch battled against the barons and the church and gave liberty
to the commoners only because they offered him funds to pay for
his wars. Liberty was therefore the accidental product of monarchical ambition and a system that Hume had termed a 'barbarous
monarchy, not regulated by any fixed maxims, or bounded'.[30] In different times superstition had raised the clergy to power while a
weak king raised the nobility. The people had, then, always been
weak and susceptible to being dominated by the other elements of
the constitution. This was happening in her own time, Wollstonecraft said, when laws and customs were 'melting' into 'darkness and
ignorance'.[31] The measure of a government or society was the
extent to which natural rights were being respected. She believed
these rights were given to humans by God as rational creatures
'above the brute creation by their improvable faculties'. They could
never legitimately be taken away, so that a father could dissipate a
child's inheritance but never 'sell him for a slave, or fetter him with
laws contrary to reason'.[32]

Rights facilitated a reckoning, and Wollstonecraft indicted Britain
accordingly. In politics the rich had everything and the poor no
rights of any kind. They were squeezed unceasingly by taxes while
their representatives in the House of Commons were 'often purchased by the crown' and corrupted by money.[33] Money bought
influence and this in turn bought offices in the army, in politics and
in the church. This was a fact about contemporary Britain, yet
Burke talked of virtue and liberty, as if either existed. Liberty, Wollstonecraft argued, only meant the security of property in Britain.
This was 'the definition of English liberty. And to this selfish principle every nobler one is sacrificed.' The laws defended the rich
alone while 'the man who lives by the sweat of his brow has no
asylum from oppression.' Hence the press gang, which forced ordinary subjects into the navy, the game laws, which justified the
execution of those who hunted deer, and the decoy field, which

ensured the poor man saw his crop destroyed because the rich man wanted to attract birds for shooting to his own nearby plot: 'Game devour the fruit of his labour; but fines and imprisonment await him if he dare to kill any or lift up his hand to interrupt the pleasure of his lord.' In Britain the poor had become 'the live stock of an estate, the feather of hereditary nobility'. The result was a 'silent majority of misery'.[34] In addition to the lack of rights for the poor, those who had different beliefs to the established church were persecuted by being locked out of normal society. Much worse still was the position of chattel slaves. Wollstonecraft argued that slavery infringed natural rights, every idea of justice and 'the common principles of humanity, not to mention Christianity'.[35]

Wollstonecraft was furious with Burke for questioning Price's patriotism and for identifying him as a dangerous radical and would-be fomenter of violence. This was because Price defended the rights of the people in the constitution and Wollstonecraft found a contradiction in Burke because his hero William Blackstone also argued that 'the succession of the King of Great Britain depends on the choice of the people, or that they have a power to cut it off.'[36]

Most marked in Wollstonecraft's assessment of Britain was her assault on the noble class. She praised the French for abolishing rank on the grounds that, 'Inequality of rank must ever impede the growth of virtue, by vitiating the mind that submits or domineers.'[37] Proof could be found in Europe, where the growth of civilization had been 'very partial', with loose morals and a false sentimentality pervasive. Wollstonecraft's description of contemporary mores was very much in the manner of Rousseau's indictment of Paris in earlier decades. But the source of the malaise for Wollstonecraft was 'hereditary property – hereditary honours'.[38] Turning men who owned land into tyrants because of their wealth and social position had had disastrous consequences for the states of Europe. In France, the use of arbitrary *lettres de cachet* could ensure imprisonment without trial. Equally, children could be imprisoned at the whim of parents if they refused to marry a fellow noble.[39]

In Britain the laws of primogeniture and entail ensured that only the eldest male mattered in a family. Family control over marriages meant that men behaved like rakes, seeking sex and debauching women while waiting for the formal betrothal intended only to secure the noble line. If male morals went to pot, women were equally tainted by the system, forced to behave coquettishly in order to impress a potential suitor. Wollstonecraft considered such behaviour to be both pitiful and dangerous, weakening morality to the point of turning the rich into feverish and unreasoning fools.[40] Equally, the landed interest, being idle and deluded, became obsessed with military valour and war, rather than anything useful for society. Being dominant, their manners and culture were disastrously aped by the middle class. False patriotism and a lust for war was the outcome. Wollstonecraft called it 'a destructive mildew that blights the fairest virtues; benevolence, friendship, generosity, and all those endearing charities which bind human hearts together, and the pursuits which raise the mind to higher contemplations'.[41] Instead, the barbarous and feudal institution of property enabled 'the elder son to overpower talents and depress virtue'.[42] Again Wollstonecraft called Burke 'deluded' for making noble families the pillar of the state while 'luxury and effeminacy' had corrupted them to the point of what she termed 'idiotism'.[43] Noble culture, pervasive across the whole of society, led people of all ranks to turn to stealing, gaming, drunkenness and prostitution.[44] That Burke lauded such a culture was horrific because it was tantamount to encouraging poison ivy, as beautiful as it might be to look at, to insidiously destroy the trunk of a tree.[45] What Burke praised as a 'liberal descent', meaning the rule of wise and sensible men with a stake in Britain, was for Wollstonecraft a corrupt cabal whose loose conduct 'obliterated instead of inspiring native dignity, and substituted a factitious pride that disembowelled the man'.[46]

Despite the state of the world and of Britain in particular, Wollstonecraft had faith that 'a glorious change' could occur by giving the people true liberty, an experiment that was being undertaken in France. There had never been a true enlightenment because liberty 'has never yet received a form in the various governments that have been established on our beauteous globe; the demon of property has ever been at hand to encroach on the sacred rights of men, and to fence round with awful pomp laws that war with justice'.[47] Wollstonecraft's enlightenment, it has to be admitted, smacked of puritanism. She dreamed of the transformation that would occur 'if men were more *enlightened!*'. The world would be cleaner, people would work more and be more industrious, and they would emulate the behaviour of the moral rather than the depraved. The clergy, instead of pursuing their own interests, would serve the people of the parish, guiding them and educating them. The result would be a country where 'domestic comfort, the civilizing relations of husband, brother, and father, would soften labour, and render life contented.'[48]

Creating such a moral world relied upon the exercise of reason, which ultimately taught that virtue led to happiness. The cultivation of reason was 'an arduous task' but Wollstonecraft had faith that 'if virtue is to be acquired by experience, or taught by example, reason, perfected by reflection, must be the director of the whole host of passions, which produce a fructifying heat, but no light, that you would exalt into her place.'[49] The notion of reason and liberty working together to solve problems and foster social improvement and general happiness harked back to Shelburne's point to Price that he was looking for someone who could define laws self-evidently for the common good of all and hence beyond contestation. Decades before this had led the Shelburne Circle to look to Turgot's science of legislation. Wollstonecraft was not arguing that this science had now become a reality, but rather stating that the best hope of so doing lay in trusting the French to undertake a grand experiment in politics. Burke's unwillingness to do so meant that he had no solutions to offer.

From Burke's perspective, the problem with Wollstonecraft was that she was as far away as Price or anyone else from precisely defining the public good, the laws that embodied everyone's interest and that would be recognized to be doing so. She was putting her trust in the unknown while even Price had worked on books defining the common good; hers, by contrast, was a species of enthusiasm bordering on the superstitious, because it lacked an engagement with existing law and was destructive rather than positive in intention. Wollstonecraft's counter-argument was that grotesque inequality had made such a mess of European society that the French were right to abolish aristocracy, that they were just in their redistribution of church land and wealth to the poor.[50] Wollstonecraft said she knew that the policies being put into practice by the National Assembly in France were the right ones – this of course was the perspective of 1790 and 1791. The actions of revolutionaries had proved that giving liberty to the people was the best means of creating a new world. Liberty was itself a transmission mechanism. As she put it, 'Such a glorious change can only be produced by liberty. Inequality of rank must ever impede the growth of virtue, by vitiating the mind that submits or domineers; that is ever employed to procure nourishment for the body, or amusement for the mind.'[51] Burke had placed his faith in a noble elite whom she called 'the profligates of rank, emasculated by hereditary effeminacy'.[52] Wollstonecraft placed her faith in men 'who had no titles to sacrifice', remembering that titles were 'the corner-stone of despotism'.[53]

IV

Wollstonecraft's devotion to Price was underlined by the nature of her personal attacks on Burke.[54] She called Burke mistaken, vain, venal, jealous of Price and a hypocrite, himself an example of what was wrong with British politics, being a placeman and defender of corruption, debauchery and tyranny. Burke's portrayal of Marie Antoinette during the October Days was vicious because he insinuated that Price would have been happy to see popular violence.[55] Burke, if he was not always in pursuit of 'the throne of fame' would have supported the French Revolution.[56] If Price's hopes for the future were 'utopian reveries' since 'the world is not yet sufficiently civilized to adopt such a sublime system of morality', Burke was wrong to castigate them as dangerous. How, after all, could something be amiss with the doctrine of a 'benevolent mind' who was 'tottering on the verge of the grave' and ought to be praised for having never in his life 'dreamt of struggling for power or riches'.[57] It was evident that Price's optimistic speculations about the future were altogether shared by Wollstonecraft. She went so far as to argue that society could not exist if there was not equality between members: 'Among unequals there can be no society . . . if the basis of friendship is mutual respect, and not a commercial treaty.'[58] Faith was vital in events in France because here was an opportunity to attain 'more virtue and happiness than has hitherto blessed our globe'.[59]

The full extent of equality envisaged by Wollstonecraft became clear in the book that soon followed the *Rights of Men*, *A Vindication of the Rights of Woman*.[60] Although many of the arguments of the response to Burke were reiterated, there was a confidence about the future that was new and an expectation that the transformation of social mores was speedily to be anticipated. Such a tone was due entirely to what at the time was seen as the real success of the French Revolution. The events of 1789–91 were seen by radicals to have shown purposive social and political reform to be possible and self-sustaining. The people of France were better off, the state was stronger rather than having collapsed, and nay-sayers like Burke were being refuted daily. Wollstonecraft's was one of a wave of books written on the assumption that France had turned itself into a model for the globe, well worthy of emulation. This was why *A Vindication of the Rights of Woman* was dedicated to the cleric and slippery politician Charles-Maurice de Talleyrand-Périgord, who had recently launched a plan of national education for France which Wollstonecraft hoped to improve upon. Wollstonecraft wrote *A Vindication of the Rights of Woman* at high speed, in a matter of months, for the good reason that she perceived an enlightenment never before experienced in human societies taking shape all around her.

Wollstonecraft's *Vindication of the Rights of Woman* called for equality between the sexes based on a complete transformation of the woman's role in contemporary society. Women had, she argued, been conditioned into a state of 'barren blooming', meaning purposeless or useless aspiration and activity – her description focused especially on the upper echelons.[61] As example was the refusal to eat as a proof of 'delicacy'.[62] For equality to exist, women had to cease to be women as they were presently shaped. Manners and culture were geared to turning women into 'alluring mistresses' rather than 'affectionate wives and rational mothers'. The pursuit of love and desire prevented understanding, she wrote, being 'bubbled by this specious homage' to sexual intercourse with eminent and socially superior men.[63] She argued that women, in pursuing the goal of being sexually desirable in order to make a good marriage, had been formed frivolous, meek and pathetic. Women had been made to sacrifice body and mind to 'libertine notions of beauty, to the desire of establishing themselves'. They had become, according to Wollstonecraft, more like children than adults. Her disgust for the system and its product was absolute. Modern British women were appropriate only for the brothel: 'they dress; they paint, and nickname God's creatures. Surely these weak beings are only fit for a seraglio!'[64] Worse still, the system as it was constructed turned women into despots towards one another. Deceit and cunning were deployed to defeat rivals by ruining their confidence and sense of self.[65] In a memorable passage Wollstonecraft described the extent of the degradation. Women were 'rendered foolish or vicious' by their ignorance. Both sexes were being corrupted by 'wealth, idleness, and folly' so that men considered 'love as a selfish gratification'; they were not friends with their lovers because relations were false and affected. Marriage could not be the positive institution it ought to be in such circumstances. Rather, there was a complete collapse of morality because, 'Virtue flies from a house divided against itself – and a whole legion of devils take up their residence there.'[66]

Wollstonecraft called the pursuit of fashion 'a badge of slavery'.[67] The term is important because women were forced, by the structures of male power surrounding them, to behave as they did.[68] Women had become akin to colourful birds whose impressive plumage could not hide the fact of their being in cages.[69] The result was that women had become shadows of their potential selves since, 'The grand source of female folly and vice has ever appeared to me to arise from narrowness of mind.'[70] Women in contemporary society were forced to become altogether 'creatures of sensation'. This was ensured by the literature and music consumed within a culture Wollstonecraft termed 'gallantry'. She attacked the portrayal of women serving the needs of men alone in so many novels and by numerous poets.[71] What Wollstonecraft called an 'overstretched sensibility' was the result – the modern term would be co-dependency – limiting the powers of the mind and preventing 'intellect from attaining that sovereignty which it ought to attain to render a rational creature useful to others, and content with its own station'. The neglect of the intellect meant that women became slaves to passion, because the intellect alone could calm the passions.[72]

The assault on current mores continued to the end of *A Vindication of the Rights of Woman*. Girls were taught from infancy that 'beauty is woman's sceptre, the mind shapes itself to the body.' Women roamed around gilt cages if they were lucky, around prisons if not so fortunate.[73] But the broader point Wollstonecraft was making was that people, men and women together, considered themselves civilized while what it amounted to in terms of social practice was a partial civilization, if not barbarism, entrenching fake and purposeless ways of life, aspirations and conduct under the guise of terms such as sensibility, politeness and progress. The question to be asked was, given that people were 'educated in slavish dependence, and enervated by luxury and sloth, where shall we find men who will stand forth to assert the rights of man?'[74] For women, a moral revolution was required so that they would be able to recognize and abandon such behaviour, so that they would be able to orient themselves into full citizens.

Writing in 1792, Wollstonecraft was sure that if women were

given liberty, were directed by her own writing, that of others and by a new education system, then the kinds of behaviour she termed 'virtuous' would become habitual, creating an entirely different culture between the sexes. As she put it, 'brutal force has hitherto governed the world.' What she called 'the science of politics' was in its infancy. Yet she had high hopes because 'as sound politics diffuse liberty, mankind, including woman, will become more wise and virtuous.'[75] It was time 'to effect a revolution in female manners, time to restore to them their lost dignity and make them, as a part of the human species, labour by reforming themselves to reform the world'.[76] Wollstonecraft identified the actions of men within a culture of misogyny to be the central impediment to the realization of an altered world. But men too were victims, being themselves corrupted and degraded by cultures which valued rank and money above utility and social worth.[77]

The excessive love of money was a passion which Wollstonecraft always disdained. Commercial societies were full of misery, experiencing a false freedom 'which has been bartered for splendid slavery'. Men sought money as a route to pre-eminence, obtaining pleasure by 'commanding flattering sycophants'. Liberty itself had become an idea associated with what Wollstonecraft termed 'mock patriotism'. Money bought rank and together this translated into positions for men, most of whom did not deserve them, in the army, navy and the church. Idle men who contributed little to society were valued, and men whose profession was the pursuit of war. Wollstonecraft condemned mercenaries and standing armies as incompatible with liberty. War and commerce were tied together in the search for riches and glory by monarchs, by merchants drawing wealth from luxuries sold in towns that were dens of iniquity, and by men who committed atrocities in the pursuit of empire.[78] In a republican register, Wollstonecraft attacked the history of monarchy as key to the dominion of vice and the subjection of women. Behind monarchy lay aristocracy, another source of iniquity and moral abandonment. Wollstonecraft admitted that after she had challenged 'the sacred majesty of Kings' it was not surprising for her then to argue that the 'great subordination of rank constitutes its power, is highly injurious to morality'.[79]

Wollstonecraft held that 'preposterous distinctions of rank' rendered 'civilization a curse', by dividing the world between 'voluptuous tyrants, and cunning envious dependents'. In turn every class of people focused on maintaining their station and status while neglecting social duties.[80] With social duties neglected, monarchy and aristocracy, ever seeking their own interests, fed a culture of sensuality and excess, turning aspiring men into servile parasites and vile panderers and women into cyphers, appendages to the mighty and servants of their sensual pleasures and therefore akin to slaves.[81] Drawing once more upon Hume, exactly as she had in *A Vindication of the Rights of Men*, Wollstonecraft asserted that the people had become a force in politics in the battles between monarch, nobility and church. Commerce and agriculture had given them status and wealth. Yet the people – and this was where Wollstonecraft departed from Hume – were now prevented from rising by the traditional orders and authorities.

Wollstonecraft called the monarch, nobility and church despots 'compelled, to make covert corruption hold fast the power which was formerly snatched by open force'. Prevailing dominant institutions and cultural powers were a 'baneful lurking gangrene' that was 'quickly spread by luxury and superstition, the sure dregs of ambition'. The man who served as an 'indolent puppet of a court' turned himself into 'a luxurious monster, or fastidious sensualist', serving as a model ultimately for the common people to emulate, establishing a cultural contagion that was itself an 'instrument of tyranny'.[82] Wollstonecraft quoted a long passage from Smith's *Theory of Moral Sentiments* underlining the fact that authority and power in the present derived from rank and nobility achieved by the prowess of ancestors, rather than any virtue or capacity among their descendants.[83] Due to the nature of current forms of government, 'wealth and female softness equally tend to debase mankind.'[84] Women in general and the rich of both sexes had all the follies and vices of civilization 'and missed the useful fruit'.[85]

Following the line of the Shelburne Circle, directly in the manner of Price, Wollstonecraft described contemporary Britain as a mercantile system, passing legislation and enacting policy for the benefit of the figure in office rather than for the public good. What she called 'the whole system of British politics' was engaged in 'multiplying dependents and contriving taxes which grind the poor to pamper the rich'. Wars were fought for the benefit of the elite, for their offices and wealth and desire for greater patronage.[86] The lack of a moral culture in Britain was the root cause of the malaise. States in general 'have mostly been governed by arts that disgrace the character of man'. Morality was 'polluted in the national reservoir' and sent off 'streams of vice to corrupt the constituent parts of the body politic'.[87] It was therefore the case that in Britain liberty had been lost and the rulers and the people were increasingly barbarous. The 'whole system of representation' had become 'only a convenient handle for despotism'. Taxes levied upon necessities funded 'an endless tribe of idle princes and princesses to pass with stupid pomp before a gaping crowd, who almost worship the very parade which costs them so dear.'[88]

The solution was to allow women 'to be rational creatures', to 'acquire virtues which they may call their own'.[89] Wollstonecraft was less clear about precisely the kinds of behaviour that would flourish in the new moral world of equality. Although several passages emphasizing the point were removed from the first edition, Wollstonecraft had asserted that men and women *were* different and that their roles in society would always be distinctive. What Wollstonecraft emphasized in the first instance was for women to become better wives and better mothers.[90] An example was that women 'would be contented to love but once in their lives; and after marriage calmly let passion subside into friendship'. They would become more modest, less jealous, cause fewer social conflicts and get on better with men and their neighbours. The virtues of chastity, modesty, public-spiritedness and everything that promoted social happiness could be expected to flourish.[91]

Such goals were to be achieved by legislators making laws so that individuals had an interest in behaving virtuously, rather than allowing the 'feculent stream of wealth that has muddied the pure rills of natural affection'.[92] She imagined a system of laws in which men would fulfil the duties of a citizen. If a man failed to enact the duties expected of him, he would be derided by the watching public. While he was undertaking the roles of civil life, his wife, also described as an 'active citizen', would manage her family, educate her children and assist her neighbours. The conclusion Wollstonecraft drew was that if an effort was made to make women 'rational creatures, and free citizens' they would 'quickly become good wives, and mothers', so long as men did not 'neglect the duties of husbands and fathers'.[93] This was her vision of equality.

Wollstonecraft, observing events in France from Britain, was sure that the acquisition of political liberty by the French people was leading to the alteration of the relationship between men and women. As she put it, once liberty was granted women 'will quickly become wise and virtuous, as men become more so; for the improvement must be mutual'.[94] Under the first revolutionary constitution only men had voting rights and women were termed 'passive' citizens akin to men without property; but they *were* citizens nevertheless. Wollstonecraft's point was that since women were as active as men in society in general the fact that they were passive in terms of being legislators mattered little. Women did not need to make the laws themselves. Wollstonecraft admitted that she could not see how things would change precisely but had faith in a system of national education in which men and women attended day schools together and were taught the benefits of morality, virtue and the duties associated with citizenship. Women would then be likely to cease to be confined to 'merely domestic pursuits'.[95] France was the key to everything as Wollstonecraft was certain that her vision was in the process of being realized. It was also being tested.

V

Wollstonecraft's brave new revolutionary world rested on what she called morals 'fixed on immutable principles' and a passionate belief that if reason reigned in the world the result would be far greater virtue.[96] Virtue too had a precise meaning, as much about avoiding particular practices as adhering to others. Wollstonecraft hated lust, vanity, wantonness and selfishness. She had a vision of what she termed 'purity', which meant greater chastity, modesty, social peace and a focus on duty.[97] This highly moralized culture was expected to emerge in revolutionary France, replacing the debauched morals of the Old Regime. Wollstonecraft was keen to move to France to see her philosophy being realized at firsthand as soon as she had completed *A Vindication of the Rights of Woman*. In characteristically iconoclastic fashion, and following the mores of straightforwardness she preached, she planned to go to Paris in the summer of 1792 with the man she was then infatuated with, the artist Henry Fuseli. Wollstonecraft's hope was that the two of them would move along with his wife Sophia, whom she offered a ménage à trois. When this was rejected out of hand, Wollstonecraft travelled alone in December 1792, remaining at Paris until April 1794.[98] She found numerous fellow travellers, forming a group of cosmopolitans supportive of Brissot and the Girondins in the Legislative Assembly, including Paine and the poet and Dissenter Helen Maria Williams.[99]

In Paris, Wollstonecraft met Gilbert Imlay, and soon fell madly in love. Imlay was an American merchant, ambitious projector and rake who went through a phase of being a committed republican and revolutionary. One of his schemes was to seize Spanish Louisiana for the French and via Thomas Cooper of Manchester he presented the project to Brissot.[100] Imlay contributed to saving Wollstonecraft from prison after the August 1793 law criminalizing British subjects living in France, which was one of the reasons why Paine was arrested in December 1793. As some British subjects were executed by the French authorities, Imlay may have saved her from death. She began to use his surname and he declared her, falsely, to be his wife, allowing her to claim to be an American. By this time Imlay appears to have abandoned politics for the pursuit of money, moving to Le Havre for business reasons in November 1793. In fact, as the best account of Imlay's life reveals, he was ever a conman and had even invested in the transport of slaves in 1786 while professing to be an enemy of slavery.[101] Although she was now pregnant with his child, Wollstonecraft did not join Imlay until February 1794, giving birth to their daughter Fanny Imlay, named after Fanny Blood, in May 1794. Imlay refused to play the role of the husband or father, abandoning Wollstonecraft repeatedly before moving to London in September 1795. Abandoning is probably the wrong term – Imlay probably always felt Wollstonecraft to be peripheral, someone to be used and discarded. Yet when she joined him in England in April 1795, she sought to help him by pursuing his lawsuit against the Norwegian captain Ellefsen, who was accused of stealing a cargo of silver. She travelled from Hull to Scandinavia as his agent under the name Mary Imlay, with their daughter.[102] By the end of 1795 and back in London, she discovered that Imlay was in a relationship with another woman. Ending the connection was, she wrote 'the most serious event of my life'.[103]

Wollstonecraft's relationship with Imlay formed part of her experiment in the transformation of morals in conditions of revolution. She made this clear in letters describing her attempt to live a purer and domesticated life in which she would play the role of the devoted wife and mother, support Imlay in his work, and communicate openly and honestly in love and in friendship. She had worked during her life to become independent and had become so. She now sought 'the simple pleasures that flow from passion and affection'.[104] She and Imlay contributed differently to domestic arrangements but were equal partners. The plan at one point was clearly to farm together in North America. As she said in a letter of December 1794, 'I should have been content, and still wish, to retire with you to a farm.'[105] Instead, Imlay betrayed this simple, domestic vision: he failed to support Wollstonecraft and their daughter, embracing commerce and trade, rather than love and duty. This led Wollstone-craft to express her fury in letters that were marked by candour and by increasing frustration that Imlay was refusing to behave in accordance with the principles of liberty and equality that she thought they were both devoted to. In a typical letter she repeated her view of 'men in general', that they were 'systematic tyrants, and that it is the rarest thing in the world, to meet with a man with sufficient delicacy of feeling to govern desire'. She complained of Imlay's failure to supply 'the necessaries of life', including a servant, which she needed in order to cope with the baby.[106]

But above all she railed against Imlay's pursuit of money. As she wrote to him, '[give me] any thing but commerce, which debases the mind, and roots out affection from the heart.'[107] When she arrived alone in Le Havre she noted that the house where she and Fanny were lodging, belonging to the Havrais family, 'smelt of commerce from top to toe'. The lesson was that 'the demon of traffic will ever fright away the loves and graces.'[108] Her letters charted the progress of Imlay's moral degradation. Initially he had sought only moderate wealth, which to Wollstonecraft amounted to a thousand pounds for the procurement of a farm in America. Then Imlay declared the acquisition of such a sum to be insufficient, and that he had to scheme and toil to procure far more in order to live in luxury. This led him to his ultimate position, confessing that riches alone mattered to him. Wollstonecraft noted that it was evident that Imlay 'did not know himself' – one of the deadliest of sins in her view – and the result was his lusting after lucre, guaranteeing the complete corruption of his heart.[109] Part of her exasperation derived from a failure to comprehend how another person could be, as she put it, 'embruted by trade, and the vulgar enjoyments of life'.[110] Imlay needed to use his imagination to battle against the baser passions. If reason was insufficient, then the imagination could be called upon to sustain the love of liberty and equality. Imagination was, she said, 'the mother of sentiment, the great distinction of our nature, the only purifier of the passions'. Imagination was a sympathy that could lead to true rapture, 'rendering men social by expanding their hearts, instead of leaving them leisure to calculate how many comforts society affords'.[111]

How precisely imagination was going to operate to cure Imlay from selfishness remained unclear. This was probably why Wollstonecraft's central feelings continued to be anxiety and agony. She admitted to Imlay that the French Revolution had had a major impact upon her and that she was now experiencing the force of his own persecution; he was burning up 'her vital stream'. It had been 'such a period of barbarity and misery'. Her projects for a better world described in her books had been refuted by the descent of the Revolution. Personal happiness together, the rational life of equality and empathy she had also planned out, and hoped to realize with Imlay, had been ruined by the primacy of his base passions, leading him to reject her and their child. Her thoughts turned to suicide, again drawing a parallel with the terror that had tarnished the French Revolution: 'I wish one moment that I had never heard of the cruelties that have been practised here, and the next envy the mothers who have been killed with their children.'[112] Writing from Gothenburg in early July 1795 she again threatened to put an end to it all. Gazing at the sea she 'longed to bury my troubled bosom in the less troubled deep'. The parallel she drew was highly significant. She asserted, with Marcus Junius Brutus, that 'the virtue I had followed too far, was merely an empty name!'[113] Rather than experiencing moral reformation undergirding and guaranteeing political liberation and the progress of equality, the hopes of the French Revolution had collapsed. Fighting Caesars failed. Burke had seen far further than any contemporary. Rather than meeting a man with whom she could live a moral life, Wollstonecraft had lost her independence. She found herself 'dependent on a man, whose avidity to acquire a fortune has rendered him callous to every sentiment connected with social or affectionate emotions'.[114] Wollstonecraft put into practice what she had threatened in her letters, attempting to kill herself first when she returned to Britain from France, and again on her return from Sweden.[115]

Despite domestic turmoil Wollstonecraft nevertheless completed a book seeking to make sense of the French Revolution, which her friend Johnson published in 1794 as *An Historical and Moral View of the Origin and Progress of the French Revolution; and the Effect it has Produced in Europe*.[116] Partly it was an attempt by Wollstonecraft to generate funds for herself and Fanny in the light of Imlay's behaviour but it was more an attempt to address the issue of why she had been so wrong in both of her *Vindication* books about what was happening in France. The book's structure was complicated, with a narrative of events at Paris accompanied by reflections on the behaviour of numerous prominent revolutionary actors combined with more general reflections, inserted randomly through the work, addressing the question of why the Revolution had resulted in chaos and massacre rather than order and virtue. The Terror required explanation; as Wollstonecraft put it, it was important to understand 'the violent, the base, and nefarious assassinations, which have clouded the vivid prospect that began to spread a ray of joy and gladness over the gloomy horizon of oppression'. Terror had chilled 'the sympathizing bosom' and palsied intellectual vigour.[117]

VI

Wollstonecraft's response to the conundrum of the Terror was ultimately the same as that of every member of the Shelburne Circle. Manners were not yet ready for liberty, and reform should have proceeded far more gradually. She made the point that 'the revolutions of states ought to be gradual; for during violent or material changes it is not so much the wisdom of measures, as the popularity they acquire by being adapted to the foibles of the great body of the community, which gives them success.'[118] Almost all of the peoples of Europe, and especially the French under the absolute monarchy of the Old Regime, were 'strictly speaking, slaves; bound by feudal tenures, and still more oppressive ecclesiastical restraints; the lord of the domain leading them to slaughter, like flocks of sheep; and the ghostly father drawing the bread out of their mouths by the idlest impositions'.[119] The Crusades and the Protestant Reformation had in turn 'freed many of the vassals' and made the clergy more moral and wise. But across the continent of Europe liberty was threatened or in decline. In the republics of Genoa and of Venice addiction to luxury and selfishness, termed by Wollstonecraft 'lascivious pleasures', had put an end to liberty. Across Switzerland and in Sweden it was a mercenary aristocracy, in the Netherlands corrupt commercial mores of 'the covetous Hollanders', and in Corsica the jealousy of neighbouring France had come to dominate the island. Italy, Spain and Portugal, 'cowering under a contemptible bigotry, which sapped the remains of the rude liberty they had enjoyed, formed no political plans'. Germany had suffered military despotism for longer than any other European state while Russia remained barbaric and voluptuous, where 'grandeur and parade of a palace are mistaken for the improvement of manners, and the false glory of desolating provinces for wisdom and magnanimity.'[120] France, ripe for revolution because enlightenment had been experienced to a limited extent, had equally experienced a 'vile despotism', with monarchs debauched or slaves to their mistresses, and a fake noble culture of eloquence and honour which in reality was self-serving and corrupt in spreading luxury and depravity together. This was why the people finally rose 'like a vast elephant, terrible in his anger, treading down with blind fury friends as well as foes.'[121]

At the same time, there were then grounds for optimism, even if the victory was always going to be slow and tortured, because through history enlightenment could be identified to be seeking toleration and peace. Wollstonecraft formulated a genealogy of liberty with the goal of establishing a new science of politics capable of restoring and then maintaining enlightenment. Wollstonecraft's genealogy started with the ancients. They were rightly to be admired but had no respect for rights and an excessive love of war and patriotism, turning them into civil tyrants who neglected social duties. Bad morals or voluptuousness stopped 'the progress of civilization' in Greece and at Rome.[122] 'The first social systems were certainly founded by passion; individuals wishing to fence round their own wealth or power, and make slaves of their brothers to prevent encroachment.'[123] The printing press, travel and commerce gave the moderns singular advantages, facilitating the spread of knowledge, but the superstitious belief in privileged classes prevented progress. John Locke defined toleration more completely than hitherto and his ideas were the origin of the Declaration of the Rights of Man.[124] The writings of Fénelon were full of ideas promoting the happiness of the people, combating the lust for war and glory of the then reigning monarch Louis XIV.[125] Wollstonecraft listed among Locke's followers in France, Voltaire, Rousseau, the physiocrats and Turgot, all of whom promoted enlightenment in the form of toleration and civil liberties. Rousseau, she wrote, 'depicted the evils of a priest-ridden society, and the sources of oppressive inequality'.[126] Quesnay's physiocrats were 'the first champions for civil liberty'.[127] Turgot she termed an 'excellent man' who 'greatly contributed to produce that revolution in opinion, which, perhaps, alone can overturn the empire of tyranny'.[128] The experience of fighting on the side of liberty in America then convinced many Frenchmen that they too ought to enjoy it. They all faced 'the serious folly of superstition' in the form of a reverence for rank, a superficial culture valuing display and luxury.[129]

If enlightenment existed in France the difficulty was that the general culture was depraved and divided, characterized by 'intrigue and finesse' and a 'tragic and comic' culture of raillery, luxury, ridicule and selfishness. No social group trusted any other. Politics continued to be dominated by self-interest. Wollstonecraft argued that 'vain glorious ambition, mixing with the abortions of giddy patriotism, acts as the most fatal poison to political disquisitions, during seasons of public ferment.'[130] Truly enlightened views only grew slowly because there was no virtuous emulation. Rather, what existed in France Wollstonecraft called 'polished slavery' and an 'inordinate love of pleasure, as led the majority to search only for enjoyment, till the tone of nature was destroyed'.[131] Individuals from 1789 had to be blamed for failing to challenge existing French culture, from the concert of prominent revolutionaries such as Lafayette and Mirabeau, who were typically French in their narcissism to Louis XVI, a 'hapless' and 'sensual bigot', and his useless ministers such as Necker, to the plots of evil power-seekers such as the duc d'Orléans.[132] France was too divided by the corruptions of the court and the debauchery of aristocratic and clerical mores. For Wollstonecraft, the French nobility were 'the most corrupt and ignorant set of men in the world'.[133] She wrote that, 'The inveterate pride of the nobles, the rapacity of the clergy, and the prodigality of the court, were, in short, the secret springs of the plot, now almost ripe, aimed at the embryo of freedom through the heart of the national assembly.'[134] This culture ensured a lust for luxury and self-ishness among the lower ranks which allowed a mob to became active in politics to the point where brutality predominated.[135] The 'rich and poor were separated into bands of tyrants and slaves' so that when the slaves acquired power, suddenly and unexpectedly, their retaliation was always going to be 'terrible'.[136] Equally, because the division of ranks was absolute before 1789, the poor did not know how to live well. It was significant, Wollstonecraft claimed, that the French had no word for 'comfort', the moderate wealth and stable life that ought to have been the first goal of the poor, who instead imitated their betters in excess, the pursuit of extremes and of personal enrichment.[137] It also ensured that the leaders of the National Assembly, who ought to have been preaching a gospel of new behaviour, either lacked the skills to realize the revolution or could not break free from the long-standing culture of the Old Regime.[138]

The failure of the revolutionaries to cast off traditional political cultures and practices meant that they tended to recreate aristocracy and the laws they passed failed to stamp out corruption. Equally, from the National Assembly onwards, leading politicians were deluded, having so little experience either of liberty or virtue. One major mistake was that they believed they could perfect government and society. They 'selected from books only the regulations proper for a period of perfect civilization'. They sought to put into practice Hume's idea of a perfect commonwealth, one of his most famous essays, which, as Hume said, only made sense with circumstances entirely different to those of France.[139] Equally, they misunderstood both Rousseau's *Contrat social* and his *Second Discourse on the Origin of Inequality among Men*, because such philosophers' reforms only made sense if erected on the basis of a general culture of virtue rather than selfishness.[140] The result was failure and the unleashing of anarchy as the people became more frustrated that their new leaders amounted to old masters with altered names.

Wollstonecraft admitted to weeping over those who felt the snap of the guillotine at their heels, 'fleeing from the despotism of licentious freedom'. The term licentious was the key. She believed French manners in general had become debased before the French Revolution. Revolution was bound to fail because manners had not been reformed before political rebellion was initiated. Liberty would only be established when there was a change of opinion, when moral behaviour became the norm. With a different end in sight, Wollstonecraft sounded like Martin Luther in her vitriolic barrages against contemporary mores. Private virtue had to become the guarantee of patriotism, rather than seeing what Wollstonecraft called 'mock patriotism', one of her most-used phrases, meaning the pursuit of selfish interests in the guise of the public good; in France there were far too many 'mock patriots of the day declaiming about public reform, merely to answer sinister purposes'.[141] Wollstonecraft's assertions sometimes read like one of her letters to Imlay. Her book attacked 'the folly, selfishness, madness, treachery, and more fatal mock patriotism' that were 'the common result of depraved manners, the concomitant of that servility and voluptuousness'. If the higher orders in France evinced such behaviour, the tragedy was that Imlay too was exhibiting it and following them, rather than the rule of reason and the path of virtue.[142] 'Embruted' was the term she used again to describe Imlay's trajectory and that of the revolutionaries, where both ought to have been going in the opposite direction, towards domesticity, selflessness and virtue.[143] Perhaps Wollstonecraft's most distinctive idea was to tie domesticity and enlightenment together.[144] Men and women who were happy in their homes and with their children, independent and equal in their spheres, would never turn brutish, superstitious and fanatic.[145]

The major lesson for Wollstonecraft was that revolution as a political tactic had for ever to be abandoned. As she put it: 'All sudden revolutions have been as suddenly overturned, and things thrown back below their former state.' It took time to change the world. Even Moses, Wollstonecraft noted, after forty years could not get the Jewish people to the promised land because, just like in France, 'the first generation had perished in their prejudices.'[146] The French Revolution and its descent into terror made sense for the related reason that every government that changed 'from absolute despotism to enlightened freedom' was likely to 'be plunged into anarchy, and have to struggle with various species of tyranny before it is able to consolidate its liberty'. Liberty would only be enjoyed when 'the manners and amusements of the people are completely changed.'[147] Yet Wollstonecraft's core philosophy had evidently not changed, praising Stoicism and condemning epicureanism.[148] Her aim remained the banishment of 'the narrow opinions of superstition', and the promotion of 'enlightened sentiments of masculine and improved philosophy', meaning schemes for the reformation of manners.[149] This entailed, above all else, a moral revolution to establish a true community of the virtuous. Government would only become legitimate once citizens habitualized a set of practices that led to true happiness. The French Revolution had occurred when the wrong culture predominated, one of personal interest rather than the real patriotism of principle and self-sacrifice.[150] The Terror was explicable because the French had 'neither sufficient purity of heart nor maturity of judgement to conduct [the revolution] with moderation and prudence'.[151]

There was a substantial difference, however, in *An Historical and Moral View of the Origin and Progress of the French Revolution* compared to her earlier books, all of which were written before she had moved to France. No reader of the times could miss it and it begged a series of further questions for Wollstonecraft. In all her previous work the granting of liberty to the people did the work in establishing the conditions for virtue. To realize her philosophy, there was now a complete reversal of this transition mechanism: virtue had to come before liberty. Equally, revolution was the last means to be countenanced to carry out moral transformation. As a political tactic, revolution was henceforth not to be trusted, something that Brissot and Clavière had been saying since the 1780s. Wollstonecraft's tactics became focused upon education and upon the spreading of the enlightened word through books such as her own. But she also formulated a genealogy of progress in order to give a new history of enlightenment. This asserted that, despite all the evidence to the contrary, reason and virtue were gaining ground and had been so doing for centuries. As she put it, 'intellectual improvement' was 'gradually proceeding to perfection' to the point that the 'sincerity of principles' was 'hastening the overthrow of the tremendous empire of superstition and hypocrisy, erected upon the ruins of gothic brutality and ignorance'.[152] Perhaps she was thinking of Macaulay and of her own genius. But Wollstonecraft found it easy to define bad behaviour. The difficulty lay in proving the victory of the principles of virtue and reason held to be capable of replacing brutality and again in explaining how such positive behaviour would become the norm.

Wollstonecraft also changed her stance from *A Vindication of the Rights of Men* and the *Vindication of the Rights of Woman* regarding Britain. British culture and politics had in each work received as much vitriol as she now directed against the French. Unlike Paine, who continued to condemn the British, Wollstonecraft, like so many supporters of the French Revolution, now felt that she had been too harsh on her own country. Britain had, after all, never experienced anything truly akin to the Terror, whatever Pitt's critics asserted. In the *Historical and Moral View*, therefore, she praised Britain as a land where liberty had been nurtured and continued to exist rather than where it had merely been enjoyed briefly and then lost. While the rest of Europe had 'groaned under the weight of the most unjust and cruel laws, the life and property of Englishmen were comparatively safe'.[153] Liberties were far from perfect – again Wollstonecraft mentioned the press gang for the poor – but Britain had 'the best existing constitution' of which the people were rightly proud.[154] The manners of the nobles were praised for being less those of a caste, as they were in France and Italy. One of the reasons was that in Britain the landed and the commercial interests had intermingled. In a remarkable sentence Wollstonecraft said that it was 'monied interest, from which political improvement first emanates'.[155] France lacked a monied interest and its nobility and clergy were both removed from the people and entirely self-serving. Wollstonecraft still criticized Britain as a state where they mistakenly presumed the existing constitution to be perfect. She also said that it could be simplified, and more importantly Britons needed to 'promote and maintain the freedom of mankind'.[156] North America too merited praise for carrying out a successful revolution without descent into terror or fanaticism. There were few lessons for Europe, however, because America existed 'in a situation very different from the rest of the world'.[157]

Wollstonecraft claimed that she knew exactly what to do to change the world successfully. It could not be done by the people taking up arms, by a revolution which gave power to a new species of aristocrat. Optimism about future progress was coupled with the gradual permeation through the people of virtuous manners, which she termed enlightenment. This entailed 'a more enlightened moral love of mankind' supplanting or challenging the dominion of physical affections. It was 'the image of God implanted in our nature'.[158] Such a language harked back to the influence of Price upon Wollstonecraft. The optimism about aristocracies falling away and all bad laws collapsing, because they weakened states, was redolent of Price's final sermons praising events in France, fully certain that the true moral world was waiting for him after death in the realm of Christ. Wollstonecraft sounded very like Price when she claimed that 'man may contemplate with benevolent complacency and becoming pride, the approaching reign of reason and peace.'[159]

Even 'Colossian strides' of progress could be identified 'hastening the overthrow of oppressive tyranny and contumelious ambition'.[160]

Something Price would never have shared was Wollstonecraft's especially positive account of Germany. Education in Germany had been made useful, meaning tending towards the public good, rather than focusing upon 'dead languages', and Wollstonecraft predicted that the Germans would become 'in the course of half a century, the most enlightened people in Europe'. The Germans were fortunate in having simple manners and 'honesty of heart', creating a bulwark against 'that inundation of riches by commercial sources, that destroys the morals of a nation before it's [sic] reason arrives at maturity'.[161] Wollstonecraft praised Frederick the Great of Prussia as a ruler who had encouraged such an education, avoided the excesses of commercial society, and attempted to introduce a milder government more supportive of liberty.[162] The lesson was that it was through 'teaching men from their youth to think, that they will be enabled to recover their liberty; and useful learning is already so far advanced, that nothing can stop its progress'.[163] Members of Shelburne's Circle would have asked where any evidence for such a future lay, especially given the history of the French Revolution.

Wollstonecraft did argue, however, that, if time was on her side, it was vital nevertheless to promote 'true political science' promoting 'a civilization of manners'. This was especially vital in Britain, being the freest state capable of serving as a model to others. Political science had to be combined with political economy in order to get rid of national debts, poverty and the desire for foreign wars.[164] Giving advice to the republicans still seeking to make a success of the French Revolution, she said that it would only happen if Paris rapidly crumbled 'into decay'.[165] There was too much luxury and too much debauchery at Paris. France had to become more of an agricultural state more suited to virtue. Such a point reflected Wollstonecraft's major fear for the future, despite her attempt at optimism: commerce could, she said, establish a new aristocracy of the rich, as debauched and selfish as the aristocracy of land, sword and church they replaced, who would in turn create a servile class beneath them, largely ignorant because the division of labour 'renders the mind entirely inactive'. Wollstonecraft had clearly been reading Smith's *Wealth of Nations* and she referenced the pin industry as an example of labourers turned near brutes because of the basic and repetitive tasks required in their daily work. The world would not be improved until most of the people were independent in the sense of enjoying moderate wealth, the only route 'to the perfection of reason, and the establishment of rational equality'.[166] Like Smith she worried about the mercantile system or 'aristocracy of wealth which degrades mankind'.[167]

VII

Did Wollstonecraft really believe the central thrust of *An Historical and Moral View of the Origin and Progress of the French Revolution* that virtue and liberty would trickle through populations, make progress together and ensure the future of enlightenment? There are reasons for scepticism. Wollstonecraft admitted to failing to convert Imlay, a real-life experiment in turning a man away from what she called 'old propensities' towards 'I and virtue'. Wollstonecraft in one of her final letters said she had initially had faith in Imlay's 'magnanimity of character' being sufficient to enable him 'to conquer himself'.[168] She might have been writing about the French Revolution in admitting to Imlay that 'you are not what you appear to be.'[169] A genuine pessimism was underlined by the fragmentary 'Letter on the Present Character of the French Nation', which Godwin published the year after her death. Here too she underlined the horrors of the Terror and stated that she only wished the history of liberty and virtue in France had been different. Underlining the extent to which all dreams had been dashed, she also warned of a new challenge to enlightenment in the form of the nobility of birth being replaced by an aristocracy of riches.[170]

Wollstonecraft admitted she had been wrong about the progress of civilization and had underestimated the force of epicurean philosophy in France, which taught selfishness and the satisfaction of the baser passions and had been entrenched in national habits at every social level. She blamed epicureanism for fostering a culture of the pursuit of luxury and debauchery. Wollstonecraft went so far as to state that events in France had led her to consider the possibility that evil was the great spring of human action, although she claimed she had not in consequence become an atheist. Despite their avowed support for revolution in popular demonstrations and in all of their assemblies, the French had displayed the same lust for office, status and power as characters who had come to prominence under the Old Regime. Every man, she said, during the Revolution had sought to turn himself into a petty tyrant. Frenchmen had turned France into a dunghill and behaved like strutting cocks.[171]

Wollstonecraft's other work of the time was similarly pessimistic, the account of her Scandinavian voyage published as *Letters from Sweden, Norway and Denmark*. Here she warned once more of the dangers of an aristocracy of the wealthy making people servile, thereby preventing necessary progress towards reason and virtue.[172] She was critical of mores across Scandinavia, seeing no home for liberty and equality in these countries. The tone she employed, which Godwin considered profound and affecting, was one of a realistic believer in a cause who had lost her faith, not because she had changed her values but because circumstances had proved revolutionary aspirations to be utopian. The state of the world was dreadful, and the dream had died. In a letter to her friend from Paris, Gustav, Graf von Schlabrendorf, of May 1796, Wollstonecraft wrote that she had 'almost learnt to hate mankind'.[173]

The fact was that the French Revolution had shattered reformist philosophies. Wollstonecraft's commitment to it had been complete. She had anticipated a world of new and harmonious social relationships coming into being, even to the point of making men and women equal by law, in civil life and in the home, if not in politics. Enlightenment, in the form of peace and toleration, to be enjoyed to a degree unsurpassed in recorded history, by means of a nation coming together through revolution, had seemed so close to being realized. Yet the experiment in passing laws for the equality of men, against a background of campaigns for the equality of women, led to war, intolerance and instability. The defeat of the French Revolution, not only because of the descent into violence but because a republic erected on rights continued to violate them more egregiously than the Old Regime, was recognized to be total, leaving gapingly open the issue of which tactics were sufficient to prevent the end of enlightenment.

The trickle-down theory of virtuous manners, spreading from good works or moral examples, had not convinced Wollstonecraft herself. Godwin was open about this, arguing that he had been mistaken in his *Enquiry Concerning Political Justice*, having too readily been intoxicated by French republicanism, and that his opinions had altered. Part of this change was due to Wollstonecraft. There was a marked reverence for private life and domestic virtue in Godwin's works of 1797 and 1798.[174] There were also concerns about the dangers of commercial society in fostering poverty and avarice.[175] At the same time, Godwin would not have agreed with Wollstonecraft about the condition of Britain. Godwin had been prominent in the battle against what many saw to be Pitt's own terror, the attack on civil liberties from the early 1790s seeking to prevent the circulation of ideas or the gathering of persons supportive of reform or revolution. Godwin railed against Pitt's suspension of the Habeas Corpus Act, his use of spies and his war on unguarded words in any debate about politics, however private.[176] He accused the prominent patriot and anti-Jacobin campaigner John Reeves of repudiating British liberties enshrined in the Bill of Rights of 1689. When the treason trials were launched against many of Godwin's friends he came to their aid, accusing Pitt and his ministers of turning tyrant and abandoning the constitutional guarantee of the right to fair trial while invading the private lives and censoring the private thoughts of Britons.[177] Godwin's point was that Britons, traditionally secure in and jealous of their liberties, were becoming xenophobic bigots and servile prey for demagogues and projectors. Wollstonecraft did admit that the English had 'lost the common sense that used to distinguish them'.[178] But Godwin's sense of the loss of national character was far deeper, marking a profound malaise in political culture equivalent to the failure of revolutionary ideas in France. Pitt's Britons were alien to Godwin, akin to deluded monsters.

Godwin's deep depression about politics derived from the presentation in Britain of his and Wollstonecraft's position on France as meaning that they were enemies of the state and British traditions of liberty. As Thomas Rowlandson put it in a widely circulated print 'The Contrast', supporters of the French Revolution favoured 'Atheism, Perjury, Rebellion, Treason, Anarchy, Murder, Equality, Madness, Cruelty, Injustice, Treachery, Ingratitude, Idleness, Famine, National & Private Ruin. Misery'.[179] Such prints avoided the standard portrayal of the French revolutionaries as starving and destitute, to be compared to fat Britons living well and without the threat of murder hanging over them. Rather, Rowlandson and other artists such as James Gillray presented Britons as moderates, governed in accordance with justice and the law, and the French as wild fanatics who lived in anarchy and were turning into savages. 'The Contrast' was sold cheaply and widely distributed by John Reeves' 'Association for Protecting Liberty and Property against Republicans and Levellers', established on 20 November 1792 at the Crown and Anchor tavern in the Strand.[180] It was Reeves who made opposition to Paineite republican cosmopolitanism an English nationalist crusade. For Reeves, modern democrats and republicans had to be identified as corroders of morality and government. Englishness had been established during the Reformation and now comprised Protestantism and moderation by means of a unique political culture generating a unique 'temper of mind'. Reeves openly declared 'I am not a *Citizen of the World,* so as to divide my affection with strangers.' Rather, he was an Englishman with 'more goodness of heart and Good Sense than any other in the world, and who are the happiest, because they make the best use of both'.[181]

Reeves was certain that the French Revolution was replicating with greater violence the evils of the seventeenth-century wars within England and between England, Scotland and Ireland. During this period the English had fallen foul of the projects of the Scottish 'Presbyterian Covenantors' and their 'Puritanical Brethren', asserting 'Calvin's plan of church government [or] Presbytery by Divine Right'. The consequence, as in the 1640s, was the loss of 'security of property, freedom of person or the peace and quiet so much sighed after' until rational 'Government of Monarchy' was restored.[182] Reeves felt Godwin, Paine, Wollstonecraft and their tribe to be so dangerous because they were risking a national descent into civil war. Pitt's government was underestimating the danger. Through Reeves, English liberty was everywhere associated with peace and prosperity in vivid images showing the populace what would happen if Fox or Shelburne and their friends returned to power. Fire, burning buildings and scenes of pandemonium predominate in prints such as James Gillray's 'Promis'd Horrors of the French Invasion, or Forcible reasons for negotiating a regicide peace', showing French troops marching up St James's Street after burning Buckingham Palace, Burke being tossed by a bull named the Duke of Bedford, while members of the royal family either lay murdered or were being butchered. On the balcony on the right of the image, above the door of Brooks' Club, Shelburne happily guillotined his enemies while Magna Carta was being torched. The choice was either to experience such horrors or to continue the war against revolutionary France and its republican ideology.[183]

Although Wollstonecraft and Godwin were themselves critical of the course of the French Revolution, they were branded as friends of terror. Association with French forms of liberty was described as insane. It was also futile and self-defeating, because anyone who followed the path of reform would, if they succeeded in coming to power, end up dead. Hence James Gillray's print dated 16 February 1797 with the title 'The tree of liberty must be planted immediately!', showing the bloody head of Fox on a pike, his eyes concealed by a cap inscribed 'Libertas'.[184] Around the base of the pike were heaped the heads of the Foxites who continued to support the French Revolution, ranging from James Maitland, 8th Earl of

Lauderdale, to Charles Mahon, 3rd Earl Stanhope, Sheridan and the lawyer Thomas Erskine. Among the heads too were extra-parliamentary supporters such as Horne Tooke and John Thelwall. Most of these men were Godwin's friends. Although the frenzy of the treason trials was history and French republicanism was tarnished, Wollstonecraft and Godwin found themselves in a time of patriotism and xenophobia in which they were othered as Britons-turned-French, not only alien but likely treacherous, republican fifth columnists.

VIII

Amid such turbulence and notoriety, when they were being branded as fools and terrorists, whose works had been refuted by the passage of events, Godwin and Wollstonecraft married on 29 March 1797 at St Pancras Church. The event shocked many of their friends. Godwin had denounced the institution of marriage in the *Enquiry Concerning Political Justice*. Wollstonecraft was incorrectly presumed to have been married to Imlay, whose name she regularly adopted. Yet, their marriage was supposed to lead not only to domestic happiness but to putting their minds together on the great challenge of the day – whether any vestige of enlightenment could be salvaged in France or in Britain. So Wollstonecraft's death on 10 September 1797 shattered Godwin. His grief led him to seek to use Wollstonecraft's example as a message of hope to reformers, an example of genius whose values never changed even as her projects were dashed, and her life was tragically cut short. Wollstonecraft had, after all, lived honestly and unapologetically, challenging convention, seeking the true equality she believed in. Unfortunately, Godwin's *Memoirs of the Author of a Vindication of the Rights of Woman*, published the year after her death, had a disastrous impact upon Wollstonecraft's reputation. Her private life and enjoyment of sex, descriptions of her lovers and her radical thoughts about equality were revealed to the world, seemingly realized in a life lived freely and against convention. Her eighteenth-century critics concluded that her death was an act of God because her sins against morality were so great.

The Wollstonecraft who had witnessed the French Revolution might have been unsurprised that someone who had defended virtue and reason with such ardour was redescribed for generations as an amoral slattern in hock to the vilest passions.[185] Many were nevertheless horrified at Godwin's action. The poet Robert Southey said he had stripped his dead wife naked.[186] For Godwin, the response to his *Memoir* confirmed that British culture was debased, having turned enthusiastic and fanatic in a manner that paralleled the failure of the French Revolution. Wollstonecraft had never addressed the point Hume made about the likelihood of national character turning towards superstition during the end of enlightenment. Godwin now diagnosed enthusiasm as the problem that had to be overcome if enlightenment was ever to be established once again. His first historical novel, *St Leon: A Tale of the Sixteenth Century* (1799), which described religious wars as perennial and a phenomenon that had to be overcome for peace and toleration to be realized, was an acknowledgement of the reality of the end of enlightenment while liberty in Britain was lost and the French republican experiment close to death.[187]

The last point is significant. Generations have reified French revolutionary republicanism. Karl Marx went so far as to argue that the process followed by the French during the 1790s was intrinsic to the structure of each and every revolution, a necessary event in the process of creating a socialist and ultimately communist utopia. As part of the inherited radical toolkit, however, revolution had always been questioned as a political tactic. For Commonwealthmen, calling the people to arms was something to be contemplated only in conditions of dire necessity. Scepticism became the dominant register concerning revolution before the end of the century. To contemporaries, including Paine, Wollstonecraft and Godwin, the French Revolution failed to create an egalitarian society. Legions of disabused former revolutionaries by the mid-1790s saw enthusiasm, superstition and fanaticism to be defining everyday politics. Cosmopolitans had turned terrorist. Advocates of rights initiated massacres. Self-proclaimed moderates called for war to the death. Two self-proclaimed free states battled one another on the grounds that their own liberty would be imperilled unless the enemy state was annihilated. War and terror were justified as the means of creating free societies on Earth.

IO.

And by Confusion Stand

I

Adam Smith's account of Hume's irreligious death caused a stir in 1776. Smith soon considered himself to have been tarred by association with Hume's unapologetic heterodoxy. His worry, acute for someone of Smith's delicate temperament, was still there at his own death in 1790, when the French Revolution was widely seen to be a direct result of assaults upon Christianity. It was one reason why Smith asked for his own papers to be burned. But Smith, while hiding any link with unorthodox religion opinions, remained a Humean in his view of the contemporary world. He was deadly serious when he contrasted an imagined 'natural progress of opulence' with the 'unnatural and retrograde order' of his own time.[1] Smith inherited the idea of a natural or what might be termed republican history of development – republican because it encompassed the good of all the people, rather than that of a single individual or of a narrow group within society – from Hume. It was no accident that Smith ended the *Wealth of Nations* with a Humean flourish, demanding that Britain ought, in the light of the failure to persuade its colonies to contribute to the costs of defence and governance, 'accommodate her future views and designs to the real mediocrity of her circumstances.' Underlining the mediocrity of Britain's actual resources was coupled with condemnation of the 'showy equipage of the empire'.[2]

Within such a context, the accusation that followers of Hume were closet revolutionaries was widespread. In certain respects this was accurate: if you accepted the dire situation of liberty in Britain you would be more sympathetic to radical projects to change the world. And we have seen many cases where an acceptance of such an evaluation led to a wholehearted embrace of the French Revolution at its outset. Samuel Taylor Coleridge was typical in this, along with his great friend and fellow poet William Wordsworth.[3] Yet, in his prominent Bristol Lectures of 1795, Coleridge revealed that his politics were changing, moving to a position Hume had expounded, that the lust for liberty could easily become fanatical.[4] Coleridge condemned the French for 'wading to their Rights through Blood, and marking the track to Freedom by Devastation', arguing that 'French Freedom is the Beacon, which while it guides to Equality, should shew us the Dangers that throng the road.'[5] The source of the trouble, he argued, had been the passion of religious enthusiasm, infecting Jacobins – 'the ardour of undisciplined benevolence seduces us into malignity.' In Robespierre's case enthusiasm created 'a wild and dreadful Tyrant . . . [he] despotized in all the pomp of Patriotism, and masqueraded on the bloody stage of Revolution, a Caligula with the cap of Liberty on his head'.[6] For Coleridge there was a clear parallel between 'the majority of Democrats' and 'Infidels in religion' in their misunderstanding of politics and society:

> The majority of Democrats appear to me to have attained that portion of knowledge in politics, which Infidels possess in religion. I would by no means be supposed to imply, that the objections of both are equally unfounded, but that they both attribute to the system which they reject, all the evils existing under it; and that both contemplating truth and justice 'in the nakedness of abstraction' condemn constitutions and dispensations without having sufficiently examined the natures, circumstances, and capacities of their recipients.[7]

Coleridge held it to be obvious that creating a republic or taking radical action to reform a state was akin to the process of reinvigorating a religious community or establishing a new church. Both were beset by difficulties, not least the danger that the people would follow a self-serving projector, promising an easy path to utopia, and soon turn upon those labelled enemies. For Coleridge, too, a democratic element of any constitution, while necessary for the protection of the people, still risked a state turning Caesarist, populist or theocratic. And the forces that might be relied upon to contain fanaticism were weaker, Coleridge acknowledged, in conditions of global commerce where luxury bred self-interest and traditional social ties were lacking in growing towns or newly established factories.

Coleridge argued that if the French Revolution had not bettered the world but rather the opposite, then Britain's own recent history had to be understood as a reason for the Revolution's violent turn. In response he fostered the great Romantic aspiration of seeking other sources of liberty and happiness, often thinking imaginatively beyond politics, commerce and the dealings of nations, turning instead to the individual and their experience outside of society.

II

When William Blake sketched a new Jerusalem built on the ruins of London, with walls to impede Satan's armies, he too was embarking on a Romantic project that envisioned that which comes *after* the Enlightenment, as did the writer Madame de Staël, in her book *Germany* (*De l'Allemagne*), which explored the new Romantic philosophies and writing in the hope of rebuilding Europe along different lines.[8] On its publication in 1810, de Staël's work tellingly drew the ire of Napoleon Bonaparte, by then emperor of the French, who had all the copies he could find destroyed; just four survived. Madame de Staël, like Coleridge, Blake, Paine, Wollstonecraft and Brissot, had initially supported revolutionary action. But she expressed forcefully in her subsequent writings the first substantial lesson of the end of enlightenment, that revolutions initiated to restore liberty and reason themselves unleashed intolerance and the justification of terror. That the French Revolution had built

Bonaparte, a new emperor beyond Caesar or Cromwell, was, she believed, evidence enough. During the Reformation, murder was justified as necessary for the saving of souls. In the 1790s, killing was justified, from kings downward, as necessary for freeing individuals, nations or humanity as a whole. With toleration abandoned, peace and stability suddenly rare, Enlightenment had ended. The French Revolution provided proof. Up to the bloody events in Paris and across France, many contemporaries would have said that religious war remained in memory only and as such enlightenment remained, at least in part; but the ideological divisions that caused the civil and international wars of the 1790s were redolent precisely of the religious conflict of the past. Coleridge, like many, came to recognize that Hume's prophesies had come to pass. New species of fanaticism tied to the idea of liberty and shot through with xenophobic nationalism spread across Europe. Bonaparte's armies were at their head.

Gibbon's worst fears for the cultures of old Europe, and especially the weaker states, were more than realized. If states like Poland-Lithuania and Corsica had been dismembered before the 1780s, recall that the surviving republics of Venice, Genoa, Lucca, the Grisons, Switzerland, Geneva, Ragusa and the Dutch *all* lost their independence during the French Revolutionary and Napoleonic Wars. After the creation of the French-puppet Cisalpine Republic in northern Italy in 1797, and after Switzerland was transformed into the Helvetic Republic and Geneva annexed to France in 1798, the journalist Jacques Mallet Du Pan, in his *Essai historique sur la destruction de la Ligue et de la liberté helvétiques* (1798), wrote that the French destruction of Switzerland had left 'only rocks, ruins, and demagogues'. Mallet Du Pan reputedly called the French 'the vilest people in the history of Europe since the fall of the Roman Empire'.[9] No republic put up much of a fight.[10] The tiny rocky outcrop calling itself the Republic of San Marino, in the Apennine range facing Italy's Adriatic coast, alone survived. The decline of the republican political form that had played such a major role in the history of Europe was of profound significance to contemporaries. Smaller states, so long a part of the European landscape, were now endangered species. Even substantial states, like Poland-Lithuania, were wiped off the map in the 1790s. As the new century dawned, more and more simply ceased to exist.[11]

Among the greatest tragedies was the fate of republican France itself. The First French Republic appeared to have created a new force in modern politics, a republican patriotism so powerful that it resisted all military challenge. Such a force had helped establish a state that was imperial both in its conquest of territory but also, peculiarly, in its seduction of common populaces throughout Europe. The First French Republic, whatever the rhetoric linking it to historic sister republics, was different to all comparable republics and free states.[12] Indeed, it shared more in common with the surviving imperial monarchies, who were similarly disposed to expanding their borders. But at heart, it was unique and ignored the normal rules of politics. It lacked hierarchical orders, a national church, and a productive economy founded upon a stable currency, while its citizens and people appeared to be willing to undergo any hardship, such was their love for their country.

Many Dutch, Swiss and Italians were keen to drink the heady republican draft and turn themselves French. Indeed, at times in the 1790s the spread of this republican ideology across Europe looked like the progress of a new hyper-popular religion. Although civil liberties were being violated across France, the political liberty and equality enjoyed by the people outweighed everything else. Countless observers, men and women who had dedicated their lives to the cause of political change, died confused and despondent, having lived into a time when politics had once more turned upside down. For others, French republicanism remained the grandest project in human history, offering a bright future of liberty and equality. Its failure in many respects allowed it to be understood for the first time, because the transformation of a republic or democracy into a monarchy or despotism was entirely explicable to Europeans familiar with the path of parallel polities throughout history.

Revolutions had traditionally been associated with fanatic

religious leaders or generals. In the French case, although generals quickly became prominent in national politics after the outbreak of war in 1792, successive republican governments appeared, whatever other crises they faced, to have avoided this fate. Burke could not understand the apparent stability of a republic seemingly without foundations. Ultimately, nor could Paine, Godwin or Wollstonecraft; to their minds, the successive French revolutionary republics suffered domestic disaster too regularly. If Burke had lived a further five years, he might have died relieved, if not contented, because of the rise of Bonaparte. Bonaparte turned France into the most formidable empire of the day, turning much of Europe into a universal monarchy ruled from Paris.[13] Advocates of expansive republics had made heroes of republican generals and Bonaparte was a classic case. Paine, due to accompany Bonaparte in the invasion of Britain, praised him as a republican moralist whose armies avoided rapine and who would always allow the peoples he conquered to choose their own government. The pinnacle of Bonaparte's career, Paine hoped, would be turning Britain into a republic.[14]

But Bonaparte, having risen through the consular constitution of 1799, modelled on republican Rome, soon turned his own republic into a monarchy. He first used a referendum in February 1800 to increase his powers as First Consul. Afterwards, he proclaimed the First French Empire and crowned himself in front of Pope Pius VII on 2 December 1804. He went on to behave exactly as emperors always had, making monarchs of his relations in the Netherlands, Tuscany, Westphalia, Naples and Spain. The empire saw a return to personal and increasingly regional rule, as Bonaparte's relations jostled for power, and a new Swedish royal line was established through the former marshal and minister of war, Jean Bernadotte.[15]

We have seen that the return of an imperial figure to rule what had been Europe's longest standing monarchy, for some represented a return to political normality. The rise of a general as a solution to the problem of the failure of popular or democratic government had occurred many times before. As an explicable process, it was a lot less frightening than the rule of republican patriots who appeared to have permanently altered the inherited rules of political life. Multiple histories were written likening Bonaparte to Caesar or other republican generals turned sovereign such as Cromwell, finding a meaning and context for recent upheavals no longer without parallel.[16] Bonaparte presented himself as fulfilling the promise of the Revolution with regards to liberty, while establishing the long-sought-for order that the republicans of the 1790s had failed to deliver.[17]

Such a line was accepted only by the deluded. In Bonaparte's France, politics and life quickly returned to the past: Catholicism was revived, the press censored and military police sauntered the streets. Former aristocrats rediscovered their titles, and the newly ennobled recipients of the *Légion d'honneur* enjoyed their elevated status. Bonaparte presented himself as a patriotic monarch in the mould of the early physiocratic ideal of the legal despot, making laws for the good of mankind. This was the aspiration behind the Code Napoleon of rational and benevolent laws, a project Turgot would have favoured. But whatever the dress in which Bonaparte clothed himself, Turgot, the physiocrats and every member of the Shelburne Circle would have cried foul at the harnessing of the republican patriotism generated by the French Revolution in pursuit of empire by war. Republican patriotism was transmuted by Bonaparte into French nationalism. His armies were cosmopolitan, but only in the service of the First French Empire. Propaganda and restrictions on civil liberties were deployed to increase French faith in their state and emperor. Madame de Staël was an early victim, hounded out of France to her father and mother's house in Coppet; an exile convinced that assassins would end her life.[18]

III

The most tangible shock of the end of enlightenment was the survival of Britain. Eighteenth-century minds would have been surprised above all else at Britain's trajectory, had they been able to see into the future. Those who had embraced revolution as a means of preserving enlightenment, including Paine and Macaulay, naturally turned away from Britain. To them, it was a monster and pariah state rather than a free and tolerant polity. The perception of Burke as a fellow traveller, and the perception of Shelburne and his friends as fellow revolutionaries, was because they too were all critics of the growth of fanaticism and corruption within Britain. What horrified Paine most about the British response to the French Revolution was that they became blind to their own faults.[19] He continued to assert that the British economy rested upon a corrupt nobility promoting empire, using exploitative and immoral state-funded companies to mercilessly abuse native populations and free born Britons. Such an edifice, he argued in his *Decline and Fall of the English System of Finance* (1797), could not stand.

But Paine ignored the fact that many prominent British politicians and thinkers were fully aware that theirs was an economy of corruption. Pitt seemingly accepted that although he was not corrupt himself it was acceptable for those who served him, such as his treasury secretary George Rose or the patronage secretary John Robinson, to make vast sums while in office. Wartime bureaucracy, bribery in the naval dockyards, and egregious expenditure within the general administration – all increased exponentially.[20] Drawing upon evidence or rumour, French commentators followed Paine relentlessly in ridiculing perfidious Albion and British pretensions to freedom, justice and prosperity.[21] Against all odds, however, Britain did maintain itself and its empire.

A difference between perceptions of Britain in the eighteenth and nineteenth centuries needs to be underlined. Hume had anticipated Britain's imminent collapse. He saw Smith's mercantile system in the government and the nation and believed that the size of the public debt and the corruption caused by the wealth of empire would be too much to bear. Many times, it looked as if Hume was going to be proved correct. Having lost the North American colonies and suffered defeat in war, having experienced the crisis of the Regency after George III fell, seemingly irrecoverably, into mental illness, Britain in the 1780s had ended in chaos. Over the next decade, established jeremiad literature continued to predict that the British Carthage was about to succumb to the French Rome.[22] The French traveller Volney's book *The Ruins of Empires*, first published in French in 1791, was speedily translated into English and saw eleven editions between 1793 and 1822, with Anglophobe readers seeing decline and Britain to be synonymous.[23] After the French Republic declared war at the end of February 1793, Britain fought constantly across the globe until 1814, with only the brief respite of the Peace of Amiens between March 1802 and May 1803. Economic circumstances became so constrained in an era defined by a fear of invasion that in February 1797 the Bank of England suspended specie payments, the obligation to debtors to redeem their investments by payment of gold. War did not cease, and the costs of financially supporting Britain's allies grew ever greater. By 1815, the debt level was at 200 per cent of GDP, still the highest figure in British history.

All the luminaries of the Enlightenment era would have been astounded by the stability of the British state through the final decades of the eighteenth century and into the nineteenth. According to enlightenment political logic, Britain should never have been able to weather the storms it faced, to defeat all comers at war, expand as an empire, generate more revenue from commerce than any other society, and yet not take any of the recommended steps to dismantle the mercantile system which had so horrified the Shelburne Circle. Ministers in London survived the creation of a domestic revolutionary movement inspired by France. An aborted revolution on the other side of the Irish Sea occurred in 1798, leading to the Acts of Union of 1800–01 that brought together the Kingdom of Great Britain and the Kingdom of Ireland. Seven successive coalitions against France between 1793 and 1815 were sustained by British funds. Imperial France was defeated twice, after the Battle of Leipzig in 1814, and again after Bonaparte's brief return from his exile at Elba, the Hundred Days which culminated at Waterloo. The Congress of Vienna, which sought to restore peace after more than a generation of war, saw the great monarchies of Europe, Prussia, Austria and above all Russia redraw the continental map. The autocratic states worked with France, now a free constitutional monarchy, and with Britain, the leading global economic power. The Old Swiss Confederacy and the Dutch Republic, the most prominent of European republics, were not restored.

Yet it tended to be the republicans whose states had fallen victim first to the French Revolution and then to Bonaparte that turned to Britain. They began to argue that Britain might become a model nation, being a monarchical republic and a large state, and therefore having the potential to survive into the future, unlike the militarily weak miniature polities. Key to this new view of Britain was the history of Scotland. A prominent advocate was François d'Ivernois, a Genevan lawyer who had come to Britain because of Shelburne in 1782, and in the 1790s, as Sir Francis d'Ivernois, served William Windham, the secretary at war under Pitt, in combating anti-British propaganda pouring out of revolutionary France. D'Ivernois argued that Europe had nothing to fear from British commerce, as natural as any form of trade, entailing neither dominion nor a challenge to liberty.[24] Small states, d'Ivernois held, could safely become like Scotland. In 1707, Scotland had given up political sovereignty for economic development, becoming involved in a greater union that had transformed Britain's prospects. The results, he argued, were remarkable. If you were a Protestant seeking the education of your sons, you would no longer send them to Leiden or Utrecht, but rather to Edinburgh, Glasgow, Aberdeen or St Andrews. Scottish culture was held to be more vibrant than ever; it had certainly not been crushed by that of England, while it had been transformed economically. A successful transition was being made of a poor state with a feudal aristocracy into a commercial state with large cities, ample towns and middling ranks. A populace characterized by moderate wealth was said to have been created, sustained by an advanced and improving agricultural system.[25]

For d'Ivernois's friends such as Pierre Prévost, from 1793 professor of theoretical philosophy at the Genevan Academy, and

Marc-Auguste Pictet, Scotland proved that Britain was not a purely mercantile system as depicted by Paine.[26] Since the union, Scotland, for them a previously little known and backward country, had become an epicentre of research and a beacon of civilization. When Pictet visited Scotland in 1801, he was astonished at the philosophical life, the commercial progress, the cutting-edge use of machinery, the building of canals and the vibrancy of urban living.[27] In 1796, Pictet became a founder member of the monthly journal the *Bibliothèque Britannique*, translating and publishing extracts from British periodicals, memoirs, transactions of learned societies and the books of prominent authors.[28] Via the pages of the *Bibliothèque Britannique*, the writings of a number of English, Irish and Scottish authors, including Jeremy Bentham, Maria Edgeworth and Dugald Stewart, were communicated to a broader audience. The Genevans were entirely committed to the example of Scotland, being their solution to the problem of small state survival in the midst of imperially minded commercial monarchies. In consequence, when d'Ivernois and Charles Pictet attended the Congress of Vienna, responsible for determining the future of the formerly independent republic, they justified Geneva becoming a Swiss canton on the grounds that it would become like Scotland within a greater Britain.[29] The verdict of the Genevans was that Britain might be a mercantile system abroad, but at its core was a cosmopolitan relationship between a rich state and a once-poor state, England and Scotland.

The test case for the Anglo/Welsh-Scottish experiment was the union between Britain and Ireland in 1800, suddenly vital after the national rebellion of the United Irishmen in 1798. The expectation was that Ireland would not be crushed culturally. Nor would Ireland suffer from the loss of the liberty embodied by its Dublin parliament. Rather, in return for losing a parliament, Ireland would gain economic development. It would, like Scotland, see the collapse of its feudal nobility. Towns would grow. Learning and politeness would follow in a culture that remained distinctly Irish. For many observers it was obvious that if Ireland followed Scotland and became united within a greater Britain, another small and weak state would be transformed, while always being safe from invasion and foreign interference.[30] After the union occurred, d'Ivernois quickly claimed that it had been a roaring success: Ireland, he argued, had developed more rapidly even than Britain in the years that followed.[31]

In practice the union of Britain and Ireland proved to be different to that with Scotland of 1707. George III refused Catholic emancipation, despite the requests of his ministers. In consequence most of the populace of Ireland, because of their religious beliefs, did not enjoy the civil liberties of fellow Britons.[32] Cynics saw the protestant elite in Ireland being incorporated into a mercantile system of the rich. Lesser mortals lost out.[33] Britain was bringing Ireland into a mercantile system just as it had Scotland a century before, making secure a polity geared to the expansion of a trading empire globally, by any means necessary, readying itself for the inevitable time that it would be challenged in war by a would-be imperial rival.

For those who rejected the positive view of the Anglo/Welsh-Scottish or Anglo/Welsh-Irish unions, the tragedy of the end of enlightenment was that the British, however much they battled against the French Revolution, had themselves turned revolutionary in their xenophobia, nationalism and warlike patriotism. A war between free states had occurred, the significance of which paralleled the Peloponnesian Wars between the city states of Sparta and Athens, or the Punic Wars between Carthage and Rome. Both the free states of Britain and France defined themselves against one another but were mirror images in their mutual loathing.[34] Burke's final hope expressed in his *Letters on a Regicide Peace* had come to pass. British national character was intertwined with the pursuit of war against enemy states whose ideologies were believed to be fanatic, projecting and enthusiastic. Britons considered themselves superior because of their military strength, suddenly vaunted and held to be a product both of their political culture and their mixed and moderate constitution. A Europe consumed by war, and then by domestic division, was the outcome.

Bonaparte recognized that to defeat the British he had to create his own mercantile system, an empire so great, with markets so extensive, backed up by xenophobic patriotic nationalism, that it would be militarily invincible. This project led to the creation of the Continental System, which attempted to blockade and destroy Britain's trade between 1806 and 1814. Alas for Bonaparte, this dedication to mercantile empire led to war with Russia in 1812, and ultimately to his defeat and banishment. Bonaparte and Pitt were not returning to the state of the world as it had been, with William and Mary of England battling Louis XIV's France in 1689.[35] The nature of empire had changed, now seeking markets and wealth for investors and companies supported by their national states, promising riches to their populations and greatness through war and dominion.

Hume failed in his estimation of the capacity of trading empires to fight wars successfully, on their ability to draw upon a loyal populace ready to die for their state. Mercantile systems, it was held, should not have been able to maintain themselves. That they did is the key fact of modern global history.[36]

IV

None of those who experienced the end of enlightenment gave up on the belief that liberty and enlightenment *had* to be tied together. All the historical figures whose views we have recovered accepted that religious and other kinds of fanaticism would return sooner or later under conditions of despotism. It was acknowledged that absolute monarchies and autocratic empires could develop strategies of enlightenment – and had indeed done so in the process of putting an end to the wars of religion. But despotism would always itself turn fanatic. There was an outpouring of anger in the mid-1790s at Burke's justification of Britain's alliance and subsidy of the states that destroyed Poland-Lithuania. Life in a free state, however much corruption there was or however desperate life became in circumstances of perpetual political crisis, was always preferred to a life where tyrants had the power to dispose of their critics, which would sooner or later be exercised.

Bonaparte's actions in the early years of the century reinforced the contrast between free states and tyrannies. The execution of the duc d'Enghien after a sham trial, accused of conspiring with the British against Bonaparte, was one example.[37] Another was the murder of Toussaint Louverture, the great liberator of the French colony of Saint-Domingue. Bonaparte restored slavery in 1802 and attempted to recover Saint-Domingue for the French Empire, sending a vast invasion force under his brother-in-law Charles-Victoire-Emmanuel Leclerc, which battled Toussaint's forces to the point of surrender. As French troops were decimated by yellow fever, Toussaint began to plan to battle for liberty once more; a political genius, he recognized it was wise to negotiate not only with the French, but the Spanish and British, too. Leclerc then tricked Toussaint into a meeting and deported him to France; he died imprisoned in a cold cell in the Jura mountains in 1803. After genocidal conflict and grotesque massacres, Toussaint's former deputy Jean-Jacques Dessalines defeated the French and proclaimed the independent state of Haiti in 1804, serving himself as governor for life and then emperor. If Bonaparte failed in Haiti, he continued to pursue critics closer to home, including Jean Peltier, through the British courts for libel, de Staël and many others.[38]

James Mackintosh, one of Burke's most vociferous early critics, successfully defended Peltier at trial, arguing that British liberty was superior to that of revolutionaries or Bonapartists. Britain might be imperfectly free, but the monstrous empire of France had destroyed Europe, violating every facet of the law of nations.[39] After a 'long series of conflicts between the greatest power in the world and the only free press now remaining in Europe', Britain remained a defender of 'smaller states . . . devoted . . . to the arts of peace, to the cultivation of literature and the improvement of reason'. Liberty in Britain, Mackintosh concluded, was the only hope for enlightenment and the survival of what he called 'the European Commonwealth'.[40]

Numerous former diehard revolutionaries followed Mackintosh

and de Staël in portraying Britain as the model free state, the only place where liberty could be maintained. The task of the era which followed the Enlightenment was to save Britain from its worst elements, including the mercantile system, reforming the polity so that the public good was pursued by legislators, independently of the sinister interests of churches, classes or corporations.[41] Many of those who began to call themselves liberals, such as Benjamin Constant (1767–1830) or Jean-Charles-Léonard Simonde de Sismondi (1773–1842), had been critical of Britain in their early years. But they acknowledged that Britain's ultimate success as a free state, the battling of the French Revolution and then the French Empire, meant that strategies for preventing descent into republican fanaticism, despotism or religious fury were to be found in British history, culture and law. The task was to apply them to other parts of the world, including Europe, Spanish America and the autocratic empires, and any place willing to fight to be free.[42]

V

There is a widespread assumption among scholars, philosophers and the educated public that we can trace intellectual currents straightforwardly from past to present. If you want to know about rights you study Thomas Aquinas, Francisco Suárez, Hobbes or Wollstonecraft. If you need a compendium of ideas about justice, it is Aristotle or Grotius. As a devotee of conservatism or free market capitalism you might very well dip into Smith or Burke. For the darker side of humanity or defences of reason-of-state, see Machiavelli or Giovanni Botero. Above all, if you want justifications of reason, toleration and moderation, you look to Montesquieu and to Hume. For rights, democracy and equality, go to the Founding Fathers of the United States or leading French revolutionaries. Philosophically, many see themselves to be Kantians or Utilitarians, the two great philosophies of the late eighteenth century, founded respectively by Kant and Bentham.

The assumption is that eighteenth-century authors would, if

beamed across time into the present, recognize and appreciate that many of their hopes and dreams about politics had been realized. They would praise the creation of democracies defending human rights. They would applaud the extent of toleration and the break-up of empire, even if the latter had been largely within living memory. They might accept that war remained part of the human condition, but the extent of social and technological progress would no doubt overwhelm them. Many of our intellectuals would seek to congratulate their ancestors on establishing the foundations of our world: many global traditions of revolution, we might tell them, can be charted from their historical moment, and so too can traditions of gradual reform, the basis of breathtaking technological and social progress that deserves to be lauded.[43]

But for Hume, Bentham, Kant and a host of Enlightenment fig-ures, the key fact about their times was the failure of their reformist philosophies, the great sciences of the statesman or legislator erected by natural jurists across early modern Europe. Systems of natural jurisprudence geared to maintaining toleration and peace no longer had solutions to the problems of the times. Superstition and enthusiasm translated from religion into politics promoted both nationalism and militant revolutionary republicanism. Far from being tolerant, each ideology found violence against others entirely justifiable if it maintained the independence of a state or the sanctity of a republic. Social homogeneity in large cities and large states was seen to be the norm for both nationalists and repub-licans. A mercantile system of corrupt merchants and politicians no longer needed to seek empire directly. If the economy of another state could be controlled in the sense of being forced to pursue pol-icies in accordance with the interests of foreign owners of capital, there might well be no need to intervene directly. The people in a subject state could even be encouraged to see themselves to be living freely in a democracy, enjoying human rights, if they renounced control over their own economic destinies. The 'world crisis' that shifted power to Western Europe and especially Britain by the end of the eighteenth century, had shocking implications. It reversed traditional expectations about the inability of corrupt economies or commercial empires to maintain themselves by war.[44] Instead war really did become, as Clausewitz later put it, 'a real political instrument, a continuation of political commerce'.[45]

The great evil of the mercantile system was its propagation of this violence to secure the resources its merchants required to generate profits or to limit the economic power of rival states. From an eighteenth-century perspective, the outbreak of successive world wars, increasingly global in nature, would have been no surprise, being the natural conclusion of such a system, as well as clear instances, to their minds, of republican or democratic fanaticism. As most enlightenment philosophers were highly sceptical about the capacity of the people to rule, they might well have described the states we call democracies to be in fact plutocracies. As we have seen, it was commonplace in the eighteenth century to argue that if you wanted to secure the rule of the rich over the poor the obvious means was representative government. Unaware of rife corruption, people were easily deluded into thinking that they enjoyed real power.[46] And regardless, in the eighteenth century as today, there was a sense that the poor tended to look up to the wealthy, to seek to emulate them, and so to vote for them. The rich and the famous, it was held, would always be more likely to win elections than someone unknown, however much they were dedicated to the true interests of the social body. Representative government in the context of a mercantile system, it is said, never makes the people free. Yet given the history of democratic or autocratic populism, the most stable free states continue to be modelled on Britain, not that the critiques of this free state have ever gone away.

Those battling to prevent the end of enlightenment worried about the loss of cultural diversity, the loss of alternative political or economic systems, and the identification of happiness with the ever-growing consumption of luxury goods. They worried that their own world was a return to the past: to times of division, turbulence, sacrifice, war and death. Enlightenment figures saw what we call modern politics largely in religious terms, with politicians in free states presenting themselves as latter-day priests. They were concerned that fanatics had won the day, with enthusiasm the most powerful force in social intercourse. Political puritanism, they believed, had defeated enlightenment.

Eighteenth-century actors had concerns about their own past and likely future that resonate with post-humanist assessments of our own. In turn there are implications for our own politics, and the way we see our past. Enlightenment commentators were fully aware of the effects of what we now term global trade and democratic civilization. Globalization and democracy were touted by their advocates as forces to be relied upon to restore toleration and peace, because neither the people in power nor merchants seeking trade would willingly embrace war. One of the revelations of the eighteenth century was the ease by which popular government could be corrupted by dangerous projectors, the prophets and men of system who convinced the people that war and conflict were worth it, being vital for national flourishing. Equally, critics argued that merchants were willing to embrace war if it offered more profit; they were never naturally pacific. Fortunately, unlike in the present, they could only with difficulty liquidate their assets and move across borders. For those who still believed commonwealth assumptions to be relevant, this was significant because the rich men who had caused or were embroiled in crisis could not avoid its consequences. Like all other members of the nation state, they were stuck. As they were likely to have their wealth invested in the land of the country they resided in, they also had an interest, it was believed, in the public good.

From an end of enlightenment perspective, the final decades of the eighteenth century saw forms of globalization and democracy become dominant that were manipulated by self-serving politicians, merchants and bankers, and employed to seduce a credulous populace into accepting total war. The perspective of many living through this period was that fanaticism, enthusiasm and superstition had infested the political realm. New species of false religion abounded in the form of an excessive love for luxury, power or liberty. Such fevers in the political body had been seen before but in the late eighteenth century their advocates began to dominate the political landscape. Moderation was abandoned and the traditional strategies defending peace began to fail. Critics identifying the end of enlightenment perceived the worship of authority, wealth or power to be everywhere and to be dangerously influencing political action in states that once defined themselves as free. The consequence was social collapse, the justification of violence, the abandonment of laws sustaining toleration and the outbreak of war.

Such a world was not ultimately theirs, because solutions were found in the most unlikely of quarters, liberal philosophies derived from the experience of the following generation, battling for liberty in different continents and circumstances. Across the world, but especially in South America, North America, Europe and Britain, new groups in the early nineteenth century fought to stop mercantile systems from causing wars and spreading chaos, establishing a version of enlightenment different to that of the past. The choices faced were brutal. Alexis de Tocqueville, for all his praise of liberty and equality in the United States in his book *Democracy in America*, watched in horror as the Native American Choctaws crossed the Mississippi, the remnant of a people near destroyed by a mercantile system. Tocqueville wrote that 'their calamities were of an ancient date, and they knew them to be irredeemable.'[47] Yet Tocqueville saw no alternative to the dominion of large commercial empires, accepting the French invasion of Algeria despite the grotesque abuse of civilians.[48] He planned to write a history of British India, hoping to understand mercantile systems and their likely future, but ultimately abandoned the project.

Once again we live in a world that has suffered an end of enlightenment, as the strategies formulated after 1945 to prevent civil and international violence, fanaticism and chaos from breaking out again have gradually failed or been abandoned.[49] Accepting the transformatively positive effects of commerce, science and technology, we must remember that from an enlightenment perspective there is little purpose in emphasizing alone the path of progress. It is much more important to foresee crisis, to formulate strategies for the moments of social break down, when war and fanaticism dominate the public sphere. Equally, there is little to be gained from turning against history, censoring and condemning national histories for being responsible for the ills of the present. History alone supplies answers, rejecting the past for its flaws is to go blindly into the future.

One of the remarkable facts about the post-1945 period was a renaissance of research concerned with the eighteenth century. Some of the greatest scholars were Jewish – the list is long but includes Isaiah Berlin, Peter Gay, Judith Shklar, Frank E. Manuel, Ralph A. Leigh and Theodore Besterman. Many had miraculously survived the Holocaust and all lost friends and family to the fascist genocide. Rather than turning against European history, they sought lessons for the present in the history of fanaticism and the strategies of enlightenment that were formulated to prevent it. We need to follow them and battle for enlightenment anew.

Acknowledgements

The End of Enlightenment is dedicated to the recently departed John Pocock. John read early drafts of the book; engaging with his singular historical imagination inspired many of the interpretative claims here made. Alongside Quentin Skinner, John in many ways founded the modern discipline of intellectual history and they have each helped and supported me more than I can say. In addition, I need to emphasise a special obligation to two now departed luminaries of the field, Donald Winch and István Hont.

The End of Enlightenment began life as Carlyle Lectures at the University of Oxford between January and March 2019. A significant debt of gratitude is owed to the incomparable George Garnett and everyone involved in organising the series. A second is to the fellows and staff of Nuffield College for hosting me, especially Cécile Laborde, David Miller and Claire Bunce. Turning lectures into a book has caused me, as always, to draw upon the labours of many friends including Béla Kapossy, Knud Haakonssen, Michael Sonenscher, Brian Young, Ian Hunter, James Harris, Colin Kidd, Lasse Andersen, Lina Weber, John Robertson, Pamela Clemit, Gabriel Sabbagh, Peter Ghosh, Philip Schofield, Rosario Lopez, David Armitage, Richard Bourke, Koen Stapelbroek, Stefan Collini, Keith Tribe, David Allan, Amy Westwell, Peter Madill, Cailean Gallagher, Max Skjönsberg, Jamie Gianoutsos, Doohwan Ahn, Avi Lifschitz, John Marshall, John Hudson, Ann Thomson, Andreas Hess, Ali Ansari, Paul Myles, Synne Myreboe, Minchul Kim, Rachel Hammersley, Ariane Fichtl, Cesare Cuttica, David Coates, Anna Plassart, Jason Isbit, Sophie Scott-Brown, Caroline Humfress, Dario Castligione, Manuela Albertone, Jim Livesey, Joon Hyung Kim, Isaac Nakimovsky, Frances Nethercott, Rory Cox, Robin Mills, Ryan Walter, Alan Macfarlane, Michael Drolet, Camila Vergara, Valerie Wallace, Karie

Schultz, Davide Caddedu and Chandrika Kaul. Jess Whatmore, Emilie Aebischer, Joon Hyung Kim and Elizabeth Shannon acted as research assistants. My scholarly debts are broader, listed in *Anarchists, Terrorists and Republicans* (2019), including to students at St Andrews who take the 'Revolutions and Empires' final-year module and the MLitt in Intellectual History. Staff at the Institute and School of History, especially Elsie Johnstone and Lorna Harris, have been endlessly supportive.

A Leverhulme Trust fellowship for the project 'Death and the Philosophers' proved invaluable for the completion of the book. I have been writing about many of the figures discussed in *The End of Enlightenment* for a long time and, although the argument here is new, I've inevitably drawn upon such work. But I need to thank my great friend Béla Kapossy especially for allowing me to use our jointly authored writing on Edward Gibbon and republicanism. A bibliography for *The End of Enlightenment* can be found on the St Andrews Institute of Intellectual History website.

I want to send a special thank you to Casiana Ionita and Edward Kirke; they embraced the daunting challenge of teaching me to write for a trade audience and have been wonderful, displaying to a high degree the very enlightenment virtues of patience, calm and toleration. I can't sufficiently express my appreciation to them and to the broader Penguin team including Noosha Alai-South, Anna Wilson and Penelope Vogler.

As always, by far the greatest of my debts by far go to my wife Ruth Woodfield and our sons Jess, Kim and Davy Whatmore.

Notes

Introduction

1 James Boswell, 'An Account of my last interview with David Hume Esq.', *Boswell in Extremes, 1776–1778*, ed., Charles McWeiss and Frederick A. Pottle (New York: Mc Graw-Hill, 1970), 11. On the influence of Hume, see John C. Laursen, 'David Hume and the Danish Debate about the Freedom of the Press in the 1770s', *Journal of the History of Ideas* (1998), 167–72; James Fieser, ed., *Early Responses to Hume's Moral, Literary and Political Writings* (Bristol: Thoemmes Continuum, 1999), 2 vols.; Mark G. Spencer, *David Hume and Eighteenth-Century America: The Reception of Hume's Political Thought in America, 1740–1830* (Rochester, NY: 2005); Peter Jones, ed., *The Reception of David Hume in Europe* (London and New York: Thoemmes Continuum, 2005); Ben Dew, '"Waving a *Mouchoir à la* Wilkes": Hume, Radicalism and the North Briton', *Modern Intellectual History* (2009), 235–60; Ryu Susato, 'Hume as an *Ami de la liberté*: The Reception of His "Idea of a Perfect Commonwealth"', *Modern Intellectual History* 13/3 (2016), 569–96; Danielle Charette, 'Hume's "Idea of a Perfect Commonwealth" and Scottish political thought of the 1790s', *History of European Ideas* 48/1 (2022), 78–96.

2 On Hume's closeness to Smith and the issue of the latter's willingness or otherwise to publish posthumously Hume's *Dialogues concerning Natural Religion*, see Felix Waldmann, 'Adam Smith on David Hume's *Dialogues concerning Natural Religion*: An Unnoticed Fragment', *Scottish Historical Review* 100 (2021), 138–50.

3 Adam Smith, LL.D., to William Strachan, Esq., 9 November 1776, in 'The Correspondence of Adam Smith', ed., Ernest C. Mossner and Ian Simpson Ross, *The Glasgow Edition of the Works and Correspondence of Adam Smith: VI* (Oxford: Oxford University Press, 1987), 219.

4 'Draft of Preface to a Volume of David Hume's History', cited in Ernest Mossner, *The Life of David Hume* (Oxford: Oxford University Press, 1980), 306–7.

5 Duncan Shaw, *A Comparative View of the Several Methods of Promoting Religious Instruction: From the Earliest Down to the Present Time; from Which the Superior Excellence of That Recommended in the Christian Institutes, Particularly from the Illustration of Scripture History and Characters, Is Evinced and Demonstrated* (London: Richardson and Urquhart 1776), I, 247–67.

6 Daniel MacQueen, *Letters on Mr. Hume's History of Great Britain* (Edinburgh: Sands, Donaldson, Murray and Cochran, 1756), 5–35.

7 Hugh Trevor-Roper, 'The Religious Origins of the Enlightenment', *Religion, the Reformation and Social Change* (London: Macmillan, 1967), 193–236; Ole Peter Grell and Roy Porter, eds., *Toleration in Enlightenment Europe* (Cambridge: Cambridge University Press 2000); Wendy Brown, *Regulating Aversion: Tolerance in the Age of Identity and Empire* (Princeton, NJ: Princeton University Press, 2008); Roy Porter, *Enlightenment: Britain and the Creation of the Modern World* (London: Allen Lane, 2001); Denis Lacorne, *The Limits of Tolerance: Enlightenment Values and Religious Fanaticism* (New York: Columbia University Press, 2019), trans. C. Jon Delogu and Robin Emlein.

8 John R. Knott, 'John Foxe and the Joy of Suffering', *Sixteenth Century Journal* 27/3 (1996), 721–34; John N. King, ' "The Light of Printing": William Tyndale, John Foxe, John Day, and Early Modern Print Culture', *Renaissance Quarterly* 54/1 (2001), 52–85.; Thomas S. Freeman, 'Fate, Faction, and Fiction in Foxe's Book of Martyrs', *Historical Journal* 43/3 (2000), 601–23; Elizabeth Evenden and Thomas S. Freeman. 'Print, Profit and Propaganda: The Elizabethan Privy Council and the 1570 Edition of Foxe's "Book of Martyrs" ', *English Historical Review* 119, no. 484 (2004), 1288–1307; Elizabeth Evenden and Thomas S. Freeman, *Religion and the Book in Early Modern England: The Making of John Foxe's 'Book of Martyrs'*.

9 Daniel Ternois, *Jacques Callot (1592–1635): Actes du Colloque* (Paris: Musée du Louvre, 1993); Klincksieck. Howard G. Brown, *Mass Violence and the Self: From the French Wars of Religion to the Paris Commune* (Ithaca, NY: Cornell University Press, 2018).

10 David Hume, *A Letter from a Gentleman to His Friend in Edinburgh (1745)*, eds., Ernest C. Mossner and John V. Price (Edinburgh: Edinburgh University Press, 1967), 34. For Hume's religious beliefs see J. C. A. Gaskin, *Hume's Philosophy of Religion*, second edn (London: Macmillan, 1988); Richard Serjeantson, 'David Hume's *Natural History of Religion* (1757) and the End of Modern Eusebianism', in Sarah Mortimer and John Robertson, eds., *The Intellectual Consequences of Religious Heterodoxy 1600–1750* (Leiden: Brill, 2011), 267–95; Jennifer Smalligan Marusic, 'Refuting the Whole System? Hume's Attack on Popular Religion in *The Natural History of Religion*', *Philosophical Quarterly* 62 (2012), 715–36; James Moore, 'The Eclectic Stoic, the Mitigated Sceptic', *Rivista di storia della filosofia (1984–)* 62/3 (2007), 133–69. On the theological context, see M. A. Stewart 'Revealed Religion: the British Debate' and 'Arguments for the existence of God: The British Debate', in Knud Haakonssen, ed., *The Cambridge History of Eighteenth-Century Philosophy* (Cambridge: Cambridge University Press, 2006), 683–709, 710–30. More broadly, see J. C. D. Clark, *English Society 1660–1832: Religion, Ideology and Politics during the Ancien Régime* (Cambridge: Cambridge University Press, 2000); Brian Young, 'Religious History and the Eighteenth-Century Historian', *Historical Journal* 43/3 (2000), 849–68.

11 J. G. A. Pocock, 'Hume and the American Revolution: The Dying Thoughts of a North Briton', *Virtue, Commerce, and History – Essays on Political Thought and History, Chiefly in the Eighteenth Century* (Cambridge: Cambridge University Press, 1985), 125–41.

12 For Hume's worries about the excess of liberty, see Duncan Forbes, *Hume's Philosophical Politics* (Cambridge: Cambridge University Press, 1975), and Knud Haakonssen, 'The Structure of Hume's Political Theory', in David Fate Norton and Jacqueline Taylor, eds., *The Cambridge Companion to Hume* (Cambridge: Cambridge University Press, 2008), 341–80. For context, see H. T. Dickinson, *Liberty and Property: Political Ideology in Eighteenth-Century Britain* (London: Methuen, 1977); J. G. A. Pocock, *The Machiavellian Moment: Florentine Political Thought and the Atlantic Republican Tradition* (Princeton, NJ: Princeton University Press, 2016).

13 On Hume, see Ryu Susato, ' "Refinement" and "Vicious Luxury":
Hume's Nuanced Defence of Luxury', *Hume's Sceptical Enlightenment*
(Edinburgh: Edinburgh University Press, 2015), 92–130. For context
see István Hont, 'Needs and Justice in the *Wealth of Nations* ', in István
Hont and Michael Ignatieff, *Wealth and Virtue: The Shaping of Political
Economy in the Scottish Enlightenment* (Cambridge, Cambridge Univer-
sity Press, 1983), 1–44; 'The Language of Sociability and Commerce:
Samuel Pufendorf and the Foundations of Smith's Four Stages
Theory', in Anthony Pagden, ed., *Languages of Political Theory in Early
Modern Europe* (Cambridge: Cambridge University Press, 1986), 253–
76; *Politics in Commercial Society: Jean-Jacques Rousseau and Adam Smith*,
eds., Béla Kapossy and Michael Sonenscher (Cambridge, MA: Harvard University Press, 2015).

14 M. N. Pearson, *Merchants and Rulers in Gujarat: The Response to the Por-
tuguese in the Sixteenth Century* (Berkeley, CA: University of California
Press, 1976), *Before Colonialism: Theories on Asian-European Relations,
1500–1750* (Oxford: Oxford University Press, 1988), and, ed., *Trade Cir-
culation and Flow in the Indian Ocean World* (Basingstoke: Palgrave
Macmillan, 2015); Sanjay Subrahmanyam Sanjay, *Improvising Empire:
Portuguese Trade and Settlement in the Bay of Bengal 1500–1700* (Delhi:
Oxford University Press, 1990).

15 Jonathan Israel, *Dutch Primacy in World Trade 1585–1740* (Oxford and New
York: Clarendon Press and Oxford University Press, 1989); Brandon
Pepijn, *War, Capital, and the Dutch State (1588–1795)* (Leiden: Brill, 2015).

16 Richard Bonney, ed., *Economic Systems and State Finance* (Oxford and
New York: Clarendon Press, 1995) and, ed., *The Rise of the Fiscal State
in Europe, c. 1200–1815* (Oxford: Clarendon Press, 1999); Bartolomé Yun-
Casalilla, Patrick K. O'Brien and Francisco Comín Comín, eds., *The
Rise of Fiscal States: A Global History, 1500–1914* (Cambridge: Cambridge
University Press, 2012).

17 James D. Tracy, ed., *The Rise of Merchant Empires: Long Distance Trade
in the Early Modern World 1350–1750* (Cambridge: Cambridge University
Press, 1990) and James D. Tracy, ed., *The Political Economy of Merchant
Empires: State Power and World Trade, 1350–1750* (Cambridge: Cambridge
University Press, 1991).

18 John Brewer, *The Sinews of Power: War Money and the English State 1688–1783* (London: Unwin Hyman, 1989); Lawrence Stone, *An Imperial State at War: Britain from 1689 to 1815* (London: Routledge, 1994); Aaron Graham and Patrick Walsh, *The British Fiscal-Military States 1660– c. 1783* (London: Routledge, 2016).

19 Michael Roberts, *The Military Revolution, 1560–1660: An Inaugural Lecture Delivered before the Queen's University of Belfast* (Belfast: Queen's University, 1956); Geoffrey Parker, *The Military Revolution: Military Innovation and the Rise of the West, 1500–1800* (Cambridge: Cambridge University Press, 1996); Jeremy Black, *European Warfare, 1660–1815* (New Haven CT, 1994); Jeremy Black, *A Military Revolution? Military Change and European Society 1550–1800* (Basingstoke: Macmillan, 1991) and, ed., *War in the Early Modern World* (London: Routledge, 2016); John A. Lynn, 'Forging the Western Army in Seventeenth-Century France', in M. Knox and W. Murray, eds., *The Dynamics of Military Revolution 1300–2050* (Cambridge: Cambridge University Press, 2001), 35–56.

20 P. G. M. Dickson, *The Financial Revolution in England: A Study in the Development of Public Credit* (London: Macmillan, 1967); P. G. M. Dickson and John Sperling, 'War Finance, 1689–1714', in J. S. Bromley, ed., *New Cambridge Modern History, Vol. 6: The Rise of Great Britain and Russia, 1688–1715/25* (Cambridge: Cambridge University Press, 1970); Christopher Storrs, ed., *The Fiscal-Military State in Eighteenth-Century Europe: Essays in Honour of P. G. M. Dickson* (London: Routledge, 2016); Marjolein C. 't Hart, 'Mobilising Resources for War: The Dutch and British Financial Revolutions Compared', in Rafael Torres Sánchez, ed., *War, State and Development: Fiscal-Military States in the Eighteenth Century* (Pamplona: Ediciones Universidad de Navarra, 2007), 179–200.

21 J. L. Price, 'A State dedicated to War? The Dutch Republic in the 17th Century', in Andrew Ayton and J. L. Price, eds., *The Medieval Military Revolution: State, Society and Military Change in Medieval and Early Modern Europe* (London and New York: I. B. Tauris, 1995); Jonathan Israel, 'Spain, the Spanish Embargoes and the Struggle for Mastery of World Trade, 1585–1660', in *Conflicts of Empires: Spain, the Low*

Countries and the Struggle for World Supremacy, 1585–1713 (London: Hambledon Press, 1997); Marjolein C. 't Hart, *The Making of a Bourgeois State: War, Politics and Finance during the Dutch Revolt* (Manchester: Manchester University Press, 1993); J. D. Tracy, *The Founding of the Dutch Republic: War, Finance, and Politics in Holland, 1572–1588* (Oxford: Oxford University Press, 2008); Oscar Gelderblom, Abe de Jong and Joost Jonker, 'The Formative Years of the Modern Corporation: The Dutch East India Company VOC, 1602–1623', *Journal of Economic History* 73/4 (2013), 1050–76; Oscar Gelderblom and Joost Jonker, 'Completing a Financial Revolution: The Finance of the Dutch East India Trade and the Rise of the Amsterdam Capital Market, 1595–1612', *Journal of Economic History* 64/3 (2004), 641–72; Pepijn Brandon, '"The Whole Art of War is Reduced to Money": Remittances, Short-term Credit and Financial Intermediation in Anglo-Dutch Military Finance, 1688–1713', *Financial History Review* 25 (2018), 19–41.

22 Ron Harris, 'The English East India Company', in *Going the Distance: Eurasian Trade and the Rise of the Business Corporation, 1400–1700* (Princeton, NJ: Princeton University Press, 2020), 291–330; Ghulam A. Nadri, 'The English and Dutch East India Companies and Indian Merchants in Surat in the Seventeenth and Eighteenth Centuries: Interdependence, Competition and Contestation', in Adam Clulow and Tristan Mostert, eds., *The Dutch and English East India Companies: Diplomacy, Trade and Violence in Early Modern Asia* (Amsterdam: Amsterdam University Press, 2018), 125–150.

23 Michael Sonenscher, 'The Nation's Debt and the Birth of the Modern Republic: The French Fiscal Deficit and the Politics of the Revolution of 1789', *History of Political Thought* 18 (1997), 63–103, 267–325.

24 Lina Weber, 'National Debt and Political Allegiance in Eighteenth-Century Britain', *Historical Journal* 65/4 (2022), 1015–34.

25 Anon., *Les moyens de la France, pour ruiner le commerce des Hollandois, avec ses intérêts à l'égard des étrangers, présentés au roy par ses ministres* (Brussels, 1671); Maarten Prak, *The Dutch Republic in the Seventeenth Century: The Golden Age* (Cambridge, MA: Cambridge University Press, 2005); Koen Stapelbroek, 'Dutch Decline as a European Phenomenon', *History of European Ideas* 36/2, (2010), 139–52; Doohwan Ahn,

'The Anglo-French Treaty of Commerce of 1713: Tory Trade Politics and the Question of Dutch Decline', *History of European Ideas* 36/2 (2010), 167–180; Koen Stapelbroek and Antonio Trampus, 'Commercial Reform against the Tide: Reapproaching the Eighteenth-Century Decline of the Republics of Venice and the United Provinces', *History of European Ideas* 36/2 (2010), 192–202; Gregory Hanlon, *The Twilight of a Military Tradition: Italian Aristocrats and European Conflicts, 1560–1800* (London: UCL Press, 1998); Tonio Andrade and William Reger, eds., *The Limits of Empire: European Imperial Formations in Early Modern World History: Essays in Honor of Geoffrey Parker* (London: Routledge, 2017); Joris Oddens, Mart Rutjes and Arthur Weststeijn, eds., *Discourses of Decline: Essays on Republicanism in Honor of Wyger R. E. Velema* (Leiden: Brill, 2022); Robert I. Frost, *The Northern Wars: War State and Society in Northeastern Europe 1558–1721* (Harlow: Longman, 2000); Richard Butterwick, *The Polish-Lithuanian Monarchy in European Context c. 1500–1795* (Basingstoke: Palgrave Macmillan, 2001); Jerzy Łukowski, *Disorderly Liberty: The Political Culture of the Polish-Lithuanian Commonwealth in the Eighteenth Century* (London and New York: Continuum, 2010); Tomasz Gromelski, 'Liberty and Liberties in Early Modern Poland-Lithuania', in Quentin Skinner and Martin van Gelderen, eds., *Freedom and the Construction of Europe* (Cambridge: Cambridge University Press, 2013), 215–34; Regina Grafe, *Distant Tyranny: Markets, Power, and Backwardness in Spain, 1650-1800* (Princeton, NJ: Princeton University Press, 2011); James S. Grubb, 'When Myths Lose Power: Four Decades of Venetian Historiography', *Journal of Modern History* 58/1 (1986), 43–94; Avner Greif, 'Political Organizations, Social Structure, and Institutional Success: Reflections from Genoa and Venice during the Commercial Revolution', *Journal of Institutional and Theoretical Economics (JITE)/Zeitschrift für die gesamte Staatswissenschaft* 151/4 (1995), 734–40.

26 Michael Roberts, *The Age of Liberty: Sweden 1719–1772* (Cambridge: Cambridge University Press, 1986); Thomas Munck, 'Absolute Monarchy in Later Eighteenth-Century Denmark: Centralized Reform, Public Expectations, and the Copenhagen Press', *Historical Journal* 41/1 (1998), 201–24.

27 Franco Venturi, *Utopia and Reform in the Enlightenment* (Cambridge: Cambridge University Press, 1971), *The End of the Old Regime in Europe: Republican Patriotism and the Empires of the East* (Princeton, NJ: Princeton University Press, 1991); Manuela Albertone, 'Repubblica e repubbliche nella riflessione storica di Franco Venturi', *Società e storia* 29 (2006), 158–78, and 'Presentazione', *Il repubblicanesimo moderno: L'idea di repubblica nella riflessione storica di Franco Venturi* (Naples: Bibliopolis, 2006), ed. Manuela Albertone, xxxiii–li; Richard Whatmore, *Republicanism and the French Revolution: An Intellectual History of Jean-Baptiste Say's Political Economy* (Oxford: Oxford University Press, 2000) and *Against War and Empire: Geneva, Britain and France in the Eighteenth Century; Terrorists, Anarchists, and Republicans: The Genevans and the Irish in Time of Revolution* (Princeton, NJ: Princeton University Press, 2019); Michael Sonenscher, *Before the Deluge: Public Debt, Inequality, and the Intellectual Origins of the French Revolution* and *Sans-Culottes: An Eighteenth-Century Emblem in the French Revolution* (Princeton, NJ: Princeton University Press, 2008).

28 István Hont, 'Free Trade and the Economic Limits to National Politics: Neo-Machiavellian Political Economy Reconsidered', in John Dunn, ed., *The Economic Limits to Politics* (Cambridge: Cambridge University Press, 1990), 41–120. See more broadly, Hamish M. Scott, 'Diplomatic Culture in Old Regime Europe', in Hamish Scott and Brendan Simms, eds., *Cultures of Power in Europe during the Long Eighteenth Century* (Cambridge: Cambridge University Press, 2007), 59–60; Robert Oresko, G. C. Gibbs and Hamish M. Scott, eds., *Royal and Republican Sovereignty in Early Modern Europe* (Cambridge: Cambridge University Press, 1997); Lucien Bély, 'Souveraineté et souverains: La question du cérémonial dans les relations internationales à l'époque moderne', *Annuaire-bulletin de la Société de l'histoire de France* 130 (1993), 27–43; Ho-fung Hung, 'Imperial China and Capitalist Europe in the Eighteenth-Century Global Economy', *Review (Fernand Braudel Center)* 24/4 (2001), 473–513; P. J. Marshall, 'Presidential Address: Britain and the World in the Eighteenth Century: III, Britain and India', *Transactions of the Royal Historical Society* 10 (2000), 1–16; Jennifer Pitts, 'Empire and Legal Universalisms in the Eighteenth

Century', *American Historical Review* 117/1 (2012), 92–121; Felicia Gottmann, 'French-Asian Connections: The Compagnies des Indes, France's Eastern trade, and new directions in historical scholarship', *Historical Journal* 56/2 (2013), 537–52; Tamara H. Bentley, ed., *Picturing Commerce in and from the East Asian Maritime Circuits, 1550–1800: Visual and Material Culture, 1300–1700* (Amsterdam: Amsterdam University Press, 2019).

29   See Sankar Muthu, *Enlightenment against Empire* (Princeton, NJ: Princeton University Press, 2003), and Sankar Muthu, ed., *Empire and Modern Political Thought* (Amsterdam University Press, 2012).

30   Adam Smith, *An Inquiry into the Nature and Causes of the Wealth of Nations*, ed. R. H. Campbell, A. S. Skinner and W. B. Todd (Oxford: Oxford University Press, 1975), 2 vols., IV.Vii.b22, II, 575. A note cites the Abbé Raynal's *Histoire philosophique des deux Indes*, III, 385. On Portugal see Armando da Silva Saturnino Monteiro, 'The Decline and Fall of Portuguese Seapower, 1583–1663', *Journal of Military History* 65/1 (2001), 9–20; Kenneth Maxwell, 'Portugal, Europe, and the Origins of the Atlantic Commercial System, 1415–1520', *Portuguese Studies* 8 (1992), 3–16; P. A. Leupe and Mac Hacobian, 'The Siege and Capture of Malacca from the Portuguese in 1640–1641', *Journal of the Malayan Branch of the Royal Asiatic Society* 14/1 (124) (1936), i–178; P. J. Marshall, 'Early British Imperialism in India', *Past & Present* 106 (1985), 164–9, 'British Society in India under the East India Company', *Modern Asian Studies* 31/1 (1997), 89–108, and 'Western Arms in Maritime Asia in the Early Phases of Expansion', *Modern Asian Studies* 14/1 (1980), 13–28.

31   Adam Smith, *An Inquiry into the Nature and Causes of the Wealth of Nations*, eds., R. H. Campbell, A. S. Skinner and W. B. Todd, IV.Vii. b12, II, 570.

32   Ibid., IV.vii,c.103, II, 637.

33   Ibid., IV.viii,4, II, 644. See further, Keith Tribe, 'Reading Trade in the *Wealth of Nations*', *History of European Ideas* 32 (2006), 58–79; Paul Sagar, 'The Conspiracy of the Merchants', *Adam Smith Reconsidered: History, Liberty and the Foundations of Modern Politics* (Princeton NJ: Princeton, University Press, 2022), 187–211.

34 Eli F. Heckscher, *Mercantilism* (London: Routledge, 1995); Lars Magnusson, *The Political Economy of Mercantilism* (London: Routledge, 2018), and Magnusson, ed., *Mercantilist Theory and Practice: The History of British Mercantilism* (London: Routledge, 2016). For a critique, see Philip J. Stern and Carl Wennerlind, eds., *Mercantilism Reimagined: Political Economy in Early Modern Britain and Its Empire* (Oxford: Oxford University Press, 2014).

35 Farhad Rassekh, 'Comparative Advantage in Smith's *Wealth of Nations*' and Ricardo's '*Principles*: A Brief History of Its Early Development', *History of Economic Ideas* 23/1 (2015), 59–75; for the actual history, see István Hont, *Jealousy of Trade: International Competition and the Nation-State in Historical Perspective* (Cambridge MA: Harvard University Press, 2005), 68–9; Ryan Walter, *Before Method and Models: The Political Economy of Malthus and Ricardo* (Oxford: Oxford University Press, 2021); Keith Tribe, *The Economy of the Word: Language History and Economics* (New York: Oxford University Press, 2015); and for an explanation of the mis-readings, see Tribe, *Constructing Economic Science: The Invention of a Discipline 1850–1950* (New York: Oxford University Press, 2022).

36 Smith, *An Inquiry into the Nature and Causes of the Wealth of Nations*, eds. R. H. Campbell, A. S. Skinner and R. B. Todd, IV.ii.30, I, 464–5; see further, Gregory M. Collins, 'Adam Smith on the Navigation Acts and Anglo-American Imperial Relations', *History of Political Thought* 43/2 (2022), 273–304.

37 Barry R. Weingast captures the ambivalence of Smith's position nicely. See 'War, Trade, and Mercantilism: Reconciling Adam Smith's Three Theories of the British Empire' (6 September 2018), SSRN: https://ssrn.com/abstract=2915959 or http://dx.doi.org/10.2139/ssrn.2915959

38 Hume to Smith, 1 April 1776, in *The Letters of David Hume*, ed. J. Y. T. Greig (Oxford: Oxford University Press, 1932), 2 vols., II, 311: see also Ian Simpson Ross, 'The Intellectual Friendship of David Hume and Adam Smith', *Rivista di storia della filosofia*, 62/3 (2007), 345–63.

39 Smith to John Sinclair of Ulster, 14 October 1782, *The Correspondence of Adam Smith*, ed. Ernest Campbell Mossner and Ian Simpson Ross

(Oxford: Clarendon Press, 1977), 2nd edn, 262; Donald Winch, *Riches and Poverty: An Intellectual History of Political Economy in Britain, 1750–1834* (Cambridge: Cambridge University Press, 1996), 50; 'A Great Deal of Ruin in a Nation', in Peter Clarke and Clive Trebilcock, eds., *Understanding Decline: Perceptions and Realities of British Economic Performance* (Cambridge: Cambridge University Press, 1997), 30–48.

40 Smith, *An Inquiry into the Nature and Causes of the Wealth of Nations*, ed. R. H. Campbell, A. S. Skinner and R. B. Todd, IV.vii.c.65, II, 616. See further, Aaron Graham, 'Auditing Leviathan: Corruption and State Formation in Early Eighteenth-Century Britain', *English Historical Review* 128/533 (2013), 806–38.

41 For the origins, see Andrew Fitzmaurice, 'The Commercial Ideology of Colonization in Jacobean England: Robert Johnson, Giovanni Botero, and the Pursuit of Greatness', *William and Mary Quarterly* 64/4 (2007), 791–820.

42 On Clive, see H. V. Bowen, 'Clive, Robert, First Baron Clive of Plassey (1725–1774), Army Officer in the East India Company and Administrator in India', *Oxford Dictionary of National Biography*; on nabobs, see Robert Travers, 'Death and the Nabob: Imperialism and Commemoration in Eighteenth-Century India', *Past & Present*, 196 (2007), 83–124; Christina Smylitopoulos, 'Portrait of a Nabob: Graphic Satire, Portraiture, and the Anglo-Indian in the Late Eighteenth Century', *RACAR: Revue d'art Canadienne/Canadian Art Review* 37/1 (2012), 10–25.

43 Smith blamed the Company in *An Inquiry into the Nature and Causes of the Wealth of Nations*, ed. R. H. Campbell, A. S. Skinner and W. B. Todd, IV.,v.b.6, I, 527: 'The drought in Bengal, a few years ago, might probably have occasioned a very great dearth. Some improper regulations, some injudicious restraints, imposed by the servants of the East India Company upon the rice trade, contributed, perhaps, to turn that dearth into a famine.' See further P. J. Marshall, *Bengal: The British Bridgehead: Eastern India 1740–1828* (Cambridge: Cambridge University Press, 2006), 18; Rajat Datta, 'Subsistence Crises and Economic history: A Study of Eighteenth-Century Bengal', in *A Cultural History of Famine: Food Security and the Environment in India and Britain*,

ed. Ayesha Mukherjee (London: Routledge, 2019), 48; Tirthankar Roy, *How British Rule Changed India's Economy: The Paradox of the Raj* (London: Palgrave, 2019), 117.

44 Adam Smith, *An Inquiry into the Nature and Causes of the Wealth of Nations*, Book III, ch. 1, I, 380. See further, Paul Sagar, *Adam Smith Reconsidered: History, Liberty and the Foundations of Modern Politics*, 203–7.

45 George Bancroft, *History of the United States from the Discovery of the American Continent* (Boston: Little & Brown, 1841), 6th edn, 10 vols. [1838–1876], III, 233: 'The *mercantile system*, of which the whole colonial system was the essential branch, culminated in the slave trade, and in the commercial policy adopted with regard to the chief produce of slave labor.' See more broadly, Eric E. Williams, *Capitalism and Slavery* (Chapel Hill, NC, and London: University of North Carolina Press, 1944); Felix Brahm and Eve Rosenhaft, *Slavery Hinterland: Transatlantic Slavery and Continental Europe 1680–1850* (Woodbridge: Boydell & Brewer, 2016) and *Globalized Peripheries: Central Europe and the Atlantic World, 1680–1860*; Jutta Wimmler and Klaus Weber, *Peripheries: Central Europe and the Atlantic World 1680–1860* (Woodbridge: Boydell & Brewer, 2020); Toby Green, *A Fistful of Shells: West Africa from the Rise of the Slave Trade to the Age of Revolution* (London: Allen Lane, 2019); Paul Cheney, *Cul de Sac: Patrimony, Capitalism, and Slavery in French Saint-Domingue* (Chicago, IL: University of Chicago Press, 2017); Pernille Røge, *Economistes and the Reinvention of Empire: France in the Americas and Africa, c. 1750–1802* (Cambridge: Cambridge University Press, 2019); Glory Liu, *Adam Smith's America: How a Scottish Philosopher Became an Icon of American Capitalism* (Princeton, NJ: Princeton University Press, 2022).

46 Linda Colley, 'The Apotheosis of George III: Loyalty, Royalty and the British Nation 1760–1820', *Past & Present*, 102 (1984), 94–129; Gerald Jordan and Nicholas Rogers, 'Admirals as Heroes: Patriotism and Liberty in Hanoverian England', *Journal of British Studies* 28/3 (1989), 201–24; Diana Donald, *The Age of Caricature: Satirical Prints in the Reign of George III* (New Haven, CT and London: Yale University Press, 1996); Paul Langford, *Englishness Identified: Manners and Character*

1650–1850 (Oxford: Oxford University Press, 2001); Tamara L. Hunt, *Defining John Bull: Political Caricature and National Identity in Late Georgian England* (Aldershot: Ashgate, 2003); Peter Mandler, *The English National Character: The History of an Idea from Edmund Burke to Tony Blair* (New Haven, CT: Yale University Press, 2006); Derek Heater, 'Fighting Corruption and France', *Citizenship in Britain: A History* (Edinburgh: Edinburgh University Press, 2006), 66–98.

47 Fred Anderson, *Crucible of War: The Seven Years' War and the Fate of Empire in British North America 1754–1766* (London: Faber, 2000); Hamish Scott, 'The Seven Years War and Europe's "Ancien Régime"', *War in History* 18/4 (2011), 419–55; Stephen Conway, 'Continental European Soldiers in British Imperial Service, c. 1756–1792', *English Historical Review* 128/536 (2014), 79–106; Peter J. Marshall, *Problems of Empire: Britain and India, 1757–1813* (London: Routledge, 1968); Trevor Burnard and John Garrigus, 'The Seven Years' War in the West Indies', *The Plantation Machine: Atlantic Capitalism in French Saint-Domingue and British Jamaica* (Philadelphia, PA: University of Pennsylvania Press, 2016), 82–100; Justin du Rivage, 'The Seven Years' War and the Politics of Empire', *Revolution against Empire: Taxes, Politics, and the Origins of American Independence* (New Haven, CT: Yale University Press, 2017), 77–100; Paul Kelton, 'The British and Indian War: Cherokee Power and the Fate of Empire in North America', *William and Mary Quarterly* 69/4 (2012), 763–92.

48 J. C. D. Clark, 'Providence, Predestination and Progress: Or, Did the Enlightenment Fail?', *Albion: A Quarterly Journal Concerned with British Studies* 35/4 (2003), 559–89.

49 Smith said the man of system was 'so enamoured with the supposed beauty of his own ideal plan of government' that he imagined that he could 'arrange the different members of a great society with as much ease as the hand arranges the different pieces on the chess board'. He failed to consider that 'the pieces on the chess board have no other principle of motion besides that which the hand impresses upon them, but that in the great chess board of human society every single piece has a principle of motion of his own, altogether different from that which the legislature might chuse to impress upon it.' Smith,

Theory of Moral Sentiments, The Glasgow Edition of the Works and Correspondence of Adam Smith, Vol. 1: The Theory of Moral Sentiments, ed. D. D. Raphael and A. L. Macfie (Oxford: Oxford University Press, 1976), VI.ii.2.17.

50 See further, Gregory Claeys, *Utopia: The History of an Idea* (London: Thames and Hudson, 2020) and *Utopianism for a Dying Planet: Life after Consumerism* (Princeton, NJ: Princeton University Press, 2022).

51 Lawrence E. Klein and Anthony J. LaVopa, *Enthusiasm and Enlightenment in Europe 1650–1850* (San Marino, CA: Huntington Library, 1998); James Farr, 'Political Science and the Enlightenment of Enthusiasm', *American Political Science Review* 82/1 (1988), 51–69; Mark Knights, *The Devil in Disguise: Deception Delusion, and Fanaticism in the Early English Enlightenment* (Oxford: Oxford University Press. 2011); Jon Mee, *Dangerous Enthusiasm: William Blake and the Culture of Radicalism in the 1790s* (Oxford and New York: Clarendon Press, 1992) and *Romanticism Enthusiasm and Regulation: Poetics and the Policing of Culture in the Romantic Period* (Oxford: Oxford University Press, 2003).

52 Alex Schulman, 'The Twilight of Probability: Locke, Bayle, and the Toleration of Atheism', *Journal of Religion* 89, no. 3 (2009), 328–60; Jeffrey Wigelsworth, 'The Meaning of 1689: Politics and Theology, 1694–1700', in *Deism in Enlightenment England: Theology, Politics, and Newtonian Public Science* (Manchester: Manchester University Press, 2009), 14–43.

53 Jon Parkin and Timothy Stanton, *Natural Law and Toleration in the Early Enlightenment* (Oxford: Oxford University Press, 2013); J. K. Numao, 'Locke on Atheism', *History of Political Thought* 34/2 (2013), 252–72; Denis Lacorne, *The Limits of Tolerance: Enlightenment Values and Religious Fanaticism* (New York: Columbia University Press, 2019), 11–30; Geoff Kemp, 'Locke the Censor, Locke the Anti-Censor', in *Politics, Religion and Ideas in Seventeenth- and Eighteenth-Century Britain: Essays in Honour of Mark Goldie*, ed. Justin Champion, John Coffey, Tim Harris and John Marshall (Woodbridge: Boydell & Brewer, 2019), 161–80.

54 Ross Lerner, *Unknowing Fanaticism: Reformation Literatures of Self-Annihilation* (New York: Fordam University Press, 2019). More broadly,

see Diarmaid MacCulloch, *Reformation: Europe's House Divided 1490–1700* (London: Penguin, 2004); Ulinka Rublack, ed., *The Oxford Handbook of the Protestant Reformations* (Oxford: Oxford University Press, 2016); Joachim Whaley, *Germany and the Holy Roman Empire* (Oxford: Oxford University Press, 2012).

55 Paul Rycaut, *Histoire des trois derniers empereurs des Turcs depuis 1623 jusqu'à 1677* (Paris: La Veuve Louis Bilenne, 1683), vol. 3, 170; David-Augustin de Brueys, *Histoire du fanatisme de nostre temps, et le dessein que l'on avoit de soulever en France les mécontens des calvinistes* (Paris: F. Muguet, 1692).

1. The Meaning of Enlightenment

1 Anthony Pagden, *The Enlightenment: And Why It Still Matters* (Oxford: Oxford University Press, 2013); Ritchie Robertson, *The Enlightenment: The Pursuit of Happiness, 1680–1790* (London: Allen Lane, 2020).

2 The most influential in recent times is Jonathan Israel and his series *Radical Enlightenment: Philosophy and the Making of Modernity 1650–1750* (Oxford: Oxford University Press, 2001); *Enlightenment Contested: Philosophy, Modernity and the Emancipation of Man 1670–1752* (Oxford: Oxford University Press, 2006); *Democratic Enlightenment: Philosophy, Revolution and Human Rights 1750–1790* (Oxford: Oxford University Press, 2011); *Revolutionary Ideas: An Intellectual History of the French Revolution from the Rights of Man to Robespierre* (Princeton, NJ: Princeton University Press, 2014); *A Revolution of the Mind: Radical Enlightenment and the Intellectual Origins of Modern Democracy* (Princeton, NJ: Princeton University Press, 2010). See further, Thomas Munck's review 'The Enlightenment as Modernity: Jonathan Israel's Interpretation across Two Decades', *Reviews in History* (review no. 2039), DOI: 10.14296/RiH/2014/2039

3 Michel Foucault, 'What Is Enlightenment?', trans. Catherine Porter, in *Ethics: Subjectivity and Truth*, vol. 1 of *The Essential Works of Foucault, 1954–1984*, ed., Paul Rabinow (London: Allen Lane, 2000), 303. For an assessment, see John Robertson, 'Enlightenment and Modernity,

Historians and Philosophers', *International Journal for History, Culture and Modernity* 8/3–4 (2020), 278–321.

4 Darrin M. McMahon, *Enemies of the Enlightenment: The French Counter-Enlightenment and the Making of Modernity* (Oxford: Oxford University Press, 2001); Theo Jung, 'Multiple Counter-Enlightenments: The Genealogy of a Polemics from the Eighteenth Century to the Present', in Martin L. Davies, ed., *Thinking about the Enlightenment: Modernity and Its Ramifications* (New York: Milton Park, 2016), 209–26. For an opposed view, see Robert E. Norton, 'The Myth of the Counter-Enlightenment', *Journal of the History of Ideas* 68 (2007), 635–58.

5 Leo Strauss, 'Progress or Return? The Contemporary Crisis in Western Civilization', *Modern Judaism* 1/1 (1981), 17–45; 'Correspondence Concerning Modernity', trans. George Elliott Tucker, *Independent Journal of Philosophy* 4 (1983), 105–19 and 5/6 (1988), 177–92; Eric Voegelin, *From Enlightenment to Revolution* (Durham NC: Duke University Press, 1975), 32. See further, Corine Pelluchon, *Leo Strauss and the Crisis of Rationalism: Another Reason, Another Enlightenment*, trans. Robert Howse (New York: State University of New York Press, 2014); Charles Taylor, *Sources of the Self: The Making of the Modern Identity* (Cambridge, MA: Harvard University Press, 1989); Hans Joas, *The Sacredness of the Person: A New Genealogy of Human Rights* (Washington, DC: Georgetown University Press, 2013).

6 Jacob L. Talmon, *The Origins of Totalitarian Democracy* (New York: W. W. Norton, 1970 [1952]), 1–4, 249–53.

7 Isaiah Berlin, 'The Counter-Enlightenment', *The Proper Study of Mankind: An Anthology of Essays*, ed. Henry Hardy and Roger Hausheer (London: Chatto & Windus, 1997 [1973]), 243–6. On Berlin's enlightenment see Michael Ignatieff, *Isaiah Berlin: A Life* (London: Vintage, 2000), 200–250. On the impact of the fear of communism for Berlin's generation see more broadly Jonathan Haslaam, *The Spectre of War: International Communism and the Origins of World War II* (Princeton, NJ: Princeton University Press, 2021).

8 Michael Oakeshott, *Rationalism in Politics and Other Essays* (Indianapolis: Liberty Fund, 1991 [1932]).

9 John Gray, *Enlightenment's Wake: Politics and Culture at the Close of the Modern Age* (London and New York: Routledge, 1995), viii.

10 John Gray, *False Dawn: The Delusions of Global Capitalism* (London: Granta Books, 1998).

11 Jean-François Lyotard, *The Postmodern Condition: A Report on Knowledge*, trans. Geoff Bennington and Brian Massumi (Minneapolis: University of Minnesota Press, 1984 [1979]), xxiii–iv.

12 Max Horkheimer and Theodor W. Adorno, *Dialectic of Enlightenment: Philosophical Fragments*, trans. Edmund Jephcott (Stanford, CA: Stanford University Press, 2002 [1947]), xiv, 14, 18.

13 James Schmidt, 'What Enlightenment Project?', *Political Theory* 28/6 (2000), 734–57.

14 Michel Foucault, *Discipline and Punish: The Birth of the Prison*, trans., Alan Sheridan (New York: Vintage Books, [1975] 1979), 200-209.

15 Laurent Dubois, 'An Enslaved Enlightenment: Rethinking the Intellectual History of the French Atlantic', *Social History* 3/1 (2006), 1–14; Damien Tricoire, ed., *Enlightened Colonialism: Civilization Narratives and Imperial Politics in the Age of Reason* (London: Palgrave MacMillan, 2017); Jane Flax, 'Is Enlightenment Emancipatory?', in *Disputed Subjects: Essays on Psychoanalysis, Politics, and Philosophy* (New York: Routledge, 1993); Rajani Kannepalli Kanth, *Against Eurocentrism: A Transcendent Critique of Modernist Science, Society, and Morals* (New York: Palgrave Macmillan, 2005). For an opposed view, see Sharon S. Stanley, *The French Enlightenment and the Emergence of Modern Cynicism* (Cambridge: Cambridge University Press, 2012). On gender, see especially Anthony J. LaVopa, *The Labor of the Mind: Intellect and Gender in Enlightenment Cultures* (Philadelphia, PA: University of Pennsylvania Press, 2017). On contemporary thought about colonialism and empire, see Sunil M. Agnani, *Hating Empire Properly: The Two Indies and the Limits of Enlightenment Anticolonialism* (New York: Fordham University Press, 2013); Jennifer Pitts, *Boundaries of the International: Law and Empire* (Cambridge, MA: Harvard University Press, 2018).

16 Louis Sala-Molins, *Dark Side of the Light: Slavery and the French Enlightenment*, trans. John Conteh-Morgan (Minneapolis MN: University

of Minnesota Press, 2006); the original is *Les Misères des lumières. Sous la raison, l'outrage* (Paris: Robert Laffont, 1992).

17 George L. Mosse, *Toward the Final Solution: A History of European Racism* (New York: Howard Fertig, 1978); Zygmunt Bauman, *Modernity and the Holocaust* (Ithaca, NY: Cornell University Press, 1989); Lawrence Birken, *Hitler as Philosophe: Remnants of the Enlightenment in National Socialism* (Westport CT: Praeger, 1995); John Docker, 'The Enlightenment, Genocide, Postmodernity', *Journal of Genocide Research* 5/3 (2003), 339–60, and 'The Enlightenment and Genocide', *Journal of Narrative Theory* 33/3 (2003), 292–314; Jean-Claude Milner, *Les penchants criminels de l'Europe démocratique* (Paris: Verdier, 2003). Against such views, see Robert Wokler, *Rousseau, the Age of Enlightenment, and Their Legacies*, ed. Bryan Garsten with an introduction by Christopher Brooke (Princeton, NJ: Princeton University Press, 2012).

18 'Does the Enlightenment Need Defending? Steven Pinker and Homi Bhabha discuss the good, the bad and the ugly of the Enlightenment', *HowTheLightGetsIn*, 10 September 2018: https://iai.tv/articles/does-the-enlightenment-need-defending-auid-1149

19 Gareth Stedman Jones, *Karl Marx: Greatness and Illusion* (London: Penguin Books, 2018); Gregory Claeys, *Marx and Marxism* (London: Penguin Books, 2018); Stedman Jones, 'Religion and the Origins of Socialism' in I. Katznelson and G. Stedman Jones, eds., *Religion and the Political Imagination* (Cambridge: Cambridge University Press, 2010), 171–89.

20 J. W. Burrow, *A Liberal Descent: Victorian Historians and the English Past* (Cambridge: Cambridge University Press, 1981) and *A History of Histories: Epics, Chronicles, Romances and Inquiries from Herodotus and Thucydides to the Twentieth Century* (London: Allen Lane, 2007); J. G. A. Pocock, 'The Varieties of Whiggism from Exclusion to Reform: A History of Ideology and Discourse', in *Virtue, Commerce, and History: Essays on Political Thought and History, Chiefly in the Eighteenth Century*, 215–310.

21 Eric Hobsbawm, *The Age of Revolution: Europe 1789–1848* (New York: Vintage Books, 1996 [1962]); E. P. Thompson, 'Eighteenth-Century

English Society: Class Struggle without Class?', *Social History* 3/2 (1978), 133–65.

22 For a summary and critique, see Nicholas J. Rengger, *The Anti-Pelagian Imagination in Political Theory and International Relations: Dealing in Darkness* (Abingdon: Routledge, 2017), and Vassilios Paipais, ed., *The Civil Condition in World Politics: Beyond Tragedy and Utopianism* (Bristol: Bristol University Press, 2022).

23 Jürgen Habermas, *The Structural Transformation of the Public Sphere: An Inquiry into a Category of Bourgeois Society*, trans. Thomas Burger and Frederick Lawrence (Cambridge, MA: The MIT Press, 1989 [1962]). See in response, John Robertson, 'Enlightenment and Modernity', and Antoine Lilti, 'In the Shadow of the Public: Enlightenment and the Pitfalls of Modernity', *International Journal for History, Culture and Modernity* 8/3–4 (2020), 256–77.

24 Peter Gay, *The Enlightenment: An Interpretation – The Rise of Modern Paganism* (London: Weidenfeld and Nicolson, 1967) and *The Enlightenment: An Interpretation: The Science of Freedom* (London: Weidenfeld and Nicolson, 1969). For problems with Gay's approach, see John Robertson, *The Case for the Enlightenment: Scotland and Naples 1680–1760* (Cambridge: Cambridge University Press, 2005), and Annelien de Dijn, 'The Politics of Enlightenment: from Peter Gay to Jonathan Israel', *Historical Journal* 55/3 (2012), 785–805.

25 For a summary and critique of the literature, see Peter King and Richard Ward, 'Rethinking the Bloody Code in Eighteenth-Century Britain: Capital Punishment at the Centre and on the Periphery', *Past & Present* 228 (2015), 159–205, and Simon Devereaux, 'Execution and Pardon at the Old Bailey 1730–1837', *American Journal of Legal History* 57/4 (2017), 447–94.

26 Adam Smith criticized the game laws as an example of feudal oppression in his 1762 *Lectures on Jurisprudence*: LJ(A) I.54–5. 'Among other encroachments it became the rule that wild animalls should belong only to the king and those of his lords to whom he gave the power of catching them.' Ronald L. Meek, D. D. Raphael and Peter Stein, eds., *Lectures on Jurisprudence* (Oxford and New York: Clarendon Press, 1978), 23.

27 V. A. C. Gatrell, *The Hanging Tree: Execution and the English people 1770–1868* (Oxford: Oxford University Press, 1994). See also, Peter Linebaugh, *The London Hanged: Crime and Civil Society in the Eighteenth Century* (London: Allan Lane, 1991); Geoffrey Poitras, 'The Luddite Trials: Radical Suppression and the Administration of Criminal Justice', *Journal for the Study of Radicalism* 14/1 (2020), 121–66.

28 Marx and Engels, *The Communist Manifesto*, ed. Gareth Stedman Jones (London: Penguin, 2004).

29 Samuel Moyn, *The Last Utopia: Human Rights in History* (Cambridge, MA: Belknap Press of Harvard University Press, 2010); Richard Whatmore, 'Democracy and Empire', in *The Cambridge History of Democracy* (Cambridge: Cambridge University Press, 2023), ed. Christopher Meckstroth and Samuel Moyn, forthcoming.

30 H. W. Blom, J. C. Laursen and L. Simonutti, eds., *Monarchisms in the Age of Enlightenment: Liberty, Patriotism, and the Common Good* (Toronto: University of Toronto Press, 2007); László Kontler, *Translations Histories Enlightenments: William Robertson in Germany 1760–1795* (New York: Palgrave Macmillan, 2014); László Kontler and Mark Somos, *Trust and Happiness in the History of European Political Thought* (Leiden: Brill, 2018); Cesare Cuttica, László Kontler and Clara Maier, *Crisis and Renewal in the History of European Political Thought* (Leiden: Brill, 2021); Avi Lifschitz and Michael Squire, *Rethinking Lessing's Laocoon: Antiquity Enlightenment and the 'Limits' of Painting and Poetry* (Oxford: Oxford University Press, 2017); Avi Lifschitz, *Frederick the Great's Philosophical Writings*, trans. Angela Scholar (Princeton, NJ: Princeton University Press, 2020), trans., Angela Scholar; Susa Richter, Thomas Maissen and Manuela Albertone, *Languages of Reform in the Eighteenth Century: When Europe Lost Its Fear of Change* (New York: Routledge, 2020).

31 James Schmidt, ed., *What Is Enlightenment? Eighteenth-Century Answers and Twentieth-Century Questions* (Berkeley and Los Angeles, CA: University of California Press, 1996); 'Inventing the Enlightenment: Anti-Jacobins, British Hegelians and the Oxford English Dictionary', *Journal of the History of Ideas* 64/3 (2003), 421–43; 'Misunderstanding the Question "What Is Enlightenment?": Venturi, Habermas, and Foucault', *History of European Ideas* 37 (2011), 43–52. See also Graeme

Garrard, 'The War against the Enlightenment', *European Journal of Political Theory* 10 (2011), 277–86.

32 Robert Darnton, in his influential *Mesmerism and the End of the Enlightenment in France* (Cambridge, MA: Harvard University Press, 1968), noted that his book 'may help one to understand how the Enlightenment ended – not absolutely (for some still take seriously the Declaration of Independence and the Declaration of the Rights of Man and Citizen) – but historically, as a movement characterising eighteenth-century France' (viii). Darnton's argument was that Rousseau's rejection of standard ideas about rational living spread through indirect channels to cause the French Revolution. Such accounts have parallels in the work of Lynn Hunt, *Inventing Human Rights: A History* (New York: W. W. Norton, 2007), and Dan Edelstein, *The Enlightenment: A Genealogy* (Chicago, IL: Chicago University Press, 2010). See also Margaret C. Jacob, 'Reflections on the Enlightenment and Modernity: In Our Plague Year', *International Journal for History, Culture and Modernity* 8/3–4 (2020), 247–55.

33 James Schmidt, 'Enlightenment as Concept and Context', *Journal of the History of Ideas* 75/4 (2014), 677–85, and J. G. A. Pocock, 'The Concept of a Language and the *Métier d'historien*: Some Considerations on Practice', in *The Languages of Political Theory in Early-Modern Europe*, ed. Anthony Pagden (Cambridge: Cambridge University Press, 1987), 21–5.

34 J. G. A. Pocock, *Barbarism and Religion, Vol. 2: Narratives of Civil Government* (Cambridge University Press, 1999) and 'Historiography and Enlightenment: A View of Their History', *Modern Intellectual History* 5/1 (2008), 83–96.

35 Ian Hunter, *Rival Enlightenments: Civil and Metaphysical Philosophy in Early Modern Germany* (Cambridge: Cambridge University Press, 2001) and 'The University Philosophy in Early Modern Germany', in Conal Condren, Stephen Gaukroger and Ian Hunter, eds., *The Philosopher in Early Modern Europe: The Nature of a Contested Identity* (Cambridge: Cambridge University Press, 2006), 35–65.

36 Frederick C. Beiser, *The Fate of Reason: German Philosophy from Kant to Fichte* (Cambridge, MA: Harvard University Press, 1987);

Enlightenment, Revolution, and Romanticism: The Genesis of Modern German Political Thought, 1790–1800 (Cambridge, MA: Harvard University Press, 1992); *The Genesis of Neo-Kantianism, 1796–1880* (Oxford: Oxford University Press, 2014); Michael J. Sauter, *Visions of the Enlightenment: The Edict on Religion of 1788 and the Politics of the Public Sphere in Eighteenth-Century Prussia* (Leiden: Brill, 2009).

37 Geoffrey Hawthorn's *Enlightenment and Despair: A History of Sociology* (Cambridge: Cambridge University Press, 1976) is a related account of this process.

38 Geoffrey Parker, *Global Crisis: War Climate Change and Catastrophe in the Seventeenth Century – Abridged and Revised Edn* (New Haven, CT: Yale University Press, 2017); Philippe Contamine, ed., *War and Competition between States* (Oxford: Clarendon Press, 2000); Charles Carlton, *This Seat of Mars: War and the British Isles 1485–1746* (New Haven, CT: Yale University Press, 2011); J. H. Elliot, *Empires of the Atlantic World: Britain and Spain, 1492–1830* (New Haven, CT: Yale University Press, 2006); Helen Rawlings, ed., *The Debate on the Decline of Spain* (Manchester: Manchester University Press, 2012); Henry Kamen, *Spain, 1469–1714: A Society of Conflict* (London: Routledge, 2014), 4th edn; Jonathan Scott, *England's Troubles: Seventeenth-Century English Political Instability in European Context* (Cambridge: Cambridge University Press, 2000) and *How the Old World Ended: The Anglo-Dutch-American Revolution 1500–1800* (New Haven, CT: Yale University Press, 2019).

39 Scholars such as Charles Tilly have dated the constancy of European warfare to as early as 990. See Charles Tilly, ed., *The Formation of National States in Western Europe* (Princeton, NJ: Princeton University Press, 1975) and *Coercion, Capital, and European States, AD 990–1990* (Cambridge, MA: Basil Blackwell, 1990), and M. S. Anderson, *War and Society in Europe of the Old Regime 1618–1789* (London: Sutton, 1998 [1988]).

40 William Shakespeare, *As You Like It*, Act II, Scene VII, 'All the world's a stage . . .'

41 James Clifton, Leslie M. Scattone, Emine Fetvaci, Ira D. Gruber and Larry Silver, *The Plains of Mars: European War Prints, 1500–1825, from the Collection of the Sarah Campbell Blaffer Foundation* (New Haven, CT:

Yale University Press, 2009), 2. See further, John Childs, *Warfare in the Seventeenth Century* (London: Cassell & Co., 2001).

42 M. Destombes, 'A Panorama of the Sack of Rome by Pieter Bruegel the Elder', *Imago Mundi* 14 (1959), 64–73; Paul Flemer, 'Clement VII and the Crisis of the Sack of Rome', in *Society and Individual in Renaissance Florence*, ed., William J. Connell (Berkeley, CA: University of California Press, 2002), 409–34.

43 Noel Malcolm, *Agents of Empire: Knights, Corsairs, Jesuits and Spies in the Sixteenth-Century Mediterranean World* (London: Penguin, 2015).

44 Noel Malcolm, *Useful Enemies: Islam and the Ottoman Empire in Western Political Thought, 1450–1750* (Oxford: Oxford University Press, 2019); Alessandro Stanziani, *After Oriental Despotism: Eurasian Growth in a Global Perspective* (London: Bloomsbury, 2014).

45 J. R. Hale, 'Incitement to Violence? English Divines on the Theme of War, 1578–1631', in *Renaissance War Studies* (London: Hambledon Press, 1983), 487–517.

46 Geoffrey Parker, ed., *The Thirty Years' War* (London: Routledge, 1997), 2nd edn; Peter H. Wilson, *The Thirty Years' War: Europe's Tragedy* (Cambridge MA: Harvard University Press, 2009). The old account, C. V. Wedgwood, *The Thirty Years War* (London: Harmondsworth, 2016 [1938]), remains highly readable.

47 Paul Seaward, *Behemoth or The Long Parliament, Clarendon Edition of the Works of Thomas Hobbes, Vol. X* (Oxford: Oxford University Press, 2009).

48 Jennifer Powell McNutt, *Calvin Meets Voltaire: The Clergy of Geneva in the Age of Enlightenment, 1685–1798* (Farnham: Ashgate, 2013).

49 Alan W. Fisher, 'Enlightened Despotism and Islam under Catherine II', *Slavic Review* 27/4 (1968), 542–53; Eberhard Weis, 'Enlightenment and Absolutism in the Holy Roman Empire: Thoughts on Enlightened Absolutism in Germany', *Journal of Modern History* 58 (1986), 181–97; R. A. Houston, 'Literacy, Education and the Culture of Print in Enlightenment Edinburgh', *History* 78/254 (1993), 373–92; Neven Leddy, 'Mary Wollstonecraft and Adam Smith on Gender, History,

and the Civic Republican Tradition', in *On Civic Republicanism: Ancient Lessons for Global Politics*, ed. Leddy and Geoffrey C. Kellow (Toronto: University of Toronto Press, 2016), 269–81; Christy Pichichero, *The Military Enlightenment: War and Culture in the French Empire from Louis XIV to Napoleon* (Ithaca, NY: Cornell University Press, 2017).

50 David Sorkin, 'Geneva's "Enlightened Orthodoxy": The Middle Way of Jacob Vernet (1698–1789)', *Church History* 74/2 (2005), 286–305, and *The Religious Enlightenment: Protestants, Jews, and Catholics from London to Vienna* (Princeton, NJ: Princeton University Press, 2011); Brent S. Sirota, 'The Trinitarian Crisis in Church and State: Religious Controversy and the Making of the Postrevolutionary Church of England, 1687–1702', *Journal of British Studies* 52/1 (2013), 26–54; Annabel Brett, *Changes of State: Nature and the Limits of the City in Early Modern Natural Law* (Princeton, NJ: Princeton University Press, 2011); Tom Jones, *George Berkeley: A Philosophical Life* (Princeton, NJ: Princeton University Press, 2021), 174–208.

51 Lewis W. Spitz, 'Particularism and Peace Augsburg: 1555', *Church History* 25/2 (1956), 110–26; Robert von Friedeburg, 'The Making of Patriots: Love of Fatherland and Negotiating Monarchy in Seventeenth-Century Germany', *Journal of Modern History* 77/4 (2005), 881–916.

52 Quentin Skinner makes this clear in *Reason and Rhetoric in the Philosophy of Hobbes* (Cambridge: Cambridge University Press, 1996), *Hobbes and Republican Liberty* (Cambridge: Cambridge University Press, 2008) and *From Humanism to Hobbes: Studies in Rhetoric and Politics* (Cambridge: Cambridge University Press, 2018).

53 Béla Kapossy, Isaac Nakhimovsky and Richard Whatmore, eds., *Commerce and Peace in the Enlightenment* (Cambridge: Cambridge University Press, 2017); Carole Dornier, *La Monarchie éclairée de l'abbé de Saint-Pierre: Une science politique des modernes* (Liverpool: Liverpool University Press and the Voltaire Foundation, 2020); Stella Ghervas, *Conquering Peace: From the Enlightenment to the European Union* (Cambridge, MA: Harvard University Press, 2021).

54 Alexander Querengässer, 'Military Change and the Development of the Early Modern State', in *Before the Military Revolution: European Warfare and the Rise of the Early Modern State 1300–1490* (Oxford: Oxbow

Books, 2021), 205–20; John A. Lynn, 'Recalculating French Army Growth during the Grand Siècle, 1610–1715', *French Historical Studies*, 18/4 (1994), 881–906; Christopher Duffy, *The Fortress in the Age of Vauban and Frederick the Great, 1660–1789* and *Siege Warfare: The Fortress in the Early Modern World 1494–1660* (London: Routledge and Kegan Paul, 1979 and 1985); Jamel Ostwald, *Vauban under Siege: Engineering Efficiency and Martial Vigour in the War of the Spanish Succession* (Leiden: Brill, 2007); Geoffrey Parker, 'The "Military Revolution" in Seventeenth-Century Ireland' and 'The Artillery Fortress as an Engine of European Overseas Expansion, 1480–1750', in *Empire, War and Faith in Early Modern Europe* (London: Allen Lane, 2002), 169–212; David Parrott, *The Business of War: Military Enterprise and Military Revolution in Early Modern Europe* (Cambridge: Cambridge University Press, 2012).

55 J. G. A. Pocock, *Barbarism and Religion, Vol. 3: The First Decline and Fall* (Cambridge: Cambridge University Press, 2005) and 'From *The Ancient Constitution* to *Barbarism and Religion; The Machiavellian Moment*, the History of Political Thought and the History of Historiography', *History of European Ideas* 43/2 (2017), 129–46. More broadly, see Derek Croxton, *Westphalia: The Last Christian Peace* (New York: Palgrave Macmillan, 2013); Stephen D. Krasner and Daniel T. Froats, 'Minority Rights and the Westphalian Model', in *The International Spread of Ethnic Conflict: Fear, Diffusion, and Escalation*, ed. David A. Lake and Donald Rothchild (Princeton, NJ: Princeton University Press, 1988), 227–50; Annabel S. Brett, Megan Donaldson and Martti Koskenniemi, *History, Politics, Law: Thinking through the International* (Cambridge: Cambridge University Press, 2021); Martti Koskenniemi, *To the Uttermost Parts of the Earth: Legal Imagination and International Power 1300–1870* (Cambridge: Cambridge University Press, 2021).

56 T. Campanella, *A Discourse Touching the Spanish Monarchy: Laying Down Directions and Practices Whereby the King of Spain May Attain to an Universal Monarchy* (London: Philemon Stephens, 1654), 42. On Campanella, see also J. M. Headley, 'Tommaso Campanella and the End of the Renaissance', *The Journal of Medieval and Renaissance Studies* 20 (1990), 157–74; Anthony Pagden, *Spanish Imperialism and the Political Imagination* (New

Haven, CT: Yale University Press, 1990), 37–63; Peter Schröder, 'The Concepts of Universal Monarchy and Balance of Power in the First Half of the Seventeenth Century – A Case Study', in Martti Koskenniemi, Walter Rech, and Manuel Jiménez Fonseca, eds., *International Law and Empire: Historical Explorations* (Oxford: Oxford University Press, 2017), 83–100; for fears of universal monarchs, see Andrew C. Thompson, 'The Balance of Power, Universal Monarchy and the Protestant Interest', in *Britain, Hanover and the Protestant Interest, 1688–1756* (Woodbridge: Boydell & Brewer, 2006), 25–42; John Headley, 'The Demise of Universal Monarchy as a Meaningful Political Idea' in *Imperium / Empire / Reich: Ein Konzept politischer Herrschaft im deutsch-britischen Vergleich*, ed. Franz Bosbach and Hermann Hiery (Berlin and Boston: K. G. Saur, 1999), 41–58; see further, Hamish M. Scott, ' "The True Principles of the Revolution": The Duke of Newcastle and the Idea of the Old System', in Jeremy Black, ed., *Knights Errant and True Englishmen: British Foreign Policy, 1600–1800* (Edinburgh: John Donald, 1989), 59–91; John Robertson, 'Universal Monarchy and the Liberties of Europe: David Hume's Critique of an English Whig Doctrine', in Nicholas Phillipson and Quentin Skinner, eds., *Political Discourse in Early Modern Britain* (Cambridge: Cambridge University Press, 1993), 349–73; Steven Pincus, 'The English Debate on Universal Monarchy', in John Robertson, ed., *A Union for Empire, Political Thought, and the British Union of 1707* (Cambridge: Cambridge University Press, 1995), 37–72.

57 Jan De Vries, *European Urbanization 1600–1800* (London: Methuen, 1984); Christopher R. Friedrichs, *Urban Politics in Early Modern Europe* (London: Routledge, 2000); Peter Clark, ed., *Small Towns in Early Modern Europe* (Cambridge and New York: Cambridge University Press, 2002); Albrecht Classen, ed., *Urban Space in the Middle Ages and the Early Modern Age* (Berlin: Walter de Gruyter, 2009); Henk Schmal, *Patterns of European Urbanisation since 1500* (London: Taylor and Francis, 2018); Paolo Malanima, 'Urbanization', in S. Broadberry and K. O'Rourke, *The Cambridge Economic History of Modern Europe* (Cambridge: Cambridge University Press, 2010), 235–63; Andrew Lees and Lynn Hollen Lees, *Cities and the Making of Modern Europe: 1750–1914* (Cambridge: Cambridge University Press, 2010).

58 E. J. Hundert, *The Enlightenment's Fable: Bernard Mandeville and the Discovery of Society* (Cambridge: Cambridge University Press 1994); István Hont, 'The Early Enlightenment Debate on Commerce and Luxury', in Mark Goldie and Robert Wokler, eds., *The Cambridge History of Eighteenth-Century Political Thought* (Cambridge: Cambridge University Press, 2006), 379–418, and 'Luxury and the Route to Revolution in Rousseau's *Discourse on Inequality*' (unpublished paper, István Hont Papers, Special Collections, University of St Andrews); Michael Sonenscher, *Before the Deluge: Public Debt, Inequality, and the Intellectual Origins of the French Revolution* (Princeton, NJ: Princeton University Press, 2007), 173–253, and *Jean-Jacques Rousseau: The Division of Labour, the Politics of the Imagination and the Concept of Federal Government* (Leiden: Brill, 2020).

59 Maxine Berg, 'In Pursuit of Luxury: Global History and British Consumer Goods in the Eighteenth Century', *Past & Present*, 182 (2004), 85–142.

60 Neil McKendrick, John Brewer and J. H. Plumb, eds., *The Birth of a Consumer Society: The Commercialization of Eighteenth-Century England* (Bloomington IN: University of Indiana Press, 1982); Maxine Berg and Elizabeth Eger, eds., *Luxury in the Eighteenth Century: Debates, Desires and Delectable Goods* (Basingstoke: Palgrave, 2002); Michael Kwass, 'Ordering the World of Goods: Consumer Revolution and the Classification of Objects in Eighteenth-Century France', *Representations* 82/1 (2003), 87–116; *The Consumer Revolution, 1650–1800* (Cambridge: Cambridge University Press, 2022).

61 Robert J. Gorman and Vanessa B. Gorman, 'Luxury and Corruption', in *Corrupting Luxury in Ancient Greek Literature*, 7–75 (Ann Arbor, MI: University of Michigan Press, 2014); Joseph M. Levine, 'Edward Gibbon and the Quarrel between the Ancients and the Moderns', *Eighteenth Century* 26/1 (1985), 47–62.

62 John Brown, *An Estimate of the Manners and Principles of the Times, by the Author of Essays on the Characteristics, &c.* (London: L. Davis and C. Reymers, 1758), 7th edn, 2 vols, I, 27–35.

63 Joseph Addison, *Spectator*, no. 201, Saturday, 20 October, 1711, in *The Works of the Right Honourable Joseph Addison Esq.* (London: Jacob Tonson, 1721), 4 vols, III, 171.

64 See J. G. A. Pocock, 'Within the Margins: The Definition of Orthodoxy', in Roger D. Lund, ed., *The Margins of Orthodoxy: Heterodox
Writing and Cultural Response 1660–1750* (Cambridge: Cambridge University Press, 1995), 33–53; and Brian Young, *Religion and Enlightenment
in Eighteenth Century England: Theological Debate from Locke to Burke*
(Oxford: Clarendon Press, 1996).

65 Samia Al-Shayban, 'The Treaty of Utrecht and Addison's Cato: Brit-
ain's War of the Spanish Succession, Peace and the Imperial Road
Map', in *Performances of Peace: Utrecht 1713*, ed. Renger E. de Bruin,
Cornelis van der Haven, Lotte Jensen and David Onnekink (Leiden:
Brill, 2015), 123–41; Brodie Waddell, 'The Politics of Economic Dis-
tress in the Aftermath of the Glorious Revolution, 1689–1702', *English
Historical Review* 130/543 (2015), 318–51; Hannah Smith, 'Politics, Patri-
otism, and Gender: The Standing Army Debate on the English
Stage, circa 1689–1720', *Journal of British Studies* 50/1 (2011), 48–75.
More broadly, see John Childs, *The British Army of William III, 1689–
1702* (Manchester: Manchester University Press, 1987); N. A. M. Rodger,
The Command of the Ocean: A Naval History of Britain, 1649–1815
(London: Penguin, 2006).

66 Joseph Addison, *Spectator*, no. 126, Wednesday, 25 July 1711, *The Works
of the Right Honourable Joseph Addison Esq,* III, 75–6.

67 On Trenchard and Gordon, see p. 123.

68 John Trenchard and Thomas Gordon, *Cato's letters: Or, Essays on Liberty, Civil and Religious, and Other Important Subjects*, ed. Ronald
Hamowy (Indianapolis, IN: Liberty Fund, 1995), 2 vols., II, 852–3.

69 Lois G. Schwoerer, 'The Role of King William III of England in the
Standing Army Controversy – 1697–1699', *Journal of British Studies* 5/2
(1966), 74–94; Gary W. Cox, 'War, Moral Hazard, and Ministerial
Responsibility: England after the Glorious Revolution', *Journal of
Economic History* 70/1 (2011), 133–61; Daniel Baugh, 'Parliament, Naval
Spending and the Public: Contrasting Financial Legacies of Two
Exhausting Wars, 1689–1713', *Histoire & Mesure* 30/2 (2015), 23–49.
More broadly, see Julian Hoppit, *Britain's Political Economies: Parlia-
ment and Economic Life, 1660–1800* (Cambridge: Cambridge University

Press, 2017); Justin A. Champion, *The Pillars of Priestcraft Shaken: The Church of England and Its Enemies 1660–1730* (Cambridge: Cambridge University Press, 1992).

70 Daniel Defoe, *An Essay upon Projects* (London: Thomas Cockerill, 1697), 4. See further, Julian Hoppit, 'Attitudes to Credit in Britain, 1680–1790', *Historical Journal* 33/2 (1990), 305–22, and *Risk and Failure in English Business 1700–1800* (Cambridge: Cambridge University Press, 1987); Natasha Glaisyer, *The Culture of Commerce in England, 1660–1720*, *Royal Historical Society Studies in History* (Woodbridge: Boydell Press, 2006).

71 William Thomas Morgan, 'The Origins of the South Sea Company', *Political Science Quarterly* 44/1 (1929), 16–38; William A. Pettigrew, 'Free to Enslave: Politics and the Escalation of Britain's Transatlantic Slave Trade, 1688–1714', *William and Mary Quarterly* 64/1 (2007), 3–38; Kathleen S. Murphy, 'Collecting Slave Traders: James Petiver, Natural History, and the British Slave Trade', *William and Mary Quarterly* 70/4 (2013), 637–70.

72 Julian Hoppit, 'The Myths of the South Sea Bubble', *Transactions of the Royal Historical Society* 12 (2002), 141–65; Richard A. Kleer, 'Riding a Wave: The Company's Role in the South Sea Bubble', *Economic History Review* 68/1 (2015), 264–85; Patrick Kelly, ' "Industry and Virtue versus Luxury and Corruption": Berkeley, Walpole, and the South Sea Bubble Crisis', *Eighteenth-Century Ireland / Iris an Dá Chultúr* 7 (1992), 57–74.

73 Antoin E. Murphy, *John Law: Economic Theorist and Policy-Maker* (Oxford: Oxford University Press, 1997), 51–66.

74 Thomas E. Kaiser, 'Money, Despotism, and Public Opinion in Early Eighteenth-Century France: John Law and the Debate on Royal Credit', *Journal of Modern History* 63/1 (1991), 1–28; John Shovlin, 'Jealousy of Credit: John Law's "System" and the Geopolitics of Financial Revolution', *Journal of Modern History* 88/2 (2016), 275–305; Rebecca L. Spang, 'The Ghost of Law: Speculating on Money, Memory and Mississippi in the French Constituent Assembly', *Historical Reflections / Réflexions Historiques* 31/1 (2005), 3–25.

75 Lina Weber, 'Bound by debt: Political arguments concerning state finance in Great Britain and the Dutch Republic, 1694–1795' (unpublished PhD, University of Amsterdam, 2019).

76 William Wagstaff, 'The State and Condition of Our Taxes Considered', *Miscellaneous Works of Dr William Wagstaffe, Physician to St Bartholomew's-hospital, Fellow of the College of Physicians, and of the Royal Society: To Which is Prefix'd His Life, and an Account of His Writings* (London: Jonah Boyer et al., 1726), 2nd edn, 169.

2. David Hume and the End of the World

1 James Moore, 'Hume's Political Science and the Classical Republican Tradition', *Canadian Journal of Political Science / Revue Canadienne de Science Politique* 10/4 (1977), 809–39; Neil McArthur, 'General Laws and Civilized Government', in *David Hume's Political Theory: Law, Commerce and the Constitution of Government* (Toronto: University of Toronto Press, 2007), 57–81.

2 Ross Carroll, *Uncivil Mirth: Ridicule in Enlightenment Britain* (Princeton, NJ: Princeton University Press, 2021), 85–118; Ashley Walsh, 'The Civil Faith of Common Sense: David Hume', in *Civil Religion and the Enlightenment in England, 1707–1800* (Woodbridge: Boydell & Brewer, 2020), 108–36.

3 István Hont, 'The "Rich Country–Poor Country" Debate in Scottish Political Economy', *Jealousy of Trade*, 267–324, 'The "Rich Country–Poor Country" Debate Revisited: The Irish Origins and French Reception of the Hume Paradox', in Margaret Schabas and Carl Wennerlind, eds., *Hume's Political Economy* (London: Routledge, 2007), 222–342; M. Sonenscher, 'Property, Community, and Citizenship', in Mark Goldie and Robert Wokler, eds., *The Cambridge History of Eighteenth-Century Political Thought* (Cambridge: Cambridge University Press, 2006), 465–96, and Sonenscher *Before the Deluge*, 34–94, 159–72, 179–222, 266–334.

4 David Hume, 'Of Superstition and Enthusiasm', *Essays Moral, Political, Literary*, ed. and with a foreword, notes and glossary, Eugene

F. Miller, with an appendix of variant readings from the 1889 edition by T. H. Green and T. H. Grose, revised edn. (Indianapolis, IN: Liberty Fund, 1987), 73.

5 Ibid., 76–7.

6 Ibid., 78.

7 Robert G. Ingram, *Reformation without End: Religion, Politics and the Past in Post-Revolutionary England* (Manchester: Manchester University Press, 2018).

8 On Puritanism, see John Coffey, *John Goodwin and the Puritan Revolution: Religion and Intellectual Change in Seventeenth-Century England* (Woodbridge: Boydell & Brewer, 2006); *The Oxford History of Protestant Dissenting Traditions, Vol. I: The Post-Reformation Era, c.1559–1689*, ed. John Coffey (Oxford and New York: Oxford University Press, 2020); *The Cambridge Companion to Puritanism*, ed. John Coffey and Paul C-H. Lim (Cambridge: Cambridge University Press, 2008).

9 David Hume, *The History of England from the Invasion of Julius Caesar to the Revolution in 1688* (Indianapolis IN: Liberty Fund, 1983 [1778]), 6 vols., IV, 145–6. The Dissenting minister Caleb Flemming adopted Hume's comment as the epigraph to his *The Palladium of Great Britain and Ireland: Or Historical Strictures of Liberty, from before the Reformation Down to the Present Times. Which Prove, to Whom and to What It Has Chiefly Owed Its Origin and Preservation, in These Islands* (London: C. Henderson, T. Becket and P. A. de Hondt, 1762). See further, Tom Pye, 'Histories of Liberty in Scottish Thought, 1747–1787' (PhD dissertation, Cambridge University, 2018).

10 Anon. [Pierre Jurieu], *Les soupirs de la France esclave qui aspire à la liberté* (Amsterdam: n. p., 1689).

11 Edward Stillingfleet, *A Discourse concerning the Idolatry Practised in the Church of Rome, and the Hazard of Salvation in the Communion of It: In Answer to Some Papers of a Revolted Protestant. Wherein a Particular Account Is Given of the Fanaticisms and Divisions of That Church* (London: Henry Mortlock, 1672), 2nd edn, and the response, Anon. [Serenus Cressy], *Fanaticism Fanatically Imputed to the Catholic Church, by Doctour Stillingfleet: And the Imputation Refuted and Retorted by S. C. a Catholick* (London: n. p.: 1672).

12 Jacques-Bénigne Bossuet, *Premier avertissement aux protestans sur les lettres du ministre Jurieu contre l'histoire des variations, le christianisme flétri, & le socinianisme* [sic] *autorisé par ce ministre. Par messire Jacques Benigne Bossuet* (Paris: La Veuve de Sébastien Mabre-Cramoisy, 1689).

13 Guy Rowlands, *The Dynastic State and the Army under Louis XIV: Royal Service and Private Interest, 1661–1701* (Cambridge: Cambridge University Press, 2002)

14 Hume to Abbé Le Blanc, September 1754, *The Letters of David Hume*, I, 194. See further, Duncan Forbes, *Hume's Philosophical Politics* (Cambridge: Cambridge University Press, 1975), 145–72; 'Sceptical Whiggism, Commerce and Liberty', in *Essays on Adam Smith*, ed. A. Skinner and T. Wilson (Oxford: Clarendon, 1975), 179–202; 'The European, or Cosmopolitan, Dimension in Hume's Science of Politics', *British Journal for Eighteenth-Century Studies* 1 (1978), 57–60; James Moore, 'Hume's Political Science and the Classical Republican Tradition', *Canadian Journal of Political Science / Revue Canadienne De Science Politique* 10/4 (1977), 809–39.

15 David Hume, 'Of Liberty and Despotism', in *Essays Moral, Political, Literary*, ed., Eugene F. Miller, 93. The essay title remained until the reissue of the *Essays* entitled *Essays and Treatises on Several Subjects* appearing at London and Edinburgh in 1753–54, and then became 'Of Civil Liberty' in the *Four Dissertations* (1757) and subsequent editions of the *Essays and Treatises on Several Subjects* (from 1758).

16 David Hume, 'Of Liberty and Despotism', in *Essays Moral, Political, Literary*, ed. Eugene F. Miller, 94.

17 Georg Cavallar, 'The Law of Nations in the Age of Enlightenment: Moral and Legal Principles', *Jahrbuch Für Recht Und Ethik / Annual Review of Law and Ethics* 12 (2004), 213–29; Mads Langballe Jensen, 'The Law of Nations', in *The Cambridge Companion to Pufendorf*, ed. Knud Haakonssen and Ian Hunter (Cambridge: Cambridge University Press, 2022), 236–62.

18 Julia Rudolph, *Common Law and Enlightenment in England 1689–c. 1750* (Woodbridge: Boydell & Brewer, 2013); Marie Seong-Hak Kim, *Custom Law and Monarchy: A Legal History of Early Modern France*, 1st edn (Oxford: Oxford University Press, 2021); Knud Haakonssen,

'Early-Modern Natural Law', in *Cambridge Companion to Natural Law Jurisprudence*, ed. George Duke and Robert P. George (Cambridge: Cambridge University Press, 2017), 76–102; Linda Colley, *The Gun, the Ship, and the Pen: Warfare, Constitutions and the Making of the Modern World* (London: Profile, 2021).

19 David Hume, 'Of Liberty and Despotism', in *Essays Moral, Political, Literary*, ed., Eugene F. Miller, 93.

20 William Doyle, *Aristocracy and Its Enemies in the Age of Revolution* (Oxford: Oxford University Press, 2009).

21 William Doyle, *Venality: The Sale of Offices in Eighteenth-Century France* (Oxford and New York: Clarendon Press, 1996).

22 On the French reform context, see Ryan Hanley, *The Political Philosophy of Fénelon* (Oxford: Oxford University Press, 2020); Charles Woolsey Cole, *Colbert and a Century of French Mercantilism* (New York: Columbia University Press, 1939), 2 vols.; Lionel Rothkrug, *Opposition to Louis XIV: The Political and Social Origins of the French Enlightenment* (Princeton, NJ: Princeton University Press, 1965); Nannerl Keohane, *Philosophy and State in France: The Renaissance to the Enlightenment* (Princeton, NJ: Princeton University Press, 1980); Catherine Larrère, *L'invention de l'économie au XVIII siècle. Du droit naturel à la physiocratie* (Paris: Presses Universitaires de France, 1992); Paul Cheney, *Revolutionary Commerce, Globalization and the French Monarchy* (Cambridge, MA: Harvard University Press, 2010).

23 Hume, 'Of the Rise and Progress of the Arts and Sciences', in *Essays Moral, Political, Literary*, ed., Eugene F. Miller, 119.

24 Albert O. Hirschman, *The Passions and the Interests: Political Arguments for Capitalism before Its Triumph* (Princeton, NJ: Princeton University Press, 1977) and *Rival Views of Market Society and Other Recent Essays* (New York: Viking, 1986); Catherine Larrère, 'Montesquieu et le «doux commerce»: Un paradigme du libéralisme', *Cahiers d'histoire: Revue d'histoire critique* 123 (2014), 21–38; Arnault Skornicki, 'La France des lumières et l'humanisme commercial: Bilan et perspectives historiographiques', *Histoire, économie et société* 32/4 (2013), 75–89; Michael Sonenscher, *Capitalism: The Story behind the Word* (Princeton NJ: Princeton University Press, 2022).

25 For attempts to maintain peace, see John Shovlin, *Trading with the Enemy: Britain, France, and the 18th-Century Quest for a Peaceful World Order* (New Haven, CT: Yale University Press, 2021), and Paul Cheney, 'A False Dawn for Enlightenment Cosmopolitanism? Franco-American Trade during the American War of Independence', *William and Mary Quarterly* 63/3 (2006), 463–88.

26 Hume, 'Of the Populousness of Ancient Nations', *Essays Moral, Political, Literary,* ed., Eugene F. Miller, 406, 414.

27 Anon. [Nicholas Barbon], *A Discourse of Trade* (London: The Author, 1690), A3–A4.

28 Montesquieu, *Considérations sur les causes de la grandeur des Romains et de leur decadence* (Paris: Huart, Clousier & Guillyn, 1734), 9–10: 'Le monde de ce terns-là n'étoit pas comme notre monde d'aujourd'hui: les Voyages, les Conquêtes, le Commerce, l'établissement des grands Etats, les Inventions des Postes, de la Boussole & de l'Imprimerie, une certaine Police générale ont facilité les communications & établi parmi nous un Art qu'on appelle la Politique. Chacun voi d'un coup d'oeil tout ce qui se remue dans l'univers & pour peu qu'un peuple montre d'ambition il éffraye d'àbord tous les autres.'

29 Ibid., 157: 'Le Peuple de Rome . . . regardoit le Commerce & les Arts comme les choses propres aux seuls Esclaves.' The translation is from *Reflections on the Causes of the Rise and Fall of the Roman Empire* (Glasgow: T. Glas and W. Gray, 1752), 3rd edn, 78.

30 Christopher Brooke, 'Eighteenth-Century Carthage', in Béla Kapossy, Isaac Nakhimovsky and Richard Whatmore, eds., *Commerce and Peace in the Enlightenment* (Cambridge: Cambridge University Press, 2017), 110–24.

31 Montesquieu, *Considérations sur les causes de la grandeur des Romains et de leur decadence*, 33–34: 'Les Puissances établies par le Commerce peuvent subsister longtemps dans leur médiocrité, mais leur grandeur est de peu de durée: elles s'élevent peu-à-peu & sans que personne s'en aperçoive car elles ne sont aucun act particulier qui fasse du bruit & signaller leur puissance: mais lorsque la chose est venue au point qu'on ne peut plus s'empêcher de la voir, chacun cherche à priver cette nation d'un avantage qu'elle n'a pris, pour ainsi dire, que par

surprise.' For the translation see *Reflections on the Causes of the Rise and Fall of the Roman Empire*, 19.

32 Montesquieu, *De l'esprit des lois*, book XXI, ch. 14, *Œuvres Complètes de Montesquieu*, ed., Roger Caillois, II, 632: 'On n'a jamais remarqué aux Romains de jalousie sur le commerce. Ce fut comme nation rivale, et non comme nation commerçante, qu'ils attaquèrent Carthage.'

33 E. C. Mossner, 'Hume's Early Memoranda, 1729–1740: The Complete Text', *Journal of the History of Ideas* 9/4 (1948), 492–518, citation at 508.

34 Hume, 'Of Civil Liberty', *Essays Moral, Political, Literary*, ed., Eugene F. Miller, 87.

35 Ibid., 88.

36 John Keay, *The Honourable Company: A History of the English East India Company* (London: Harper Collins, 1993); Koen Stapelbroek, '"The Long Peace": Commercial Treaties and the Principles of Global Trade at the Peace of Utrecht', in *The 1713 Peace of Utrecht and Its Enduring Effects*, ed. A. H. A. Soons (Leiden: Brill, 2015) and 'Between Utrecht and the War of the Austrian Succession: The Dutch Translation of the British Merchant of 1728', *History of European Ideas* 40 (2014), 1026–43; Philip J. Stern, *The Company-State: Corporate Sovereignty and the Early Modern Foundations of the British Empire in India* (Oxford: Oxford University Press, 2011).

37 William Temple, *Observations upon the United Provinces of the Netherlands* (London: Jacob Tonson, 1705), 7th edn, 259. See further, Ida J. A. Nijenhuis, '"Shining Comet, Falling Meteor": Reflections on the Dutch Republic as a Commercial Power during the Second Stadholderless Era', in Jan A. F. de Jongste, Augustus J. Veenendaal, eds., *Anthonie Heinsius and the Dutch Republic, 1688–1720: Politics, War, and Finance* (The Hague: Institute of Netherlands History, 2005), 115–32.

38 Paul Rapin de Thoyras, *The History of England Written in French* (London: John and Paul Knapton), 3rd edn, 2 vols., II, 638.

39 Koen Stapelbroek, 'Dutch Decline as a European Phenomenon', *History of European Ideas* 36/2 (2010), 139–52, and Iain McDaniel, 'Enlightened History and the Decline of Nations: Ferguson, Raynal, and the contested legacies of the Dutch Republic', *History of European Ideas* 36/2 (2010), 203–16.

40 Koen Stapelbroek, 'From Jealousy of Trade to the Neutrality of Finance: Isaac de Pinto's "System" of Luxury and Perpetual Peace', in *Commerce and Peace in the Enlightenment*, 78–109.

41 Hume, 'Of Luxury', *Essays Moral, Political, Literary*, ed., Eugene F. Miller, 271. This essay was given the title 'Of Refinement in the Arts' in editions of Hume's essays from 1760.

42 William Temple, *Observations upon the United Provinces of the Netherlands (1672)*, ed., George Clark (Oxford: Clarendon Press, 1972), 123–6; Richard Cantillon, *Essay on the Nature of Trade in General (1730–4)*, ed. and trans., Henry Higgs (London: Macmillan & Co. for the Royal Economic Society, 1931), 246–7. See further, István Hont, 'The "Rich Country– Poor Country" Debate in Scottish Classical Political Economy', in István Hont and Michael Ignatieff, eds., *Wealth and Virtue: The Shaping of Political Economy in the Scottish Enlightenment*, 271–316.

43 Hume, 'Of Civil Liberty', *Essays Moral, Political, Literary*, ed., Eugene F. Miller, 92

44 Hume, 'Of Public Credit', *Essays Moral, Political, Literary*, ed., Eugene F. Miller, 360–61. See further, Duncan Forbes, *Hume's Philosophical Politics*, 174–5.

45 Hume, 'Of Public Credit', *Essays Moral, Political, Literary*, ed., Eugene F. Miller, 364.

46 Ibid., 362.

47 Hume to Strahan, 25 June 1771, *The Letters of David Hume*, II, 244.

48 Caroline A. Robbins, *The Eighteenth-Century Commonwealthman: Studies in the Transmission, Development and Circumstance of English Liberty Thought from the Restoration of Charles II until the War with the Thirteen Colonies* (Indianapolis IN: Liberty Fund, 2004 [1959 and 1987]); J. G. A. Pocock, *The Ancient Constitution and the Feudal Law: A Study of English Historical Thought in the Seventeenth Century: A Reissue with a Retrospect* (Cambridge: Cambridge University Press, 1987); Isaac Kramnick, 'Augustan Politics and English Historiography: The Debate on the English Past, 1730–35', *History and Theory* 6 (1967), 33–56; R. J. Smith, *The Gothic Bequest: Medieval Institutions in British Thought, 1688–1863* (Cambridge: Cambridge University Press, 1987); Tom Pye, 'The Gothic Past in Scottish Thought, c. 1750–1820',

(University of Cambridge, Unpublished PhD, 2018); Philip Connell, 'British Identities and the Politics of Ancient Poetry in Later Eighteenth-Century England', *Historical Journal* 49/1 (2006), 161–92.

49 Mark Goldie, 'The Roots of True Whiggism, 1688–94', *History* of *Political Thought* I (1980), 195–236; Richard Ashcraft and M. M. Goldsmith, 'Locke, Revolution Principles, and the Formation of Whig Ideology', *Historical Journal* 26/4 (1983), 773–800.

50 Hume, *History of England*, VI, ch. LXXI, 533.

51 Hume, 'The Life of David Hume, Esq. Written by Himself', in *Essays Moral, Political, Literary*, ed., Eugene F. Miller, xxxviii.

52 Hume, *History of England*, VI, ch. LXXI, 533.

53 Teresa M. Bejan, *Mere Civility: Disagreement and the Limits of Toleration* (Cambridge, MA: Harvard University Press, 2017).

54 Duncan Forbes, 'The European, or Cosmopolitan, Dimension in Hume's Science of Politics', *British Journal of Eighteenth-Century Studies* I (1978), 57–60; Laurence L. Bongie, *David Hume: Prophet of the Counter-Revolution* (Indianapolis, IN: Liberty Fund, 2000 [1965]), 2nd edn; Donald W. Livingston, 'David Hume and the Conservative Tradition', *Intercollegiate Review* 44/2 (2009), 30–41.

55 Hume, *History of England*, IV, Appendix III, 354–5 and note: 'By the ancient constitution, is here meant that which prevailed before the settlement of our present plan of liberty. There was a more ancient constitution, where, though the people had perhaps less liberty than under the Tudors, yet the king had also less authority: The power of the barons was a great check upon him, and exercised great tyranny over them. But there was still a more ancient constitution, viz. that before the signing of the charters, when neither the people nor the barons had any regular privileges; and the power of the government, during the reign of an able prince, was almost wholly in the king. The English constitution, like all others, has been in a state of continual fluctuation.' For a related critique, see Eric Nelson, '"Barons' Wars, under Other Names": Feudalism, Royalism and the American Founding', *History of European Ideas* 43/2 (2017), 198–214.

56 See Patrick Kelly, 'The Irish Woollen Export Prohibition Act of 1699: Kearney Re-visited', *Irish Economic and Social History* 7 (1980), 22–44;

'William Molyneux and the Spirit of Liberty in Eighteenth-Century Ireland', *Eighteenth-Century Ireland* 3 (1988), 133–48; 'Recasting a Tradition: William Molyneux and the Sources of *The Case of Ireland . . . Stated* (1698)', in Jane H. Ohlmeyer, ed., *Political Thought in Seventeenth-Century Ireland* (Cambridge: Cambridge University Press, 2000), 83–106; David Armitage, *The Ideological Origins of the British Empire* (Cambridge: Cambridge University Press, 2000), 146–69; Martyn J. Powell, *Britain and Ireland in the Eighteenth-Century Crisis of Empire* (Basingstoke: Palgrave Macmillan, 2003); Nicholas Canny, *Kingdom and Colony: Ireland in the Atlantic World, 1560–1800* (Baltimore, ML, and London: Johns Hopkins University Press, 1988).

57 C. A. Bayly, 'Ireland, India and the Empire: 1780-1914', *Transactions of the Royal Historical Society* 10 (2000), 377–97.

58 K. N. Chaudhuri, *The Trading World of Asia and the English East India Company, 1660–1760* (Cambridge: Cambridge University Press, 1978); C. A. Bayly, *The New Cambridge History of India II: 1. Indian Society and the Making of the British Empire* (Cambridge: Cambridge University Press, 1988); Peter J. Marshall, *The New Cambridge History of India II: 2. Bengal: The British Bridgehead. Eastern India 1740–1828* (Cambridge: Cambridge University Press, 1987); James M. Vaughn, *The Politics of Empire at the Accession of George III: The East India Company and the Crisis and Transformation of Britain's Imperial State* (New Haven, CT: Yale University Press, 2019).

59 István Hont, *Jealousy of Trade: International Competition and the Nation-State in Historical Perspective*.

60 Richard Tuck, *Philosophy and Government 1572–1651* (Cambridge: Cambridge University Press, 1996), 31–64; *The Rights of War and Peace: Political Thought and the International Order from Grotius to Kant* (Oxford: Oxford University Press, 2000), 1–15; Jonathan Haslam, *No Virtue like Necessity: Realist Thought in International Relations since Machiavelli* (New Haven CT: Yale University Press, 2002); Horst Driezel, 'Reason-of-State and the Crisis of Political Aristotelianism: An Essay on the Development of Seventeenth-Century Political Philosophy', *History of European Ideas* 28 (2002), 163–84; Thomas Poole, *Reason-of-State: Law, Prerogative and Empire* (Cambridge: Cambridge

University Press, 2015). On Anglo-French relations, see Linda Colley, *Britons: Forging the Nation 1707–1837* (New Haven, CT: Yale University Press, 1992); Edmond Dziembowski, *Un nouveau patriotisme français, 1750–1770: La France face à l'anglaise à l'époque de la guerre de Sept ans* (Oxford: Voltaire Foundation, 1998); David A. Bell, *The Cult of the Nation in France: Inventing Nationalism 1680–1800* (Cambridge, MA: Harvard University Press, 2001).

61 Hume to William Robertson, 1 December 1763, *New Letters of David Hume*, ed. Raymond Klibansky and Ernest C. Mossner (Oxford: Oxford University Press, 1954), 76.

62 Hume to Gilbert Elliot of Minto, 12 March 1763, ibid., 69–70.

63 Hume to William Robertson, 27 November 1768, ibid., 186.

64 Hume to Jean-Charles Trudaine de Montigny, 25 May 1767, ibid., 235.

65 Marie Peters, *Pitt and Popularity: The Patriot Minister and London Opinion during the Seven Years War* (Oxford and New York: Clarendon Press, 1980).

66 Hume to Strahan, 2 January 1772, *The Letters of David Hume*, II, 251.

67 Hume to Strahan, 11 March 1771, ibid., 237.

68 Hume, 'Of the Liberty of the Press', *Essays Moral, Political, Literary*, ed., Eugene F. Miller, 13.

69 ibid., 11, quoting a speech from the Emperor Galba to his nominated successor, Piso: Tacitus, *The Histories*, 1.16.28.

70 Hume to Tobias Smollett, 18 July 1767, *The Letters of David Hume*, II, 151–2.

71 Hume to William Mure, Baron Mure of Caldwell, 18 October 1768, ibid., II, 187–9.

72 Max Skjönsberg, 'David Hume and "Of the Liberty of the Press" (1741) in Its Original Contexts', in Robert G. Ingram, Jason Peacey and Alex W. Barber, eds., *Freedom of Speech, 1500–1850* (Manchester: Manchester University Press, 2020), 171–91.

73 John Brewer, 'The Misfortunes of Lord Bute: A Case-Study in Eighteenth-Century Political Argument and Public Opinion', *Historical Journal* 16/1 (1973), 3–43; Gordon Pentland, '"We Speak for the Ready": Images of Scots in Political Prints, 1707–1832', *Scottish Historical Review* 90/229 (2011), 64–95. See more broadly, Colin Kidd, 'North Britishness and the Nature of Eighteenth-Century British Patriotisms', *Historical*

Journal 39 (1996), 361–82, and *Subverting Scotland's Past: Scottish Whig Historians and the Creation of an Anglo-British Identity 1689–c. 1830* (Cambridge: Cambridge University Press, 1993).

74 See Ira Katznelson and Gareth Stedman Jones, eds., *Religion and the Political Imagination* (Cambridge: Cambridge University Press, 2012).

75 Hume to Sir Gilbert Elliot of Minto, 3rd Baronet, 21 February 1770, *The Letters of David Hume*, II, 215–17.

76 Hume to William Strahan, 5 June 1770, ibid., 226.

77 Hume to Smith, 27 June 1772, ibid., 263.

78 Hume to Strahan, 14 November 1769, ibid., 211.

79 Hume to Strahan, 25 June 1771, ibid., 244.

80 Hume to Smith, 6 February 1770, ibid., 215.

81 Hume to Strahan, 30 January 1773, ibid., 269.

82 Hume to Strahan, 19 August 1771, ibid., 248.

83 Hume to Gilbert Elliot, 22 July 1768, ibid., 184.

3. Shelburne, His Circle and the End of Britain

1 Frank O'Gorman, 'Shelburne: A Chathamite in Opposition and in Government 1760–82?', in Aston and Campbell Orr, eds., *An Enlightenment Statesman in Whig Britain*, 117–40.

2 John Brewer, *Party Ideology and Popular Politics at the Accession of George III* (Cambridge: Cambridge University Press, 1976); J. C. D. Clark, *The Language of Liberty 1660–1832: Political Discourse and Social Dynamics in the Anglo-American World* (Cambridge: Cambridge University Press, 1994).

3 Lawrence Klein, 'Sociability, Politeness, and Aristocratic Self-Formation in the Life and Career of the Second Earl of Shelburne', *Historical Journal* 55 (2012), 653–77.

4 Shelburne to Henry Fox, 20 May 1762, Edmond Fitzmaurice, *Life of William, Earl of Shelburne, afterwards First Marquess of Lansdowne, with Extracts from his Papers and Correspondence* (London: Macmillan and Co., 1912), 2nd edn, 2 vols., I, 112.

5 See Isabel Rivers and David L. Wykes, eds., *Joseph Priestley Scientist Philosopher and Theologian* (Oxford: Oxford University Press, 2008).

6 Anon., *An Essay on the Means of Producing Moral Effects from Physical Causes: Or, of Infallibly Extirpating the Roots of National Animosity among the North and South Britons* (London: J. Williams, 1773), 4.

7 Hume, Appendix III [To the Reign of Elizabeth I], *History of England*, IV, 373n. Price cited the 1778 edition 'with the Author's Last Corrections and Improvements', IV, 475, in 'Additional Observations on the Nature and Value of Civil Liberty' in *Two Tracts on Civil Liberty, the War with America, and the Debts and Finances of the Kingdom* (London: T. Cadell, 1778), xiii–xiv.

8 Price, 'Additional Observations on the Nature and Value of Civil Liberty', in *Two Tracts on Civil Liberty, the War with America, and the Debts and Finances of the Kingdom*, 29, 38–9, 51, 154.

9 Frank O'Gorman, 'Party and Burke: The Rockingham Whigs', *Government and Opposition* 3/1 (1968), 92–110; Derek Watson, 'The Rockingham Whigs and the Townshend Duties', *English Historical Review* 84/332 (1969), 561–5; W. M. Elofson, 'The Rockingham Whigs in Transition: The East India Company Issue 1772–1773', *English Historical Review* 104/413 (1989), 947–74.

10 On the physiocrats and their view of Britain see George Weulersse, *Le Mouvement physiocratique en France de 1756 à 1770* (Paris: Éditions Mouton, 1968), 2 vols., I, 53; Kenneth E. Carpenter, *The Economic Bestsellers before 1850: A Catalogue of an Exhibition Prepared for the History of Economics Society Meeting, May 21–24, 1975, at Baker Library* (Cambridge MA: Harvard Business School, 1975); Christine Théré, 'Economic Publishing and Authors, 1566–1789', in *Studies in the History of French Political Economy: From Bodin to Walras*, ed. Gilbert Faccarello (London: Routledge, 1998), 21; Michael Kwass, 'Consumption and the World of Ideas: Consumer Revolution and the Moral Economy of the Marquis de Mirabeau', *Eighteenth-Century Studies* 37 (2004), 187–213; Michael Sonenscher, 'Physiocracy as a Theodicy', *History of Political Thought* 23 (2002), 326–39; Philippe Steiner, *La 'Science nouvelle' de l'économie politique* (Paris: Presses Universitaires de France, 1998); Loïc Charles and Philippe Steiner, 'La physiocratie parmi les origines intellectuelles de la Révolution française', *Études Jean-Jacques Rousseau* 11 (2000), 83–160; Liana Vardi, *The Physiocrats and the World of*

Enlightenment (Cambridge: Cambridge University Press, 2012); Paul Cheney, 'Physiocracy and the Politics of History', in *Revolutionary Commerce: Globalization and the French Monarchy*, 141–67.

11 Fitzmaurice, *Life of William, Earl of Shelburne*, I, 12.

12 Ibid., 5–7.

13 Ibid., 9.

14 Ibid., 7–8.

15 See S. J. Connolly, *Religion, Law and Power: The Making of Protestant Ireland, 1660–1760* (Oxford: Oxford University Press, 1995); David W. Hayton, *Ruling Ireland 1685–1742: Politics, Politicians and Parties* (Woodbridge, Suffolk: Boydell & Brewer, 2004); Ian McBride, *Eighteenth-Century Ireland: The Isle of Slaves* (Dublin: Gill and Macmillan, 2009).

16 Martyn J. Powell, 'Shelburne and Ireland: Politician, Patriot, Absentee', in Aston and Campbell Orr, eds., *An Enlightenment Statesman in Whig Britain*, 141–59.

17 For the debate about union, see Colin Kidd, *Union and Unionisms: Political Thought in Scotland, 1500–2000* (Cambridge: Cambridge University Press, 2006); Murray Pittock, *Scotland: The Global History – 1603 to the Present* (New Haven, CT: Yale University Press, 2022).

18 Clarissa Campbell Orr, 'Aunts, Wives, Courtiers: The Ladies of Bowood', in Aston and Campbell Orr, eds., *An Enlightenment Statesman in Whig Britain: Lord Shelburne in Context, 1737-1805* (Woodbridge: Boydell & Brewer, 2011), 51–78.

19 William Blake Odgers, 'Sir William Blackstone', *Yale Law Journal* 28/6 (1919), 542–66; Wilfrid Prest, *William Blackstone: Law and Letters in the Eighteenth Century* (Oxford: Oxford University Press, 2008), 119–50.

20 Nigel Aston, 'Petty and Fitzmaurice: Lord Shelburne and His Brother', in Aston and Campbell Orr, eds., *An Enlightenment Statesman in Whig Britain*, 29–50.

21 Fitzmaurice, *Life of William, Earl of Shelburne*, I, 40.

22 Ibid., 61–4.

23 Ibid., 72.

24 W. Kent Hackmann, 'William Pitt and the Generals: Three Case Studies in the Seven Years' War', *Albion: A Quarterly Journal Concerned with British Studies* 3/3 (1971), 128–37.

25 Fitzmaurice, *Life of William, Earl of Shelburne,* I, 79.

26 Ibid., 82–129.

27 John Norris, *Shelburne and Reform* (London: Macmillan, 1963), 1–17.

28 Fitzmaurice, *Life of William, Earl of Shelburne,* I, 96–7.

29 Peter D. G. Thomas, 'Barré, Isaac (1726–1802), army officer and politician', *Oxford Dictionary of National Biography.*

30 For John Dunning's speech of 6 April 1780 in the House of Commons, see *Cobbett's Parliamentary History of England: From the Earliest Period to the Year 1803* (London: Hansard, 1814), vol. 21 (1780–81), 340–47. See further, John Cannon, 'Dunning, John, first Baron Ashburton (1731–1783), barrister and politician', *Oxford Dictionary of National Biography.*

31 John Dunning, speech of 6 April 1780, *Cobbett's Parliamentary History of England: From the Earliest Period to the Year 1803,* vol. 21 (1780–81), 347–8.

32 Herbert Butterfield, *George III, Lord North and the People 1779–80* (London: G. Bell and Sons, 1949); R. Pares, 'George III and the Politicians', *Transactions of the Royal Historical Society* 1 (1951), 127–51; Ian R. Christie, 'George III and the Debt on Lord North's Election Account, 1780–1784', *English Historical Review* 78, no. 309 (1963), 715–24; William C. Lowe, 'George III, Peerage Creations and Politics, 1760–1784', *Historical Journal* 35/3 (1992), 587–609; David M. Craig, 'The Crowned Republic? Monarchy and Anti-Monarchy in Britain, 1760–1901', *Historical Journal* 46/1 (2003), 167–85; Neil York, 'George III, Tyrant: "The Crisis" as Critic of Empire, 1775–1776', *History* 94/4 (316) (2009), 434–60.

33 Fitzmaurice, *Life of William, Earl of Shelburne,* I, 80.

34 Ibid., 211–13.

35 Ibid., 142–3.

36 François Fénelon, *The Adventures of Telemachus, the Son of Ulysses. Translated from the French by John Hawkesworth* (London: W. Strahan, 1768), iii–iv.

37 Joseph Priestley to Richard Price, 21 July 1772, *The Correspondence of Richard Price,* ed. D. O. Thomas and W. Bernard Peach (Durham, NC, and Cardiff: Duke University Press and University of Wales Press, 1983–94), 3 vols., I, 132–5.

38 Joseph Priestley, *Letters to the Inhabitants of Northumberland and its Neighbourhood, on Subjects Interesting to the Author and to Them* (Philadelphia, PA: Conrad and Conrad, 1801), 26–9.

39 Blackstone to Shelburne, 27 December 1761, Fitzmaurice, *Life of William, Earl of Shelburne*, I, 219. On Franklin's links to Dissenters and London radicals, see Verner W. Crane, 'The Club of Honest Whigs: Friends of Science and Liberty', *William and Mary Quarterly* 23/2 (1966), 210–33, and more broadly, J. A. Leo Lemay, *The Life of Benjamin Franklin, Vol. 1: Journalist, 1706–1730* (Philadelphia, PA: University of Pennsylvania Press, 2006).

40 Shelburne to Franklin, 6 April 1782, *Benjamin Franklin Papers Online*, Yale University, The American Philosophical Society, and The Packard Humanities Institute, digital database, franklinpapers.org

41 See Verner W. Crane, 'Benjamin Franklin and the Stamp Act', *Colonial Society of Massachusetts, Transactions* 32 (1937), 56–77; Jack P. Greene, 'The Alienation of Benjamin Franklin – British American', *Journal of the Royal Society of Arts* 124/5234 (1976), 52–73; Alan Houston, *Benjamin Franklin and the Politics of Improvement* (New Haven CT and London: Yale University Press, 2008); Gordon S. Wood, *The Americanization of Benjamin Franklin* (New York: Penguin Books, 2004).

42 David Hume to Shelburne, 12 December 1761, *The Letters of David Hume*, I, 347–8.

43 Sophia Carteret's diary, 28 February 1766, Edmond Fitzmaurice, *Life of William, Earl of Shelburne*, I, 271–2.

44 Shelburne to Dugald Stewart, 1795, *The Collected Works of Dugald Stewart*, ed. Sir William Hamilton, (Edinburgh: Thomas Constable, 1858) 10 vols., X, 95.

45 Fitzmaurice, *Life of William, Earl of Shelburne*, I, 429–33.

46 John Bowring, 'Memoirs of Jeremy Bentham', *Tait's Edinburgh* Magazine for 1840, vol. VII (Edinburgh: William *Tate*, 1840), 697: 'Bentham's visits to Bowood were full of felicity. A few of his amusing letters, full as they are of agreeable tittle-tattle, will best shew how many pleasures were crowded into those happy days; which, in writing to the present Lord Lansdowne, Bentham called the "happiest of his life".'

47 Bentham, *The Works of Jeremy Bentham*, ed., John Bowring (Edinburgh and London: W. Tait and Simpkin, Marshall, 1843), 10 vols., X, 175.

48 John Dunning, speaking in the House of Commons, 6 April 1780, *Parliamentary History*, XXI, 346.

49 John Burnby, *An Address to the People of England, on the Increase of their Poor Rates, Dedicated to the Earl of Shelburne* (London: n. p., 1780), ii–iii.

50 On Shelburne's beliefs, see G. M. Ditchfield, 'A Christian Whig: Lord Shelburne and the Latitudinarian Tradition', in Aston and Campbell Orr, eds., *An Enlightenment Statesman in Whig Britain*, 79–96.

51 Lois G. Schwoerer, 'Locke, Lockean Ideas, and the Glorious Revolution', *Journal of the History of Ideas* 51/4 (1990), 531–48; Richard Ashcraft and M. M. Goldsmith, 'Locke, Revolution Principles, and the Formation of Whig Ideology', *Historical Journal* 26/4 (1983), 773–800; Mark Knights, 'John Locke and Postrevolutionary politics: Electoral Reform and the Franchise', *Past & Present*, 213 (2011), 41–86.

52 Geoffrey W. Rice, 'Deceit and Distraction: Britain, France, and the Corsican Crisis of 1768', *International History Review* 28, no. 2 (2006), 287–315; Theodore C. Pease, 'The Mississippi Boundary of 1763: A Reappraisal of Responsibility', *American Historical Review* 40/2 (1935), 278–86.

53 On Hume's justification of corruption, see James A. Harris, *Hume: An Intellectual Biography*, 166–186, and Max Skjönsberg, *The Persistence of Party: Ideas of Harmonious Discord in Eighteenth-Century Britain* (Cambridge: Cambridge University Press, 2021), chs. 4 and 6.

54 Pitt to Shelburne, December 1765, *Correspondence of William Pitt, Earl of Chatham*, ed. William Stanhope Taylor and Captain John Henry Pringle (London: John Murray, 1838), 4 vols., II, 359.

55 Maurice Morgann, memorandum for Shelburne on North American affairs [1767], Fitzmaurice, *Life of William, Earl of Shelburne*, I, 315–18.

56 Patrick Griffin, *The Townshend Moment: The Making of Empire and Revolution in the Eighteenth Century* (New Haven, CT: Yale University Press, 2017).

57 Stephen Conway, 'The Consequences of the Conquest: Quebec and British Politics, 1760–1774', in *Revisiting 1759: The Conquest of Canada in Historical Perspective*, ed. Phillip Buckner and John G. Reid (Toronto: University of Toronto Press, 2012), 141–65.

58 On Shelburne's policy as derived from Bute's focus upon peace and security, see Rachel Banke, 'Bute's Empire: Reform, Reaction, and the Roots of Imperial Crisis' (Unpublished PhD thesis, University of Notre Dame, 2017).

59 Shelburne to Francis Fauquier, 19 February 1767, *The Official Papers of Francis Fauquier, Lieutenant Governor of Virginia, 1758–1768: 1764–1768. Virginia Historical Society Documents*, vol. 16, ed. George Reese (Charlottesville, VA: University Press of Virginia, 1983), vol. 3, 1429–30.

60 Fitzmaurice, *Life of William, Earl of Shelburne*, I, 334.

61 Shelburne to Rochford, 4 July 1768, ibid., 371.

62 Geoffrey W. Rice, 'Great Britain, the Manila Ransom, and the First Falkland Islands Dispute with Spain, 1766', *International History Review* 2/3 (1980), 386–409.

63 Geoffrey W. Rice, 'Deceit and Distraction: Britain, France and the Corsican Crisis of 1768', *International History Review* 28/2 (2006), 287–315.

64 Luke Long, 'James Boswell and Corsica 1728–1768: The Development of British Opinion during the Corsican Revolt', *History of European Ideas* 45/6 (2019), 817–41.

65 Mount Stuart to Shelburne, 20 August 1768, Fitzmaurice, *Life of William, Earl of Shelburne*, I, 384.

66 T. B. Macaulay, 'The Life of Robert Lord Clive; Collected from the Family Papers Communicated by the Earl of Powis. By Major-General Sir John Malcolm, KCB., 3 vols. 8vo. London: 1836', *Edinburgh Review* 70 (January 1840); P. J. Marshall, *East Indian Fortunes: The British in Bengal in the Eighteenth Century* (Oxford: Clarendon Press, 1976); P. Lawson and B. Lenman, 'Robert Clive, the Black Jagir and English Politics', *Historical Journal* XXVI (1983).

67 Lansdowne House MSS cited in Fitzmaurice, *Life of William, Earl of Shelburne*, I, 295.

68 Shelburne to Pitt, 5 October 1766, ibid., 295.

69 George McGilvary, *Guardian of The East India Company: The Life of Laurence Sulivan* (London: Bloomsbury, 2005); James M. Vaughn, *The Politics of Empire at the Accession of George III: The East India Company and the Crisis and Transformation of Britain's Imperial State* (New Haven, CT: Yale University Press, 2019).

70 Thomas Bartlett, 'The Augmentation of the Army in Ireland 1767–1769', *English Historical Review* 96/380 (1981), 540–59.

71 Vincent T. Harlow, *The Founding of the Second British Empire, 1763–1793* (London: Longmans, 1952), 2 vols.

72 Fitzmaurice, *Life of William, Earl of Shelburne*, I, 69.

73 Ibid., 36.

74 Ibid., 80.

75 Smith, *An Inquiry into the Nature and Causes of the Wealth of Nations*, ed. R. H. Campbell, A. S. Skinner and R. B. Todd, III.i.9, I, 380.

76 Shelburne to Richard Price, 29 September 1786, *Correspondence of Richard Price*, III, 64.

77 Ibid., 86.

78 Bentham to Jacques-Pierre Brissot, 25 November 1791, *The Correspondence of Jeremy Bentham: October 1788 to December 1793*, ed. Alexander Taylor Milne (London: Athlone Press, 1981), IV, 341–2.

79 Fitzmaurice, *Life of William, Earl of Shelburne*, I, 405.

80 Jeremy Black, *Pitt the Elder* (Cambridge: Cambridge University Press, 1992).

81 Shelburne speech in the House of Lords, 4 May 1770, *Parliamentary History*, XVI, 966.

82 Basil Williams, *The Life of William Pitt, Vol. 1: Earl of Chatham* (London: Cass, 1913), 246–313.

83 Shelburne speech in the House of Lords, 4 May 1770, *Parliamentary History*, XVI, 966, 1026.

84 Shelburne speech in the House of Lords, 22 November 1770, ibid., 114.

85 Pitt to Calcraft, 28 November 1770, *Correspondence of William Pitt*, IV, 32.

86 Nicholas Rogers, *Whigs and Cities: Popular Politics in the Age of Walpole and Pitt* (Oxford and New York: Oxford University Press and Clarendon Press, 1989); Bob Harris, *Politics and the Nation: Britain in the*

Mid-Eighteenth Century (Oxford: Oxford University Press, 2002); Troy O. Bickham, *Making Headlines: The American Revolution as Seen through the British Press* (DeKalb IL: Northern Illinois University Press, 2009); Marie Peters, 'Early Hanoverian Consciousness: Empire or Europe?', *English Historical Review* 122/497 (2007), 632–68.

87 Shelburne to Pitt, 25 February 1771, Fitzmaurice, *Life of William, Earl of Shelburne*, II, 223.

88 Shelburne to Pitt, 9 April 1774, ibid., 223–4

89 Morellet, *Lettres de l'abbé Morellet [. . .] à Lord Shelburne, depuis marquis de Lansdowne, 1772–1803*, ed. Edmond Fitzmaurice (Paris: E. Plon, Nourrit et Cie, 1898), I, ch. 6, vi, ix; E. S. Roscoe, 'An Eighteenth-Century Abbé in England: Morellet and Shelburne', *Contemporary Review* 142 (1932), 357–69; Dorothy Medlin and Arlene P. Shy, 'Enlightened Exchange: The Correspondence of André Morellet and Lord Shelburne', in Kathleen Hardesty Doig and Dorothy Medlin, eds., *British-French Exchanges in the Eighteenth Century* (Newcastle: Cambridge Scholars Publishing, 2007), 34–82.

90 Richard van der Bergh and Christophe Salvat, 'Scottish Subtlety: André Morellet's Comments on the Wealth of Nations', *European Journal of the History of Economic Thought* 8/2 (2001), 146–85.

91 Shelburne to Pitt, 13 April 1772, Fitzmaurice, *Life of William, Earl of Shelburne*, II, 263.

92 Shelburne to Pitt, 12 June 1773, ibid., 264.

93 Richard Price, *Four Dissertations: On Providence. On Prayer. On the Reasons for Expecting That Virtuous Men Shall Meet after Death in a State of Happiness. On the Importance of Christianity, the Nature of Historical Evidence, and Miracles* (London: A. Millar and T. Cadell, 1767).

94 Richard Price, *A Review of the Principal Questions and Difficulties in Morals: Particularly Those Relating to the Original of Our Ideas of Virtue, Its Nature, Foundation Reference to the Deity, Obligation, Subject Matter and Sanctions* (London: T. Cadell., 1769), 2nd edn; *Observations on Reversionary Payments: On Schemes for Providing Annuities for Widows, and for Persons in Old Age; on the Method of Calculating the Values of Assurances on Lives; and on the National Debt to Which Are Added Four Essays on Different Subjects in the Doctrine of Life-Annuities and Political*

Arithmetick (London: T. Cadell, 1772); *An Appeal to the Public on the National Debt* (London: T. Cadell, 1772).

95 Shelburne, 31 October 1776, *Parliamentary History*, XVIII, 1384–91.

96 Shelburne, 17 March 1778, ibid., XIX, 924–5.

97 Shelburne, 2 June 1778, ibid., 1267.

98 Barré to Shelburne, 1779, Fitzmaurice, *Life of William, Earl of Shelburne*, II, 35.

99 Shelburne to Price, 5 September 1779, ibid., 40.

100 Shelburne speech, 2 June 1779, *Parliamentary History*, XX, 666.

101 Shelburne speech in the House of Lords, 1 December 1779, ibid., II, 44.

102 Shelburne speech in the House of Lords, 1 December 1779, ibid., XX, 1156.

103 Loïc Charles, 'French "New Politics" and the Dissemination of David Hume's Political Discourses on the Continent, 1750–1770', in *David Hume's Political Economy*, 181–202.

104 Takumi Tsuda, '*Laissez Faire, Laissez Passer*: Its Prototypes in the Cases of Marquis d'Argenson and Vincent de Gournay', *Economic Review* 30/3 (1979), 217–27; Takumi Tsuda, ed., *Mémoires et lettres de Vincent de Gournay*, Economic Research Series no. 31, The Institute of Economic Research, Hitotsubashi University (Tokyo: Kinokuniya Company, 1993); Christine Théré, Loïc Charles and Frédéric Lefebvre, *Le cercle de Vincent de Gournay: Savoirs économiques et pratiques administratives en France au milieu du XVIIIe siècle* (Paris: INED, 2011).

105 On the *Lettres sur la liberté du commerce des grains* (1770) and the *Réflexions sur la formation et la distribution des richesses* and their impact, see Emma Rothschild, *Economic Sentiments: Adam Smith, Condorcet, and the Enlightenment* (Cambridge, MA: Harvard University Press, 2001); Joseph Tissot, *Turgot: Sa vie, son administration, ses ouvrages* (Paris: Didier, 1862); Pierre Henri Goute and Gérard Klotz, 'Turgot: A Critic of Physiocracy? An Analysis of the Debates in *Éphémémerides du citoyen* and in Correspondence with Dupont', *European Journal of the History of Economic Thought* 22/3 (2015), 500–533.

106 Edgar Faure, *La Disgrâce de Turgot: 12 Mai 1776* (Paris: Gallimard, 1961).

107 Franklin's correspondence with Turgot and Price can be found in the *Benjamin Franklin Papers* Online. See especially, Price to Franklin, 22

December 1780, and also Yiftah Elazar, 'The Downfall of All Slavish Hierarchies: Richard Price on Emancipation, Improvement, and Republican Utopia', *Modern Intellectual History* 19/1 (2022), 81–104.

108 See Dorothy Medlin, *André Morellet and the Idea of Progress* (Oxford: Voltaire Foundation, 1980) and *André Morellet and the Trudaines* (Oxford: Voltaire Foundation, 2005).

109 Pierre-Samuel Dupont de Nemours, *De l'exportation et de l'inportation* [sic] *des grains. Mémoire lû à la Société Royale d'agriculture de soissons par M. du Pont l'un des associés* (Soissons and Paris, P. G. Simon, 1764), 145.

110 Dupont de Nemours, 'Notes à propos d'observations sur les règlemens de commerce et sur le système de finances adopté en Angleterre', *Journal de l'agriculture, du commerce et des finances*, November 1765; 'Histoire abrégée des finances de l'Angleterre', *Éphémérides du citoyen*, IV, 1769; *De l'origine et progrès d'une science nouvelle* (London and Paris: Desaint, 1768), 25–30; 'Situation actuelle du commerce anglais dans plusieurs de ses différentes parties', *Journal de l'agriculture, du commerce et des finances*, December 1765; *Mémoires sur la vie et les ouvrages de M. Turgot, ministre d'état, seconde partie, contenant son ministère aux finances et sa retraite* (Philadelphia, PA, and Paris: n. p., 1782), 126, 132.

111 Ibid., 171, 196.

112 Turgot, 'Réflexions rédigées à l'occasion du mémoire sur la manière dont la France & l'Espagne doit envisiger les suites de la querelle entre la Grande-Bretagne & ses colonies', in Filippo Mazzei, *Recherches historiques et politiques sur les États-Unis de l'Amérique septentrionale . . . par un citoyen de Virginie, avec quatre lettres d'un bourgeois de New-Heaven sur l'unité de la legislation* (Colle and Paris: Froullé, 1788), 4 vols., III, 217–82.

113 Mazzei to John Adams, 31 May 1781, Margherita Marchione, ed., *Philip Mazzei: Selected Writings and Correspondence, Vol. 1: 1765–1788* (Prato: Cassa di risparmi e depositi di Prato, 1983), 280.

114 Mazzei, 'Reflections tending to predict the outcome of the present War (April 1781)', ibid., 304–308.

115 Vaughan, 'Reflections Occasioned by a Memoir of Count Vergennes, Respecting the Light in Which France and Spain Ought to View the Consequences of the Dispute between Great Britain and Her Colonies. By the Late M. Turgot. [Translated from the French.]', *The Repository:*

Containing Various Political, Philosophical, Literary, and Miscellaneous Articles (London: W. Justins, 1789), vol. 2, 251–81. Shelburne wrote to Richard Price on 29 November 1786 that, 'I have been so much struck with Mr. Turgot's Life, that I have sent it to a friend of ours to get it translated and publish'd': *The Correspondence of Richard Price*, III, 93. See further Giancarlo de Vivo and Gabriel Sabbagh, 'The First Translator in English of Turgot's *Réflexions sur la formation et la distribution des richesses*: Benjamin Vaughan', *History of Political Economy* 47 (2015), 185–99, and Kenneth E. Carpenter, 'Benjamin Vaughan's Contributions Unveiled: A Bibliography', *History of European Ideas* 44/3 (2018), 297–343.

116 Donald Winch, *Adam Smith's Politics: An Essay in Historiographic Revision* (Cambridge: Cambridge University Press, 1978), 141–63.

117 Shelburne, *Parliamentary History*, XVIII, 162, 448, 722, 920, 1083, 1220; XIX, 850–56.

118 Turgot to Price, 22 March 1778, in Honoré-Gabriel Riqueti de Mirabeau, *Considerations on the order of Cincinnatus; To Which Are Added, as Well Several Original Papers Relative to That Institution, as Also a Letter from the Late M. Turgot, Comptroller of the Finances in France, to Dr Price, on the Constitution of America; and An Abstract of Dr. Price's Observations on the Importance of the American Revolution* (London: J. Johnson, 1785), 155–63.

119 Ibid., 170–72.

120 Ibid., 194–7.

121 Shelburne to Richard Price, 22 November 1786, *The Correspondence of Richard Price*, III, 86–7.

122 André Morellet, *Lettres de l'abbé Morellet de l'Académie française à Lord Shelburne, depuis marquis de Lansdowne, 1772–1803*, ed. Edmond Fitzmaurice (Paris: Librairie Plon, 1898), Morellet to Shelburne, 12 March 1776, 102; 30 December 1777, 130–35. On Saint-Pierre see most recently Carole Dornier, *La Monarchie éclairée de l'abbé de Saint-Pierre: Une science politique des Modernes*.

123 André Morellet to Shelburne, 1 April 1783 (letter 788), *Correspondance générale d'Helvétius: Vol. IV, 1774–1800 / Lettres 721–855, suivies de lettres relevant des périodes des trois premiers volumes et découvertes depuis leur parution*, ed. Peter Allan, Alan Dainard, Marie-Thérèse Inguenaud,

Jean Orsoni and David Smith (Toronto, Buffalo and Oxford: University of Toronto Press and Voltaire Foundation, 1998), 97–9.

124 Pierre-Edouard Lémontey, 'Eloge', in Morellet, *Mémoires inédits de l'abbé Morellet* (Paris: Librairie Française de l'Advocat, 1822), 2 vols., I, ix.

125 Benjamin Vaughan to Shelburne, 3 October 1782, Charles C. Smith, ed., 'Letters of Benjamin Vaughan', *Proceedings of the Massachusetts Historical Society*, 2nd ser, 17 (1903), 406–38 (cited at 409).

126 Richard B. Morris, 'The Great Peace of 1783', *Proceedings of the Massachusetts Historical Society* 95 (1983), 29–51.

127 Franklin to Benjamin Vaughan, 10 July 1782, *Benjamin Franklin Papers*.

128 Benjamin Vaughan to Shelburne, 4 December 1782, Charles C. Smith, ed., 'Letters of Benjamin Vaughan', *Proceedings of the Massachusetts Historical Society*, 2nd ser., 17 (1903), 421.

129 Benjamin Vaughan to Shelburne, 18 January 1783, ibid., 437.

130 Benjamin Vaughan to Shelburne, 4 December 1782, ibid., 421.

131 Andrew Stockley, 'Shelburne, the European Powers, and the Peace of 1783', in *An Enlightenment Statesman in Whig Britain: Lord Shelburne in Context, 1737–1805*, 177–94.

132 Fitzmaurice, *Life of William, Earl of Shelburne*, II, 264; Morellet, *Mémoires inédits de l'abbé Morellet*, I, 27.

133 Andrew Kippis, *Considerations upon the Provisional Peace Treaty with America and the Preliminary Articles of Peace with France and Spain* (London: T. Cadell, 1783), 2nd edn, 5, 79–81.

134 Shelburne, *The Speech of the Right Honourable the Earl of Shelburne, in the House of Lords, on Monday, February 13, 1783, on the Articles of Peace* (Ipswich: Charles Punchard, 1783), 4.

135 A. Stockley, *Britain and France at the Birth of America: The European Powers and the Peace Negotiations of 1782–1783* (Exeter: Exeter University Press, 2001), 111–13, 135–8, 204–08.

136 Shelburne, *The Substance of the Speech of the Marquis of Lansdowne, in the House of Lords, On the 14th of December, 1790; On the Subject of the Convention with Spain, Which Was Signed on the 28th of October, 1790* (London: J. Debrett, 1790), 7. On commercial treaties see Antonella Alimento and Koen Stapelbroek, eds., *The Politics of Commercial Treaties in the*

Eighteenth Century: Balance of Power, Balance of Trade (London: Palgrave, 2017).

137 Shelburne to Morellet, 1802, Fitzmaurice, *Life of William, Earl of Shelburne*, II, 430–31.

138 Ibid., 18.

139 Jacques-Pierre Brissot, *Un defenseur du peuple: À l'empereur Joseph II sur son réglement concernant l'émigration*, 35–8.

140 Mirabeau, *Doutes sur la liberté de l'Escaut réclamée par l'empereur: Sur les causes & sur les conséquences probables de cette réclamation. Par le comte de Mirabeau. Avec une carte du cours de l'Escaut, depuis Anvers jusqu' à la mer* (London: G. Faden, J. Robson and P. Elmsley, 1785), 21: 'disparoître à jamais les jalousies nationales'.

141 Mirabeau, *Doubts concerning the Free Navigation of the Scheld Claimed by the Emperor, and the Probable Causes and Consequences of That Claim. In Which the Views of His Imperial Majesty, and of the Empress of Russia Are Clearly Pointed Out, and the Characters of Those Great Potentates are Exhibited in a New, and Interesting Light* (London: W. Faden, J. Robson and P. Elmsley, 1785), i–vi. Note the spontaneous English version published by the same London publishers; Samuel Romilly; *The Memoirs of the Life of Sir Samuel Romilly*, 3rd edn, (London: John Murray, 1842, 2 vols., I, 81), wrote that, 'His [Mirabeau's] pamphlet on the opening of the Scheldt was Benjamin Vaughan's.' Gabriel Sabbagh has convincingly argued that the tract is in the polemical style of Mirabeau, a point supported by the fact that it originally appeared in French. Vaughan may have been in touch with Mirabeau during the composition as a fellow member of Shelburne's Circle. On Vaughan's involvement, see further, Kenneth E. Carpenter, 'Benjamin Vaughan's Contributions Unveiled: A Bibliography', *History of European Ideas* 44/3 (2018), 297–343.

142 William Eden and Gerard de Rayneval, *Treaty of Navigation and Commerce between His Britannick Majesty and the Most Christian King: Signed at Versailles, the 26th of September, 1786* (London: T. Harrison and S. Brooke, 1787), 3.

143 Dupont de Nemours, *Lettre à la chambre du commerce de Normandie, sur le mémoire qu'elle a publié relativement au traité de commerce avec l'Angleterre* (Rouen and Paris: Moutard, 1788), 74–5.

144 Shelburne to Richard Price, 22 November 1786, *Correspondence of Richard Price*, III, 87–8.

145 William Eden, Lord Aukland, *The Journal and Correspondence of William, Lord Auckland: With a Preface and Introduction by . . . the Bishop of Bath and Wells* (London: R. Bentley, 1861), 2 vols., I, 164–71.

146 Selwyn H. H. Carrington, 'The American Revolution and the British West Indies' Economy', *Journal of Interdisciplinary History* 17/4 (1987), 823–50.

147 Benjamin Franklin to Benjamin Vaughan, 26 July 1784, *Benjamin Franklin Papers*.

148 Price to Franklin, 5 November 1785, *The Correspondence of Richard Price*, II, 319.

149 Shelburne to Price, 7 October 1784, ibid., 228–9.

150 Price to William Eden, 15 June 1785, ibid., 289.

151 Price to Thomas Jefferson, 21 March 1785, ibid., 268–9.

152 Munro Price, 'The Dutch Affair and the Fall of the Ancien Régime, 1784–1787', *Historical Journal* 38/4 (1995), 875–905; F. L. Nussbaum, 'The Formation of the New East India Company of Calonne', *American Historical Review* 38/3 (1933), 475–97; G. C. Bolton and B. E. Kennedy, 'William Eden and the Treaty of Mauritius, 1786–7', *Historical Journal* 16/4 (1973), 681–96.

153 Richard Price to Shelburne, 10 November 1787, *Correspondence of Richard Price*, III, 152–4.

154 William Eden, Lord Auckland, *The Journal and Correspondence of William, Lord Auckland* I, 172–76; J. H. Rose, 'Great Britain and the Dutch Question in 1787–1788', *American Historical Review* 14/2 (1909), 262–83.

155 Benjamin Vaughan to Benjamin Franklin, 4 March 1789, *Benjamin Franklin Papers*.

156 Benjamin Vaughan, *New and Old Principles of Trade Compared, or, A Treatise on the Principles of Commerce between Nations* (London, J. Johnson and J. Debrett, 1788), 2–3.

157 Bentham, 'Letters of Anti-Machiavel to the Public Advertiser', *The Works of Jeremy Bentham*, ed., John Bowring, X, 312–18; Stephen

Conway, 'Bentham versus Pitt: Jeremy Bentham and British Foreign Policy 1789', *Historical Journal* 30 (1987), 791–809.

158 Anon. [Vaughan], *Collection of Testimonies in Favor of Religious Liberty in the Case of the Dissenters, Catholics and Jews* (London: C. Dilly, Poultry, J. Johnson, 1790).

159 Benjamin Vaughan to Shelburne, 15 July 1790, Fitzmaurice, *Life of William, Earl of Shelburne*, II, 462–4.

160 Anon. [Vaughan], *Letters on the Subject of the Concert of Princes, and the Dismemberment of Poland and France. First published in the* Morning Chronicle . . . *1793. With Corrections and Additions. By a Calm Observer* (London: C. G. & J. Robinson, 1793); *The Essence of the Calm Observer: On the Subjects of the Concert of Princes, the Dismemberment of Poland, and the War with France* (London: W. Williams, 1793).

161 Anon. [Vaughan], *Two Papers by the Calm Observer, Not Printed in the collection of His Letters extracted from the* Morning Chronicle (London: n.p., 1795), advertisement. Robertson's comment can be found in *The History of the Reign of the Emperor Charles V: With a View of the Progress of Society in Europe, from the Subversion of the Roman Empire, to the Beginning of the Sixteenth Century. In Three Volumes. By William Robertson. D.D. Principal of the University of Edinburgh, and Historiographer to His Majesty for Scotland. A New Edition* (Dublin: W. Whitestone, W. Sleater, M. Hay, D. Chamberlaine, J. Potts, J. Hoey, L. L. Flin, J. Williams, W. Colles, W. Wilson, J. Porter, W. Walhead, T. T. Faulkener, J. Exshaw, 1777), 3 vols., I, 25.

162 On the context, see Michael Lobban, 'Treason, Sedition, and the Radical Movement in the Age of the French Revolution', *Liverpool Law Review* 22 (2000), 205–34.

163 Craig C. Murray, 'Benjamin Vaughan (1751–1835). The Life of an Anglo-American intellectual' unpublished PhD thesis, Columbia University, 1972, 342–3.

164 Ibid., 335.

165 Samuel Vaughan to Benjamin Vaughan, 13 August 1795, ibid., 341.

166 Ibid., 342–4.

167 Albert Mathiez, 'Robespierre et Benjamin Vaughan', *Annales révolutionnaires* 9/1 (1917), 1–11.

168 Craig C. Murray, 'Benjamin Vaughan (1751–1835)', 345–8.

169 Ibid., 348–80.

170 Bentham to Shelburne, 24 August 1790, *The Correspondence of Jeremy Bentham: October 1788 to December 1793*, ed. Alexander Taylor Milne (London: Athlone Press, 1981), 12 vols., IV, 145–70.

4. Catharine Macaulay and the End of Liberty

1 James Gillray, 'Guy-Vaux & Judas-Iscariot', 14 August 1782 (British Museum Collections).

2 Gabriel Glickman, 'Political Conflict and the Memory of the Revolution in England 1689–c. 1750', *The Final Crisis of the Stuart Monarchy: The Revolutions of 1688–91 in Their British, Atlantic and European Contexts*, ed. Tim Harris and Stephen Taylor (London: Boydell & Brewer, 2013), 243–72.

3 Philip Hicks, 'Catharine Macaulay's Civil War: Gender, History, and Republicanism in Georgian Britain', *Journal of British Studies* 41/2 (2002), 170–98.

4 Bridget Hill, *The Republican Virago: The Life and Times of Catharine Macaulay, Historian* (Oxford: Clarendon Press, 1992), 107–23.

5 Anon. [Thomas Watson], 'An Irregular Ode, Respectfully Inscrib'd to Mrs Macaulay', *Six Odes Presented to That Justly-Celebrated Historian, Mrs. Catharine Macaulay, on Her Birth-day, and Publicly Read to a Polite and Brilliant Audience, Assembled April the Second, at Alfred-House, Bath, to Congratulate That Lady on the Happy Occasion* (Bath and London: R. Cruttwell et al., 1777), 24.

6 On Macaulay in context see Karen O'Brien, *Women and Enlightenment in Eighteenth-Century Britain* (Cambridge: Cambridge University Press, 2009); J. G. A. Pocock, 'Catharine Macaulay: Patriot Historian', in *Women Writers and the Early Modern British Political Tradition*, ed. H. Smith, (Cambridge: Cambridge University Press, 1998), 243–58.

7 Karen Green, 'Catharine Macaulay's Enlightenment Faith and Radical Politics', *History of European Ideas* 44/1 (2017), 35–44.

8 Macaulay, *A History of England from the Accession of James I to That of the Brunswick Line, Vol. I* (London: J. Nourse; R. and J. Dodsley; and W. Johnston, 1763), 8 vols., I, vii.

9 Rachel Hammersley, *The English Republican Tradition and Eighteenth-Century France: Between the Ancients and the Moderns* (Manchester: Manchester University Press, 2010).

10 Catharine Macaulay, *The History of England from the Accession of James I to the Elevation of the House of Hanover, Vol. V: From the Death of Charles I to the Restoration of Charles II* (London: Edward and Charles Dilly, 1771), V, 382.

11 Ibid., 383.

12 John Milton, *A Complete Collection of the Historical, Political and Miscellaneous Works of John Milton*, ed. John Toland (Amsterdam: n. p., 1698); Algernon Sidney, *Discourses concerning Government* (London: n. p., 1698); *Memoirs of Edmund Ludlow Esq in Two Volumes* (London: n. p. 1698); *Memoirs of Lieutenant General Ludlow: The Third and Last Part* (Bern: n. p., 1699); *The Oceana of James Harrington, and His Other Works: Som Whereof Are Now First Publish'd from His Own Manuscripts. The Whole Collected, Methodiz'd, and Review'd, with an Exact Account of His Life Prefix'd, by John Toland* (London: n. p., 1700). On Toland's manipulations of texts, see Blair Worden, 'Whig History and Puritan Politics: The Memoirs of Edmund Ludlow, Revisited', *Historical Research* 75 (2002), 209–37; Justin Champion, *Republican Learning: John Toland and the Crisis of Christian Culture, 1696–1722* (Manchester: Manchester University Press, 2003); Katherine A. East, *The Radicalization of Cicero: John Toland and Strategic Editing in the Early Enlightenment* (London: Palgrave, 2017).

13 Anon. [Walter Moyle and John Trenchard], *An Argument, Shewing, That a Standing Army Is Inconsistent with a Free Government, and Absolutely Destructive to the Constitution of the English Monarchy* (London: n. p., 1697), 2.

14 Thomas Gordon, ed., *The Works of Tacitus. In Four Volumes. To Which Are Pre-fixed, Political Discourses upon that Author by Thomas Gordon. The Second Edition, corrected* (London: T. Woodward and J. Peele, 1737) and, ed., *The Works of Sallust, Translated into English with Political Discourses*

upon that Author. To Which Is Added, a Translation of Cicero's Four Orations against Catiline* (London: R. Ware, 1744).

15 Robert Molesworth, 'The Translator's Preface', *Franco-Gallia: Or, An Account of the Ancient Free State of France, and Most Other Parts of Europe, before the Loss of Their Liberties. Written Originally in Latin by the Famous Civilian Francis Hotoman, in the Year 1574 and Translated into English by the Author of the Account of Denmark, Second Edition (London, 1721)*, in Robert Molesworth, *An Account of Denmark with Francogallia and Some Considerations for the Promoting of Agriculture and Employing the Poor*, ed. Justin Champion (Indianapolis, IL: Liberty Fund, 2001), 171–90.

16 Macaulay to Capel Lofft, 12 November 1789, *The Correspondence of Catharine Macaulay*, ed. Karen Green (Oxford: Oxford University Press, 2019), 285: 'I never was a Trinitarian but I acknowledge to you that I Worship Jesus Christ as the Lord of all the human race and as a Being deserving of all the honours which God can confer on any of his Creatures.'

17 Sarah Hutton, 'Liberty, Equality and God: The Religious Roots of Catharine Macaulay's Feminism', in *Women, Gender and Enlightenment*, ed. S. Knott and B. Taylor (Basingstoke: Palgrave Macmillan, 2005), 538–50; Karen Green, *Catharine Macaulay's Republican Enlightenment* (New York: Routledge, 2020).

18 Catharine Macaulay, *An Address to the People of England, Scotland, and Ireland, on the Present Important Crisis of Affairs* (London: Edward and Charles Dilly, 1775), 2nd edn, 9.

19 Macaulay, *The History of England from the Accession of James I to the Elevation of the House of Hanover*, V, 383.

20 Ibid., 378–9.

21 Ibid., 380.

22 Ibid., 380–81.

23 Catharine Macaulay, *Loose Remarks on Certain Positions to Be Found in Mr. Hobbes's Philosophical Rudiments of Government and Society. With a Short Sketch of a Democratical Form of Government, in a Letter to Signior Paoli* (London: T. Davies, Robinson and Roberts, and T. Cadell, 1767).

24 Ibid., 35.

25 Peter D. G. Thomas, 'Sawbridge, John (1732–1795), politician', *Oxford Dictionary of National Biography Online.*

26 Robert Edge Pine, Catharine Macaulay, National Portrait Gallery, 5856. Macaulay's brother's portrait was destroyed but an engraving can be seen in H. von Erffa & A. Staley, *The Paintings of Benjamin West*, 1986, no. 694.

27 Catharine Macaulay, *Observations on a Pamphlet Entitled 'Thoughts on the Cause of the Present Discontents'* (London: Edward and Charles Dilly, 1770), 4th edn, 6–7.

28 Ibid., 12–13.

29 Ibid., 13.

30 Ibid., 14.

31 Ibid., 15–19.

32 Ibid., 31.

33 Ibid., 8–9.

34 Macaulay, *An Address to the People of England, Scotland, and Ireland, on the Present Important Crisis of Affairs*, 2nd edn, 6.

35 Ibid., 2nd edn, 11.

36 Ibid., 2nd edn, 10, 15.

37 Ibid., 18–19.

38 Ibid., 23–24. On Burgh, see Carla H. Hay, 'Burgh, James (1714–1775), educationist and author', *Oxford Dictionary of National Biography.*

39 Macaulay, *An Address to the People of England, Scotland, and Ireland, on the Present Important Crisis of Affairs*, 2nd edn, 26.

40 Ibid., 2nd edn, 29–30.

41 Macaulay, *A History of England, from the Revolution to the Present Time, in a Series of Letters to the Reverend Doctor Wilson* (Bath: R. Cruttwell, 1778), 2–6, 369–70.

42 Ibid., 421. On Walpole and opposition to him see Quentin Skinner, 'The Principles and Practice of Opposition: The Case of Bolingbroke versus Walpole', in Neil McKendrick, ed., *Historical Perspectives: Studies in English Thought and Society in Honour of J. H. Plumb* (London: Europa Publications, 1974), 93–128; Christine Gerrard, *The Patriot Opposition to Walpole: Politics, Poetry and National Myth, 1727–1742* (Oxford: Oxford University Press, 1994).

43 Macaulay, *A History of England, from the Revolution to the Present Time, in a Series of Letters to the Reverend Doctor Wilson*, 73–5, 378–9.

44 Ibid., 287–9.

45 Ibid., 351, 372.

46 Ibid., 314–15.

47 Ibid., 315.

48 Catharine Macaulay, *The History of England from the Accession of James I to the Revolution* (London: A. Hamilton, 1783), VIII, 334–5.

49 Ibid., 335.

50 James Burgh to Catharine Macaulay, 17 February 1769, *The Correspondence of Catharine Macaulay*, ed. Karen Green, 89.

51 Catharine Macaulay to James Burgh, 4 March 1769, Ibid., 90.

52 David Steuart Erskine to Catharine Macaulay, 2 July 1766, Ibid., 42.

53 Macaulay, *The History of England from the Accession of James I to the Revolution*, VIII, 335.

54 Ibid., 335–6.

55 On Chatham's popularity, see Carol Lynn H. Knight. 'A Certain Great Commoner: The Political Image of William Pitt, First Earl of Chatham, in the Colonial Press', *Proceedings of the American Philosophical Society* 123/2 (1979) 131–42; Jeremy Black, *Pitt the Elder* (Cambridge University Press, 1992).

56 Bolingbroke, *Letters on the Spirit of Patriotism: On the Idea of a Patriot King: And on the State of Parties, at the Accession of King George the First* (London: A. Millar, 1749). On Bolingbroke's politics and their context see Doohwan Ahn, 'From "Jealous Emulation" to "Cautious Politics": British Foreign Policy and Public Discourse in the Mirror of Ancient Athens (ca. 1730–ca. 1750)', in David Onnekink and Gijs Rommelse, eds., *Ideology and Foreign Policy in Early Modern Europe (1650–1750)* (Farnham: Ashgate, 2011), 93–130.

57 Macaulay, *The History of England from the Accession of James I to the Revolution*, VIII, 336.

58 Ibid.

59 Hamish M. Scott, 'The Seven Years War and Europe's "Ancien Régime"', *War in History* 18/4 (2011), 419–55.

60 Catharine Macaulay to John Collett Ryland, August 1773, *The Correspondence of Catharine Macaulay*, ed. Karen Green, 188.

61 Ibid., 189.

62 Catharine Macaulay to Henry Marchant, 22 October 1774, Ibid., 147.

63 The American Commissioners to Charles-Guillaume-Frédéric Dumas, 10 April 1778, *Benjamin Franklin Papers Online*. See also James R. Tanis, 'The Dutch-American Connection: The Impact of "The Dutch Example" on American Constitutional Beginnings', in Stephen L. Schecter and Richard B. Bernstein, eds., *New York and the Union: Contributions to the American Constitutional Experience* (Albany NY: New York State Commission on the Bicentennial of the United States Constitution, 1990), 22–8.

64 For Pufendorf's critique of republics see his *An Introduction to the History of the Principal Kingdoms and States of Europe*, trans. Jodocus Crull, (Indianapolis IL: Liberty Fund, 2013), ed. Michael J. Seidler 299–307. On Pufendorf, see Timothy J. Hochstrasser, *Natural Law Theories in the Early Enlightenment* (Cambridge: Cambridge University Press, 2000); Knud Haakonssen, 'Between God and Nature: Pufendorf on Power and Liberty' January 3 2017, and Ian Hunter, 'Response to Haakonssen' Posted: January 5 2017, https://oll.libertyfund.org/pages/lm-pufendorf

65 Carla H. Hay, 'Catharine Macaulay and the American Revolution', *Historian* 56/2 (1993), 301–16.

66 James B. Bell, *The Imperial Origins of the King's Church in Early America, 1607–1783* (Basingstoke: Palgrave, 2004) and *A War of Religion: Dissenters, Anglicans, and the American Revolution* (Basingstoke: Palgrave, 2008).

67 Carla H. Hay, 'John Sawbridge and "Popular Politics" in Late Eighteenth-Century Britain', *Historian* 52/4 (1990), 551–65.

68 John Adams to Catharine Macaulay, 28 December 1774, *The Correspondence of Catharine Macaulay*, ed. Karen Green, 123.

69 Gordon S. Wood, *The Creation of the American Republic, 1776–1787* (Chapel Hill NC: University of North Carolina Press, 1969) and *The Radicalism of the American Revolution* (New York: Knopf, 1992).

70 Dwight Boehm and Edward Schwartz, 'Jefferson and the Theory of Degeneracy', *American Quarterly* 9/4 (1957), 448–53; Manuela Albertone, *National Identity and the Agrarian Republic: The Transatlantic Commerce of Ideas between America and France (1750–1830)* (Farnham: Ashgate, 2014), 85–94; Mark Somos, *American States of Nature: The Origins of Independence 1761–1775* (New York: Oxford University Press, 2019).

71 Samuel Adams to John Scollay, 30 December 1780, *The Writings of Samuel Adams*, ed. Harry Alonzo Cushing (New York: G. P. Putnam's Sons, 1904–08), 4 vols., IV, 236–8.

72 Adam Smith, *An Inquiry into the Nature and Causes of the Wealth of Nations*, ed. R. H. Campbell, A. S. Skinner and R. B. Todd, V, iii. 90, II, 944.

73 Eric Nelson, *The Royalist Revolution: Monarchy and the American Founding* (Cambridge, MA: Harvard University Press, 2014). Macaulay fits Nelson's interpretation very well in her desire to give near unlimited power to patriotic heroes like Chatham.

74 Condorcet, *Vie de Turgot* (London: n. p., 1786), 259–60. The translation is from *The Life of M. Turgot, Comptroller General of the Finances of France, in the Years 1774, 1775 and 1776*, 341.

75 Gilbert Chinard, *L'Amérique et le rêve exotique dans la littérature française au XVIIe et XVIIIe siècle* (Paris: Hachette, 1913).

76 Durand Echeverria, *Mirage in the West: A History of the French Image of American Society to 1815* (Princeton NJ: Princeton University Press, 1957).

77 Catharine Macaulay to George Washington, June 1790, *The Correspondence of Catharine Macaulay*, ed. Karen Green, 278.

78 Catharine Macaulay to Mercy Otis Warren, April 1790, ibid., 171.

79 William Winterbotham, *An Historical, Geographical, Commercial, and Philosophical View of the American United States, and of the European Settlements in America and the West-Indies* (New York: John Reid, 1796), 4 vols., I, 364.

80 James Wilson and Thomas McKean, *Commentaries on the Constitution of the United States of America: With that Constitution Prefixed, in Which are Unfolded, the Principles of Free Government, and the Superior Advantages of Republicanism Demonstrated* (London: J. Debrett, 1792), 127.

81 Thomas Branagan, *Serious Remonstrances, Addressed to the Citizens of the Northern States, and Their Representatives: Being an Appeal to Their Natural Feelings & Common Sense; Consisting of Speculations and Animadversions, on the Recent Revival of the Slave Trade, in the American Republic: With an Investigation Relative to the Consequent Evils Resulting to the Citizens of the Northern States from That Event. Interspersed with a Simplified Plan for Colonizing the Free Negroes of the Northern, in Conjunction with Those Who Have, or May Emigrate from the Southern States, in a Distant Part of the National Territory: Considered as the Only Possible Means of Avoiding the Deleterious Evils Attendant on Slavery in a Republic* (Philadelphia: Thomas T. Stiles, 1805), 100.

82 Ronald Meek, *Social Science and the Ignoble Savage* (Cambridge: Cambridge University Press, 1976); István Hont, 'Adam Smith's History of Law and Government as Political Theory', in Richard Bourke and Raymond Geuss, eds., *Political Judgement: Essays for John Dunn* (Cambridge: Cambridge University Press, 2009), 131–71.

83 David Ramsay, *The History of the American Revolution* (London: n. p., 1790), 2 vols., II, 58.

84 Edward Cooke, *Arguments for and against an Union between Great Britain and Ireland Considered* (London: John Stockdale, 1798), 12.

85 Charles Brockden Brown, 'Thoughts on the Probable Duration of the American Republic', *Literary Magazine, and American Register* 2/9 (9 June 1804), 215–16.

86 Ibid.,

87 Eliga H. Gould, *Among the Powers of the Earth: The American Revolution and the Making of a New World Empire* (Cambridge MA: Harvard University Press, 2012).

88 Delba Winthrop, 'Tocqueville on Federalism', *Publius* 6/3, (1976), 93–115.

89 Hume to David Hume the Younger, 8 December 1775, *The Letters of David Hume*, II, 306.

90 Catharine Macaulay, *The History of England; From the Revolution to the Present Time in a Series of Letters to a Friend* (Bath: R. Cruttwell, 1778), 2 vols., I, 78.

91 David Hume to Catharine Macaulay, 29 March 1764, *The Correspondence of Catharine Macaulay*, ed., Karen Green, 38.

92 Karen Green, 'Catharine Macaulay as Critic of Hume', in *Rethinking the Enlightenment*, ed. Martin Lloyd and Geoff Bowden (Lanham MD: Lexington Books, 2018), 113–30.

93 Alan M. S. J. Coffee, 'Catharine Macaulay's Republican Conception of Social and Political Liberty', *Political Studies* 65/4 (2017), 844–59.

94 Hume to David Hume the Younger, 8 December 1775, *The Letters of David Hume*, II, 306. On Harrington's influence in Britain and France, see Rachel Hammersley, *The English Republican Tradition and Eighteenth-Century France*; *James Harrington: An Intellectual Biography* (Oxford: Oxford University Press, 2019).

95 Macaulay, *Observations on the Reflections of the Right Hon. Edmund Burke, on the Revolution in France: In a Letter to the Right Hon. the Earl of Stanhope* (London: C. Dilly, 1790).

96 Catharine Macaulay to Samuel Adams, 1 March 1791, *The Correspondence of Catharine Macaulay*, ed., Karen Green, 217.

97 Jean Egret, *La révolution des notables: Mounier et les monarchiens, 1789* (Paris: A. Colin, 1950); Aurelian Craiutu, 'The Radical Moderates of 1789: The Tragic Middle of the French Monarchiens', in *A Virtue for Courageous Minds: Moderation in French Political Thought, 1748–1830* (Princeton NJ and Oxford: Princeton University Press, 2012), 69–110; Pestel Friedemann, 'Monarchiens et monarchie en exil: Conjontures de la monarchie dans l'émigration française, 1792–1799', *Annales Historiques de la Révolution Française*, 382 (2015), 3–29.

98 Hill, *The Republican Virago: The Life and Times of Catharine Macaulay, Historian*, 128–9.

5. Edward Gibbon and the End of the Republics

1 Patricia Craddock, *Edward Gibbon, Luminous Historian 1772–1794* (Baltimore, ML and London: Johns Hopkins University Press, 1989); Peter Ghosh, 'Gibbon Observed', *Journal of Roman Studies* 81 (1991), 132–56; 'The Conception of Gibbon's *History*', in R. McKitterick and

R. Quinault, eds., *Edward Gibbon and Empire* (Cambridge: Cambridge University Press, 1997), 271–316; J. G. A. Pocock, *Barbarism and Religion, Vol. I: The Enlightenments of Edward Gibbon 1737–1764* (1999); *Vol. II: Narratives of Civil Government* (1999), *Vol. III: The First Decline and Fall* (2003); *Vol. IV: Barbarians, Savages and Empires* (2005), *Vol. V: Religion: – The First Triumph* (2010), *Vol. VI: Barbarism – The Triumph in the West* (2015; all Cambridge: Cambridge University Press); David Womersley, *Gibbon and the 'Watchmen of the Holy City': The Historian and His Reputation, 1776–1815* (Oxford: Clarendon Press, 2002) and, ed. with John Burrow and John Pocock, *Edward Gibbon: Bicentenary Essays* (Oxford: Voltaire Foundation, 1997). Womersley, introduction to Edward Gibbon, *The History of the Decline and Fall of the Roman Empire*, ed. Womersley, (London: Allen Lane, Penguin Press, 1994), vols.

2 Pocock, *Barbarism and Religion, Vol. 1: The Enlightenments of Edward Gibbon, 1737–1764* (Cambridge: Cambridge University Press, 2001), 50–71, 167–274.

3 Patricia Craddock, *Young Edward Gibbon: Gentleman of Letters* (Baltimore, ML and London: Johns Hopkins University Press, 1982). The following section is greatly indebted to the work of my good friend Professor Béla Kapossy of the University of Lausanne and our 'Gibbon and Republicanism', in *The Cambridge Companion to Edward Gibbon*, ed. Karen O'Brien and Brian Young (Cambridge: Cambridge University Press, 2018), 28–46.

4 Henri Vuilleumier, *Histoire de l'Église réformée du Pays de Vaud sous le régime bernois* (Lausanne: La Concorde, 1927–33), vol. IV.

5 Edward Gibbon, *Memoirs of My Life*, 86. See further Béla Kapossy and Béatrice Lovis, eds., *Edward Gibbon et Lausanne: Le pays de vaud à la rencontre des lumières européennes* (Gollion: Infolio éditions, 2022).

6 Patricia B. Craddock, *Young Edward Gibbon: Gentleman of Letters* (Baltimore: Johns Hopkins University Press, 1982), 52–120; Michel Baridon, *Edward Gibbon et le mythe de Rome: Histoire et idéologie au siècle des Lumières* (Paris: Honoré Champion, 1977), 41–64, 80–124; Ernest Giddey, 'Gibbon à Lausanne', in Pierre Ducrey, ed., *Gibbon et Rome à la lumières de l'historiographie moderne* (Geneva: Droz, 1977) 23–45; Giuseppe Giarrizzo, *Edward Gibbon e la cultura europea del settecento*

(Naples: Istituto per gli Studi Storici, 1954); Girolamo Imbruglia, ed., *Ragione e immaginazione: Edward Gibbon e la storiografia europea del Settecento* (Naples: Liguori, 1996); Edward Gibbon, *Essai sur l'étude de la litterature: A Critical Edition*, ed. *Robort Manllin* (Oxford: Voltaire Foundation, 2010).

7 Ernest Giddey, *L'Angleterre dans la vie intellectuelle de la Suisse romande au XVIIIe siècle* (Lausanne: Bibliothèque historique vaudoise, 1974).

8 Gibbon, *Memoirs of My Life*, 210.

9 William and Clara de Charrière de Sévery, *La vie de société dans le Pays de Vaud à la fin du dix-huitième siècle: Salomon et Catherine de Charrière de Sévery et leurs amis* (Lausanne: George Bridel, 1911–12), 2 vols.; Georges-Alfred Bonnard, 'L'importance du deuxième séjour de Gibbon à Lausanne dans la formation de l'historien', in Louis Junod and Sven Stelling-Michaud, eds., *Mélanges d'histoire et de littérature offerts à Monsieur Charles Gilliard* (Lausanne : F. Rouge, 1944), 401–20; Brian Norman, *The Influence of Switzerland on the Life and Writings of Edward Gibbon* (Oxford: Voltaire Foundation, 2002).

10 Maria-Cristina Pitassi, *De l'orthodoxie aux lumières: Genève 1670–1737* (Geneva: Labor et Fides, 1992); Martin I. Klauber, 'The Drive toward Protestant Union in Early Eighteenth-Century Geneva: Jean-Alphonse Turrettini on the "Fundamental Articles" of the Faith', *Church History* 61 (1992), 334–49; Jennifer Powell McNutt, *Calvin Meets Voltaire: The Clergy of Geneva in the Age of Enlightenment, 1685–1798* (Farnham: Ashgate, 2013).

11 Abraham Stanyan, *An Account of Switzerland: Written in the Year 1714* (London: Jacob Tonson, 1714), 191.

12 William Coxe, *Sketches of the Natural, Civil, and Political State of Swisserland; In a Series of Letters to William Melmoth, Esq.* (London: J. Dodsley, 1779).

13 John Campbell, *The Present State of Europe*, 3rd edn (London: Thomas Longam et al., 1752), 466.

14 Gisela Bock, Quentin Skinner and Maurizio Viroli, eds., *Machiavelli and Republicanism* (Cambridge: Cambridge University Press, 1990); Paul Rahe, *Republics: Ancient and Modern* (Chapel Hill, NC: University

of North Carolina Press, 1992); Martin van Gelderen and Quentin Skinner, eds., *Republicanism: A Shared European Heritage* (Cambridge: Cambridge University Press, 2002), 2 vols.

15 Béla Kapossy, *Iselin contra Rousseau: Sociable Patriotism and the History of Mankind* (Basel: Schwabe Verlag, 2006); André Holenstein, Thomas Maissen and Maarten Prak, *The Republican Alternative: The Netherlands and Switzerland Compared* (Amsterdam: Amsterdam University Press, 2008).

16 E.H. Kossmann, 'Dutch Republicanism', in Franco Venturi, *L'età dei Lumi: Studi storici sul settecento europeo in onore di Franco Venturi* (Naples: Jovene, 1985), 2 vols., I, 453–86; Margaret C. Jacob and Wijnand W. Mijnhardt, eds., *The Dutch Republic in the Eighteenth Century: Decline, Enlightenment, and Revolution* (Ithaca, NY: Cornell University Press, 1992); Jacques Berchtold and Michel Porret, eds., *Être riche au siècle de Voltaire: Actes du colloque de Genève, 18–19 juin 1994* (Geneva: Droz, 1996); Michael Böhler, Etienne Hofmann and Simone Zurbuchen, eds., *Republikanische Tugend: Ausbildung eines Schweizer Nationalbewusstseins und Erziehung eines neuen Bürgers – Actes du 16e colloque de l'Académie suisse des sciences humaines et sociales* (Geneva: Slatkine, 2000).

17 Gasparo Contarini, Sebastiano Erizzo, Nicolò Crasso, Bartolomeo Cavalcanti and Donato Giannotti, *Della Republica, et magistrati di Venetia. Libri cinque di M. Gasparo Contarini, che fu poi cardinale. Con vn ragionamento intorno alla medesima di M. Donato Gianotti fiorentino. Colle annotazioni sopra li due sudetti auttori* [sic] *di Nicolo Crasso, et I discorsi de' gouerni ciuili di M. Sebastiano Erizzo, & 15 discorsi di M. Bartolomeo Caualcanti, aggiuntoui vn discorso dell'eccellenza delle republiche. All'illustriss. & eccellentis. sig. il sig. Giovanni di Zamoscia Zamoiski* (Venice: Francesco Storti, 1650).

18 Wyger Velema and Arthur Weststeijn, eds., *Ancient Models in the Early Modern Republican Imagination* (Leiden: Brill, 2017).

19 Edward Gibbon, *Miscellanea gibboniana: Journal de mon voyage dans quelques endroits de la Suisse, 1755*, ed., Georges A. Bonnard, Gavin De Beer, Louis Junod (Lausanne: Librairie de l'Université, 1952), 12, 18, 33, 38, 41, 61, 64.

20 Brian Norman, *The Influence of Switzerland*, 88–94. ADD

21 Edward Gibbon, *Miscellaneous Works of Edward Gibbon, Esquire with Memoirs of His Life and Writings, Composed by Himself*, ed. John Lord Sheffield (London: A. Strahan and T. Cadell Jun. and W. Davies, 1796), 2 vols., I, 132.

22 Algernon Sidney, *Discourses concerning Government: By Algernon Sidney, Esq; to Which Are Added, Memoirs of His Life, and an Apology for Himself, both Now First Published* (London: A. Millar, 1751), 3rd edn, frontispiece and vii. The frontispiece appears in the second edition of 1704 published at London by John Darby.

23 Gibbon, *Memoirs of My Life*, 142.

24 Gibbon, *The Miscellaneous Works of Edward Gibbon, Vol. 3* (London: John Murray, 1814), 239–30.

25 Ibid., 252: 'La liberté lui étoit chère, et cette independence qui nait de l'égalité des fortunes et du sentiment de ses forces, étoit le premier resort de son âme'.

26 Ibid., 283: 'spectacle plus rare et plus digne de la nature humaine'.

27 Ibid., 299: 'Le négociant sent que des hommes libres par leur nature sont unis par leurs vesoins réciproques. L'esprit du commerce ne peut fleurir qu'à l'ombre des loix.'

28 On Bern see Béla Kapossy, 'Bern und das Europa der Aufklärung', in *Cercle de Grande Société 1759–2009*, ed. G. von Erlach (Bern: Licorne Verlag, 2010), 15–31, and 'Neo-Roman Republicanism and Commercial Society: The Example of Eighteenth-Century Berne', in Quentin Skinner and Martin van Gelderen, eds., *Republicanism: A Shared European Heritage* (Cambridge: Cambridge University Press, 2002), 2 vols., II, 227–47; Stefan Altorfer-Ong, *Staatsbildung ohne Steuern: Politische Ökonomie und Staatsfinenzen im Bern des 18. Jahrhunderts* (Baden: Hier und Jetzt, 2010).

29 Graham Nattrass, 'The Swiss War of 1812 in contemporary sources', *British Library Journal* 19/1 (1993), 11–33.

30 Charles de Secondat, baron de Montesquieu, *Œuvres Complètes*, ed. Roger Caillois (Paris: Gallimard, 1949–51), 2 vols., II, 120.

31 Edward Gibbon, *Miscellanea gibboniana: Journal de mon voyage dans quelques endroits de la Suisse, 1755*, 56.

32 Ibid., 58.

33 Gibbon, 'La Lettre de Gibbon sur le gouvernement de Berne', Ibid.;
    cf., Brian Norman, *The Influence of Switzerland*, 21–32.

34 Pierre Morren, *La vie lausannoise au XVIIIe siècle, d'après Jean Henri
    Polier de Vernand, lieutenant baillival* (Geneva: Labor et Fides, 1970), 110.

35 Regula Wyss and Martin Stuber, 'Paternalism and Agricultural
    Reform: The Economic Society of Bern in the Eighteenth Century',
    in Koen Stapelbroek and Jan Marjanen, eds., *The Rise of Economic Soci-
    eties in the Eighteenth Century* (London: Palgrave Macmillan, 2012),
    157–81. See also, Kapossy, *Iselin contra Rousseau: Sociable Patriotism and
    the History of Mankind* (Basel: Schwabe, 2006) 103–72.

36 Gibbon, *Miscellanea gibboniana. Journal de mon voyage dans quelques
    endroits de la Suisse, 1755*, 124: 'on ose penser et l'on sache vivre'.

37 Ibid., 131: 'Des Barbares ils sont devenus civilises, d'ignorans éclairés,
    et de pauvres, riches. Je vois des villes où il y avoit des deserts et les
    forets defrichées se sont converties en champs fertils.'

38 Ibid., 130: 'le fonds de cette Constitution est demeuré dans toutes les
    revolutions, et rien de plus libre que ce fonds. Ces états, leurs mem-
    bres et leurs droits se conserverent toujours et par-tout, et par-tout ils
    étoient les mêmes.'

39 Ibid., 126: 'chaque ordre de Citoyens, chaque partie de l'état y ait ses
    representants interessés à s'opposer à toute loi qui fut nuisible à ses
    droits, ou contraite à son Bonheur, puisqu'eux-mêmes en sentiroient
    les premiers ses mauvais effets.'

40 Edmund Burke, *Reflections on the Revolution in France* (London: J. Dod-
    sley, 1791), 8th edn, 288.

41 Gibbon, *Memoirs of My Life*, 185.

42 Ibid., 184–5.

43 Holroyd to William Eden, 22 August 1787, *The Journal and Correspond-
    ence of William Lord Auckland* (London: Richard Bentley, 1861), 2 vols.,
    I, 436.

44 Edward Gibbon to Dorothea Gibbon, 6 June 1780, *The Letters of
    Edward Gibbon*, ed., J. E. Norton (London: Cassell, 1956), 3 vols., II, 242.

45 Gibbon to Dorothea Gibbon, 8 June 1780, Ibid., 243.

46 Ibid.

47 Pocock, *Barbarism and Religion: Vol. 6, Triumph in the West* (Cambridge: Cambridge University Press, 2015). See also, Brian Young, ' "Scepticism in Excess": Gibbon and Eighteenth-Century Christianity', *Historical Journal* 41 (1998), 179–99; 'John Jortin, ecclesiastical history, and the Christian republic of letters, *Historical Journal* 55 (2012), 961–81.

48 Gibbon to Thomas Cadell, 17 November 1790, *The Letters of Edward Gibbon*, III, 210. Gibbon noted on mentioning Smith that, 'I heard of his death with more concern than surprise. What a loss to letters, philosophy, and mankind!'.

49 Gibbon to Holroyd, 5 February 1791, Ibid., 216.

50 Gibbon to Holroyd, 31 May 1791, Ibid., 229–30.

51 Womersley, 'Gibbon's Unfinished History: The French Revolution and English Political Vocabularies', *Historical Journal* 35 (1992), 63–89.

52 Gibbon to Holroyd, 25 September 1789, *The Letters of Edward Gibbon*, III, 171.

53 Gibbon to Dorothea Gibbon, 6 December 1789, *ibid.*, 176.

54 Gibbon, *Memoirs of My Life: Edited from the Manuscripts by Georges A. Bonnard* (London: Thomas Nelson, 1969), 86.

55 Gibbon to Lord Chancellor Loughborough, 23 February, 1793, *The Letters of Edward Gibbon* III, 321–2: 'a valuable testimony of his esteem for our constitution; and the testimony of a sagacious and impartial stranger may have taught some of our countrymen to value the political blessings which they have been tempted to despise.'

56 Gibbon to Alexander Wedderburn, Baron Loughborough, 23 February 1793, Ibid., 321–2.

57 Gibbon to Holroyd, 4 April 1792, Ibid., 253.

58 Ibid., 254.

59 Gibbon to Dorothea Gibbon, 18 May 1791, Ibid., 227.

60 Gibbon to Holroyd, 1 January 1793, Ibid., 308.

61 Ibid., 308.

62 Gibbon to Holroyd, 30 May 1792, Ibid., 258.

63 J. G. A. Pocock, 'Gibbon and the Invention of Gibbon: Chapters 15 and 16 Reconsidered', *History of European Ideas* 35 (2009), 209–16.

64 Amos Hofman, 'Opinion, Illusion, and the Illusion of Opinion: Barruel's Theory of Conspiracy', *Eighteenth-Century Studies* 27/1 (1993), 27–60; Michael Taylor, 'British Conservatism, the Illuminati, and the Conspiracy Theory of the French Revolution, 1797–1802', *Eighteenth-Century Studies* 47/3 (2014), 293–312.

65 Robert Hall, *Modern Infidelity Considered with Respect to Its Influence on Society: In a Sermon, Preached at the Baptist Meeting, Cambridge* (Cambridge: M. Watson, 1800), 41–2.

66 Ibid., 42–3.

67 Ibid., 63.

68 John Campbell, *The Perpetual Duration of Christianity Established by Historic Proof: A Sermon Preached before the Society in Scotland, for Propagating Christian Knowledge, at Their Anniversary Meeting, Thursday, 5th June 1800* (Edinburgh: J. Ritchie, 1801), 32–3, citing, 'On the infidelity of Mr. Gibbon', *Evangelical* magazine, November 1798.

69 Arthur Young, *The Autobiography of Arthur Young with Selections from His Correspondence*, ed. M. Betham-Edwards (London: Smith, Elder & Co., 1898), 258–9.

70 Burke to the Abbé Barruel, 1 May 1797, *The Correspondence of Edmund Burke*, ed. Thomas W. Copeland, Peter J. Marshall, John A. Woods et al. (Cambridge, and Chocago, IL: Cambridge University Press and University of Chicago Press; 1958–1978), 10 vols., X, 39.

71 David Womersley, 'Gibbon's *Memoirs*: Autobiography in Time of Revolution', in *Gibbon: Bicentenary Essays*, ed. D. J. Womersley (Oxford: The Voltaire Foundation, 1997), 347–405, and *Gibbon and the 'Watchmen of the Holy City': The Historian and His Reputation, 1776–1814* (Oxford: Oxford University Press, 2002).

72 Holroyd to Eden, 10 May 1786, *The Journal and Correspondence of William Lord Auckland*, I, 371.

73 Gibbon to Holroyd, 23 August 1792, *The Letters of Edward Gibbon*, III, 268.

74 Gibbon to Holroyd, 12 September 1792, Ibid., 269.

75 Gibbon to Holroyd, 4 April 1792, Ibid., 254.

76 Gibbon to Holroyd, 30 May 1792, Ibid., 257.

77 Holroyd to Gibbon, 17 October 1792, *The Private Letters of Edward Gibbon* (London: John Murray, 1896), 2 vols., II, 321.

78 Gibbon to Holroyd, 5 October 1792, *The Letters of Edward Gibbon*, III, 276.

79 Gibbon to Holroyd, 13 October 1792, *The* Ibid., 280.

80 Gibbon to Holroyd, 10 November 1792, Ibid., 291.

81 Gibbon to Holroyd, 25 November 1792, Ibid., 303.

82 Gibbon to Holroyd, 18 February 1793, Ibid., 319.

83 Ibid.

84 Ibid.

85 Gibbon to Lady Elizabeth Foster, 4 May 1793, Ibid., 329.

86 Gibbon, *Miscellaneous Works of Edward Gibbon, Esquire: With Memoirs of his Life and Writings, Composed by Himself*, I, 181.

87 Ibid.

6. Edmund Burke and the End of Europe

1 J. G. A. Pocock, *The Machiavellian Moment: Florentine Political Thought and the Atlantic Republican Tradition* (Princeton, NJ: Princeton University Press, 2016 [1975]), 423–61.

2 E. A. Reitan, 'The Civil List in Eighteenth-Century British Politics: Parliamentary Supremacy versus the Independence of the Crown', *Historical Journal* 9/3 (1966), 318–37; Thomas W. Copeland, 'The Reputation of Edmund Burke', *Journal of British Studies* 1/2 (1962), 78–90; F. P. Lock, 'Unpublished Burke Letters (III), 1763–96', *English Historical Review* 118/478 (2003), 940–82.

3 Edmund Burke, *Letter to a Noble Lord: The Writings and Speeches of Edmund Burke*, ed. Paul Langford, William B. Todd, P. J Marshall et al. (Oxford: Clarendon Press, 1981–1997), 9 vols., IX, 165.

4 Nicholas Robinson, *Edmund Burke: A Life in Caricature* (New Haven, CT and London: Yale University Press, 1996); Jonathan M. Pettinato, 'Jeers, Jingo, and Jesuits: Britishness, Edmund Burke, and Crises of Empire in Eighteenth-Century Britain', *Eighteenth-Century Ireland / Iris an Dá Chultúr* 30 (2015), 93–121.

5 F. P. Lock, *Edmund Burke I: 1730–1784* (Oxford: Oxford University Press, 1998).

6 J. G. A. Pocock, 'The Political Economy of Burke's Analysis of the French Revolution', in *Virtue, Commerce and History: Essays on Political Thought and History, Chiefly in the Eighteenth Century*, 193–212; 'Edmund Burke and the Redefinition of Enthusiasm: The Context as Counter-Revolution', in F. Furet and M. Ozouf, eds., *The French Revolution and the Creation of Modern Political Culture, Vol. Three: The Transformation of Political Culture 1789–1848* (Oxford: Pergamon, 1990), 19–43.

7 Edmund Burke to the Duke of Richmond, 17 November 1772, *The Correspondence of Edmund Burke*, ed. T. W. Copeland et al., (Chicago, IL: Chicago University Press, 1958–78), 10 vols.

8 Richard Bourke, *Empire and Revolution: The Political Life of Edmund Burke* (Princeton, NJ: Princeton University Press, 2015), 247n.

9 Compare F. Canovan, *The Political Economy of Edmund Burke: The Role of Property in His Thought* (New York: Fordham University Press, 1995), 6, 13–15, 116–17, 158, and Donald Winch, *Riches and Poverty: An Intellectual History of Political Economy in Britain, 1750–1834* (Cambridge: Cambridge University Press, 1996), 170–220.

10 J. C. D. Clark, Introduction to Burke, *Reflections on the Revolution in France* (Stanford, CA: Stanford University Press, 2001); Ryu Susato, 'The Idea of Chivalry in the Scottish Enlightenment: The Case of David Hume', *Hume Studies 33* (2007), 155–78; Sora Sato, *Edmund Burke as Historian: War, Order and Civilisation* (London: Palgrave Macmillan, 2017). Note that references to Burke's *Reflections on the Revolution in France* are to *Writings and Speeches*, VIII, 53–293.

11 Richard Bourke, *Empire and Revolution: The Political Life of Edmund Burke*, 140, 108n, 181.

12 Edmund Burke, *Reflections, Writings and Speeches*, VIII, 130.

13 Ibid., 57.

14 Edmund Burke, *A Vindication of Natural Society, Writings and Speeches*, I, 129–84.

15 William Burke and Edmund Burke, *An Account of the European Settlements in America: In Six Parts* (London: R. and J. Dodsley, 1757), 2 vols., II, 22–4, 38–48, 284–5.

16 William Knox, *The Present State of the Nation: Particularly with Respect to Its Trade, Finances &c.* (London: J. Almon, 1769), 34–6, 71.

17 Burke, *Observations on a late Present State of the Nation*, *Writings and Speeches*, II, 112.

18 Ibid., 112, 116.

19 Ibid., 151.

20 Ibid., 175.

21 Burke, *Thoughts on the Cause of the Present Discontents*, *Writings and Speeches*, II, 252-3.

22 Ibid., 262.

23 Ibid., 256.

24 Ibid., 253.

25 Ibid., 274, 283.

26 Ibid., 284–5.

27 Edmund Burke to Charles Watson-Wentworth, 2nd Marquess of Rockingham, 23 August 1775, *Correspondence of Edmund Burke*, III, 189–96.

28 Burke to Adrian Heinrich von Borcke, 17 January 1774, Ibid., II, 512–14. For Burke's highly significant fascination with Poland, see Anna Plassart, 'Edmund Burke, Poland, and the Commonwealth of Europe', *Historical Journal* 63/4 (2020), 885–910.

29 Burke, 'Speech of Edmund Burke, Esq. on presenting to the House of Commons (on the 11th of February 1780) a Plan for the Better Security of the Independence of Parliament, and the Oeconomical Reformation of the Civil and Other Establishments', *Writings and Speeches*, III, 486–90.

30 Burke to Rockingham, 23 August 1775, *Correspondence of Edmund Burke*, III, 189–196.

31 Burke, 'Speech on Irish Trade, House of Commons, 6 May 1778', *Writings and Speeches*, IX, 522.

32 Burke, 'Speech on Declaratory Resolution', 3 February 1766, Ibid., 45–51; 'Speech on American Taxation', 19 April 1774, Ibid., 429–32, 460–62.

33 Burke to the Duke of Richmond, 26 September 1775, *Correspondence of Edmund Burke*, III, 219.

34 Burke, 'Speech on the Use of Indians', 6 February 1778, Ibid. *Speeches*, III, 356.

35 Burke, 'Speech on Restoring Lord Pigot', 22 May 1777, Ibid., V, 40.

36 P. J. Marshall, 'The Personal Fortune of Warren Hastings', *Economic History Review* 17/2 (1964), 284–300.

37 Burke, 'Speech on Nabob of Arcot's Debts', *Writings and Speeches*, VI, 491–2.

38 F. P. Lock, *Edmund Burke, Vol. 2: 1784–1797* (Oxford: Oxford University Press, 2006).

39 William Dent, 'Alexander the Great Conquering all the World', 1788 (British Museum Collections).

40 James Sayers, 'Carlo Khan's Triumphal Entry into Leadenhall Street', 5 December 1783, British Museum Collections Online.

41 Burke to William Baker, 22 June 1784, *Correspondence of Edmund Burke*, V, 154.

42 Burke to Charles-Jean-François Depont, November 1789, Ibid., VI, 41–2.

43 Burke, *Appeal from the New to the Old Whigs* (1791), *Writings and Speeches*, IV, 365–477.

44 Burke, *Thoughts on French Affairs* (1791), *Writings and Speeches*, VIII, 174, 369–72.

45 Burke, *Reflections on the Revolution in France*, *Writings and Speeches*, VIII, 253–9.

46 Burke to Sir Philip Francis, 20 February 1790, *Correspondence of Edmund Burke*, VI, 188–92.

47 Thomas Mercer to Edmund Burke, 19 February 1790, Ibid., 93.

48 Burke to Thomas Mercer, 26 February 1790, Ibid., 93–4.

49 Linda M. G. Zerilli, 'The "Furies of Hell": Woman in Burke's "French Revolution"', in *Signifying Woman: Culture and Chaos in Rousseau, Burke, and Mill* (New York: Cornell University Press, 1994), 60–94.

50 Burke, *Reflections*, *Writings and Speeches*, VIII, 127.

51 Burke to Edmund Sexton Pery, 18 July 1778, *The Correspondence of Edmund Burke*, IV, 5–10.

52 Burke to Richard Bright, 8–9 May 1789, Ibid., V, 470–71.

53 Burke to Richard Bright, 18 February 1790, Ibid., VI, 82–4.

54 Burke to Henry Dundas, 1st Viscount Melville, 30 September 1791, ibid., 419–20.

55 Burke, *Second Letter on a Regicide Peace* (1796), *Writings and Speeches*, IX, 265.

56 Burke, *First Letter on a Regicide Peace* (1796), ibid., 219.

57 David Bromwich, *The Intellectual Life of Edmund Burke* (Cambridge, MA: Harvard University Press, 2014).

58 Burke, *The Correspondence of Edmund Burke*, VI, 238–9

59 Ibid., VIII, 254.

60 Robert Bisset, *The Life of Edmund Burke: Comprehending an Impartial Account of His Literary and Political Efforts, and a Sketch of the Conduct and Character of His Most Eminent Associates, Coadjutors, and Opponents* (London: George Cawthorn, 1800), 2 vols. See also, Richard Bourke, *Empire and Revolution: The Political Life of Edmund Burke*.

61 Burke, *Reflections, Writings and Speeches*, VIII, 130–31.

62 Ibid., 290.

63 Burke, 'A Letter to a Member of the National Assembly, François-Louis, Thibault de Menonville (May 1791)', ibid., 297.

64 Jesse Norman, *Edmund Burke: Philosopher, Politician, Prophet* (London: William Collins, 2013); Gregory M. Collins, *Commerce and Manners in Edmund Burke's Political Economy* (Cambridge: Cambridge University Press, 2020).

65 Burke, *Third Letter on a Regicide Peace* (1797), *Writings and Speeches*, IX, 351.

66 Burke to William Wyndam Grenville, 1st Baron Grenville, 19 September 1792, ibid., 217.

67 Burke to William Wyndam Grenville, 1st Baron Grenville, 18 August 1792, *The Correspondence of Edmund Burke*, VII, 177.

68 Burke to Richard Burke, 17 October 1792, ibid., 271–2.

69 Burke, *First Letter on a Regicide Peace* (1796), *Writings and Speeches*, IX, 190–91.

70 Burke to French Laurence, 12 May 1797, *The Correspondence of Edmund Burke*, IX, 332.

71 Edmund Burke, *Three Memorials on French Affairs: Written in the Years 1791, 1792 and 1793* (Dublin: 1797), 53.

72 Burke, *First Letter on a Regicide* (1796), *Writings and Speeches*, IX, 191.

73 Richard Burke to William Wentworth-Fitzwilliam, 4th Earl Fitzwilliam, 29 July 1790, *The Correspondence of Edmund Burke*, VI, 125–30.

74 Burke to William Wentworth-Fitzwilliam, 4th Earl Fitzwilliam, 5 June 1791, ibid., 273.

75 Burke, *First Letter on a Regicide* (1796), *Writings and Speeches*, IX, 199.

76 Burke to French Laurence, 12 May 1797, *The Correspondence of Edmund Burke*, IX, 333.

77 Burke, *First Letter on a Regicide Peace* (1796), *Writings and Speeches*, IX, 192.

78 Peter J. Stanlis, 'Edmund Burke and the Law of Nations', *American Journal of International Law* 47/3 (1953), 397–413; David Armitage, 'Edmund Burke and Reason-of-State', *Journal of the History of Ideas* 61/4 (2000), 617–34; Iain Hampsher-Monk, 'Edmund Burke's Changing Justification for Intervention', *Historical Journal* 48/1 (2005), 65–100; Richard Bourke, 'Edmund Burke and the Politics of Conquest', *Modern Intellectual History* 4/3 (2007), 403–32; Anna Plassart, 'Edmund Burke, Poland and the Commonwealth of Europe', *Historical Journal* details.

79 Burke, *First Letter on a Regicide Peace* (1796), *Writings and Speeches*, IX, 248–9.

80 Ibid., 243.

81 Ibid., 246–7.

82 Burke to French Laurence, 11 April 1797, *The Correspondence of Edmund Burke*, IX, 307.

83 Richard Bourke, 'Edmund Burke and the Politics of Conquest', *Modern Intellectual History* 4:3 (2007), 403–32; I. Hampsher-Monk, 'Edmund Burke's Changing Justification for Intervention', *Historical Journal* 48/1 (2005), 65–100.

84 Burke, *First Letter on a Regicide Peace* (1796), *Writings and Speeches*, IX, 196, 238.

85 Ibid., 257.

86 Burke to Thomas Keogh, 17 November 1796, *The Correspondence of Edmund Burke*, IX, 115.

87 Burke to French Laurence, 18 November 1796, ibid., 116–20.

88 'The Science of Politics after the French Revolution: The Case of James Mackintosh', in *Beyond the Enlightenment: Scottish Intellectual Life, 1790–1914*, ed. Aileen Fyfe and Colin Kidd (Edinburgh: Edinburgh University Press, 2023), 70–85.

7. Jacques-Pierre Brissot and the End of Empire

1 Jacques-Pierre Brissot, *J.P. Brissot, député du département d'Eure-et-Loire, à ses commettans, sur la situation de la convention nationale sur l'influence des anarchistes, et les maux qu'elle a causés, sur la nécessité d'anéantir cette influence pour sauver la république* (Paris: P. Provost, Gorsas, Mathé, 1793).

2 Marisa Linton, *The Politics of Virtue in Enlightenment France* (New York: Palgrave McMillan, 2001) and *Choosing Terror: Virtue, Friendship and Authenticity in the French Revolution* (Oxford: Oxford University Press, 2013); Rachel Hammersley, *French Revolutionaries and English Republicans: The Cordeliers Club, 1790–1794* (Woodbridge, Suffolk: Boydell & Brewer, 2005). On the use of the 'Marseillaise' by Girondins like Brissot, see Alfred Chabaud, 'La Marseillaise: Chant patriotique "girondin"', *Annales historiques de la Révolution française* 13/77 (1936), 460–67.

3 Jacques-Pierre Brissot, *À ses commettans*, 67–72. On the invasion of Belgium see Patricia Chastain Howe, 'Charles-François Dumouriez and the Revolutionizing of French Foreign Affairs in 1792', *French Historical Studies* (1986), 367–90, and *Foreign Policy and the French Revolution: Charles-François Dumouriez, Pierre Lebrun and the Belgian Plan 1789–1793* (Macmillan Basingstoke: Palgrave, 2008), 158–9; Sophie Wahnich, 'Les républiques-sœurs, débat théorique et réalité historique, conquêtes et reconquêtes d'identité républicaine', *Annales historiques de la Révolution française* 296 (1994), 165–77.

4 Jacques-Pierre Brissot, *The Life of J. P. Brissot, Deputy from Eure and Loire, to the National Convention. Written by Himself. Translated from the French* (London: J. Debrett 1794), 60.

5 Simon Burrows, *Blackmail, Scandal, and Revolution: London's French Libellistes, 1758–1792* (Manchester: Manchester University Press, 2006).

6 R. Darnton, 'The Grub Street Style of Revolution: J.-P. Brissot, Police Spy', *Journal of Modern History* 40 (1968), 301–27 (reprinted in *The Literary Underground of the Old Regime*, pub. details 41–70); 'The Brissot Dossier', *French Historical Studies* 17 (1991), 191–205.

7 H. T. Mason, ed., *The Darnton Debate: Books and Revolution in the Eighteenth Century* (Oxford: Voltaire Foundation, 1999). For Brissot's debt to classical sources and especially Cicero see Ariane Viktoria Fichtl, *La Radicalisation de l'idéal républicain: Modèles antiques et la Révolution française* (Paris: Classiques Garnier, 2020), 87–177.

8 R. Darnton, 'Trends in Radical Propaganda on the Eve of the French Revolution (1782–1788)' (Oxford: unpublished DPhil, 1964).

9 Patrice Gueniffey, 'Cordeliers and Girondins: The Prehistory of the Republic?', in Biancamaria Fontana, ed., *The Invention of the Modern Republic* (Cambridge: Cambridge University Press, 1994), 86–106, R. Halévi 'Les Girondins avant la Gironde', in François Furet and Mona Ozouf, eds., *La Gironde et les Girondins* (Paris: Editions Payot, 1991), 137–68, 437–64; Bette W. Oliver, *Jacques Pierre Brissot in America and France, 1788–1793: In Search for Better Worlds* (Lanham MD: Lexington Books, 2016); François Furstenberg, *When the United States Spoke French: Five Refugees Who Shaped a Nation* (New York: Allen Lane, 2014).

10 Cl. Perroud, *J.P. Brissot: Correspondance et papiers, précédés d'un advertissement et d'une notice sur sa vie* (Paris: A. Picard et fils, 1912), xlviii. Jacques-Pierre Brissot de Warville, *New Travels in the United States of America, 1788*, ed. Mara Soceanu Vamos and Durand Echeverria (Cambridge, MA: Harvard University Press, 1964).

11 Jacques-Pierre Brissot, *Mémoires, 1754–1793*, ed., Cl. Perroud (Paris: A. Picard & Fils, 1911), 2 vols., I, 38; L. Loft, 'The Roots of Brissot's Ideology', *Eighteenth-Century Life* 13 (1989), 21–34; 'The Transylvanian Peasant Uprising of 1784, Brissot and the Right to Revolt: A Research Note', *French Historical Studies* 17 (1991), 209–18; *Passion, Politics and Philosophie: Rediscovering J.-P. Brissot* (Westport, CT: Greenwood 2002), 28–9, 55–63.

12 Jacques-Pierre Brissot, *Lettres philosophiques sur st. paul: sur sa doctrine, politique, morale & religieuse & sur plusieurs points de la religion chrétienne, considérés politiquement* (Neuchâtel: [Société typographique], 1783); *Bibliotheque philosophique du législateur, du politique, du jurisconsulte; Ou choix des meilleurs discours, dissertations, essais, fragments, composés sur la législation criminelle par les plus célebres écrivains, en françois, anglois, italien, allemand, espagnol, &c. pour parvenir à la réforme des loix pénales dans tous les pays, traduits & accompagnés de notes & d'observations historiques. Par J.P. Brissot de Warville* (Paris: Desauges, 1782–1785), 10 vols.; *Rome jugée et l'autorité legislative du pape anéantie: Pour servir de réponse aux bulles passées, nouvelles et futures du pape, etc.* (Paris: Buisson, 1791).

13 Rachel Hammersley, *French Revolutionaries and English Republicans: The Cordeliers Club 1790–1794* (Woodbridge, Suffolk: Boydell Press, 2005); Fichtl, *La Radicalisation de l'idéal républicain: Modèles antiques et la Révolution française,*

14 For the broader movement, see Janet Polasky, *Revolutions without Borders: The Call to Liberty in the Atlantic World* (New Haven CT and London: Yale University Press, 2015).

15 Brissot, *Mémoires*, II, 125.

16 Ibid., I, 38.

17 Loft, Brissot, 5.

18 Jacques-Pierre Brissot, *Bibliothèque philosophique*, I, xi.

19 Jacques-Pierre Brissot, *J.P. Brissot: Correspondance et papiers*; Jean François-Primo, *La jeunesse de J.-P. Brissot* (Paris: B. Grasset, 1932).

20 Linguet to Brissot, undated (Perroud dates it after 20 June 1776), *Correspondance et papiers*, 1–2.

21 Jacques-Pierre Brissot, *Théorie des lois criminelles* (Berlin: n. p., 1781), ii–iii.

22 Ibid., xv–xvi.

23 Brissot responded to two prize-essay questions set by the Academy of Châlon-sur-Marne: *S'il était dû des indemnités par la société à un accusé dont l'innocence avait été reconnue*; and *Quelles pourraient être en France les lois pénales les moins sévères et cependant les plus efficaces pour contenir et réprimer le crime par des châtiments prompts et exemplaires en ménageant l'honneur et la liberté des citoyens?*.

24 The best account of Brissot's manuscript is James Burns, 'Jacques-Pierre Brissot: From Scepticism to Conviction', *History of European Ideas* 38/4 (2012), 508–26. Brissot stated '*on est toujours dans les tenebres. [N]ous n'avons pas penetré les erreurs de nos peres [. . .] nous les avons échangées contre de nouvelles erreurs.*'

25 Brissot, *De la verité, ou Méditations sur les moyens de parvenir à la vérité dans toutes les connaissances humaines* (Neuchâtel: Société Typographique de Neuchâtel, 1782), 3–11.

26 Brissot advised Voltaire not to be envious of Rousseau in the *Bibliothèque* (V, 76) but was full of praise for Voltaire (V, 108).

27 Brissot, *De la verité*, 12.

28 Ibid., 211–12.

29 Brissot, *Rome jugée et l'autorité legislative du pape anéantie* (Paris, 1791 [1784–5]), 32, 40, 47; *Lettres philosophiques sur St. Paul* (Neuchâtel, 1783), 25, 41–2.

30 Brissot, *Rome jugée*, 20–21.

31 Brissot, *Lettres philosophiques*, 89.

32 Ibid., 2, 103–4.

33 Brissot, *Bibliothèque philosophique*, V, 56–7.

34 Villar to Brissot, 15 March 1783, 24 September 1783, *Correspondance*, 47–50, 74. In the *Mémoires* (I, 147) Brissot said he had been seduced by Linguet, but came to see that he was an apologist for monsters like the Roman Emperor Nero. Yet Brissot praised Linguet in the *Bibliothèque philosophique*, I, xx; 'De la décadence du barreau', *Bibliothèque philosophique*, IX, 77; 'Le Sang innocent vengé', *Bibliothèque philosophique*, VI, 390.

35 Ellery said he compiled the index for the *Annales* after leaving the *Courier* in 1780.

36 *Lettre de M. Linguet à M. le Comte de Vergennes* (London, 1777), 46–7.

37 On Vergennes, see Munro Price, *Preserving the Monarchy: The Comte of Vergennes, 1774–1787* (Cambridge: Cambridge University Press, 1995); John Hardman and Munro Price, eds., *Louis XVI and the Comte de Vergennes: Correspondence, 1774–1787* (Oxford: Voltaire Foundation, 1999); Hamish M. Scott, 'Louis XVI and Vergennes', *International History Review* 21/4, 941–4. See too, Simon Burrows, 'Despotism without

Bounds: The French Secret Police and the Silencing of Dissent in London, 1760–1790', *History* 89/4 (296) (2004), 525–48.

38 D. Gay Levy, *The Ideas and Careers of Simon-Nicolas-Henri Linguet* (Urbana, IL: University of Illinois Press, 1980), 186–94.

39 Jacques-Pierre Brissot, *Testament politique de l'angleterre* (Philadelphia, PA: n. p., 1780), 9–11, 24–8: 26 'l'éclat d'un empire n'annonce souvent que sa chûte prochaine.'

40 Brissot, *Mémoires*, I, 321–2.

41 Jacques-Pierre Brissot, *Théorie des lois criminelles*, I, 221; *Correspondance sur ce qui interesse le bonheur de l'homme et de la société le bonheur* (London: 1783), 2 vols., no. 2, I, 85; no. 2, II, 104–5.

42 Brissot, *De la verité, ou Méditations sur les moyens de parvenir à la verité dans toutes les connaissance humaines* (n.p., 1782), 251–6.

43 Brissot, *Bibliothèque philosophique*, III, 234–5.

44 Brissot, *Correspondance sur ce qui interesse le bonheur de l'homme et de la société*, no. 2, II, 80.

45 Ibid., no. 1, II, 27; *Bibliothèque philosophique*, I, xxxi–ii; III, 184; V, 55.

46 Ibid., III, 17, 23; IX, 300.

47 Ibid., V, 379.

48 Brissot, *The London Literary Lyceum; or, An Assembly and Correspondence Established at London, for Promoting the Union and Facilitating the Communication of Intelligence between the Literati of All Nations, and for the Publication of an Account of the Actual State of the Arts and Sciences in England, under the Direction of J.-P. Brissot de Warville* (London, 1783).

49 Pahin de Champlain de La Blancherie, *Les nouvelles de la république des lettres et des arts, ouvrage périodique par M. Pahin de Champlain de La Blancherie* (Paris: Ruault, 1777).

50 F. Dupont to Brissot, 7 May 1783, *Correspondance*, 53; Brissot, *Recherches philosophiques sur le droit de propriété* (n.p., 1780), 2, 8, 33, 40, 106.

51 Brissot to Vergennes, 13 February 1784, *Correspondance*, 81–2. Brissot enclosed a copy of the *Correspondance sur ce qui interesse le bonheur de l'homme et de la société le bonheur*.

52 James Dybikowski, 'David Williams (1738–1816) and Jacques-Pierre Brissot: Their Correspondence (Continued)', *National Library of Wales Journal* (1987), 167–190, 184. For the initial meeting of Williams

and Paine, see David Williams to Brissot, Sep. 2, 1788, in James Dybikowski, 'David Williams (1738–1816) and Jacques-Pierre Brissot: Their Correspondence', *National Library of Wales Journal* (1987), 71–97, 88.

53 Catharine Macaulay, *Nouveau précis de l'histoire d'Angleterre depuis les commencemens de cette monarchie jusqu'en 1783* (Paris, 1783).

54 Brissot to Charles-Alexandre de Calonne, 4 April 1786, *Correspondance*, 90–92. Brissot offered Calonne, then in charge of state finances, his book attacking the British Empire, *Tableau de la situation des Anglais dans les Indes orientales*, as a propaganda piece and requested an office, such as historiography of the French navy (*historiographe de la marine française*), on the grounds of having published so many 'useful books for France'.

55 Simon Burrows, 'The Innocence of Jacques-Pierre Brissot', *Historical Journal* 46/4 (2003), 843–71.

56 Brissot, *Mémoires*, I, 274, II, 28–9; Perroud, ed., *J.-P. Brissot: Correspondance et papiers*, 108.

57 Jacques-Pierre Brissot, *Le Philadelphien à Geneve, ou Lettres d'un Américain sur la dernière révolution de Genève, sa constitution nouvelle, l'émigration en Irlande, &c. pouvant servir de tableau politique de Genève jusqu'en 1784* (Dublin: n. p., 1783).w

58 Rousseau, *Considérations sur le government de Pologne*, in C. E. Vaughan, ed., *Political Writings of Jean-Jacques Rousseau* (Cambridge: Cambridge University Press, 2015), 2 vols., II, 442: 'Grandeur des nations, étendue des États: première et principale source des malheurs du genre humain, et surtout des calamités sans nombre: qui minent et détruisent les peuples polices.' The translation is from Victor Gourevitch, ed., *Rousseau: The Social Contract and Other Later Political Writings* (Cambridge: Cambridge University Press, 1997), 197.

59 Richard Whatmore, *Anarchists, Terrorists and Republicans*, 256–313.

60 Richard Whatmore, *Against War and Empire: Geneva, Britain and France in the Eighteenth Century*, 142, 177.

61 Clavière and Brissot, *Observations d'un républicain sur les différens systèmes d'administrations provinciales, Particulièrement sur ceux de Mm. Turgot et Necker, et sur le bien qu'on peut en espérer dans les gouvernemens* (Lausanne: n. p., 1787), 113.

62 Brissot, *Mémoires*, I, 274.

63 Ibid., ii, 28–9: 'un fonds inépuisable d'idées neuves, d'idées grandes et propres à captiver les esprits . . . le talent de les exprimer lui marquait. Il ignorait l'art de l'analyse; point d'ordre dans ses idées, point de clarté dans son style. Il pensait supérieurement, il fallait qu'un autre écrivît pour lui. C'était une mine intarissable de diamants bruts: il fallait un metteur en œvie.' Further portraits of Clavière as 'un honnête et vertueux citoyen' can be found in Cl. Perroud, ed., *J.-P. Brissot, Correspondance et Papiers*, 108, and *De la France et des Etats-Unis ou de l'importance de la Révolution de l'Amérique pour Le bonheur de la France: Des rapports de ce royaume & des Etats-Unis, des avantages réciproques qu'ils peuvent retirer de leurs liaisons de commerce, & enfin de la situation actuelle des Etats-Unis* (London: n. p., 1787), 28.

64 Brissot, *Mémoires*, I, 293.

65 Brissot, *Mémoires*, II, 30.

66 Simon-Nicolas-Henri Linguet, *Nouvelles considérations sur l'ouverture de l'escaut. Par M. Linguet. Pour servir de suite à la dissertation du même auteur* (Brussels: Francq, 1784)

67 Jacques-Pierre Brissot, *Un defenseur du peuple: À l'Empereur Joseph II sur son réglement concernant l'émigration, ses divers réformes, &c.* (Dublin: n. p., 1785), 1–38; *Seconde lettre d'un défenseur du peuple à l'Empereur Joseph II, sur son règlement concernant l'émigration, et principalement sur la révolte des valaques* (Dublin: n. p., 1785), 16–19.

68 Ibid., 35–8, 45–50.

69 Whatmore, *Anarchists, Terrorists and Republicans*, 171–2, 285–9.

70 James Burns, 'Bentham, Brissot and the Challenge of Revolution', *History of European Ideas* (2009), 35/2, 217–26; Emmanuelle de Champs, *Enlightenment and Utility: Bentham in French, Bentham in France*.

71 Jennifer Pitts, 'Legislator of the World? A Rereading of Bentham on Colonies', *Political Theory* 31/2 (2003), 200–234.

72 Jacques-Pierre and Clavière Brissot, *Point de banqueroute, ou, lettres à un créancier de l'état: Sur l'impossibilité de la banqueroute nationale, les moyens de ramener le crédit & la paix, & sur la dette considérée rélativement à la révocation des deux impôts, à la guerre de hollande & à celle de turquie: Avec des notes intéressantes* (London: n. p., 1788), 3rd edn, 119, 136–7. See

further, Allan Potofsky, 'The Political Economy of the French-American Debt Debate: The Ideological Uses of Atlantic Commerce, 1787 to 1800', *William and Mary Quarterly* 6/3 (2006) 489–516.

73 Jean Bénétruy's classic book *L'atelier de mirabeau: Quatre proscrits genevois dans la tourmente révolutionnaire* (Geneva: Jullien, 1962) should really be entitled '*L'atelier de Clavière*'.

74 Brissot and Clavière, *De la France et des États-Unis ou de l'importance de la Révolution de l'amérique pour le bonheur de la France.*

75 On Franklin's 'Poor Richard', see William Pencak, 'Politics and Ideology in "Poor Richard's Almanack" ', *Pennsylvania Magazine of History and Biography* 116/2 (1992), 183–211; Alfred Owen Aldridge, 'Benjamin Franklin and the "Pennsylvania Gazette" ', *Proceedings of the American Philosophical Society* 106/1 (1962), 77–81, and 'Jacques Barbeu-Dubourg, a French Disciple of Benjamin Franklin', *Proceedings of the American Philosophical Society* 95/4 (1951): 331–92.

76 D. P. Resnick, 'The Société des Amis des Noirs and the Abolition of Slavery', *French Historical Studies*, 7/4, (1972), 558–69. Cl. Perroud, 'La Société française des Amis des Noirs', *Révolution française*, LXIX (1916), 122–47; Léon Cahen, 'La Société des Amis des Noirs et Condorcet', *Révolution française*, L (1906), 481–511; Jean Vidalenc, 'La Traite des nègres en France au début de la Révolution (1789–93)', *Annales historiques de la Révolution française*, XXIX (1957), 56–69; Lawrence C. Jennings, 'The Interaction of French and British Antislavery, 1789–1848', *Proceedings of the Meeting of the French Colonial Historical Society* 15 (1992), 81–91. Caroline Oudin-Bastide and Philippe Steiner, *Calculation and Morality: The Costs of Slavery and the Value of Emancipation in the French Antilles* (New York and Oxford: Oxford University Press, 2019). Jefferson refused Brissot's invitation to join. See *The Papers of Thomas Jefferson*, ed. Julian P. Boyd (Princeton, NJ: Princeton University Press, 1955), vol. 12, 577–8.

77 Michel-Guillaume-Jean de Crèvecoeur [anglicized to J. Hector St. John de Crèvecoeur], *Letters from an American Farmer and Sketches of Eighteenth-Century America*, ed., Albert E. Stone (Harmondsworth: Penguin, 1986); Norman S. Grabo, 'Crèvecoeur's American: Beginning the World Anew', *William and Mary Quarterly* 48/2 (1991), 159–72.

78 Brissot to Thomas Jefferson, 8 March 1787, enclosing 'Prospectus de la Société gallo-américaine': 'L'utilité des deux mondes: voilà le but de cette Société, tout ce qui se rapporte à ce but, pourra fixer son attention. Elle sera composée d'hommes de tout pays, de toute profession, de toute religion, pourvu qu'ils soient capables de s'occuper constamment & sérieusement du bien de l'humanité.' *The Papers of Thomas Jefferson, Digital Edition,* ed. Barbara B. Oberg and J. Jefferson Looney (Charlottesville, VA: University of Virginia Press, Rotunda, 2008). On Jefferson's related views see Drew R. McCoy, *The Elusive Republic: Political Economy in Jeffersonian America* (Chapel Hill, NC: University of North Carolina Press, 1980). For the broader context see Manuela Albertone, *National Identity and the Agrarian Republic: The Transatlantic Commerce of Ideas between America and France (1750–1830)* pub. details.

79 David A. Bell, *The Cult of the Nation in France: Inventing Nationalism 1680–1800,* esp. ch. 5.

80 Brissot, *Nouveau voyage dans les etats-unis de l'amérique septentrionale: Fait en 1788* (Paris: Buisson, 1791).

81 On Dumont see Cyprian Blamires, *The French Revolution and the Creation of Benthamism* (London: Palgrave Macmillan, 2008); Richard Whatmore, *Against War and Empire: Geneva, Britain and France in the Eighteenth Century*; Emmanuelle de Champs, *Enlightenment and Utility: Bentham in French, Bentham in France* (Cambridge: Cambridge University Press, 2015).

82 Dumont, *Souvenirs sur Mirabeau et sur les deux premières assemblées législatives,* ed. J. L. Duval (Paris: Charles Gosselin and Hector Bossange, 1832), 298: 'une horloge qui retarde'.

83 Jacques Necker, *De la Révolution Française: Par M. Necker* ([London]: n. p., 1796).

84 Michael Sonenscher, ed., *Political Writings: Including the Debate between Sieyès and Tom Paine in 1791* (Indianapolis, IN: Hackett, 2003).

85 Dumont, *Souvenirs sur Mirabeau,* 101–3.

86 Brissot, *Nouveau voyage dans les états-unis de l'amérique septentrionale: Fait en 1788,* New Voyage, i, 130, 146, 150, 157, said morals were due, like Rousseau, to the rustic life.

87 Joseph Guadet, 'Recherches historiques sur les Girondins', in François Buzot, *Mémoires sur la Revolution française, par Buzot . . .; précédés d'un précis de sa vie et de recherches historiques sur les girondins, par M. Guadet* (Paris: Pichon and Didier, 1828), 44n.

88 Marisa Linton, *Choosing Terror: Virtue, Friendship and Authenticity in the French Revolution*.

89 Brissot, *Second discours de J.P. Brissot, sur la nécessité de faire la guerre aux princes allemands* (Paris, December 1791), 27. See also, J.-P. Brissot, 'Sur la justice de la guerre contre l'Autriche', *Chronique du mois, ou Cahiers patriotiques* (May 1792), 41–53, 52 ('c'est ici la guerre de la justice contre l'oppression, de la liberté contre le despotisme; et cette guerre est sacrée').

90 Thomas Kaiser, 'From the Austrian Committee to the Foreign Plot: Marie-Antoinette, Austrophobia, and the Terror', *French Historical Studies* 26/4 (2003), 579–617.

91 Whatmore, *Against War and Empire: Geneva, Britain, and France in the Eighteenth Century* (2012), 251. Clav Fr cit Nov 91. Nov 91, De l'état de nos finances, into cercle social Nov 91 to July 93. Supports annexation of Geneva to prevent the false assignats in December 1792.

92 Ellery, *Brissot de Warville*, 310–12; *J. P. Brissot, député à la convention nationale: À tous les républicains de France; sur la Société des Jacobins de Paris* (Paris: L'imprimerie du Patriote François, 1792), 8.

93 Lewis Goldsmith, *The Revolutionary Plutarch: Exhibiting the Most Distinguished Characters, Literary, Military and Political, in the Recent Annals of the French Republic* (London: John Murray, 1805), 3rd edn, 3 vols., I, 228.

94 Ibid., 30–37.

95 Ibid., 40–41.

96 Brissot, *Rapport sur les hostilités du roi d'Angleterre, et du stadhouder des Provinces-Unies, et sur la nécessité de déclarer que la République françoise est en guerre avec eux* (Paris: Convention Nationale, [1 February] 1793).

97 Brissot, *À tous les républicains de France: Sur la Société des Jacobins de Paris* (Cercle Social: Paris, 1792).

98 Fichtl, *La Radicalisation de l'idéal républicain. Modèles antiques et la Révolution française*, 261–70.

99 Brissot, *The Life of J. P. Brissot, Deputy from Eure and Loire, to the National Convention. Written by himself. Translated from the French*, details 60.

8. Thomas Paine and the End of Revolution

1 On Paine, see Eric Foner, *Tom Paine and Revolutionary America* (New York: 1976); A. Owen Aldridge, *Thomas Paine's American Ideology* (Delaware, DE: 1984); Bernard Vincent, *Thomas Paine, ou La religion de la liberté* (Paris: 1987); D. A. Williams, *Paine and Cobbett: The Transatlantic Connection* (Kingston: 1988); Gregory Claeys, *Thomas Paine: Social and Political Thought* (London: 1989) and 'Republicanism and Commerce in Britain, 1796–1805, in *Journal of Modern History* 66 (1994), 249–90; Mark Philp, *Paine* (Oxford: 1989); Jack R. Fruchtman, *Paine: Apostle of Freedom* (New York: 1994) and *The Political Philosophy of Thomas Paine* (Baltimore, MD: 2009); David Wootton, 'The Republican Tradition: from Commonwealth to Common Sense', *Republicanism, Liberty and Commercial Society, 1649–1776* (Stanford, CT: 1994), 1–44; John Keane, *Tom Paine: A Political Life* (London: Bloomsbury, 1995); Maurice Ezran, *Thomas Paine: Le combattant des deux révolutions, américaine et française* (Paris: 2004); Edward Larkin, *Thomas Paine and the Literature of Revolution* (Cambridge: 2005); Harvey J. Kaye, *Thomas Paine and the Promise of America* (New York: 2005); Vikki J. Vickers, *'My Pen and My Soul Have Ever Gone Together': Thomas Paine and the American Revolution* (New York: 2005); Craig Nelson, *Thomas Paine: Enlightenment, Revolutions, and the Birth of Modern Nations* (New York: 2005); Christopher Hitchens, *Thomas Paine's 'Rights of Man': A Biography* (New York: 2007); Carine Lounissi, *La pensée politique de Thomas Paine en contexte: Théorie et pratique* (Paris: Honoré Champion, 2012) and *Thomas Paine and the French Revolution* (London: Palgrave Macmillan, 2018); J. C. D. Clark, *Thomas Paine: Britain, America, and France in the Age of Enlightenment and Revolution* (Oxford: Oxford University Press, 2018).

2 Etienne Dumont, *Souvenirs sur Mirabeau et sur les deux premières assemblées législatives*, ed. J. Bénétruy (Paris: Presses universitaire de France, 1950), 180.

Notes

3 Thomas Paine, *The American Crisis*, No. II, 13 January 1777, in Philip Foner, ed. *The Complete Writings of Thomas Paine* (New York: Citadel Press, 1945), 2 vols., I, 72.

4 Diary entry for 3 March 1797, in *The Writings of Theobald Wolfe Tone 1763–98*, ed. T. W. Moody, R. B. McDowell and C. J. Woods (Oxford: Clarendon Press, 1998–2007), 3 vols., III, 29–30. On Tone see Marianne Elliott, *Wolfe Tone: Prophet of Irish Independence* (New Haven CT and London: Yale University Press, 1989).

5 Katey Castellano, 'William Cobbett, "Resurrection Man": The Peterloo Massacre and the Bones of Tom Paine', in *Commemorating Peterloo: Violence, Resilience and Claim-Making during the Romantic Era*, ed. Michael Demson and Regina Hewitt (Edinburgh: Edinburgh University Press, 2019), 183–204. See also Michael L. Bush, *Thomas Paine and the Polity of the Blood* (Canterbury: Mot Juste, 2023), appendix on Paine's bones.

6 Thomas Paine, 'To the Legislature and the Executive Directory of the French Republic', *Agrarian Justice* (1797), *The Complete Writings of Thomas Paine*, I, 606–08.

7 Michael T. Davis, 'The Vilification of Thomas Paine: Constructing a Folk Devil in the 1790s', in *Liberty, Property and Popular Politics: England and Scotland, 1688–1815. Essays in Honour of H. T. Dickinson*, ed. Michael T. Davis and Gordon Pentland (Edinburgh: Edinburgh University Press, 2016), 176–93.

8 Thomas Paine, *The Age of Reason*, in Philip S. Foner, ed., *The Complete Writings of Thomas Paine* (New York: Citadel Press, 1945), 2 vols., I, 467, 498, 597.

9 On Cobbett, see Ian Dyck, *William Cobbett and Rural Popular Culture* (New York: Cambridge University Press, 1992), and Matthew Roberts, 'William Cobbett's Anti-"Feelosofee"', in *Democratic Passions: The Politics of Feeling in British Popular Radicalism, 1809–48* (Manchester: Manchester University Press, 2022), 25–57.

10 Paine described his arrest in an autobiographical interlude at the end of the first part of *The Age of Reason: The Complete Writings of Thomas Paine*, I, 512–14.

11 Thomas Paine, *Letter to George Washington* (30 July 1796), *The Complete Writings of Thomas Paine*, II, 698–9.

12 The best account of Paine's arrest, survival and aftermath in Paris is Lounissi, *Thomas Paine and the French Revolution*, 181–222.

13 Thomas Paine, 'Remarks on the Political and Military Affairs of Europe' (1806), 'Remarks on English Affairs' (1805) and 'Of the English Navy' (1807), in *The Complete Writings of Thomas Paine*, II, 615–17, 684–7, 687–8.

14 Hedva Ben-Israel, *English Historians on the French Revolution* (Cambridge: Cambridge University Press, 1968).

15 Paine to Jefferson, 30 January 1806, *The Complete Writings of Thomas Paine*, II, 1474.

16 Ian Dyck, 'From "Rabble" to "Chopsticks": The Radicalism of William Cobbett', *Albion: A Quarterly Journal Concerned with British Studies* 21/1 (1989), 56–87; James Grande, *William Cobbett, the Press and Rural England: Radicalism and the Fourth Estate, 1792–1835* (Palgrave Studies in Nineteenth-Century Writing and Culture, 2014).

17 Thomas Paine, 'Common Sense; Addressed to the Inhabitants of America: On the Following Interesting Subjects. I. Of the Origin and Design of Government in General, with Concise Remarks on the English Constitution. II. Of Monarchy and Hereditary Succession. III. Thoughts on the Present State of American Affairs. IV. Of the present ability of America, with some Miscellaneous Reflections' (1776), *The Complete Writings of Thomas Paine*, I, 4; 'An Essay for the Use of New Republicans' (1792), II, 542–7, 'On the Existence of God', *Discourse to the Society of Theophilanthropists, Paris* (1797), II, 748–56.

18 William Cobbett, *William Cobbett Selected Writings. Vol. 5: A History of the Protestant Reformation in England and Ireland 1824–1826*, ed., Leonora Nattrass (London: Pickering and Chatto, 1998).

19 Paine, *The Age of Reason* (1794), *The Complete Writings of Thomas Paine*, I, 463, 464–82.

20 Jay E. Smith, 'Thomas Paine and the *Age of Reason's* Attack on the Bible', *Historian* 58/4 (1996), 745–61; Nathalie Caron, *Thomas Paine contre l'imposture des prêtres* (Paris: Editions l'Harmattan, 1998); David C. Hoffman, ' "The Creation We Behold": Thomas Paine's "The Age of Reason" and the Tradition of Physico-Theology', *Proceedings of the American Philosophical Society* 157/3 (2013), 281–303;

Seth Perry, '*Paine Detected* in Mississippi: Slavery, Print Culture, and the Threat of Deism in the Early Republic', *William and Mary Quarterly* 78/2 (2021), 313–38; Clark, *Thomas Paine: Britain, America, and France in the Age of Enlightenment and Revolution*, 360–418.

21 Robert E. Schofield, *The Enlightened Joseph Priestley: A Study of His Life and Work from 1773 to 1803* (University Park, PA: Pennsylvania State University Press, 2004), 377–8.

22 Paine, *Letter to George Washington, The Complete Writings of Thomas Paine*, II, 692–706. For context, see Rachel Hope Cleves, *The Reign of Terror in America: Visions of Violence from Anti-Jacobinism to Antislavery* (New York: Cambridge University Press, 2009).

23 Marc Belissa, 'La légende grise des dernières années de Thomas Paine en Amérique, 1802–1809', *Annales Historiques de la Révolution française* 360 (2010), 133–72. On Paine and the Quakers, see Clark, *Thomas Paine: Britain, America, and France in the Age of Enlightenment and Revolution*, 21–2, 53, 57, 82, 94–5, 123, 154, 163–4. For the refusal of burial as a Quaker see 82–3.

24 Anon., 'Paine and Cobbett', *Freeman's Journal* (Cooperstown, NY:), 18 October 1819, 3 cited in Heather Thomas, 'The Bones of Thomas Paine', Library of Congress: blogs.loc.gov/headlinesandheroes/2019/04/the-bones-of-thomas-paine/

25 Paine, 'The American Crisis', No. I, 23 December 1776, *The Complete Writings of Thomas Paine*, I, 50.

26 Vikki J. Vickers, '*My Pen and My Soul Have Ever Gone Together': Thomas Paine and the American Revolution* (London: Routledge, 2006).

27 Colin Brent, Deborah Gage and Paul Myles, *Thomas Paine in Lewes 1768–1774: A Prelude to American Independence* (London: Thomas Paine Society UK, 2020); Paul Myles, *The Rise of Thomas Paine: And The Case of the Officers of Excise* (London: Thomas Paine Society UK, 2018).

28 Thomas 'Clio' Rickman, *The Life of Thomas Paine* (London: Rickmann, 1819), 38.

29 Philip Ziesche, 'Thomas Paine and Benjamin Franklin's French Circle', in *Paine and Jefferson in the Age of Revolutions*, ed. Simon P. Newman and Peter S. Onuf (Charlottesville VA: University of Virginia Press, 2013), 121–36.

30 Paine, *Common Sense, The Complete Writings of Thomas Paine*, I, 7–8.

31 Ibid., 22–3.

32 Ibid., 18–24.

33 Ibid., 30–31.

34 Clark, *Thomas Paine*, 37n, 77, 92–7. The anonymous 'African Slavery in America' of 1775, presumed to have been written by Paine, was probably authored by the Quaker Anthony Benezet. See Clark, 'Appendix: Paine De-attributions', 419–26, reference to this work at 420; Gregory Claeys, 'Note on Thomas Paine's Collected Works in Progress', *Journal of Early American History* 6/2–3 (2016), 109–12.

35 On slavery and the Founding Fathers, see Francis D. Cogliano, *Thomas Jefferson: Reputation and Legacy* (Edinburgh: Edinburgh University Press, 2006); Thomas S. Kidd, *Thomas Jefferson: A Biography of Spirit and Flesh* (New Haven, CT: Yale University Press, 2022).

36 Paine, 'The American Crisis', No. VI, 20 October 1778, *The Complete Writings of Thomas Paine*, I, 131–8.

37 William A. Speck, *A Political Biography of Thomas Paine* (London: Pickering & Chatto), 76–7.

38 Paine, *Letter to George Washington, The Complete Writings of Thomas Paine*, II, 695.

39 Speck, *Paine*, 79–80.

40 Paine, 'American Crisis', No. 11, *The Complete Writings of Thomas Paine*, I, 208–16.

41 Munro Price, 'The Dutch Affair and the Fall of the Ancien Régime, 1784–1787', *Historical Journal* 38/4 (1995), 875–905.

42 Paine, 'Prospects on the Rubicon: Or an Investigation into the Causes and Consequences of the Politics to Be Agitated at the Next Meeting of Parliament' (1787), *The Complete Writings of Thomas Paine*, II, 634.

43 Paine, 'Prospects on the Rubicon', ibid., 645.

44 Ibid., 633–634.

45 Ibid., 650.

46 Paine to Shelburne, 20 November 1787, published in Paine, *A Collection of Unknown Writings*, ed. Hazel Burgess (Basingstoke: Palgrave Macmillan, 2010), 59.

47 Paine, *Rights of Man: Being an Answer to Mr Burke's Attack on the French Revolution* (1791), *The Complete Writings of Thomas Paine*, I, 249; 'Lettre à MM. Chabroud et Chapelier', *Le Républicain, ou Le défenseur du gouvernement représentatif, par une société des républicains*, no. 2 (July 1791), 31.

48 Paine to Kitty Nicholson Few, 6 January 1789, *The Complete Writings of Thomas Paine*, II, 1276.

49 Paine called for a national convention, arguing that this was necessary because no English constitution existed, in *Letter Addressed to the Addressers on the Late Proclamation* (1792), ibid. 469–511. The *Letter* was published on 18 October 1792.

50 *Rights of Man* was published on 21 February 1791 by Joseph Johnson. Johnson then had a change of heart, fearing prosecution, and withdrew the book from sale. The Fleet Street publisher J. S. Jordan stepped in and *Rights of Man* appeared on 16 March.

51 Paine, *Rights of Man*, dedication to Washington, *The Complete Writings of Thomas Paine*, I, 244.

52 Paine, *Rights of Man*, preface to the French edn, ibid., 247–9.

53 Ibid., 277.

54 Letters to Mary Berry, 3 April and 26 July, 1791, *The Yale Edition of Horace Walpole's Correspondence* ed. W. S. Lewis, (New Haven, CT: Yale University Press, 1937–83), 48 vols., VI, 239, 319. See further, Gregory Claeys, 'The French Revolution Debate and British Political Thought', *History of Political Thought* (spring 1990), 59–80.

55 Paine, *Rights of Man*, *The Complete Writings of Thomas Paine*, I, 364.

56 Ibid., 260.

57 Ibid., 293.

58 Ibid., 294n.

59 Edmund Burke, 'Thoughts on French Affairs', December 1791, *Writings and Speeches*, VIII, 341–2.

60 Paine, *Rights of Man*, *The Complete Writings of Thomas Paine*, I, 299.

61 Ibid., 338.

62 Paine, *Rights of Man, Part Second, The Complete Writings of Thomas Paine*, I, 369. On the intellectual context in America and Britain, see J. R. Pole, *Political Representation in England and the Origins of the*

American Republic (London: Macmillan, 1966); Richard R. Beeman, *The Varieties of Political Experience in Eighteenth-Century America* (Philadelphia, PA: University of Pennsylvania Press, 2004).

63 Paine, *Rights of Man, The Complete Writings of Thomas Paine*, I, 267.

64 Paine, *Letter Addressed to the Addressers on the Late Proclamation, Rights of Man, The Complete Writings of Thomas Paine*, II, 483.

65 Paine, *A Letter to Mr Secretary Dundas: In Answer to his Speech on the Late Proclamation. By Thomas Paine* (1792), *The Complete Writings of Thomas Paine*, II, 452. See further, Gareth Stedman Jones, *An End to Poverty?: A Historical Debate* (New York: Columbia University Press, 2014).

66 Paine, *Rights of Man, The Complete Writings of Thomas Paine*, I, 343.

67 Ibid., 282.

68 Ibid., 331–2.

69 Ibid., 336–7.

70 Ibid., 341.

71 Ibid., 344.

72 Ibid., 344.

73 Ibid., 344.

74 Gouverneur Morris, *The Diary and Letters of Gouverneur Morris, Minister of the United States, to France: Member of the Constitutional Convention Etc.*, ed. Anne Cary Morris (London: Kegan, 1889), 2 vols., July 4 1791, I, 429.

75 Paine to the Abbé Sieyès (1791), Paine, *The Complete Writings of Thomas Paine*, II, 520.

76 Thomas 'Clio' Rickman, *Life of Thomas Paine* (London: Rickman, 1819), 100–101.

77 Albert Goodwin, *The Friends of Liberty: The English Democratic Movement in the Age of the French Revolution* (London: Hutchinson, 1979), 188; Clark, *Thomas Paine: Britain, America, and France in the Age of Enlightenment and Revolution*, 288–92.

78 On Paine's trial see John Barrell and Jon Mee, eds., *Trials for Treason and Sedition, 1792–1794. Vol. I, Introduction and Trials of Thomas Paine (1793), John Frost (1794) and Daniel Isaac Eaton (1794)* (London: Pickering and Chatto, 2006). See more broadly, John Barrell, *The Spirit of*

Despotism: Invasions of Privacy in the 1790s (Oxford: Oxford University Press, 2006).

79 Paine, *Letters to the Citizens of the United States* (1802), letter 1, *The Complete Writings of Thomas Paine*, II, 912.

80 Lounissi, *Thomas Paine and the French Revolution*, 211–12.

81 Paine, *Rights of Man, Part Second, The Complete Writings of Thomas Paine*, I, 352.

82 Ibid., 356.

83 Ibid., 396.

84 Ibid., 399.

85 Ibid., 355–6.

86 Ibid., 443.

87 Ibid., 443.

88 Ibid., 448–9.

89 Ibid., 448.

90 Ibid., 447.

91 Ibid., 448.

92 Ibid., 448–9.

93 Ibid., 449.

94 Ibid., 449.

95 Ibid., 449.

96 Ibid., 387n.

97 Ibid., 404–05.

98 Ibid., 414.

99 Ibid., 421.

100 Ibid., 421.

101 Ibid., 422.

102 Ibid., 439.

103 Ibid., 332.

104 Paine, 'Address to the People of France', *The Complete Writings of Thomas Paine*, II, 540.

105 Ibid., 538–9.

106 Paine 'Answer to Four Questions on the Legislative and Executive Powers' (1792), *The Complete Writings of Thomas Paine*, II, 521.

107 David Dickson, 'Paine and Ireland', in Dickson, Dáire Keogh and Kevin Whelan, eds., *The United Irishmen: Republicanism, Radicalism and Rebellion* (Dublin: Lilliput Press, 1993), 135–50; Ann Thomson, 'Thomas Paine and the United Irishmen', *Études irlandaises* (1991), 109–20.

108 Thomas Moore, *The Life and Death of Lord Edward Fitzgerald* (London: Rees, Orme, Brown, Green, & Longman, 1832), 2 vols.; Emma Vincent Macleod, 'British Attitudes to the French Revolution', *Historical Journal* 50/3 (2007), 689–709.

109 Marianne Elliott, *Partners in Revolution: The United Irishmen and France* (New Haven, CT: Yale University Press, 1982), 60–73.

110 John Epps, *The Life of John Walker, M. D.* (London: Whittaker, Treacher and Co., 1831), 134.

111 T. Wolfe Tone, James Smith, and Lionel D. Woodward, 'Les projets de descente en Irlande et les réfugiés irlandais et anglais en France sous la Convention: D'après des documents inédits', *Annales historiques de la Révolution française*, 8e Année, no. 43 (Janvier–Février 1931), 1–30. For the impact on Britain see Mark Philp, ed., *The British Response to the Threat of Invasion, 1797–1815* (Aldershot: Ashgate, 2006).

112 Paine, 'To the People of England on the Invasion of England' (1798) and 'To the Council of 500' (1798), *The Complete Writings of Thomas Paine*, II, 675–83, 1403.

113 Paine, 'The Eighteenth Fructidor. To the People of France and the French Armies' (1797), *The Complete Writings of Thomas Paine*, II, 594–612.

114 Alfred Owen Aldridge, 'Thomas Paine's Plan for a Descent on England', *William and Mary Quarterly* 14/1 (January 1957), 74–84; Lounissi, *Thomas Paine and the French Revolution*, 264–74 and 293–8 on later invasion proposals.

115 Paine to General Brune, November 1799, *The Complete Writings of Thomas Paine*, II, 1403–05.

116 For their response to Paine, see Seth Cotlar, *Tom Paine's America: The Rise and Fall of Transatlantic Radicalism in the Early Republic* (Charlottesville, VA: University of Virginia Press, 2011).

117 Paine to Mr Secretary Dundas, 6 June 1792, and 'The Eighteenth Fructidor. To the People of France and the French Armies' (1797), *The Complete Writings of Thomas Paine*, II, 449.

118 Ibid., 595.

119 Paine, *Rights of Man, Part Second, The Complete Writings of Thomas Paine*, I, 451–2.

120 Lounissi, *Thomas Paine and the French Revolution*, 209–19.

121 Paine to Thomas Jefferson, 25 December 1802, in Moncure Daniel Conway, *The Life of Thomas Paine: With a History of His Literary, Political and Religious Career in America, France, and England* (New York: Putnam, 1909), 2 vols., II, 313. On Jefferson's empire of liberty, see Eliga H. Gould, *Among the Powers of the Earth: The American Revolution and the Making of a New World Empire* (Cambridge MA: Harvard University Press, 2012).

122 John Swanwick, member of the House of Representatives for Pennsylvania, attacking the proposed Jay Treaty between Britain and the United States in April 1796, *The Debates and Proceedings in the Congress of the United States: With an Appendix Containing Important State Papers and Public Documents, and All the Laws of a Public Nature: with a Copious Index . . . Fourth Congress, First Session, Comprising the Period from 7 December 1795, to 1 June 1796 inclusive* (Washington: Gales and Seaton, 1849), 997.

123 Burke, *First Letter on a Regicide Peace* (1796), *The Writings and Speeches*, IX, 191–7, 238–42, 248–57.

9. Mary Wollstonecraft and the End of Equality

1 On Wollstonecraft's philosophy and its impact, see Virginia Sapiro, *A Vindication of Political Virtue: The Political Theory of Mary Wollstonecraft* (Chicago, IL: University of Chicago Press, 1992); Lena Halldenius, *Mary Wollstonecraft and Feminist Republicanism: Independence Rights and the Experience of Unfreedom* (London: Pickering & Chatto, 2015); Sandrine Bergès and Alan Coffee, eds., *The Social and Political Philosophy of Mary Wollstonecraft* (Oxford: Oxford University Press, 2016); Sylvana Tomaselli, *Wollstonecraft: Philosophy Passion and Politics* (Princeton, NJ: Princeton University Press, 2021).

2 Pamela Clemit and Gina Luria Walker, introduction to their edn of William Godwin, *Memoirs of the Author of a Vindication of the Rights of*

Woman (Peterborough, Ontario: Broadview Press, 2001). See more broadly, *The Letters of William Godwin, Vol. II: 1798–1805*, ed., Pamela Clemit (Oxford: Oxford University Press, 2014).

3 Cora Kaplan, 'Mary Wollstonecraft's Reception and Legacies', in Claudia Johnson, ed., *The Cambridge Companion to Mary Wollstonecraft* (Cambridge: Cambridge University Press, 2002), 246–70; Sandrine Bergès, Eileen M. Hunt and Alan Coffee, *The Wollstonecraftian Mind* (Abingdon: Routledge, 2019); Nancy E. Johnson and Paul Keen, *Mary Wollstonecraft in Context* (Cambridge: Cambridge University Press, 2020).

4 William Godwin, *Enquiry concerning Political Justice and its Influence on General Virtue and Happiness*, (London 1793), 2 vols. I, 118.

5 Knud Haakonssen, *Enlightenment and Religion: Rational Dissent in Eighteenth-Century Britain* (Cambridge: Cambridge University Press, 1996); Ralph Stevens, *Protestant Pluralism: The Reception of the Toleration Act, 1689–1720* (Woodbridge: Boydell & Brewer, 2018); Robert G. Ingram and William Gibson, *Religious Identities in Britain 1660–1832* (London: Routledge, 2017).

6 On Price's views, see Jack Fruchtman Jr, *The Apocalyptic Politics of Richard Price and Joseph Priestley: A Study in Late Eighteenth-Century English Millennialism, Transactions of the American Philosophical Society* 73, part 4 (Philadelphia PA: American Philosophical Society, 1983).

7 Wollstonecraft to Joseph Johnson, summer 1788, in Janet M. Todd and Marilyn Butler, eds., *The Works of Mary Wollstonecraft* (London: Pickering and Chatto, 1989), 6 vols., VI, 358. References to the *Works* is henceforth *MWW*.

8 Mark Philp, *Godwin's Political Justice* (London: Duckworth, 1986), 35.

9 Peter H. Marshall, *William Godwin* (New Haven CT: Yale University Press, 1984).

10 W. Stafford, 'Dissenting Religion Translated into Politics: Godwin's "Political Justice"', *History of Political Thought* 1/2 (1980), 279–99; Gregory Claeys, 'The Concept of "Political Justice" in Godwin's Political Justice: A Reconsideration', *Political Theory* 11/4 (1983), 565–84; Robert M. Maniquis, 'Godwin's Calvinist Ghosts: Political Justice and Caleb Williams', in *Godwinian Moments: From the Enlightenment to*

Romanticism, ed. Robert M. Maniquis and Victoria Myers (Toronto: University of Toronto Press, 2011), 25–58.

11 Wollstonecraft, 'As for Rousseau's remarks, which have since been echoed by several writers, that they have naturally, that is from their birth, independent of education, a fondness for dolls, dressing, and talking – they are so puerile as not to merit a serious refutation', *A Vindication of the Rights of Woman*, MWW, V, 111.

12 Godwin, *Memoirs of the Author of a Vindication of the Rights of Woman* (London; Joseph Johnson, 1798), 2nd edn, 5–10.

13 On Wollstonecraft's early life, see Claire Tomalin, *The Life and Death of Mary Wollstonecraft* (New York: Penguin, 1992 [1974]), revised edn; Janet Todd, *Mary Wollstonecraft: A Revolutionary Life* (London: Phoenix Books, 2000). For an evaluation of the biographies, see Brenda Ayres, *Betwixt and Between: The Biographies of Mary Wollstonecraft* (New York: Anthem Press, 2017).

14 Caroline Franklin, *Mary Wollstonecraft: A Literary Life* (New York: Palgrave Macmillan, 2004). The title of the 1788 edition of the *Education of Daughters* speaks volumes: *Mrs Wollstonecraft's Thoughts on the Education of Daughters: With Reflections on Female Conduct in the More Important Duties of Life: To Which Is Added Fenolon [Sic] Archbishop of Cambray's Instructions to a Governess and an Address to Mothers* (Dublin: P. W. Sleater, 1788). Note the linkage with Fénelon's moral injunctions.

15 Barbara Taylor, 'Mary Wollstonecraft and the Wild Wish of Early Feminism', *History Workshop* 33 (1992), 197–219; Eileen Hunt Botting, 'Human Stories', in *Wollstonecraft, Mill, and Women's Human Rights* (New Haven, CT: Yale University Press, 2016), 204–48.

16 Wollstonecraft's *A Vindication of the Rights of Men, in a Letter to the Right Honourable Edmund Burke; Occasioned by his Reflections on the Revolution in France* (London: Joseph Johnson, 1790) was a reply to Edmund Burke's *Reflections on the Revolution in France* (1790); it appeared in two editions in November and December 1790, MWW, V, 44, n. 22.

17 See Godwin, *Memoirs of the Author of a Vindication*, 96–7. On Johnson and his impact, see Helen Braithwaite, *Romanticism, Publishing and Dissent:*

Joseph Johnson and the Cause of Liberty (Basingstoke: Palgrave Macmillan, 2003); Daisy Hay, *Dinner with Joseph Johnson: Books and Friendship in a Revolutionary Age* (Princeton, NJ: Princeton University Press, 2022).

18 Godwin wrote of the encounter in his *Memoirs of the Author of a Vindication*, 97: 'Mary and myself parted, mutually displeased with each other. I had not read her Rights of Woman. I had barely looked into her Answer to Burke, and been displeased, as literary men are apt to be, with a few offences, against grammar and other minute points of composition. I had therefore little curiosity to see Mrs. Wollstonecraft, and a very great curiosity to see Thomas Paine. Paine, in his general habits, is no great talker; and, though he threw in occasionally some shrewd and striking remarks; the conversation lay principally between me and Mary. I, of consequence, heard her, very frequently when I wished to hear Paine.'

19 Jon Mee, ' "The Use of Conversation": William Godwin's Conversable World and Romantic Sociability', *Studies in Romanticism* 50/4 (2011), 567–90.

20 William Godwin to [?Thomas Brand Hollis] [3–16 March 1791], *The Letters of William Godwin, Vol. I: 1778–1797*, ed. Pamela Clemit (Oxford: Oxford University Press, 2011), 52.

21 Godwin to Paine [7 November 1791]: ibid., 64–6.

22 See Pamela Clemit, 'Godwin's Political Justice', in *The Cambridge Companion to British Literature of the French Revolution in the 1790s*, ed. Pamela Clemit (Cambridge: Cambridge University Press, 2011), 86–100; *The Letters of William Godwin, Vol. I: 1778-1797*, ed. Pamela Clemit (Oxford: Oxford University Press, 2011).

23 Wollstonecraft, *A Vindication of the Rights of Woman*, MWW, V, 260.

24 Bridget Hill, 'The Links between Mary Wollstonecraft and Catharine Macaulay: New Evidence', *Women's History Review* 4/2 (1995), 177–92.

25 Wollstonecraft, *A Vindication of the Rights of Men*, MWW, V, 57.

26 Ibid., 58.

27 Ibid., 57.

28 Ibid., 59.

29 Ibid., 59.

30 Ibid., 11, citing David Hume, *The History of England* (1778), I, xvi, 499–500.

31 Wollstonecraft, *A Vindication of the Rights of Men*, MWW, V, 13–14.

32 Ibid., 14.

33 Ibid., 21.

34 Ibid., 15.

35 Ibid., 50–51.

36 Ibid., 19–20.

37 Ibid., 46.

38 Ibid., 10.

39 Ibid., 22.

40 Ibid., 22–3.

41 Ibid., 23.

42 Ibid., 24.

43 Ibid., 24.

44 Ibid., 25.

45 Ibid., 10.

46 Ibid., 42.

47 Ibid., 9.

48 Ibid., 56.

49 Ibid., 31.

50 Ibid., 48–50.

51 Ibid., 46.

52 Ibid., 40.

53 Ibid., 47.

54 Ibid., 44.

55 Ibid., 26–9.

56 Ibid., 44.

57 Ibid., 18.

58 Ibid., 39.

59 Ibid., 48.

60 R. M. Janes, 'On the Reception of Mary Wollstonecraft's *A Vindication of the Rights of Woman*', *Journal of the History of Ideas* 39/2 (1978), 293–302.

61 Wollstonecraft, *A Vindication of the Rights of Woman*, MWW, V, 73.

62 Ibid., 112–13.

63 Ibid., 73.

64 Ibid., 76.

65 Ibid., 77.

66 Ibid., 265.

67 Ibid., 86.

68 See further, Hannah Dawson, 'Fighting for My Mind: Feminist Logic at the Edge of Enlightenment', *Proceedings of the Aristotelian Society* 118/3 (2018), 275–306.

69 Wollstonecraft, *A Vindication of the Rights of Woman*, *MWW*, V, 125.

70 Ibid., 124.

71 Ibid., 120.

72 Ibid., 130.

73 Ibid., 113.

74 Ibid., 114.

75 Ibid., 106.

76 Ibid., 114.

77 Ibid., 133.

78 Ibid., 82–7.

79 Ibid., 84–5.

80 Ibid., 215.

81 Ibid., 93, 105.

82 Ibid., 84–5.

83 Ibid., 127–8.

84 Ibid., 120.

85 Ibid., 129.

86 Ibid., 214.

87 Ibid., 249.

88 Ibid., 217.

89 Ibid., 120.

90 Ibid., 189.

91 Ibid., 198, 208.

92 Ibid., 216.

93 Ibid., 250.

94 Ibid., 247.

95 Ibid., 245.

96 Ibid., 264.

97 Ibid., 265–6.

98 On Wollstonecraft at Paris, see Janet Todd, *Mary Wollstonecraft: A Revolutionary Life*, 202–25.

99 Godwin, *Memoirs of the Author of a Vindication*, 105.

100 O. F. Emerson, 'Notes on Gilbert Imlay, Early American writer', *Publications of the Modern Language Association of America* 39 (1924), 406–39; J. L. Fant, 'A Study of Gilbert Imlay (1754–1828): His Life and Works' (PhD diss., University of Pennsylvania, 1984).

101 Wil Verhoeven, *Gilbert Imlay: Citizen of the World* (London: Pickering & Chatto, 2008).

102 Per Nyström, *Mary Wollstonecraft's Scandinavian Journey* (Gothenburg: Kungl. Vetenskaps- och Vitterhets-Samhället, 1980).

103 Wollstonecraft to Imlay, December 1795, *MWW*, VI, 437.

104 Wollstonecraft to Imlay, 9 January 1795, ibid., 397.

105 Wollstonecraft to Imlay, 30 December 1794, ibid., 398.

106 Ibid., 398.

107 Ibid., 398.

108 Wollstonecraft to Imlay, 17 August 1794, ibid., 384.

109 Wollstonecraft to Imlay, 10 February 1795, ibid., 402.

110 Wollstonecraft to Imlay, 22 September 1794, ibid., 388.

111 Wollstonecraft to Imlay, 22 September 1794, ibid., 388.

112 Wollstonecraft to Imlay, 10 February 1795, ibid., 402.

113 Wollstonecraft to Imlay, 3 July 1795, ibid., 418.

114 Wollstonecraft to Imlay, 19 February 1795, ibid., 403.

115 Deborah Weiss, 'Suffering, Sentiment, and Civilization: Pain and Politics in Mary Wollstonecraft's "Short Residence"', *Studies in Romanticism* 45/2 (2006), 199–221.

116 Steven Blakemore, 'Wollstonecraft and the French Revolution', in Blakemore, ed., *Crisis in Representation: Thomas Paine, Mary Wollstonecraft, Helen Maria Williams, and the Rewriting of the French Revolution* (London: Associated University Presses, 1997), 89–101.

117 Wollstonecraft, *An Historical and Moral View of the Origin and Progress of the French Revolution*, *MWW*, VI, 6.

118 Ibid., 166.
119 Ibid., 113.
120 Ibid., 114.
121 Ibid., 28.
122 Ibid., 15, 21.
123 Ibid., 18.
124 Ibid., 16.
125 Ibid., 26.
126 Ibid., 18.
127 Ibid., 19.
128 Ibid., 19.
129 Ibid., 18.
130 Ibid., 143.
131 Ibid., 147.
132 Ibid., 74, 183, 206.
133 Ibid., 75.
134 Ibid., 76.
135 Ibid., 210.
136 Ibid., 234.
137 Ibid., 230–31.
138 Ibid., 141–2, 165, 232–3.
139 Ibid., 166.
140 Ibid., 61.
141 Ibid., 108.
142 Ibid., 6.
143 Ibid., 6.
144 But see Sandrine Bergès, 'A Republican Housewife: Marie-Jeanne Phlipon Roland on Women's Political Role', *Hypatia* 31/1 (2016), 107–22.
145 Alan M. S. J. Coffee, 'Freedom as Independence: Mary Wollstonecraft and the Grand Blessing of Life', *Hypatia* 29/4 (2014), 908–24; Lisa Curtis-Wendlandt, Paul Richard Gibbard and Karen Green, eds., *Political Ideas of Enlightenment Women: Virtue and Citizenship* (London: Routledge, 2016).
146 Wollstonecraft, *An Historical and Moral View of the Origin and Progress of the French Revolution*, MWW, VI, 183.

147 Ibid., 213.

148 Ibid., 228.

149 Ibid., 6.

150 Ibid., 141.

151 Ibid., 219.

152 Ibid., 7.

153 Ibid., 16.

154 Ibid., 16.

155 Ibid., 70.

156 Ibid., 113.

157 Ibid., 20.

158 Ibid., 21.

159 Ibid., 17.

160 Ibid., 17.

161 Ibid., 116.

162 Ibid., 117.

163 Ibid., 117.

164 Ibid., 117, 180–83.

165 Ibid., 229.

166 Ibid., 234.

167 Ibid., 233.

168 Wollstonecraft to Imlay, December 1795, *MWW*, VI, 437.

169 Wollstonecraft to Imlay, March 1796, ibid., 438.

170 Mary Wollstonecraft, 'Letter on the Present Character of the French Nation', ibid., 444. It was first published by Godwin in the second volume of 'Letters and Miscellaneous Pieces', which formed the fourth volume of the *Posthumous Works of the Author of a Vindication of the Rights of Woman*, which Joseph Johnson published in 1798.

171 Wollstonecraft, 'Letter on the Present Character of the French Nation', *MWW*, VI, 445–46.

172 Wollstonecraft, *Letters from Sweden, Norway and Denmark*, ibid., 344.

173 Wollstonecraft to Gustav, Graf von Schlabrendorf, 13 May 1796, *The Collected Letters of Mary Wollstonecraft*, ed. Janet Todd (New York: Columbia University Press, 2004), 341.

174 William Godwin, *The Enquirer: Reflections on Education, Manners and Literature in a series of essays* (London: G. G. and J. Robinson, 1797), ix–x.

175 William Godwin, 'Of Riches and Poverty' and 'Of Avarice and Profusion', in ibid., 161–84.

176 Godwin, *Enquiry concerning Political Justice*, 1st edn, dated 7 January 1793, and 'The Trial of Daniel Crichton for Seditious and Treasonable Words', 'Letters of Mucius in *The Morning Chronicle*' in Jack W. Marken and Burton R. Pollin, eds., *Uncollected Writings (1785–1822): Articles in Periodicals and Six Pamphlets, One with Coleridge's Marginalia* by William Godwin (Gainesville, FL: Scholars' Facsimiles & Reprints, 1968), 111–28.

177 Godwin, 'Grand Jury Inquiry into Treason, October 1794' and *Considerations on Lord Grenville's and Mr Pitt's Bills, Concerning Treasonable and Seditious Practices, and Unlawful Assemblies* (London: November 1795), in *Uncollected Writings (1785–1822)*, 129–280.

178 Wollstonecraft to Archibald Hamilton Rowan, 12 September 1796, *The Collected Letters of Mary Wollstonecraft*, ed., Janet Todd, 361–2.

179 Thomas Rowlandson, 'The Contrast', 1 January 1793, British Museum Collections. See more broadly, Mark Philp, *Reforming Ideas in Britain: Politics and Language in the Shadow of the French Revolution, 1789–1815* (Cambridge: Cambridge University Press, 2014).

180 Boyd Hilton, *A Mad, Bad, and Dangerous People? England 1783–1846* (Oxford: Clarendon Press, 2006), 69; Jennifer Mori Jennifer, 'Languages of Loyalism: Patriotism, Nationhood and the State in the 1790s', *English Historical Review* (2003), 33–58.

181 John Reeves, *Thoughts on the English Government. Addressed to the Quiet Good Sense of the People of England. In a Series of Letters. Letter the First* (London: J. Owen, 1795), 2.

182 Ibid., 36. See further, Marilyn Morris, 'Court Culture, Royalist Ritual, and Popular Loyalism', in *The British Monarchy and the French Revolution* (New Haven, CT: Yale University Press, 1998), 134–59.

183 James Gillray's 'Promis'd Horrors of the French Invasion, or Forcible Reasons for Negotiating a Regicide Peace', 20 October 1796, British Museum Collections.

184 James Gillray, 'The Tree of Liberty Must be Planted Immediately!', 16 February 1797, British Museum Collections.

185 On Wollstonecraft's reputation, Katherine Binhammer, 'The Sex Panic of the 1790s', *Journal of the History of Sexuality* 6/3 (1996), 409–34; Janet M. Todd, 'The Biographies of Mary Wollstonecraft', *Signs* 1/3 (1976), 721–34; Rosemarie Zagarri, 'The Rights of Man and Woman in Post-Revolutionary America', *William and Mary Quarterly*, 55/2, (1998), 203–30.

186 William Taylor, *Containing His Correspondence of Many Years with the Late Robert Southey Esq., and Original Letters from Sir Walter Scott and Other Eminent Literary Men*, ed. J. W. Robberds (London: John Murray, 1843), 2 vols., II, 507.

187 I am indebted to Pamela Clemit for this point and for bringing *St Leon* to my attention. See her edition in the World's Classics series (Oxford: Oxford University Press, 1994).

10. And by Confusion Stand

1 Adam Smith, *An Inquiry into the Nature and Causes of the Wealth of Nations*, ed. R. H. Campbell, A. S. Skinner and R. B. Todd, III.i.7–9, I, 379–80.

2 Ibid., V.iii.92, II, 946–7.

3 Nicholas Roe, *Wordsworth and Coleridge: The Radical Years* (Oxford: Oxford University Press, 2018), 2nd edn, 1–200.

4 Jon Mee, 'Anxieties of Enthusiasm: Coleridge, Prophecy, and Popular Politics in the 1790s', *Huntington Library Quarterly* 60/1–2 (1997), 179–203; Peter Kitson, 'Coleridge, the French Revolution, and "The Ancient Mariner": Collective Guilt and Individual Salvation', *Yearbook of English Studies* 19 (1989), 197–207.

5 Samuel Taylor Coleridge, 'Conciones ad Populum: Introductory Address', *The Bristol Lectures of 1795, Coleridge's Writings: Vol. 1: On Politics and Society*, ed., John Morrow (Princeton, NJ: Princeton University Press, 1991), 26.

6 Ibid., 28.

7 Ibid., 28–9.

8 Biancamaria Fontana, *Germaine de Staël: A Political Portrait* (Princeton, NJ: Princeton University Press, 2016).

9 Cyprian Blamires, *The French Revolution and the Creation of Benthamism*, 123.

10 Pierre Serna, Antonino De Francesco and Judith A. Miller, *Republics at War 1776–1840: Revolutions, Conflicts and Geopolitics in Europe and the Atlantic World* (Basingstoke: Palgrave Macmillan, 2013).

11 Jennifer Pitts, *A Turn to Empire: The Rise of Imperial Liberalism in Britain and France* (Princeton, NJ: Princeton University Press, 2005).

12 Thomas L. Pangle, *The Spirit of Modern Republicanism: The Moral Vision of the American* Founders *and the Philosophy of John Locke* (Chicago, IL: Chicago University Press, 1988); Isaac Kramnick, *Republicanism and Bourgeois Radicalism: Political Ideology in Late Eighteenth-Century England and America* (Ithaca, NY and London: Cornell University Press, 1990); Michael P. Zuckert, *Natural Rights and the New Republicanism* (Princeton, NJ: Princeton University Press, 1994); Johnson Kent Wright, *A Classical Republican in Eighteenth-Century France: The Political Thought of Mably* (Stanford, CA: Stanford University Press, 1997); Keith Michael Baker, 'Transformations of Classical Republicanism in Eighteenth-Century France', *Journal of Modern History* 73/1 (2001), 32–53; Dan Edelstein, *The Terror of Natural Right: Republicanism, the Cult of Nature, and the French Revolution* (Chicago, IL: University of Chicago Press, 2009).

13 David A. Bell, *The First Total War: Napoleon's Europe and the Birth of Warfare as We Know It* (Boston, MA and New York: Mariner Books, 2007).

14 Thomas Paine, *A Letter to the English People, on the Invasion of England*, 7–10.

15 Gustav von Schlabrendorf, *Bonaparte and the French People under His Consulate, Translated from the German* (London: Tipper and Richards, 1804), preface.

16 Willem Lodewyk Van-Ess, *The life of Napoleon Buonaparte . . . with a Concise History of The Events, That Have Occasioned His Unparalleled Elevation, and a Philosophical Review of His Manners and Policy as a Soldier, a*

Statesman, and a Sovereign: Including Memoirs and Original Anecdotes of the Imperial Family, and the Most Celebrated Characters That Have Appeared in France during the Revolution (London: W. Day, 1810), 4 vols., III, 312.

17 Martin Lyons, *Napolean Bonaparte and the Legacy of the French Revolution* (London: Macmillan, 2009).

18 Germaine de Staël, *Mémoires de Madame de Staël (Dix années d'exil): Ouvrage posthume. Nouvelle édition précédée d'une notice sur la vie et les ouvrages de Madame de Staël*, ed., Necker de Saussure (Paris: G. Charpentier, 1882).

19 Felix Freeman [Anon.], *A View of the Present State of France; With a Retrospect of the Past; Wherein the True Interests of the Continental Powers, and the Blessings of Our Constitution, Are Clearly Demonstrated* (Edinburgh: Oliver and Co., 1807), 4–9.

20 Philip Harling, *The Waning of 'Old Corruption': The Politics of Economical Reform in Britain, 1779–1846*, 64–5, 68–71, 74–81.

21 Albert Sorel, *Europe and the French Revolution: The Political Traditions of the Old Régime* (New York: Anchor Books, 1971); Norman Hampson, *The Perfidy of Albion: French Perceptions of England during the French Revolution* (Basingstoke: Macmillan, 1998).

22 David Hartley, *Arguments on the French Revolution and the Means of Peace* (Bath: R. Cruttwell, 1794), 5, 80–82; Anon., *A Query Whether Certain Political Conjectures and Reflections of Dr Davenant . . . Be or Be Not Applicable to the Present Crisis* (London: P. Elmsly and J. Debrett, 1795), 89–90; William Morgan, *Facts Addressed to the Serious Attention of the People of Great Britain Respecting the Experience of the War and the State of the National Debt* (London: J. Debrett, T. Cadell and W. Davies, 1796); John Bowlder, *Reform or Ruin: Take Your Choice* (London: J. Hatchard, 1798) and *Sound an Alarm to All the Inhabitants of Great Britain, from the Least to the Greatest* (London: J. Wright, 1798).

23 Constantin-François Chassebeuf de Volney, *Les Ruines, ou Méditations sur les révolutions des empires* (1791). See Colin Kidd and Lucy Kidd, introduction to Volney, *The Ruins* (Cambridge: Cambridge University Press, 2023); Alexander Cook, 'Reading Revolution: Towards a History of the Volney Vogue in Britain', in C. Charle, J. Vincent and J. Winter, eds., *Anglo-French Attitudes: Comparisons and Transfers*

between English and French Intellectuals since the Eighteenth Century (Manchester: 2007), 125–46.

24 D'Ivernois, *Réflexions sur la guerre, en réponse aux Réflexions sur la paix addressées à Mr Pitt et aux Français* (London: P. Elmsley, 1795), 30–89, 100, 143, 145–57; O. Karmin, *Sir Francis d'Ivernois (1757–1842), sa vie, son oeuvre et son temps* (Geneva: Revue historique de la Révolution française et de l'Empire, 1920), 295–310.

25 D'Ivernois, *Histoire de l'administration des finances de la République française: Pendant l'année 1796. Par Sir Francis d'Ivernois* (London: n. p., 1796), 132–3; *Historical and Political Survey of the Losses Sustained by the French Nation in Population, Agriculture, Colonies, Manufactures and Commerce, in Consequence of the Revolution and the Present War* (London: J. Wright, 1799), 34, 260, 466.

26 Pierre Prévost, *Cours de rhétorique et de belles-lettres, par Hugues Blair, . . . traduit de l'anglais par M. Pierre Prévost* (Manget and Cherbuliez: Geneva, 1808), 4 vols., I, xvi.

27 Marc-Auguste Pictet, *Voyage de trois mois, en Angleterre, en Écosse, et en Irlande pendant l'été de l'an IX* (Geneva: Bibliothèque Britannique, 1802), 53–88.

28 David M. Bickerton, *Marc-Auguste and Charles Pictet, the 'Bibliothèque britannique' (1796–1815) and the Dissemination of British Literature and Science on the Continent* (Geneva: Slatkine, 1986); Jean Cassaigneau and Jean Rilliet, *Marc-Auguste Pictet ou Le Rendez-vous de l'Europe universelle, 1752–1825* (Geneva: Slatkine, 1995).

29 This section draws on Richard Whatmore, 'Liberty, War and Empire: Overcoming the Rich State–Poor State Problem, 1789–1815', in Béla Kapossy, Isaac Nakhimovsky and Richard Whatmore, eds., *Commerce and Peace in the Enlightenment*, 216–43.

30 Mallet du Pan, *The British Mercury; or, Historical and Critical Views of the Events of the Present Times, Vol. 2. Number IX* (London : T. Cadell et al., 1798).

31 François d'Ivernois, *Effects of the Continental Blockade upon the Commerce, Finances, Credit and Prosperity of the British Islands* (London: J. Hatchard et al., 1810), 3rd edn, xxi, 121–37.

Notes

32 Donald J. McDougall, 'George III, Pitt, and the Irish Catholics, 1801–1805', *Catholic Historical Review* 31/3 (1945), 255–81; J. G. A. Pocock, 'Monarchy in the Name of Britain: The Case of George III', *Monarchisms in the Age of Enlightenment: Liberty, Patriotism, and the Common Good*, ed. Hans Blom, John Christian Laursen and Luisa Simonutti, 285–302.

33 Isaac Cruikshank, 'A Flight across the Herring Pool', 20 June 1800, British Museum Collections.

34 Günther Lottes, 'Radicalism, Revolution and Political Culture: An Anglo-French Comparison', in Mark Philp, ed., *The French Revolution and British Popular Politics* (Cambridge: Cambridge University Press, 1991).

35 For a sense of the changes during this period and indeed after, see the collection Julian Hoppit, Duncan Needham and Adrian Leonard, eds., *Money and Markets: Essays in Honour of Martin Daunton* (Woodbridge: Boydell Press, 2019).

36 Albert Sorel, *Europe and the French Revolution: The Political Traditions of the Old Régime* (New York: Anchor Books, 1971); Norman Hampson, *The Perfidy of Albion: French Perceptions of England during the French Revolution* (Basingstoke: Macmillan, 1998).

37 Sidney B. Fay, 'The Execution of the Duc D'Enghien I', *American Historical Review* 3/4 (1898), 620–40, and 'The Execution of the Duc D'Enghien II', *American Historical Review* 4/1 (1898), 21–37.

38 On Peltier, see Hélène Maspéro-Clerc, 'Un journaliste émigré jugé a Londres pour diffamation envers le premier consul', *Revue d'histoire moderne et contemporaine (1954)* 18/2 (1971), 261–81; Mark Salber Phillips, 'Burke, Mackintosh, and the Idea of Tradition', in *Society and Sentiment: Genres of Historical Writing in Britain, 1740–1820* (Princeton, NJ: Princeton University Press, 2000), 220–56; Simon Burrows, 'Culture and Misperception: The Law and the Press in the Outbreak of War in 1803', *International History Review* 18/4 (1996), 793–818.

39 James Mackintosh, *The Trial of John Peltier, Esq. for a Libel against Napoleon Buonaparte* (London: Peltier, 1803), 127, 148–80.

40 Ibid., 85, 91–3.

41 Gregory Conti, *Parliament the Mirror of the Nation: Representation, Deliberation and Democracy in Victorian Britain* (Cambridge: Cambridge University Press, 2019); William Selinger, *Parliamentarism: From Burke to Weber* (Cambridge: Cambridge University Press, 2019); James Stafford, *The Case of Ireland: Commerce, Empire and the European Order, 1750–1848* (Cambridge: Cambridge University Press, 2022).

42 Helena Rosenblatt, *The Lost History of Liberalism: From Ancient Rome to the Twenty-First Century* (Princeton, NJ: Princeton University Press, 2018); Nicola Miller, *Republics of Knowledge: Nations of the Future in Latin America* (Princeton, NJ: Princeton University Press, 2020).

43 David Armitage and Sanjay Subrahmanyam, eds., *The Age of Revolutions in Global Context, c. 1760–1840* (Basingstoke: Palgrave Macmillan, 2009); Joanna Innes and Mark Philp, eds., *Re-imagining Democracy in the Age of Revolution: America, France, Britain, Ireland, 1750–1850* (Oxford: Oxford University Press, 2013) and *Re-Imagining Democracy in the Mediterranean, 1780–1860* (Oxford: Oxford University Press 2018); Arthur Burns and Joanna Innes, eds., *Rethinking the Age of Reform: Britain 1780–1850* (Cambridge: Past and Present Publications, 2003); Philip Harling and Peter Mandler, 'From "Fiscal-Military" State to Laissez-faire State, 1760–1850', *Journal of British Studies* 32 (2014), 44–70. For a defence of progress see Steven Pinker, *Enlightenment Now: The Case for Reason, Science, Humanism, and Progress* (London: Allen Lane, 2018).

44 C. A. Bayly, *Imperial Meridian: The British Empire and the World 1780–1830* (London: Routledge, 1989) and *The Birth of the Modern World, 1780–1914: Global Connections and Comparisons* (Oxford: Blackwell Publishers, 2004).

45 Carl von Clausewitz, *On War*, trans. Col. J. J. Graham with an introduction and notes by Col. F. N. Maude (London: Kegan Paul, Trench, Trubner & Co., 1918), 3 vols., I, 24.

46 Camila Vergara, *Systemic Corruption: Constitutional Ideas for an Anti-oligarchic Republic* (Princeton, NJ: Princeton and Oxford, 2020).

47 Alexis de Tocqueville, *De la démocratie en Amérique* (Brussels: Louis Hauman, 1835), 2 vols., I, 317–18. The translation is from *Democracy in*

America . . . Translated by Henry Reeve . . . With an Original Preface and Notes, by John C. Spencer . . . Third American Edition (New York: George Adlard, 1839), 2 vols., I, 338.

48 Jennifer Pitts, 'Empire and Democracy: Tocqueville and the Algeria Question', *Journal of Political Philosophy* 8 (2000), 295–318.

49 Tony Judt, *Ill Fares the Land: A Treatise on Our Present Discontents* (London and New York: Allen Lane, 2010).

Index

ALLEN LANE

an imprint of

PENGUIN BOOKS

Also Published

Quinn Slobodian, *Hayek's Bastards*

Didier Eribon, *The Life, Old Age, and Death of a Working-Class Woman*

Richard Overy, *Rain of Ruin: Tokyo, Hiroshima and the Surrender of Japan*

Herman Pontzer, *Adaptable: The Surprising Science of Human Diversity*

Michael Lewis, *Who is Government?: The Untold Story of Public Service*

Fara Dabhoiwala, *What Is Free Speech?: The History of a Dangerous Idea*

Owen Hatherley, *The Alienation Effect: How Central European Émigrés Transformed the British Twentieth Century*

Shon Faye, *Love in Exile*

Bill Gates, *Source Code: My Beginnings*

Emily Callaci, *Wages for Housework: The Story of a Movement, an Idea, a Promise*

Kenneth Roth, *Righting Wrongs: Three Decades on the Front Lines Battling Abusive Governments*

Selena Wisnom, *The Library of Ancient Wisdom: Mesopotamia and the Making of History*

Agnes Callard, *Open Socrates: The Case for a Philosophical Life*

Manu S. Pillai, *Gods, Guns and Missionaries: The Making of the Modern Hindu Identity*

Minoo Dinshaw, *Friends in Youth: Choosing Sides in the English Civil War*

Marcus Bull, *The Great Siege of Malta*

Stephan Malinowski, *The Hohenzollerns and the Nazis: A History of Collaboration*

Ariel Zeleznikow-Johnston, *The Future Loves You: How and Why We Should Abolish Death*

Lee Seong-bok, *Indeterminate Inflorescence: Notes from a poetry class*

Robin Wall Kimmerer, *The Serviceberry: An Economy of Gifts and Abundance*

David Graeber, *The Ultimate Hidden Truth of the World*

Andrew Roberts, *Churchill: Walking with Destiny*

Jordan B. Peterson, *We Who Wrestle With God: Perceptions of the Divine*

Tim Blanning, *Augustus The Strong: A Study in Artistic Greatness and Political Fiasco*

Lionel Barber, *Gambling Man: The Wild Ride of Japan's Masayoshi Son*

Caleb Carr, *My Beloved Monster*

Helen Castor, *The Eagle and the Hart: The Tragedy of Richard II and Henry IV*

James Rebanks, *The Place of Tides*

Jean-Baptiste Fressoz, *More and More and More: An All-Consuming History of Energy*

N A M Rodger, *The Price of Victory: A Naval History of Britain: 1815 – 1945*

Lluís Quintana-Murci, *Human Peoples: On the Genetic Traces of Human Evolution, Migration and Adaptation*

Sunil Amrith, *The Burning Earth: An Environmental History of the Last 500 Years*

Diarmaid MacCulloch, *Lower than the Angels: A History of Sex and Christianity*

Claude Béata, *The Interpretation of Cats: And Their Owners*

Jerry Brotton, *Four Points of the Compass: The Unexpected History of Direction*

Serhii Plokhy, *Chernobyl Roulette: A War Story*

Richard J. Evans, *Hitler's People: The Faces of the Third Reich*

Alexis Pauline Gumbs, *Survival is a Promise: The Eternal Life of Audre Lorde*

Nate Silver, *On the Edge: The Art of Risking Everything*

Webb Keane, *Animals, Robots, Gods: Adventures in the Moral Imagination*

Helen Charman, *Mother State: A Political History of Motherhood*

Anne Applebaum, *Autocracy, Inc.: The Dictators Who Want to Run the World*

Anil Ananthaswamy, *Why Machines Learn: The Elegant Maths Behind Modern AI*

Stephen Alford, *All His Spies: The Secret World of Robert Cecil*

Rob Jackson, *Into the Clear Blue Sky: The Path to Restoring Our Atmosphere*

Clare Hammond, *On the Shadow Tracks: A Journey through Occupied Myanmar*

Elias Dakwar, *The Captive Imagination: Addiction, Reality and our Search for Meaning*

Matt Parker, *Love Triangle: The Life-changing Magic of Trigonometry*

Paul Collier, *Left Behind: A New Economics for Neglected Places*

Andrew Hindmoor, *Haywire: A Political History of Britain since 2000*

Neil D. Lawrence, *The Atomic Human: Understanding Ourselves in the Age of AI*

Ruchir Sharma, *What Went Wrong With Capitalism*

Mark Gilbert, *Italy Reborn: From Fascism to Democracy*

Oleksandr Mykhed, *The Language of War*

Kelly Clancy, *Playing with Reality: How Games Shape Our World*

Shami Chakrabarti, *Human Rights: The Case for the Defence*

George Monbiot and Peter Hutchison, *The Invisible Doctrine: The Secret History of Neoliberalism (& How It Came to Control Your Life)*

Corinne Fowler, *Our Island Stories: Country Walks through Colonial Britain*